Issues in Space

Series Editors

Stacey Henderson, Adelaide Law School, The University of Adelaide, Adelaide, SA, Australia

Melissa de Zwart, Adelaide Law School, The University of Adelaide, Adelaide, SA, Australia

The 'Issues in Space' series brings together a broad range of authors and disciplines to promote a diversity of views, perspectives, and critical approaches in the space sector. This series is designed to influence the development of the domestic and global space industry while it is in its formative stage, rather than trying to redress imbalances once they are entrenched in the industry.

This series aims to particularly promote the work of authors from traditionally marginalised groups, including women, early career researchers, and others; voices that are important in discussions of the development of the space industry. The scope of this series covers a broad range of key areas and disciplines that will be explored. Fundamental areas such as: outer space, space law, space policy, space regulation, space archaeology, space ethics, space situational awareness, space traffic management, military activities in space, commercial space, dispute resolution for space activities, space courts, space security, sustained human presence in space, space resource utilisation, space governance, space settlement, armed conflict in space, space resource utilisation, space manufacturing, space tourism, private actors in space, and space mining.

Issues in Space is an interdisciplinary series in that it is devoted to space scholarship but with the added unique focus on the promotion of diversity of authors, disciplines and opinions.

G. S. Sachdeva

Crimes in Outer Space

Perspectives from Law and Justice

 Springer

G. S. Sachdeva
Professor Emeritus
Chandigarh University
Mohali, Punjab, India

ISSN 2662-902X ISSN 2662-9038 (electronic)
Issues in Space
ISBN 978-981-99-3264-1 ISBN 978-981-99-3265-8 (eBook)
https://doi.org/10.1007/978-981-99-3265-8

© The Editor(s) (if applicable) and The Author(s), under exclusive license to Springer Nature Singapore Pte Ltd. 2023

This work is subject to copyright. All rights are solely and exclusively licensed by the Publisher, whether the whole or part of the material is concerned, specifically the rights of translation, reprinting, reuse of illustrations, recitation, broadcasting, reproduction on microfilms or in any other physical way, and transmission or information storage and retrieval, electronic adaptation, computer software, or by similar or dissimilar methodology now known or hereafter developed.
The use of general descriptive names, registered names, trademarks, service marks, etc. in this publication does not imply, even in the absence of a specific statement, that such names are exempt from the relevant protective laws and regulations and therefore free for general use.
The publisher, the authors, and the editors are safe to assume that the advice and information in this book are believed to be true and accurate at the date of publication. Neither the publisher nor the authors or the editors give a warranty, expressed or implied, with respect to the material contained herein or for any errors or omissions that may have been made. The publisher remains neutral with regard to jurisdictional claims in published maps and institutional affiliations.

This Springer imprint is published by the registered company Springer Nature Singapore Pte Ltd.
The registered company address is: 152 Beach Road, #21-01/04 Gateway East, Singapore 189721, Singapore

Dedicated to
The Fraternity of Scholars in Space Law
who have helped me grow
in Academic Specialisation

Preface

It was in August 2018 that I delivered guest lectures in space law at School of Law, SRM University, Chennai. The students and the faculty were fascinated with the subject and seemed enthused for LL.M. in air and space law. I was later invited to advocate for introduction of this course before an academic committee. But it so transpired that the authorities were keen to introduce a popular subject of criminology attached to space law. It seemed a case of strange bed-fellows.

Almost around the same time, there was a media report of an alleged criminal wrongdoing committed by the US astronaut in and from outer space. This was the first case of its kind and attracted attention. Further, commercial space travel and other activities of space exploitation involving human workforce were becoming technically feasible and economically viable. This excited my mind, and a concept was conceived resulting in this volume. Although started with the modest agenda, it has fairly comprehensive coverage of topics.

Humans are after all human and wherever they go, they tend to carry their inherited psyche and mental baggage from social grooming and learning experiences. Pugnacity, ego, and revenge are just the basic instincts. So, these would also accompany humans to the space domain and planetary habitations. And under stress or provocation, these may burst open, criminally. The criminals could be individuals individually, in joint conspiracies, or collective groups and could be accused based on the character and impact of space crimes. Classifying on causations, space crimes may be impulsive reaction, illegit business interest, national prestige, strategic compulsion, or just an ill-conceived action by a non-state entity or a mercenary.

With advancing technologies of Internet of Things, artificial intelligence, robotics, cyber, and directed energy weapons prone to dual-use, misuses and abuses are possible and likely. As a result, motivations for space crimes may also become different and diverse. Further, criminal acts with these technologies can be committed from any domain to cause damage in any other domain and still remain near-incognito and almost untraceable in investigation. Their potential for dysfunction, damage, or destruction can be limitless, even to the extent of causing an apocalypse or posing an existential threat to mankind. The dangers are real and valid while international space law is nebulous and porous on such crimes.

This book flags intertwined issues related to different kinds of crimes in outer space, analyses their motivations, causations and mens rea, confusion due to different nationality of the offender and the victim, the hassles of apprehension of the criminal, extradition as necessary or elected and trial by a competent court. Not all eventual decision may be easy or binary, and international law has its own frailties considering the attributes of state sovereignty and jurisdiction. This labyrinth surely needs markers for ease of way and speed in traction.

However, it needs a caveat that the alleged offender must be treated with due dignity and appropriate sensitivity. The accused may also not be punished solely on positive law but deserves social justice keeping margins of crime for lack of knowledge, inadvertence, or no-intention vis-à-vis the victim. Further, because of national sensitivities involved, such cases deserve to be settled or adjudicated with appropriate transparency, due promptness, solemn objectivity, and high legal acumen.

A few suggestions pertaining to treaty law, governance of space domain, and dispensation of social justice have been proffered in this book. Some solutions may need more consideration or modification, to which the author humbly submits. Believably, the actions recommended are time-consuming in negotiations or to muster consensus. Hence, a pro-active approach is recommended for timely action to position suitable legal mandates, with a reasonable visualisation of the future scenario and anticipated challenges. It is a humble call and hopes to be heard in the right quarters with a gentle nudge to the law fraternity, diplomatic corps, and the political masters for a concerted and synergistic effort.

It is rather otiose to faithfully acknowledge intellectual debt one incurs during the writing of the tome because one gradually becomes oblivious to it as the project progresses. Any such failing is mine and may be condoned. Be that as it may, I must acknowledge the contributions of Prof. Sandeepa Bhatt, Shri. Y. P. Madan, Shri. V. Gopala Krishna, and Dr. Manpreet Sethi at different times and in different connections. In their own way, they have helped to augment the content and have added to its authenticity. My profound thanks to each one of them and others unmentioned.

I owe grateful thanks to the publishers in the persona of Ms. Nupoor Singh, Ms. Jayarani Premkumar and Iydah Grac. The help, advice, and encouragement by the former have indeed been sterling and timely. As for the latter, I am grateful for good coordination and hastening up of the processes. And not to forget the unseen production staff who also deserve my gratitude for all their behind-the-scene efforts.

Last but not the least, I sincerely acknowledge gracious sacrifice of common time and companionship by my wife, Chan, during different stages of research, analysis, iteration, and revision. Truly, without her willing cooperation, constant support, and affectionate nudges, this project may not have been accomplished. My loving thanks to her.

Mohali, India
May 2023

Prof. (Dr.) G. S. Sachdeva

Prologue

A Few Narratives of Space Crimes

Media has recently reported a case of alleged criminal wrongdoing committed by a US astronaut in and from outer space. This is the first publicly reported case of its kind and raises many new issues for discussion and settlement. In this instance, the US astronaut, while tenured at the International Space Station (ISS), accessed a bank account of the spouse, in individual interest and for personal benefit, making non-official use of the privileged computer system of the ISS. The estranged spouse has alleged unauthorised access to the financial data in bank account, after revocation of authorisation, as an act on invasion of privacy and identity theft.[1] The matter was reported to the Inspector General of Investigations at NASA and also to the US Federal Trade Commissioner for inquiry.

Investigations have revealed that the complainant spouse, Summer Worden, had testified wrong statement relating to date of revocation of the authorisation from McClain relating to access to the data. For this false averment, Worden has now been charged on two counts of lying. Thus, the case has turned topsy-turvy, and the accuser has become the accused.[2] Worden has defended that it was a lapse of memory and an inadvertent inaccuracy, yet she has been found guilty on two counts. No news of a court trial has been reported, and it appears that the matter has been recalled by the Department of Defense for internal trial because both parties are military officers. Hence, disposal of the case may remain confidential till declassified.

Another case of crime in space relates to a hole detected, in August 2018, in the Soyuz module of Russia which had docked with the ISS in June 2018. It was observed by the US ground control that pressure in the space station was progressively falling and suspected a leak somewhere at the space station. On inspection, the crew found a hole in the Soyuz habitation module which had docked a couple of months back.

---

[1] "Astronaut accessed estranged spouse's bank account in possible first criminal allegation from space", a report from *New York Times*, August 23, 2019.

[2] Christina Zdanowicz, "NASA astronaut's estranged wife charged with lying about claim that spouse improperly accessed account from space", *CNN*, April 9, 2020.

The existence of a hole was an unexpected surprise for all yet was quickly sealed with gauze and epoxy adhesive by the Russian crew.

The US team suspected that the hole could have been, by mistake, drilled by a ground technician before the blast but remained unpatched. The Russian investigation revealed that the 2 mm hole was pierced with a drill by unsteady human hands after the docking. Further investigation pointed the needle of suspicion towards the US astronaut who had a psychological problem, while on-board ISS and allegedly wished to return home on Earth, earlier than scheduled. This supposition appears far-fetched and has been disputed by the US authorities. Her colleagues also assert for her medical fitness and stand by her impeccable professional conduct. Acrimonious statements have been exchanged between the two states, and Russia has now threatened criminal charges against the NASA astronaut but no positive evidence pinpoints the culprit.[3] Nevertheless, the occurrence of the crime cannot be denied.

The third incident is a case of suspected negligence for activities in space. Russia wanted to upgrade its laboratory and other scientific capabilities at the ISS, and with this intent, Nauka, a multi-purpose module was docked to the downside of the ISS. After successful docking and proper latching onto the space station, the mission controllers of Roscosmos commenced performing some post-docking "reconfiguration" procedures as per the protocol.[4] It was at this stage that, suddenly and inexplicably, the thruster jets of *Nauka* module restarted and the mishap began. This malfunction resulted in the entire space station to pitch out of its normal flight position compelling the US mission's flight director to declare a "spacecraft emergency."[5]

The actual occurrence was that the space station spun one-and-a-half revolutions, i.e. about 540 degrees, before coming to a stop upside down, relative to its original position. The space station also lost altitude during this unexpected and unplanned manoeuvre. "The space station then did a 180-degree forward flip to get back to its original orientation."[6] This was achieved by the flight teams on the ground at the Johnson Space Centre in Houston, by activating thrusters on another module of the orbiting platform in corrective action. *Nauka* engines were ultimately switched off. The ISS has fortunately returned to its original pitch without any major mishap.

At that moment, there were seven astronauts on-board and at risk though escape module was available in readiness. Early reports inform that due to this glitch, the station was actually out of control for about two minutes, while communication with all the seven members of the crew was lost or disrupted for several minutes.[7] Further, a preliminary inspection of the ISS, post-mishap, reports that the space station has certainly suffered stress on the metallic structure and turtled some equipment. In the

---

[3] Eric Berger, "Russia threatens criminal charges against a NASA astronaut", *Ars technica*, November 30, 2021.

[4] "Space Station did 540-degree flip, turned upside down: Mishap more serious than earlier reported", *India Today*, August 3, 2021.

[5] *India Today*, ibid, updated report.

[6] *The New York Times*, August 3, 2021. Based on a statement by Zebulon Scoville, Flight Director at NASA's Mission Control Centre in Houston.

[7] Reporting and writing by Steve Gorman in Los Angeles and Polina Ivanova in Moscow. Editing by Mark Heinrich, Leslie Adler and Raju Gopalakrishnan for *News SCIENCE*.

beginning, NASA and Roscosmos underplayed the incident but gradually with more details trickling in, the ground mission control shudder to rethink of the happening.

Russian space agency maintains and expects us to believe that the incident was caused "due to a short-term software failure and a command was mistakenly implemented" to fire the thruster engines.[8] This explication seems implausible for the impact sustained. Inadvertence is also possible, yet it would be naive to accept such a simplistic explanation for a goof-up of monumental dimension. In fact, who caused the malfunction, whether man or machine or software application, is still to be determined with precision and finality. More revelations may be expected, but when is doubtful.[9] But God has been kind to save all so threatened by the mishap.

A Brief Discussion of Legal Issues

Be that as it may, the abovementioned narratives, still appear simple in jurisdiction and can be seized for trial in a domestic court. The McClain case, in particular, appears rather simple because complainant and respondent, both are US citizens and illegality, if any, occurred in the US quarters of the ISS or allegedly in the statements of the spouse on the Earth. Yet the factum of such a happening is a souring thought and an alarm bell for initiating remedial measures and institutionalised dispensation of justice. The other two cases are still incomplete in investigation and lack clinching evidence to initiate a proper judicial procedure against suspected perpetrators of the crimes.

Nevertheless, in the international milieu of outer space and celestial bodies, the discussed cases certainly open up new issues which will primarily depend upon the nationals involved as also the nature and character of space activity. Therefore, in future, with the advent of space tourism, commercial exploitation of celestial resources, industrial production of space-specific products, touristic resorts, and planetary habitats, possibly, far more serious and complicated crimes with multi-nationality scenarios may occur. These would confront us for a solution.

Thus, the major legal issues may pertain to jurisdiction over the accused, considerations for extradition between states with or without treaty, gathering of multi-sited evidence, competence of the court to seize the case, decision to apply which law and award of punishment on whose national legal codes: the accused or the victim. All these aspects may be viewed differently by the parties with varying perception of justice meted out. Some of these issues would need fresh explanation on crimes and adjudication through a new international agreement, new concepts of space jurisprudence, and a novel institutional solution for justice. It is proposed to consider in this book issues relating to these aspects and cognate matters in respect of crimes in space.

---

[8] *India Today*, updated version of August 4, 2021.

[9] *India Today*, ibid.

Further, given the diversity of space activities undertaken, the divergent interests of stakeholders (viz., states, public–private partnership entities, private corporations, space tourists, individual travellers, and planetary residents) may emerge in space with new traits, different behaviour, incongruent beliefs, and nuanced temperament than that exhibited on the Earth. Accordingly, the nature and complexion of crimes in space would be different and varied. Though the full range of space crimes may not be easy to visualise at present, these would certainly pose a lot of imponderables and uncertainties under the existing laws and jurisprudence. The scenario will present a peculiar predicament of a legal trilemma involving conflicts of jurisdiction over the criminal, variance in the applicable legal and procedural systems, and the incongruence in national criminal codes and punishments specified therein.

Hence, there is need to identify and mull over the lacunae in jurisdictional options and procedural application of relevant space law as also for the applicable subaltern laws. Even at the transnational level, divergences in codified laws are significant and revealing of different perceptions of crime and variations in prescribed sanctions. A small example will clarify this assertion. The crime of rape seems to have different connotations. In the Western liberal societies, rapes are minimal, while in eastern countries, rape of women is a more frequent occurrence. Though often kept under wraps, yet of late, such crimes have come to be openly reported with complaint for investigation to the police leading to a court trial of the criminal.[10]

Generally, the rape, in most countries is treated as a crime by man where the woman is deemed an innocent victim irrespective of her complicity, lack of caution, or absence of resistance. On the contrary, in Saudi Arabia, the rapist man is not an outright offender. It is the woman who is the culprit for having lost her chastity or besmirching marital fidelity and can be punished by stoning to death. Interestingly, in Russia, the women have a statutory right to even kill a rapist in an act of escape, obstruction, and self-defence. While in Israel, women are permitted to possess and carry guns for self-defence. Thus, cultural perceptions, imbibed values, societal norms, social schooling, and consequent variations in law come up in sharp relief in a comparative study that could be aptly applicable to space and celestial living.

Some Hints at Solution

The centrality of this problem of the future needs to be recognised and appreciated for appropriate solutions so that the plaintiff-victim can in an international milieu avoid juridical confrontation and navigate through the legal labyrinths of judicial procedures to approach the competent court and reconcile the divergent connotation of crime and quantum of punishment. Individual victims may not by themselves be able to easily reach the portals of competent judiciary for equity or justice. State

---

[10] For example, in India, a woman is raped every six minutes. Refer Editorial Column, "She was walking home" in *Times of India*, (Chandigarh edition) March 13, 2021.

facilitation through diplomatic services may, at times, be necessary. The travails appear cumbrous, or perhaps, insurmountable. Hence, access to appropriate court needs to be simplified in procedures and the strict requirements of *onus probandi* be loosened. This will enable dispensation of justice more practical and speedier through the competent and accessible court and with shifted evidentiary burden on the defendant. The existing regime of space law fails in appropriateness and convenience of such solicitation.

In conclusion, the scenario so limned poses a new genre of problems and a different variety of challenges that caution us to look ahead for viable solutions. An eminently suitable option to bring about such changes in procedural rules, evidentiary mandates, and norms for due protection of the accused could be to negotiate a *specialis* treaty that may facilitate handling of specificities of crimes in space under international or native laws and in a designated institution for dispensation of justice. Perhaps, an analogous regime in Air Laws could be a good guide for learning and adaptation. This becomes important because the range of crimes could be wide and their gravity, in some cases, of catastrophic dimensions. At this juncture, it may not even be possible to imagine the entire gamut of space crimes of the future and their possible impact, including acts with artificial intelligence, deploying robots, cyber techniques, directed energy gadgets or Internet of Things (IoT) that can be perpetrated from outside the domain of space, in stealth and with anonymity leaving little trail of evidence.

On this intent and with due urgency, we need to look ahead in a pro-active approach, rather than face a reactive regret, for not establishing a timely international system or putting a holistic regime of parallel justice in place before the onslaught of space crimes. Thus, it does not solely remain national or political issue but an imperative that would necessitate a new and comprehensive treaty with enduring institutional changes, including the option for an exclusive edifice for trial and justice in space crimes. Further, because of national sensitivities involved in such criminal cases, these deserve to be settled or adjudicated with due promptness, solemn objectivity and high legal acumen, in this era of virtual and mass media reporting.

This book has been conceived and designed to be reasonably prescient of problems and challenges likely to be encountered in the outer space in the near future and to evolve solutions that may help regulate activities and facilitate governance of the space domain. It thus just shows the way forward for traction with pro-active attitude. In consequence, it is this prospective visualisation of crimes in space, their jurisdictional hassles, claims to extradition, procedural intricacies, and allied wrangles that lend this book a certain dignity of initiative for stirring consciousness about rule of law and humane justice in space domain. My motto, therefore, is to plan ahead because forethought often wins. And I also believe in the Biblical fable that Noah did not build the Ark when it was raining to flood the Earth in deluge. So, permit me to recommend suitable action as a policy imperative to pro-actively work in the right direction to reach the desired goal, well in time.

Therefore, let us put our heads together to find suitable answers and suss out viable options to this ominous challenge of the near future. Some solutions have been proffered in this book, but these are merely tentative proposals that are humbly submitted and are open to debate. An articulated consideration of these calls for global dialogues, participative discussions, or a network platform of the fraternity of enthusiastic space jurists. More importantly, we need to garner legal consensus through constructive exchange of views, solicit political will to understand and act, and harness diplomatic acumen to achieve quick and effective results in a polarised world.

A wise refrain advises that you may not get the best option in a new solution but can certainly find, with an open mind, a new vision or dimension of the problem. Ergo, decision-makers in governments, politics, business, legal affairs, and other sectors of society have perforce to look ahead to control, master, and channelise the energy of evolution shaping the world of tomorrow, in satisfaction of incumbent human needs and metamorphosing allied social structuring rather than stall or retard their growth, traction, transformation, and discernible emergence. Humanity cannot wait for too long due to our inaction, laziness, or squabbles. The thrills of space tourism and the treasure of space resources are waiting for exploitation in cooperation, and the global community need not bicker about the modality of uses and benefits of appropriation. It should strive to shape an altruistic relationship of cooperation in appropriation, equitable regulatory provisions, transparent governance of space domain, and justice for crimes and disputes. That would usher in a shared future of accrued benefits from the outer space and celestial bodies for the common and collective good of all mankind. This volume is a humble contribution and a small step in that direction.

Abstract of Chapters

This book comprises twelve chapters apart from Prologue. Broadly, it covers the description and definition of anticipated crimes in outer space, narration of some near-crimes in space, possible conflicts of jurisdiction, likely wrangles of extradition, differences in legal procedures among nations, and the variance in national criminal codes which may hinder fair trial of the accused and dispensation of true justice to the victim. In order to create a holistic regime to impart objective, yet socially humane justice, there is need for a specific treaty devoted to the avowed purpose and dedicated institutional system of fair trial and dispute resolution.

Chapter 1 discusses the first media-reported crime in space that has been brought to the notice of the appropriate authorities, just short of litigation in court. The named offender being the US astronaut, then posted at the International Space Station, allegedly indulged in an irregular act of making unauthorised use of privileged network of NASA for breach of privacy and identity theft. An evaluation of the nature and subject of this crime, in the light of germane international instruments, reaches a conclusion that the instant case has no international implications on nationality or territoriality. Hence, there is no conflict of jurisdiction or variance in applicable law, and the competence of the US courts or federal authorities to decide on the case is validated.

In fact, the matter of criminal indiscretion by the alleged astronaut was reported by the complainant and referred to for consideration of the concerned federal authorities.

After due investigation, NASA has cleared McClain of the levelled charges, and on the contrary, the estranged spouse Summer Worden has been found guilty of lying on material aspects of the case before the federal agencies. However, a final decision on the trial of Worden in a civil court or an in-house action taken by military authorities has not yet been publicly announced and may remain confidential till declassified.

Along with the above case discussed in detail, two more cases of crimes have been briefly discussed to emphasise their occurrence and existence in the outer space. The second narration deals with a 2 mm hole detected in August 2018, in the Russian Soyuz spacecraft that had docked to the ISS. It has been categorically ruled out that the hole was not there before blast-off from the cosmodrome nor it is the result of a hit by a stray meteoroid. Investigation by the Russian authorities blames the US astronaut for causing this as a deliberate criminal act. This accusation has been vehemently denied by NASA. Anyway, the culprit has not been pinpointed on material evidence but merely suspected on conjectural assumptions. This may not be adequate for a judicial process. Nevertheless, the crime has occurred.

Another incident relates to a possible negligence in space which could be deemed as crime. In this case, events so happened that Russia wanted to upgrade its research laboratory at the ISS with a new multi-purpose module, Nauka. This module faced some glitches on the ground during its preparation and ultimately was launched in November 2021. It docked on the underside of the ISS, and the docking procedure was confirmed successful. After *Nauka* module had latched onto the space station and had well settled, the mission controllers in Moscow commenced performing some post-docking protocols and "reconfiguration" procedures.[11]

It was then that suddenly the thruster jets of *Nauka* module restarted and the mishap began. This malfunction resulted in the entire station to pitch out of its normal flight position compelling the US mission director to declare a "spacecraft emergency."[12] The actual occurrence was that the space station spun one-and-a-half revolutions, i.e. about 540 degrees, before coming to a stop upside down, relative to its original position. "The space station then did a 180-degree forward flip to get back to its original orientation"[13] by activating thrusters on another module of the orbiting platform in corrective action. *Nauka* engines were ultimately switched off, and the space station stabilised. At that moment, there were seven astronauts on-board and at risk. Russian space agency maintains that the incident was caused "due to a short-term software failure and a command was mistakenly implemented" to fire the thruster engines. Human inadvertence coupled with lack of due diligence is possible, yet who caused the malfunction, whether man or machine, is still to be determined. Nevertheless, negligence in space activities would be a crime.

Chapter 2 provides description of some past near-crimes that have been committed in outer space or on the celestial bodies by the US government, national space agency,

---

[11] "Space Station did 540-degree flip, turned upside down: Mishap more serious than earlier reported", *India Today*, August 3, 2021.

[12] *India Today*, ibid, updated report.

[13] *The New York Times*, August 3, 2021. Based on a statement by Zebulon Scoville, Flight Director at NASA's Mission Control Centre in Houston.

the astronauts, and a private enterprise, so euphoric and enthusiastic about their space operations. But most of these acts of misfeasance have not been properly investigated and pursued officially and authoritatively. In respect of serious indiscretions by astronauts, their misconduct, in a couple of incidents, bordered on defiance of the official controlling authority. For example, the "almost mutiny" by the crew of Apollo 7 mission could be termed rather serious in military lexicon but has been treated chivalrously and thus either condoned in consideration of their glorious achievements or has been mildly punished in non-conventional modalities.

This chapter also discusses similar acts of "mis-experiments" by the US state agency like the copper needles dipole experiment which has caused several lumps of millions of jumbled needles as debris in space. Scientific consultations, as urged in Article IX of the OST, could have possibly obviated this indiscretion. There is another instance of advertent negligence by the US private enterprise, Space X, in sending an "unsanitised" Tesla car in an experimental launch into outer space. This has been in negligence of COSPAR policy guidelines. Both incidents deserved remonstration and condemnation by other space-faring nations, but there was not even a murmur. This chapter is fairly illustrative of past cases of malfeasance by the US astronauts in space which have, technically, not been treated as crimes nor tried as offences for punishment.

Chapter 3, in a similar vein, considers acts of near-crimes by the Soviet Union and other space-faring states, their officially authorised agencies and astronauts. The activities discussed are those that seem to have misfired and could be construed as lack of due diligence or absence of appropriate international consultation, as mandated in OST.[14] Objectively viewed, consideration of this topic of past near-crimes would not have been complete unless such, and similar acts of other space-faring nations, besides the USA, were similarly researched, narrated, and highlighted. Understandably, not much material on this subject in respect of space activities by the Russian Federation and other countries is available in the public domain. Yet an earnest effort has been made to hunt for information, even from sources that may not be too reliable. The information thus culled out has been collated to ensure completeness of the topic and to avoid an accusation of partisan bias in treatment of the subject.

Some relevant cases of the USSR space missions relate to their hasty decisions that huddled for bad planning of mission and consequently caused technology failures. Embarrassing fiascos, obviously, led to delayed reporting of their failed experiments and consequential deaths of certain cosmonauts, despite spectacular and pioneering successes. A couple of biographies of Russian cosmonauts have yielded some isolated facts and informational snippets, though officially unconfirmed. A couple of cases of Chinese misadventure like the ASAT test have been included in some detail. Another case of failed experiment included in this chapter relates to the ill-conceived *beresheet* research project by Israel that possibly has contaminated the surface of the Moon with hardy living organisms having life in centuries.

---

[14] Article IX.

Chapter 4 provides a general discussion on terrestrial crimes and enunciates the ingredients of crimes, particularly the prominence of *mens rea* in accusations. This is a peculiar trait and mentality of humans while animals commit no crimes. In fact, crimes and humanity have travelled together, and, in a way, the first crime was committed by Adam in defying the Lord's command and caution. And on the Earth, the first actual crime was committed by Cain who murdered his brother Abel out of jealousy. The motivation, intention, or *mens rea* of the crime is clearly established in this legend from the scriptures.

Sociology of crimes is another subject briefly treated in the chapter alluding to theories from Boulding to Bandura. It collates research to discuss diverse hypotheses whether criminality is genetic like in criminal tribes or instinctive like possessiveness and pugnacity or comes through sympathetic learning from society or is compulsive and habitual to reflexively compel a criminal to recidivism. The chapter also traces the changing face of the types of crimes with "socio-techno-economic" evolution in society. For example, crimes of early humans related more to denial of urges, then the cause became possession and deprivation, with industrial development and growing prosperity thefts and sexual crimes increased, IT industry has caused invasion of privacy and space activities will usher a different genre of crimes of business discords, crass competition, interference in economic activity and piracy of intellectual property in space activities.

This chapter also familiarises with space crimes as an introduction to the topic. In this regard, it limns the reasons that create new, unexperienced conditions of mental pressure and thinking processes which accordingly change the causations of crimes in space, more so with long stay. And this must first be experienced to be properly appreciated. Ergo, some space crimes would deserve leniency or condonation due to specific influences of unaccustomed environment of the domain that, at times, induces unintended reflexes, throws up inexplicable responses, and causes lapses in judgment. Thus, such specificities can occur to the detriment of even usually good-natured humans in space.

Chapter 5 visualises in some detail the complexion and character of future crimes in outer space and analyses their relevance and implications arising out of novel environment and new space activities, sustainability of space domain as also the impact of crimes on the future of humanity. Another influence on persons living in multi-ethnic, culturally different, and legally variant societies in outer space could be derived from their background, grooming, and mindset. Incompatibility in living styles, misinterpretation of innocuous behaviour, and mental fixations can cause annoyance, frustration, and crimes.

First category covers the traditional, physical crimes by individual humans in space domain like causing battery, injury, murder, rape, and their lower or higher cognates. The second category could be collective crimes of law and order or conspiracy or terrorism. The third category of crimes may relate to psychological pressure or mental torture like duress, insult, defamation, et al. The fourth category could comprise interference in economic activity, competitive aggressiveness, commercial disputes, offences of spying/copying of intellectual property researched in space, and similar wrangles of business jealousy.

Further, the possibility of human rights violations in offering shelter or ensuring evacuation of space tourists, space workers, or planetary residents from space in distress or emergencies or accidents has also been alluded to. Here, the provision applicable to astronauts in the Outer Space Treaty[15] has been extended to and invoked for all types of personnel in outer space or on celestial bodies like workers, hospitality guests, or space emigrees. The Moon Agreement reiterates this mandate.[16] This aspect can seek support from International Humanitarian Law also because refusal or denial of such facility can be deemed as "torture."

Capitalising on the option of the permissive use of ASATs for repeated activity of similar nature would adversely affect the sustainability of space environment for future operations. And allied to this would be violation of a prohibition under the Space Treaty (Article IX) on introducing earthly pollutants or contamination into outer space and celestial bodies or vice versa. This has started with *Beresheet* experiment by Israel or the launch of "unsanitised" Tesla car into space and may assume more importance as breaches escalate.

Chapter 6 delineates next class of space crimes which could be perpetrated through use of kinetic and non-kinetic technologies. Non-kinetic technologies cover digital applications and directed energy devices, for example, artificial intelligence, cyber-crimes, robot attacks, digital interference, lasers, particle blasting, micro-wave exposure, etc. The peculiarity of these crimes is that these can be committed in virtual anonymity and from any platform leaving little digital footprint. These can also be committed from any domain: Earth or airspace or outer space. Further, the offender need not be present at the site of crime and generally leaves no trail of forensic evidence. Another souring but tempting angle for such crimes may be of intrusion and indulgence by non-state actors for ideological fanaticism or political motivations and to cause a blitzkrieg. Probably, future scenario may be dominated by such crimes.

Another technology that can yield to attacks on satellites in outer space relates to kinetic-kill, anti-satellite weapons like ASAT missiles, but the problem with this category of weapons is that these are not banned when destroying own assets. And states have deployed these missiles for strategic ASAT tests or for destruction of defunct satellites containing secret equipment for espionage and sensitive data so collected and stored. The reasons may be valid for confidentiality, yet the acts are impeachable. The destruction of a satellite and disintegration of the missile do lead to creation of space debris that may take centuries to degrade and vanish, whereas their nuisance value in alerts and hazard quotient for collision is significant.

The directed energy technologies can be used for benign and peaceful purposes. For example, lasers can be used to extend the range of communication for deep-space probes or can be used to beam clean energy to the Earth with many advantages. Lasers can also be used to deflect or divert the orbit of small, mineral-rich asteroids for commercial exploitation and private appropriation, irrespective of whether it will be legal and lawful or not. But this technology is susceptible to dual-use and can

---

[15] Article V.

[16] Article 10.

be beamed on own or adversary satellite to render it operationally dysfunctional, temporarily or permanently, with no signs of apparent damage.

Therefore, the misuse or abuse of laser and similar technologies needs to be curbed and loopholes plugged with a *specialis* treaty. The author is conscious of the travails connected with treaty negotiations, yet the dreaded impact of contingent possibilities seeks attention for resolution through a "prohibitory" international treaty; and in tandem, supported by an institutional mechanism of governance to tackle breaches of treaty compliances. Additionally, states may have to take on responsibility for better regulation and supervision of activities and the captains of private enterprise to take on the duty for ethical business for peaceful purposes. The potential of serious mischief or intentional abuse with ominous consequences can be discounted or ignored only at our own peril.

Chapter 7 considers the dilemma of conflicting jurisdictional issues pertaining to territoriality of crimes and nationality of criminals and glitches in the trial due to evidentiary inadequacy. It highlights, at the international plane, the absence of a universal extradition treaty and the travails in obtaining custody of the accused and bringing one to book. Contrarily, the criminal enjoys state protections under nationality and law and can thus find escape routes, legal or political or even illegal. On the other hand, the aggrieved party struggles with unnecessary and dilatory hassles of jurisdictional nuances under international law for the possibility of extradition of the accused or effective trial in the state of domicile or the territory of arrest.

In fact, extradition is a bilateral issue between states based on mutual agreement, if any existing, or becomes a matter of political discretion or strategic posturing or nationality affiliations. To our dismay, there is no universal treaty or customary law on extradition of criminals based on certain specific criteria or established tenets with a caveat for in situ trial. A contrived solution has been experimented in aviation offences that is fairly successful.[17] At the national level, however, it is easier to invoke the established principles of nationality of the criminal or territoriality of the crime or afford protection to a citizen and thus to find a competent court for suitable trial. Such cases with single nation involvement may be simpler and fewer but most space crimes are expected to be multinational in content and import.

Chapter 8 highlights that substantive laws by themselves generally lack effective enforcement and need the help of procedural laws for dispensing justice. Therefore, this chapter deals with the cumbrous procedures to apprehend and bring the culprit to justice under international law. Even though national substantive laws or criminal codes are curt and precise on description of crimes and respective sanctions yet cannot walk on their own legs. Positive laws, by nature are lame, and it is the legal procedures that impart traction and enable justice to reach the delivery end. To enable the competent courts to seize appropriate jurisdiction for trial of the accused, legal procedures are necessary to arrest the culprit and investigation by enforcement agencies to facilitate judicial proceedings in order to provide due relief to the victim. This brings to focus the importance of procedural laws in apprehension of

---

[17] The Hague Convention, 1970.

the offender, acceptance of extradition, determination of jurisdiction, facilitation of trial, and dispensation of justice.

To our disdain, these differ in different countries. Some countries proclaim that the accused is innocent till proved guilty and affords certain rights to liberty till condemned by conviction. Some others believe that the complainant is right and the defendant must carry the burden to validate innocence by disproving the levelled charges. Another couple of countries swear by their jury system which is projected as more sensitive, humane, and empathetic. And Islamic theo-laws and punishments are entirely different and strict. Be that as it may, each system has its own merits, yet each requires procedural framework for arriving at the truth and award of punishment, if found guilty. Further, judgments on economic disputes resulting in decrees would need execution, and this process till the end turns out no simpler either and needs its own chain of writ procedures to achieve finality and duly receive the ultimate benefit. At times, to reach the end can be hopelessly dilatory, frustratingly long, and beset with obstacles, which at times appear deterring and insurmountable.

Chapter 9 attempts a brief global review of divergent legal systems prevalent transnationally and their different approaches to arrive at justice. This becomes pertinent to our study as space societies, big or small, temporary or permanent, will tend to comprise multi-nationality, multi-ethnicity, and multi-cultural populations drawn from different countries having different legal systems for justice. For example, the UK, the USA,[18] Australia, and few other countries follow the jury system where the judge, as moderator, elicits and sifts facts of the case and highlights legal nuances and leaves the jury to decide on the verdict, informally taking into consideration cultural background, social ethos, humane values, and reformist approaches.

Another judicial system followed in common law countries like the USA, India, and others is adversarial system for judicial decision to reach for justice. In this system, there are two parties to litigation, each trying to prove its point either in accusation or in defence and the accused is deemed innocent till proved guilty. The judge is the adjudicator who having heard the statements of the witnesses, scrutinised the presented documents, and listened to the arguments of the counsels of the respective parties, decides in the matter to issue a judicial verdict which is executed subject to legitimate appeals.

In a parallel, inquisitorial legal system, an inquisition, is read out to the defendant to bargain the pleas of defence. This trial system operates in France, Italy, and some other countries on the principle of inquisition. Here, the complainant raises an accusation that is to be defended by the other party to turn out "not guilty." Thus, under this system, the accused is deemed guilty till proved innocent through defence arguments or valid rejection of complainant's assertions or presentation of tenable counterarguments. In this system, major evidentiary burden rests on the defendant to prove its innocence.

Yet another pseudo-religious system of justice operates among the Muslims which is managed and dispensed by the *Kazi*. The legal codes of punishment and other judicial tenets are ordained in the Quran and are treated as Shariah which is binding

---

[18] Jury system applies only in some states of the USA.

Prologue   xxi

and obligatory on the community. Islamic countries like Saudi Arabia, other Middle East nations, and certain African countries faithfully follow this system to dispense justice. Even in India, this religio-judicial system operated and related to the Muslims, during the Mughal rule. This code and the legal system applicable to crimes and criminal investigative procedures were abolished through a common criminal code and with the establishment of secular criminal courts under the British rule. A lot more details are provided in this chapter.

Chapter 10 makes a gripping narrative that attempts to highlight a more intractable problem of divergent perceptions on crimes in respective codified laws of different countries, the varying element of gravity of the offence, and differentials in punishment for these. Study of penology becomes relevant here. The incongruence in values, beliefs, and practices is glaring. Space societies, of whatever kind or purpose, will tend to comprise multi-nationality, multi-ethnicity, and multi-cultural populations living in cramped spaces with limited comforts and little privacy. Such claustrophobic living conditions with incongruent beliefs, different attitudes, varied habits, and disagreeable behaviour patterns in spacecraft or on celestial bodies are bound to constitute an inconvenient predicament that would be, to say the least, pregnant with potential for disapprovals, disputes, and quarrels. A few illustrations will prove the above assertion and validate the need to focus on such divergences. The highlighted variations could be revealing, disparate, and disturbing.

For example, Americans are touchy on privacy and would not hesitate to take legal action for violation, even if their real estate property is innocently photographed, while in many other countries, there is no such inclination or law. Again, in the USA, motor vehicles operate with left-hand drive, while most other countries use the opposite, the right-hand drive vehicles, and follow the principle of "keep to the left." And both sets of countries have different codified traffic laws. Another simple example may be that clothes spread out on balconies or even extended out beyond for drying after a wash may be a familiar sight in Singapore and some other eastern countries, yet in Dubai, it is a sort of offence that may attract enforcement action and hefty fines.

Cultural differences and living etiquette equating to strict norms require that Muslim women need to wear a certain type of head scarf (hijab) or a face covering (burqa) in public; and exclusive quarters for them is a customary injunction. Another illustration of varying views can be those relating to rape. It is a crime, generally committed by males that inflicts violation of body-personal, denies freedom of choice, causes degradation of human dignity, and infuses a feeling of defilement in women who are normally assumed as innocent victims to the commission of crime. Whereas in Saudi Arabia, it is deemed as a crime committed by a woman for losing her chastity or compromising her fidelity and may accordingly attract a punishment of stoning to death. These aspects are amply illustrated in this chapter and proved by country-wise comparison and highlighting anomalous differences.

Chapter 11 appraises the discussion contained in earlier chapters and brings in sharp relief that the challenge of space crimes is multi-dimensional in impact and international in context. It also evaluates the efficacy of the existing corpus of space law and hints at evolving space jurisprudence to confront the formidable problems and proffers solutions to the future incumbencies. Arguably, Outer Space Treaty is excellent as a fundamental *grundnorm*, enshrines enduring tenets and laudable principles, and may best be left intact and undisturbed. However, it appears set in the era of its creation with limited vision for the fast-paced traction of "techno-commercio-politico-economic" developments of the future. Thus, the OST has little resilience or content to grapple with incumbent difficulties and looming challenges.

In a way, the treaty seems to lack inherent flexibility and bears systemic inadequacies to handle ensuing posers, emerging contingencies, technological advancements and novel challenges of commercialisation, privatisation, weaponization, planetary habitations, and sustainability of space environment. It seems that the collective corpus of Space Treaty and cognate international instruments have reached a sharp bend to effectively handle upcoming challenges. The existing space legal regimen and space jurisprudence need to acknowledge and accept necessity of circumstances, yield to essentiality of purpose, and accordingly create sufficiency of germane law to minimise breach of its provisions and handle new crimes, all in the best interests of humanity.

The fast-advancing space technology and its applications are prodding for expansion and diversification of activities in the space domain, for which the existing corpus of space law falls woefully short to efficiently handle new issues, new tasks, newer ventures, and unfamiliar challenges. Revision of existing law is one option but may not help and will only cause more confusion in text and interpretation. Therefore, a call for a *nouveau lex specialis* is loud and clear. Further, stakeholders and investors would not like to wait indefinitely in uncertainty, nor benefits to and for welfare of humanity can be stalled for too long on legal inadequacies of moribund treaties. Hence, space law fraternity may rise and move fast with purpose. At the same time, with progressively expanding common responsibilities like commercial contracts for mining or lease of Astro-realty for infrastructure or management of space debris in the space domain, there appears a need for a dedicated and competent institutional set-up for professional governance under the aegis of the United Nations. Else, defiance and crimes will become the new normal in outer space domain.

Space crimes will yet be another genre of peculiar character; more so in future, with artificial intelligence, virtual internet, cyber technology, robot slaves, and digital applications that may adversely impact the functional safety of orbiting satellites breach operational security of other space activities or disturb law and order in planetary societies, to mention just a few. In the process, this chapter limns a tentative definition of space crimes. With the onslaught of such patent criminal misadventures, not to mention the likelihood of terrorism making persistent inroads, the chaos will become prominent and disorder near-insurmountable within the existing legal ecosystem and, as yet, evolving jurisprudence of outer space.

Considering that human nature has an innate tendency to rebel against impositions, controls, and authority, so also to react to one's dislikes, distastes, and disagreements, human reactions, at times, may turn violent and result in crimes. Therefore, maintenance of public order, policing duties, and enforcement of law would be exacting tasks fraught with misperception. Same way, the imponderables of jurisdictional conflicts and procedural wrangles along with divergent understanding of law codes and legal systems, in an international scenario, would tend to pose serious problems in perception and acceptance. Therefore, an honourable dispensation that exudes an image and impression about fairness and transparency of judicial process and appropriateness of punishment should appear right to both parties to the crime, the culprit, and the victim, who remain in search of justice.

Under the circumstances, the chapter titled, Some conclusions make a bold proposal for a holistic solution, wrapped up from all ends, in a lex specialis, a treaty. It is further suggested to adopt an independent institutional set-up to resolve all issues of conflicting jurisdiction, varying criminal codes, unmatched legal procedures, and allied judicial imponderables. The vision is to effectively handle contemporary problems as well as those anticipatable in the near future. Please permit me to reiterate that the suggested proposals are tentative and open to debate for corrections as also fine-tuning with amendments. It is possible that one may not view the best option in the proffered solutions but gazing eyes and open mind may give a new vision to the problem for better answers.

It is also conceded that negotiations to craft, refine, and approve of the offered suggestions will take a long time to reach consensus due to political intransigencies and diplomatic tussles. Experience tells us that evolution of law is generally slow, jerky, and noisy. Ergo, the approach here is pro-active so that a viable and credible system is put in place, in time, before exigencies crop up to clamour for specific answers with immediacy. *Non-liquet* is not a desirable answer. Therefore, wisdom lies in being forewarned of the incumbent challenges as to be fore-armed with appropriate solutions, well before the problems stare us in the face.

This volume is partly like a textbook of fundamental truths offering didactic treatment on the topics like jurisdictional disputes and procedural wrangles. A part is narration that relates to variations in law codes and legal systems; a part is collation of history of near-crimes committed in the past and some accounts gathered from not too reliable and authentic sources which nonetheless make an interesting reading for information and research. Of course, apparently, false narratives have been assiduously avoided. And lastly, a couple of chapters like Appraisal and Conclusion involve personal cogitation, thought processes, and solutions evolved by the author.

Contents

1	**Crimes in Space: Illustrative Narratives**	1
	1.1 Introduction	1
	1.2 Illustrative Narratives of Space Crimes	4
	1.3 Analysis of the McClain Case	6
	1.3.1 A Preliminary View	9
	1.3.2 Assessment of Culpability	10
	1.3.3 An Appraisal of Jurisdiction in McClain Case	11
	1.4 A Mini-Mutiny on Skylab-4	12
	1.5 The Case of a Hole in Soyuz Module at ISS	14
	1.5.1 The Detection of the Hole	14
	1.5.2 Negligence in Space Would Be a Crime	16
	1.6 Conclusion	17
2	**Past Instances of Near-Crimes in Space: The USA**	19
	2.1 State Experiments Gone Bad	20
	2.1.1 The Copper Needles Experiment	20
	2.1.2 The Misadventure of Nuclear Testing in Space	21
	2.1.3 Riskiest Missions of NASA	21
	2.1.4 Garbage Left on the Moon	22
	2.2 Collective Defiance by the Crew	23
	2.2.1 A Near-Mutiny in Space	23
	2.2.2 Mini-Mutiny on Skylab-4	24
	2.3 Impermissible Acts by Astronauts	26
	2.3.1 Throwing Away Vomit Bag into Space	26
	2.3.2 Throwing Dirty Linen into Space	27
	2.3.3 Sandwich Smuggled into Space	27
	2.3.4 Indiscipline in Space is Also a Crime	28
	2.3.5 Sex in Space Against the Rules	29
	2.3.6 A Near Disaster in Space	30
	2.4 Acts of Individual Negligence in Space	31
	2.4.1 Loss of Tool Bag in Space	31

		2.4.2	Loss of Bag Containing New Debris Shield	32
		2.4.3	Instances of Minor Lapses and Technical Failures	32
	2.5	Misfeasance by Private Player in Space Activity		33
		2.5.1	Dereliction by Private Player in Space Activity	33
		2.5.2	Disregard of Co-orbital Space Traffic	35
3	**Past Instances of Near-Crimes in Space: The Others**			37
	3.1	Acts of Indiscretion by the Soviets		37
	3.2	State Misadventures		38
		3.2.1	The Mystery of Lost Cosmonauts	38
		3.2.2	The Shady Selection of Komarov as Cosmonaut	40
		3.2.3	The Failed Moon-Shots	40
	3.3	Acts of Misconduct by *Cosmonauts*		41
		3.3.1	Sexual Misconduct in Space	41
		3.3.2	Throwing Dirty Linen into Space	41
	3.4	Abandoning Garbage on Celestial Bodies		42
	3.5	Acts of Indiscretion by Other States		43
		3.5.1	Israel's *Beresheet* Lunar Crash	43
		3.5.2	ASAT Experiments	45
		3.5.3	Negligence in Space Operations is a Crime	47
4	**Crimes and Space Crimes: A General Discussion**			51
	4.1	Introduction		51
	4.2	Crimes: A General Discussion		52
		4.2.1	Ingredients of Crime	53
		4.2.2	Analysis of Crime	55
	4.3	Sociology of Crimes		56
		4.3.1	Considerations of Victimology	60
	4.4	Space Crimes: An Introductory Discussion		62
	4.5	New Genre of Space Activities and Crimes		63
		4.5.1	Commercialisation of the ISS and Private Space Stations	64
		4.5.2	The Nature of Space Crimes	65
		4.5.3	Cargo Transportation and Space Piracy	67
	4.6	Complications Visualised in Space Scenario		68
		4.6.1	Jurisdictional Issues	68
		4.6.2	Commercialisation and Appropriation of Celestial Resources	69
		4.6.3	Different Legal Systems and National Codes	70
	4.7	A Proposed Definition of Space Crimes		71
	4.8	Solutions in Brief		74

5	**Future Crimes in Space: A Visualisation**		75
	5.1 Introduction		75
	5.2 Classification of Space Crimes		76
		5.2.1 Classification Based on Terrestrial Legal Codes	76
		5.2.2 Agents of Crime	77
		5.2.3 Impact of Space Environment on Crimes by Humans	79
	5.3 Economic Crimes in Space		81
	5.4 Crimes of International Wrongs		82
		5.4.1 Dereliction in State Responsibility Imposed Under Space Law	84
		5.4.2 Misconduct by Astronauts in Outer Space	87
		5.4.3 Special Causations of Space Crimes	88
	5.5 Types of Space Offenders		89
	5.6 Future Activities in Outer Space		90
	5.7 Crimes of the Future		92
		5.7.1 Militarisation and Weaponisation of Space Domain	93
		5.7.2 *Contamination of the Space Domain and* Vice Versa	94
		5.7.3 Israel's Lunar Crash of *Beresheet* Module	94
		5.7.4 Cockroach in Outer Space	95
		5.7.5 Dereliction by Private Player in Protection of Planetary Environment	95
		5.7.6 Nuclear Pollution in Outer Space Domain	96
		5.7.7 The Misadventures of Nuclear Testing in Space	97
		5.7.8 Nuclear Debris in Outer Space	99
	5.8 Debris Pollution of Outer Space Domain		101
		5.8.1 The Copper Needles Experiment	101
		5.8.2 Debris Scatter Through ASAT Experiments	101
	5.9 An Appraisal		103
	5.10 Conclusion		105
6	**Space Crimes Through Technology: A New Trend**		109
	6.1 Introduction		109
		6.1.1 A Brief Note on Crimes Against Humanity	111
	6.2 Cyber Technology		113
		6.2.1 Space Crimes Through Digital Technologies	113
		6.2.2 Instances of Cyber-attacks	115
	6.3 Cyber-crimes in Space		118
		6.3.1 Suspected Hacks by China	118
		6.3.2 Russian Intrusions with Cyber Technology	120
	6.4 Space Crimes with Directed Energy Technologies		122
		6.4.1 Applications of LASER Technology	123
	6.5 Advances in Artificial Intelligence		126

	6.6	Crimes by Robots	127
	6.7	Rules of Conduct for Robots	129
	6.8	Space Crimes with Anti-Satellite Technology	131
		6.8.1 A Real-Check of Technologies	134
7	**Jurisdictional Issues: An Analysis**		137
	7.1	Jurisdiction: General Discussion	137
	7.2	Examples of Crimes with Jurisdictional Issues	138
		7.2.1 Anne McClain Case	138
		7.2.2 Detection of Hole in Russian Module	140
		7.2.3 Negligence in the Nauka Case	142
	7.3	Jurisdiction Under Space Law	144
		7.3.1 The Outer Space Treaty, 1967	144
		7.3.2 *Agreement on Rescue and Return of Astronauts, Etc., 1968*	145
		7.3.3 The Liability Convention, 1972	146
		7.3.4 Space Law Accepts and Absorbs International Law	147
	7.4	Principles of Criminal Jurisdiction Under International Law	148
		7.4.1 The Territoriality Principle	148
		7.4.2 The Nationality Principle	149
		7.4.3 The Protective Principle	151
		7.4.4 The Universality Principle	151
		7.4.5 Principle of Forum Conveniens	152
	7.5	National Laws with Extra-Territorial Jurisdiction in Outer Space	152
		7.5.1 Extra-Territorial Reach of the US Domestic Law	153
		7.5.2 Extra-Territorial Reach of Other Countries	154
	7.6	Discipline On-Board Spaceships	155
	7.7	Jurisdictional Challenges from New Space Activities	156
	7.8	Division of Territorial Jurisdiction of Outer Space and Air Space	158
	7.9	Conclusion	162
8	**Legal Procedures Under International Law: A Cumbrous Process**		165
	8.1	An Analysis of Legal Procedures	165
		8.1.1 Introduction to Procedural Law	165
		8.1.2 Procedures in International Law	168
	8.2	International Court of Justice	170
		8.2.1 Support of Procedural Law	171
		8.2.2 Competence of the ICJ	172
	8.3	Extradition as a Procedural Remedy	176
	8.4	Conclusion	182

Contents

9 Diverse Legal Systems: A Global Review 185
    9.1 Divergent Legal Systems: A Global Review 187
        9.1.1 Adversarial System of Common Law Countries 188
        9.1.2 Inquisitorial System of Justice 189
        9.1.3 The Jury System for Dispensing Justice 191
        9.1.4 The Codes of *Sharia* 194
        9.1.5 A Brief Appraisal 198

10 Legal Codes and Social Norms: Divergent Perceptions 199
    10.1 Divergent Perception of Crimes 199
        10.1.1 Varied Understanding of Law 199
        10.1.2 Incomprehension of Religious Taboos and Symbols of Faith 202
        10.1.3 A Needy Hungry Commits No Crime in Stealing Food 203
        10.1.4 Harsh Punishments in Islamic Arabian Countries 204
        10.1.5 Varied Views on Sex and Prostitution 204
        10.1.6 Differential Treatment of Women 206
        10.1.7 Views on the Crime of Rape 208
        10.1.8 Views on Virginity 210
        10.1.9 Varied Opinions on Nudity 211
        10.1.10 Acceptance of Nudism in Europe 211
        10.1.11 Dignity of the Royalty is Inviolable 213
        10.1.12 Varied Notions and Supporting Laws 214
        10.1.13 Impact of Societal Ethos and Cultural Values 215
        10.1.14 The Japanese Customs and Laws 217
        10.1.15 A Miscellany 218
    10.2 In Search of Justice 220

11 Appraisal and Solutions 225
    11.1 An Appraisal 225
        11.1.1 Near Crimes by the States 226
        11.1.2 The Complexion of Future Crimes 227
        11.1.3 Challenges of Diversity and Perception 229
        11.1.4 Hassles in Adjudication of Space Crimes 230
    11.2 Proffered Solutions 231
        11.2.1 The Scenario 231
        11.2.2 The Need for a New and Specific Treaty 232
        11.2.3 Overall Governance of Outer Space Domain 234
    11.3 Support Set-up for the Outer Space Trusteeship Council 238
        11.3.1 Space Utilisation and Sustenance Regulatory Authority (SUSRA) 238
        11.3.2 Authority for Space Monitoring and Compliances 240
    11.4 International Court for Space Crimes 240
        11.4.1 Support Structure for ICSC 241
        11.4.2 Character and Competence of ICSC 242

12	**Some Conclusions**	245
	12.1 The Need for a Specialised Treaty for Space Crimes	246
	12.2 The Need for Governance of the Space Domain	248
	12.3 The Need for Sustainability of the Space Domain	248
	12.4 The Need for Judicial Set-up for Space Crimes	249
	12.5 The Need for National Legislation	251
	12.6 Timeliness of the Topic	252

About the Author

Prof. (Dr.) G. S. Sachdeva is one of the pioneer scholars on Space Law in India and has been writing on the subject for the last four decades. He has seven books to his credit and has contributed over seventy articles in edited books and law journals in India and abroad. He has Masters in Economics from Delhi School of Economics, Delhi University, Law graduation from Nagpur University, Nagpur (Gold Medallist) and Ph.D. in International Law from Jawaharlal Nehru University, New Delhi. He is currently Professor Emeritus, Chandigarh University, Mohali, Punjab; Adjunct Professor to NALSAR University of Law, Hyderabad, and was formerly Adjunct Professor, School of International Studies, JNU, New Delhi. He was Leader of a Think-tank and National Panellist for Revising of Draft Space Activities Bill (2022). He has also been selected as Member of Study Group 3.26 of International Academy of Astronautics, (IAA) Paris. He is a peer-reviewer for many reputed journals like *Astropolitics*, *Space Policy*, *Indian Journal of International Law* and others and is on the Editorial/Advisory Boards of several Indian and foreign law journals.

Chapter 1
Crimes in Space: Illustrative Narratives

1.1 Introduction

Before we embark on a discussion regarding illustrative cases of crimes in space, it will be prudent to introduce the concept of the book and the flow of ideation thereunder. Therefore, with commercial travel to space having started with flights by Virgin Galactic, Blue Origin, and SpaceX, human groupings in space appear just round the corner. To begin with, it may start with suborbital flights for gravity thrills, then orbiting space stations as entertainment dens leading to celestial hotels, and space habitats for vacationing and longer residence, respectively. Safety of commercial flights has been demonstrated and is statistically safer than shuttle-era. Further, the tariffs are also bound to become affordable with multiplicity of space carriers and ensuing competition. The space carriers are promising exhilarating view of the planet Earth in cosmic perspective and *lumiere* splendour. The touristic offers will progressively become more fun-loving, interesting and attractive, for example, a package of marriage ceremony in a space station, honey-mooning in micro-gravity, golfing on the Moon and other sports on celestial bodies.

Apart from tourists, there are going to be groups of space workers to support space infrastructure, hospitality industry, and other commercial space activities. For example, progress towards excavation and mining of celestial mineral resources has shown possibility of break-even of costs and thereafter promising profitability. To begin with, asteroids are being explored for reserves of mineral resources of vital importance to humanity that can yield good profits to private enterprise. Further, space environment offers benefits of sterile conditions for production of high-quality vaccines, zero-gravity conditions for manufacturing of uniform quality of alloys and producing bubble-free, high-end crystals for electronics.

It is to be expected that space groupings of humans and worker assemblages would be cosmopolitan with multiplicity of nationalities, ethnicities, cultural background, social values, and behavioural attitudes. Moreover, humans would carry their instincts of pugnacity, ego, and revenge, among others, even to the outer space domain. Each factor would pack the gathering with differences in perception making it endemic of conflict and resultant crimes. Added to this would be the travails of blast-off, the effects of velocity, spin, and g-factor that would make even a trained person uncomfortable and irritated, bodily and mentally. Moreover, the conditions of cramped living, claustrophobic spaces, and unergonomic work benches in mines and production sheds may in due course cause an overwhelming feeling of uneasiness that may erupt into a crime, minor or major.

The existing corpus of space law has no specific rules for handling such situations. In fact, Outer Space Treaty (OST)[1] did not visualise such contingencies and the need for remedies because the astronauts were highly trained professionals with regulated behaviour and ingrained discipline. But tourists and workers, in future, may be derived from different economic and family background and styles of living and hence may not be able to adjust well and amicably. And their stay in cramped residencies and cooped-up environment with little privacy may cause annoyance and evoke strong reaction. Added to these can be the adverse effects of unaccustomed living, pressures for productivity and a nagging feeling of the hazardous work conditions. Moreover, long contractual stay with the absence of familiar faces and personal relations may affect the psyche and behaviour. The cumulative effect of all these factors could cause provocation and, in the ultimate, crimes.

Acts of crimes in space venues may pose additional problems in adjudication due to conflicts of jurisdiction and hassles of extradition. Of course, help can be legitimately sought from the tenets of international law[2] but this may not be enough to settle emanating issues. This dilemma leads to a need for a *specialis* treaty to regulate handling of space crimes with facilitative procedures. Further, Outer Space Treaty does not permit operation of national sovereignty on the celestial bodies;[3] hence, outer space, including celestial bodies, remains an ungoverned domain with no policing of compliances or enforcement of treaty provisions. Self-seeking interpretations and vested defiance by the states and profit-enhancing compromises by private space entities can be visualised which may clamour for enforcement of rule of law as also remedial measures.

It has been argued in the book that there is an eminent need for an empowered institutional set-up in the form of a governance body for the composite outer space, including celestial bodies, which had earlier been suggested under the name of World Space Authority (WSA)[4] with a suitable Charter, professional staffing and adequate funding to administer this ungoverned domain. In the next recommendation, the authority was upgraded to World Space Organisation[5] with improved status, wider

---

[1] Treaty on Principles Governing the Activities of States in the Exploration and Use of Outer Space, including the Moon and the Other Celestial Bodies, 1967. Also referred to as Outer Space Treaty, the Treaty or OST.

[2] Outer Space Treaty, 1967, Article III.

[3] Ibid, Article II.

[4] G. S. Sachdeva, *Outer Space: Law, Policy and Governance,* New Delhi, KW Publishers, 2014, pp. 198–200.

[5] G. S. Sachdeva, *Space Commercialisation: Prospects, Challenges and Way Forward,* New Delhi, Pentagon Press LLP, 2019, pp. 38–9, 139–40. Also refer, GS Sachdeva, "Space Tourism: Some

span of control, holistic scope of action, and semi-self-sustaining organisation with powers to levy a cess on launches to generate revenue.

Now, a revised proposal has been mooted that the defunct Trusteeship Council may be revived and repurposed for the task of this governance. This organ of the UN, earlier also, has discharged a similar function and would be eminently suited for administration and management of the outer space and celestial bodies as "the province of all mankind"[6] or common heritage of mankind[7] and attend to the calls of future human migration and celestial settlements. In this role, it would be executing leases of celestial realty for hospitality uses and commercial mining of natural resources; managing spaceports and space traffic with due safety; control on space debris through mitigation and remediation; and ensure public order and promote human welfare in planetary habitats by promoting and regulating space activities in the best interest of humankind.

Again, Trusteeship Council as an executive organisation of the outer space can, at best, initiate coercive administrative action against breaches or report the crimes committed in the outer space but cannot act in judicial capacity or award punishments. Of course, the first reference would be to the concerned state to assume jurisdiction under principles of territoriality or nationality or universality or supra-territoriality, whether legislated or claimed by possession. But these parameters may not be sufficient for the purpose and may be conflicted with claims of extradition or that enough evidence for trial may not be available to the country seizing of jurisdiction. Such hassles with diplomatic processes tend to be dilatory and long drawn. So, a solution has been proffered to establish an International Court of Space Crimes (ICSC) as a specialised bench of International Court of Justice or International Criminal Court for adjudication in delayed, disputed and complex, multi-nationality cases.

It is conceded that the proffered solutions are not simple decisions but would need prolonged discussions at the UN and involved diplomatic consultations to build consensus on all the three suggestions, viz., concluding a new *specialis* treaty, deciding on resuscitation of Trusteeship Council, and establishing a specialised bench as ICSC for trial of complicated and disputed space crimes. Also, that my submissions may have to be suitably modified and subtly honed to the objectives intended through debate and discussions. Therefore, space law fraternity is urged to cogitate and comment on the wisdom and suitability of the recommendations. For the very reason of dilatory processes involved, pro-active initiatives are requested to be taken by the United Nations and the COPUOS, so that an appropriate enforcement system is put in place, and well on time, to tackle the problems contingent on the popularity of space tourism and positioning of space workforce for mining and industrial activities.

Legal Implications" in B Sandeepa Bhat, General Editor, *Space Law: The Emerging Trends*, Kolkata, Eastern Law House, 2018, pp. 122.

[6] Outer Space Treaty, Article I.

[7] Agreement Governing the Activities of States on the Moon and Other Celestial Bodies, 1979, Article 11.

It will be prudent to define the scope of this tome in the beginning itself. On the positive side, it will visualise crimes by humans in the space domain, as conventionally understood and affected by the space environment. It will also discuss business crimes which may or may not attract corporeal punishment but would certainly incur liability and compensation. The discussion also intends to allude to crimes against humanity that may be caused in the process of escalating space activities, irrespective of the mode and method of retribution. Crimes by the states in breach or defiance of treaties like weaponization as also militarisation of outer space and celestial bodies or testing of kinetic weapons like ASAT missiles causing proliferation of space debris would only be briefly alluded to. But possible scenario of defiance by states in commercial colonisation of celestial natural resources or claims to pseudo-sovereignty in establishment of heritage parks would be excluded from the purview of this book.

It equally needs clarification that the concept and content of crimes discussed here are not always the puritanical, conventional, or terrestrial crimes as defined in legal codes of countries. The crime used in this book is in the generic sense with broad connotation of defaults in commission of prohibited acts or omission to perform mandated acts, irrespective of the prescribed punishments. The broadness of usage may extend to negligent acts that need not be corporeally punished but do incur *vinculum juris* for liability or compensation as *restitutio in integrum*. Similarly, breaches of an international treaty or offensive military overtures of states may mean a threat or even start an armed conflict yet would not, technically and strictly, constitute space crimes, albeit have been discussed under the respective heading to ensure better understanding in context and for completeness of treatment of the subject. Therefore, do bear with me, at times, with slightly broad references to the terminology of crimes.

1.2 Illustrative Narratives of Space Crimes

So far, astronauts that have been sent into space in manned or crewed spaceships or stationed at International Space Station, barring fare-paying experimenters, have belonged to the defence forces of their respective countries. So has been and remains to be the practice in India.[8] The officers so deputed were deeply selected from within their cadre who were well educated, excellently trained, truly professional, really proficient, highly disciplined with motivation for the task and dedication to the mission. These were the *crème d'la crème* of their corps and uniquely fit to be elevated as astronauts. Thus, there was never a doubt about their disciplined behaviour, professional performance, flying skills, and mission achievements.

For nearly half a century of space activities, model behaviour by astronauts has been the standard of conduct and official deportment in "humanned" space flights.

---

[8] Squadron Leader Rakesh Sharma of Indian Air Force (IAF) went into outer space in Soyuz spacecraft of the Soviet Union in 1984. For the mission to the Moon in 2022 also, Air Force officers have been deputed for training in Russia. They have since returned after completion of training.

1.2 Illustrative Narratives of Space Crimes

There were no aberrations in behaviour nor any serious cases highlighting illegal conduct or assuming unauthorised routine or any grave acts of reportable indiscipline or notable defiance of authority. The norms of professional integrity and military discipline have prevailed as per the "Astronauts Code of Professional Responsibility" issued by NASA in 2008.

Regimented discipline and ingrained reflexes of the defence forces were the solemn norms among astronauts till the case of Ms. Anne McClain was reported in 2019 as "the first crime in space." The media splash was big and surprising. NASA image and military discipline were under attack. In general, it shocked the astronaut fraternity, shook the NASA authority and surprised the US government. An in-house investigation was ordered by NASA immediately, to be conducted by the Inspector General of Investigations and file a report. Of course, this case took a tumultuous turn and McClain was cleared of the accusations and her complainant spouse was charged for lying on oath.[9]

Another instance of crime in space had come to notice in August 2018. There was a hole in the Soyuz MS-09 spacecraft that was a habitation module docked to the ISS. It was detected due to falling pressure inside the Soyuz vehicle and International Space Station. The hole was filled with gauze and epoxy composites and the defect was rectified. Thereafter, there was no problem of pressure decrease or any other problem and the same Soyuz module returned to the Earth with astronauts scheduled to return as planned. Be that as it may, the reason and the cause of existence of the hole as also who did it had to be investigated as per the military rules.

The American inquiry team put it as erroneously drilled hole during servicing on the ground before blast-off. The Russians did not accept this preliminary conjecture and conducted their own investigation, the results of which have just been made public.[10] The Russian inquiry puts the blame on an American astronaut, Serena Aunon-Chancellor, who had psychological fits and suffered from depression while at the ISS and allege that circumstantially, possibly she could have committed the crime. NASA has, however, declared that she was medically fit while at the ISS, and as confirmed from the camera footage, she was nowhere near the site prior to the detection of the hole.[11]

Recently, another case has come to notice, as reported in media that a person, presumably, posed as Russian astronaut presently posted at the International Space Station. He befriended a Japanese woman, aged 65 years, resident of Shiga prefecture in Japan. Their contact started from Instagram where he had posted some of his photographs from the ISS. They first met in June 2022 and started exchanging messages. He convinced the woman of her true love and expressed a desire to return from the space assignment, marry her, and live with her.[12]

---

[9] More details later in the chapter.

[10] Eric Berger, "Russia threatens criminal charges against NASA astronaut", *Space.com*, November 30, 2021.

[11] Ibid.

[12] Poulomi Ghosh, "Russian astronaut dupes woman, seeks money to 'return to Earth'", *the Hindustan Times*, October 12, 2022, in World News column.

He then informed the lady-love that for his premature return, he will have to pay a landing fee in Japan and convinced her to remit certain amount at designated address. However, this request was repeated within a span of less than one month during which time she had transferred 4.4 million yen. Repeated requests made her suspicious of the intentions of the astronaut. The matter has been reported to the police and is under investigation. If it turns out to be true, it becomes a space crime with international ramifications of jurisdiction. In case, the conman is resident in Japan, and then it becomes a case of "romance scam." The results of investigation are awaited.[13]

But it must be accepted that humans are human and perforce carry their frailties wherever they go, even to the outer space. It is wisely said, to err is human, and it really happens in life, immaterial of the locale. This propensity gets accentuated further due to long stay in gravitation-free environment, claustrophobic spaces, unergonomic living, and consequent physiological changes. Psychological stress, pressures of work, accumulation of fatigue, and emotional distress in space also cast perceptible influence on the mind, proficiency, and behaviour of astronauts. This may, at times, exhibit itself in strange expression, unusual demeanour, or inexplicable conduct. The same possibly happened for astronaut McClain, who was additionally embroiled in her family tensions, unknown to the NASA authorities.

1.3 Analysis of the McClain Case

The reported case[14] relates to an act of commission by a NASA astronaut, Lieutenant Colonel Anne McClain, a decorated Army officer and an accomplished career flyer of vast experience who had joined NASA Astronauts Corps in 2013. She had earlier served in the Iraq war as part of her military tenure and successfully flown crucial combat missions. At the time of commission of the, so called, improper act, she was posted at the International Space Station (ISS) for six months and was officially working in American quarters there. Prior to her flight to the ISS, the astronaut was embroiled in family estrangement, had been fighting a painful separation process, and judicially contesting a parenting dispute in the USA. This very personal and private matter has, unfortunately, now spilled out into the media and the press. Anne McClain has refuted the allegations in general terms through her lawyer in the press.

McClain had contracted a same-sex lesbian marriage with Ms. Summer Worden, an Air Force Intelligence Officer with decorated past, in 2014. Worden had a son from an earlier relationship, whom McClain wanted to formally adopt while providing financial support for the upbringing and schooling of the child. Worden sternly spurned this proposal, yet McClain petitioned in a local court for shared parenting

---

[13] Ibid.
[14] Mike Baker, "A divorce battle on Earth leads to 'first crime in space'", *The Times of India*, Chandigarh edition, August 24, 2019, pp. 1 and 14.

1.3 Analysis of the McClain Case

rights and "exclusive right to designate the primary residence of the child." This petition was duly rejected by the court and custody refused. Again, during this period of estrangement and escalating disaffection, McClain accused Worden of an assault which met with outright denial from the spouse and the case was dismissed.[15]

Worden was disillusioned by this false allegation of assault as also the earlier petition on custody of the child. The situation precipitated and the relationship worsened beyond redemption. In consequence, Worden, in frustration, filed for separation and divorce in October 2018 and then followed a bitter battle for divorce with mutual recrimination. During this period of adversarial confrontation and acrimonious separation process, McClain deliberately shared on media, official astronaut portraits that featured the contentious child. Worden strongly objected to it and complained. As a result, McClain soon removed them from the internet.[16] Surprisingly, however, during training and preparations for departure to the ISS, McClain exhibited no anguish or anxiety or angst or any discernible behaviour pattern due to this reason or cause. Neither was NASA aware of these developments at that time nor had any inkling of this continuing court dispute.

In March 2019, the aggrieved spouse, Summer Worden, made a complaint to the establishment. The plaint contained criminal allegations of impropriety of identity theft and misconduct for improper access to confidential financial data and personal banking records by astronaut McClain, while on official duty on-board ISS in outer space. Worden formally lodged complaints with the Federal Trade Commissioner and Office of Inspector General of NASA, an in-house investigative authority.[17] The contention was that the official computer facility and privileged network had been misused to gain access to confidential financial data for personal and private ends. It was contended as an unauthorised action and contrary to service rules and ISS Crew Code of Conduct (CCoC) thus constituting illegality. Apparently, it was a peccant act on the part of McClain that could possibly establish *mens rea* leading to prove an element of alleged criminality in motive, intent, and action. However, NASA as a matter of policy, declined to make a statement on this issue because it normally refrains to comment on personnel or personal matters of the staff.[18]

McClain, on her part, clarified, "she was dealing with the couple's intertwined finances" and Worden had shared with her the online login credentials.[19] Of course, this disclosure of password was during the golden period of their marriage and relationship. Thus, McClain had the requisite information and explicit approval to access the account from 2015 till 31 January 2019, when the permission was formally

---

[15] Christina Zdanowicz, "NASA astronaut's estranged wife charged with lying about claim that spouse improperly accessed account from space", *CNN*, April 9, 2020.

[16] "Astronaut accessed estranged spouse's bank account in possible first criminal allegation from space", A report from *New York Times*, August 23, 2019. Also refer Chelsea Gohd, *Space.com*, August, 25, 2019. She commented that this case appears simple, cut and dried but future crimes could pose murkier situations and complex conditions for analysis.

[17] AFP report, August 25, 2019.

[18] Report by Meghan Bartels at < mbartels@space.com >

[19] Christina Zdanowicz, "NASA astronaut's estranged wife charged with lying about claim that spouse improperly accessed account from space", *CNN*, April 9, 2020.

revoked by Ms. Worden. And she had accessed Worden's personal bank account twice during this period, before revocation and termination of the authorisation. She further asserted that this action was for the welfare of their child. She reasserted that she had intended to obtain details about the finances of the estranged spouse in order to ensure availability of adequate funds for the school fees and other needs of the child, a responsibility she had been discharging for some time. "It was a normal action for me as I had been doing in the past."[20]

On the contrary, Worden reported that Ms. McClain, unauthorisedly used the ISS computer system with connectivity to NASA network to gain privileged access to personal bank account and financial status of the spouse, allegedly when the permission had been revoked. This incident was protested by Worden and indicted as identity theft among other charges. It initially transpired from the complaint that the astronaut while in space was alleged to have made an unauthorised use of the NASA-affiliated computer system from aboard the ISS to gain access into the bank's computer network solely for own advantage and personal benefit. However, McClain, in her statement to an in-house inquiry by NASA, had refuted the charges levelled against her and explained that there could be confusion and misunderstanding on both sides.[21]

It transpired during investigation by NASA that Worden had made a false statement during an inquiry interview regarding the timing of revocation of her authorisation to McClain. Moreover, McClain had made two incursions into Worden's bank account during her stay at the ISS and both these instances had occurred well before Worden's wrongly claimed revocation of authority. Incidentally, both these bank transactions had been valid, successful, and bonafide; and withdrawal of authority was not yet operative. Therefore, NASA has cleared Astronaut McClain of the charges alleged by the estranged spouse. Incidentally, she is now expected, in her next space mission, to take a Moon-walk as the first woman to step on the Moon.

In the same case, Worden, in frustration, had also filed a complaint with Federal Trade Commissioner on 19 March 2019, imputing similar wrong facts and inaccurate details. After a lengthy investigation by the public authority, Worden has been found to have lied on material evidence and vital counts by making false statements. In return, she has been charged accordingly, and the matter has been duly referred to the Department of Justice for allocating Magistrate Judge for necessary trial.

Worden on her part, has defended her mistake as sheer confusion and a memory lapse regarding date of change of password of bank account. Further, after she had become aware of this mix-up on dates, she had voluntarily returned to the authorities for admission of the confusion and submission of correct information. Perhaps, it was too late by then. If found guilty, she "could face up to five years in prison on each of the two counts and a maximum fine of $250,000, according to the Department of Justice statement."[22] Legal advice suggests to call for the records of McClain's internet usage from space, which could be "subpoenaed" in the court to aid a defence

---

[20] Christina, ibid.

[21] *New York Times* report, n. 4 ante.

[22] Christina at n. 15, ante.

1.3 Analysis of the McClain Case

plea; and may be, these reveal a new twist. As per the latest information, a Federal Grand Jury has returned the verdict on Summer Worden as guilty, in February 2021. The court has yet to confirm this verdict and award sentence.[23] But there has been near-silence on this case in the media. Efforts to approach NASA to elicit further information have failed to evoke response. Nor has Google any updates on this case. It can now be reasonably conjectured that the matter has been recalled by the US Department of Defense on the ground that both the parties belong to the military service as Army and Air Force officers, respectively. It may, therefore, have been decided to try the case by Court Martial under Military Law. In fact, most countries have military laws where all offences, other than murder, rape, and sedition, by military personnel fall within the jurisdiction of military courts. And proceedings of military Court Martials are confidential. Another possibility also exists that Summer Worden, in view of her meritorious past record, has been penalised for her indiscretion, in non-traditional manner with a punishment of much lesser severity going into the records of the officer. Further, it is equally believable that McClain, in her magnanimity and nostalgia of good times, has pleaded for leniency for her ex-spouse.

On her part, Worden was shocked with the jury indictment that accuses her for submission of false details in a formal investigation. No wonder, the case has turned topsy-turvy with accuser becoming the accused. Be that as it may, the case certainly opens up new issues and likely complications of international dimensions on jurisdiction over the accused, considerations for extradition with or without treaty between states, competence of the court to seize the case, decision to apply which law and award of punishment on whose legal codes: the accused or the victim and finally, the perception of justice meted out to the parties. Some of these issues would need new explanations in international agreements, revised jurisprudence for the space domain, and novel institutional solutions. These flagged issues have been discussed in the relevant chapters and finally presented in Conclusion.

1.3.1 A Preliminary View

Astronaut, Anne McClain, is now back on Earth and is resident in the USA after completion of her official mission at the ISS. NASA instituted an in-house inquiry by the Inspector General of Investigations into the alleged and formally complained act of misfeasance and breach of Crew Code of Conduct which came be popularly treated as the first assertion of crime in space. The investigators, on the contrary, found that the complainant spouse had made false allegation and had averred untrue statement twice before the authorities. This indiscreet action, presumably intentional, to embarrass her estranged spouse, became the cause for countercharges against the complainant Worden. She stands trial in a court now and the verdict is awaited.

---

[23] Report by Mike Baker, "Space Crime Allegation Leads to Charges Against Astronaut's Ex-Wife", in *New York Times,* April 6, 2020.

Thus, the case has turned topsy-turvy and the crime supposedly committed in space is no longer valid in law and the astronaut McClain comes out honourably clean and unblemished in this media-reported episode.

Be that as it may, and whatever be its outcome, this case can be discussed as an illustration that highlights several pertinent legal issues. The case certainly presents a perspective that raises important questions about jurisdiction and procedures and how we should handle criminal activity in future, of whatever kind or import, occurring in orbit in outer space or on celestial bodies. The subject deserves contemplation and debate to arrive at easy and viable solutions because such crimes could involve persons from different countries or nationalities that could have international implications and diverse ramifications. Undoubtedly, treaties being state-centric are approachable for relief through bureaucratic machinery, or diplomatic corps. Therefore, such cases relating to international relations and handling of judicial matters are proverbially slow in traction and dilatory in processes yielding rather delayed results.

Of course, McClain had defended herself, according to a report in New York Times,[24] by publicly asserting that it was a routine occurrence, to make sure that the couple had enough money to pay for their son's tuition fees and outstanding bills. She also claimed that she had been accessing her spouse's financial accounts and bank statements in the past also but possibly that was in better times of conjugal togetherness. She has further pleaded that this was done with *bonafide* honest intention and as such it was in furtherance of common interest and for the welfare of their six-year-old son. This circumstance seems true and actions bonafide as it turns out in the official investigation, and the underlying reasons reiterated appear to have merit and validity. Thus, it was no emotional defence based on human frailties and sentimental fervour but a ground reality of a fractured relationship and the vengeance of a wounded spouse. No wonder, some elements of dark truth sneaked in. It appears that justice will eventually prevail in this murky case.

1.3.2 Assessment of Culpability

Shorn of the genuine defence and despite the triumph of acquittal, this case with unproven allegations may be taken as an example of a moot-case of possible crimes in outer space. The construct of circumstances and the alleged act of misfeasance has apparent strains of culpability. It is clear that the irregularity or this wrongful act, if at all so, was knowingly conceived, voluntarily performed, and intentionally executed with motive and selfish advantage. It thus had a well-thought-out purpose and planned personal motivation that was intended to benefit the wrongdoer, who was reasonably conscious of the wrongdoing. She was well aware of the service rules of conduct, repercussions of the unauthorised act, and knowledge of the consequences.

---

[24] Loren Grush, "The first alleged crime committed in space raises questions about jurisdiction in orbit", August 27, 2019. < lorengrush@lorengrush >

1.3 Analysis of the McClain Case

Ostensibly, different aspects of the impugned act uncover a deliberated intent, design of an envisioned outcome, and matching physical acts which establish *prima facie* culpability. Apart from the negative essence of the overt, physical actions, their inner motivation, hidden intention, and intrinsic prodding reveal a discernible element of *mens rea*. Nonetheless, truth in the evidence is for the court to judge.

Therefore, in the instant mock case, the apparent criminality in this case may be held try-able through due process of law, in accordance with the US statutes and rules framed there under, by a competent court in the USA. Of course, as an illustration, the actual crime is simple and relates to only one country on all salient parameters comprising the litigants, the locus of event, its jurisdiction and availability of evidence. But the situation may not always be so simplistic in nationality or territoriality or the subject matter of offence or availability of evidence or the number of contestants to the dispute and their respective nationality. Future crimes in space may be far varied and diverse in nature; far complex and complicated in material evidence and the number of contesting parties hailing from different countries. Ergo, national courts may find it difficult to seize jurisdiction of the case, apprehend the accused, and muster enough evidence so easily.

1.3.3 An Appraisal of Jurisdiction in McClain Case

In order to analyse and determine jurisdiction in such cases, the wrongdoing must first be tested on the "trichotomy" of Space Treaty law and international law and domestic laws. The alleged offence, in this particular case, has occurred in American quarters of the ISS by an American astronaut making unauthorised use of American official equipment and a privileged working system and against an aggrieved American citizen. Apparently, it looks a simplistic case of domestic jurisdiction and is unreservedly the US concern, covered entirely by the US law. So has Michelle Hanlon opined in an interview to *The Verge*.[25] Her off-the-cuff views may be correct, yet we certainly need to search for judicial logic and probe legal basis even for such an obvious deductive answer to a simplistic situational crime.

Taking into account the applicable space law and facts of the reported space crime, it transpires that both the persons: complainant and the defendant, in the instant case are an American astronaut and a US Air Force officer. Allegedly, the impugned crime was committed in the US quarters of ISS. So, all the germane incidents and material evidence concur to validate that the alleged misfeasance can be validly tried by a competent court in the USA on either the principle of territoriality or the principle of nationality, or both, in deciding jurisdictional issues. Hence, the McClain case simply and squarely falls under both the principles to amply satisfy jurisdictional criteria and there arises no conflict of laws on jurisdiction. At the same time, both parties being American, there appear no conflict or hassles on extradition.

---

[25] Grush, ibid.

To clarify in the instant case, as an illustration, no infringement of any international instrument seems to have occurred; and the provision of permanent jurisdiction under Article VIII of the OST also supports the stated position. Therefore, international trial is neither mandated nor relevant. Accordingly, the trial venue rightfully shifts to domestic jurisdiction of the US courts under the principle of nationality of the parties. Further, on the principle of territoriality also, the US quarters of ISS are notionally deemed as US territory, and as the astronaut was stationed there, the aspect of jurisdiction does not get complicated. Further, the alleged offender and the relevant subject matter being present and available in the USA, the case rightly requires intervention by the US court. Hence, the domestic jurisdiction of the appropriate US courts under the germane law becomes applicable and legitimate to seize the case.

This media-reported case was treated as an illustration though it has undergone twists due to factual inaccuracies and the case has been handled by federal agencies of the USA. Nevertheless, many more complications of nationalities involved in conflict or notional territorial claims on celestial bodies or leased orbiting space hotels or celestial resorts can be imaginable pointing towards conflicting competence of international as well as domestic judicial forums. Even moot courts have evolved narratives with scenarios much more complex and intertwined with international implications and national compulsions. Permutations and combination can be worked out not only as an exercise but also because these may occur in reality to pose jurisdictional hassles necessitating a need to elect one of the competing legal systems for adjudication to impart a well-meaning perception of fair trial and due justice in the international milieu.

1.4 A Mini-Mutiny on Skylab-4

An infamous tale of defiance and of serious dimension occurred on the Skylab-4 mission. The story so goes that in 1973, Apollo programme, so successful in mission achievements, was terminated. The US government and NASA were content with the accomplishments of lunar missions and the political gains derived therefrom. So, despite the availability of Saturn V rockets, Apollo exploratory launches to the Moon were suddenly called off. As a result, Skylab programme was born that continued for four missions undertaking different tests and trials for future roadmaps.

It was December 1973, and this was the last crewed Skylab programme with the longest stay in space. It seemed the flight was bugged with glitches. Three highly annoyed astronauts aboard the US space station Skylab stopped talking to ground control on Earth for an entire day of 28 December, almost rebelling against their apathetic and inconsiderate NASA "overlords" after repeatedly complaining of being over-worked and fatigued. They clarified later that NASA had been pushing them too hard on a tight work routine with too little time to themselves even for daily personal chores.

1.4 A Mini-Mutiny on Skylab-4

So, they unilaterally, on their own, took some desired respite without official permission from the Capsule Communicator or even informal information to ground control. They went so far as to switch off their radio to remain incommunicado so that the crew could not even be contacted.[26] Thus, they spent the unscheduled holiday rather leisurely and self-indulgently. On this day of "do-not-disturb," they all took an unhurried shower, listened to music, and looked out of the window at Earth. They suddenly observed Comet Kohoutek and snapped its pictures. They also took some time to catch up on sleep to overcome fatigue. No wonder, they generally had a good time and much-wanted relaxation, both physical and mental. But the day of pleasure, paradoxically, involved an element of guilt and show of indiscipline.

It is conceded that as per the mission plan, the crew were to observe a holiday after ten days of work. But due to heavily packed work schedule, this was not to be and they missed on three free days with bickering on the next. Heavy routine was really telling on their physique and nerves; fatigue had mounted beyond forbearance and mental faculties were slowing down. And they simply conspired to take a day off disregarding the mission's reluctance for such permission. It was mutiny; though it makes a very strong labelling of the act, there is no word like strike in military parlance. Howsoever dire was their need for rest under the peculiar predicament, their modus and action were patently unauthorised and "undisciplined" where condonation is rarely granted. Let us honestly accept that indiscretions are mistakes that turn into crimes by their sensitivity and tendency towards repetition as also due to their "offensive gravity" under the military rules of discipline, regimentation, and command system.

It may be argued, on the contrary, that the facts of the case reveal a much lesser gravity of offence than the heinous mutiny. But military justice works on its own strict doctrines of discipline and haloed concepts of authority; and these respective weightings are skewed or undermined. Defence forces never really condone such conduct in itself and more importantly tend to create a precedence in deterrence for future insubordination. In this case also, perhaps, the commanders did not take the act kindly and possibly the defiant crew members were branded, if not openly, at least in their confidential dossiers. No wonder, all the three crew members never got a space sortie again.

Whatever was the style of punishment and injustice dispensed to the crew, this incident did bring about a realisation among the authorities that long stay in outer space has its own typical and mounting stress–physical, mental, and emotional–of a different kind which is not easily comprehensible because it is not experienced on the Earth. Thus, longevity of this mission highlighted a new challenge. This was a revelation and NASA, thereafter, did appreciate the psychological constraints of the astronauts and introduced flexibility in future routines. The work schedules of the crew were more humanised.

---

[26] Jonathan O'Callaghan, "The Bizarre Story Of The "Mutiny" On Board A Space Station", April 21, 2018. This story has also been repeated in Smithsonian Magazine, LA Times and Gizmodo.

1.5 The Case of a Hole in Soyuz Module at ISS

1.5.1 The Detection of the Hole

It was August 2018. The Russian vehicle, Soyuz MS-09, had flown three astronauts, Russian cosmonaut Sergey Prokopyev, European Space Agency astronaut Alexander Gerst, and NASA's Serena Auñón-Chancellor, to augment the existing crew strength at the ISS. Later, on 29 August 2018, ISS controllers at Johnson Space Centre, Houston, noticed a slight drop in pressure inside the orbiting laboratory. This variation was informed to the crew for investigation. The crew on internal inspection of the ISS traced the leak to a small hole in Russian Soyuz MS-09, which had docked to the Station in June same year. The hole was patched up on 30 August 2018, with gauze and epoxy composite by astronaut Prokopyev, the then commander of the Soyuz. With this patch repair, the minor danger was averted.

Based on the inspection report from the ISS and repair procedure from the astronaut, the Russian authorities decided to investigate the reason for leak in the pressure and who could possibly have done the sabotage. An early report from Roscosmos announced that the breach in the Soyuz wall was a drill hole of the size 2 mm (0.08 inches), possibly made by a person with apparently "a faltering hand" because of the scuff marks nearby that likely resulted when the drill slipped. Russian officials "further insinuated that the unsteady hand was likely due to the culprit drilling in micro-gravity" implying that someone among the crew was to blame.[27] They also ruled out the suggested possibility of it happening at the assembly line or testing stages of the module prior to its launch.

NASA, on the contrary, based on a video footage from the space station surveillance system, asserted that none of the US astronauts on the station were near the Russian segment where Soyuz vehicle was docked and the accusations are baseless. The Russians, however, did not accept this plea nor its basis and in reciprocal recrimination have brazenly claimed that the camera results could have been tampered with or doctored. The Russian official further allege that they "were denied the chance to examine Russian tools and administer polygraphs, or lie detector tests, on the astronauts."[28]

The Russian media has gone far to pinpoint the suspicion on an American astronaut. The Russian news agency TASS reported that Serena Aunon-Chancellor had an emotional breakdown in space and it was then that she caused the damage to the Russian spacecraft docked at the station so that she could return home to Earth ahead of schedule. NASA was upset at such personal attack on the astronaut and her

---

[27] Amy Thompson, "Russian space officials try to blame NASA astronaut for Soyuz air leak in 2018: report", Space.com, August 14, 2021.
[28] Ibid.

medical history. Crewmates have strongly commented that the disclosures and accusations are not credible. They have lauded, "Serena is an extremely well-respected crew member...and...we stand behind Serena and her professional conduct."[29]

In the latest statement, Roscosmos has confirmed that the investigation into "what or who" caused a hole has been completed. The possibility that a micro-meteoroid strike may have caused the hole is ruled out. Another possibility that it happened by error of a technician on the ground before the blast-off was also dismissed because that person would have tried to cover up the mistake by remedial measures. It is thus certain that the hole has been punctured with human effort and with the use of a drill machine which was in all likelihood available nearby. It also seems credible to assume that it was a work of shaking hands of an unstable mind in fear while doing the act. By elimination of motivation and evaluation of *mens rea*, the suspicion moves towards astronaut Serena who had "an acute psychological crisis" while on-board ISS "due to stress after an unsuccessful romantic relationship with another crew member."[30] As a result of this mental disturbance and disgruntled attitude, she possibly wanted to return home to the Earth earlier than scheduled and could have, in all probability, resorted to this act. Circumstantially derived assumptions may not turn out to be true, always.

The truth may not come out soon as NASA does not, as a matter of policy and privacy, make public comments on the professional conduct or personal life of the astronauts. In general, NASA has lauded her professional performance and defended her conduct. Mutual recrimination and diplomatic pressures, however, may go on as Roscosmos has threatened of criminal charges against a NASA astronaut. It is also stated that "All results of the investigation regarding the hole in the habitation module of the Soyuz MS-09 spacecraft [have been] transmitted to Law Enforcement officials," who would "decide whether or not to initiate a criminal case which would be akin to issuing an indictment."[31]

Proven facts and presented circumstances confirmed the existence of a hole in Soyuz module where it should not be and posed danger. Thus, evidence makes it clear that an act equivalent to crime has been committed. Only the identity of the person who committed this act has not been established beyond reasonable doubt. Such a dilemma is often confronted in investigation of terrestrial crimes. But crimes in space should be less pardonable for their possible impact and accompanying consequences. Therefore, deterrent punishments are more important to instil fear to lessen the incidents of crimes. May be, because at times, the criminal may not survive the consequences of own act.

---

[29] Ibid.

[30] Eric Berger, "Russia threatens criminal charges against a NASA astronaut", *Space.com*, November 30, 2021.

[31] Refer https://arstechnica.com/science/2021/11/russia-threatens-criminal-charges-against-a-nasa-astronaut/. Verb in parentheses has been changed in context.

1.5.2 *Negligence in Space Would Be a Crime*

The *Nauka*,[32] a multi-purpose module, was designed to serve as a research laboratory, storage unit, and airlock device to upgrade Russia's capabilities aboard the ISS. *Nauka* was launched and it docked on the underside of the ISS, though under tense operations. Anyway, docking was successfully achieved on 29 July 2021 and was so confirmed by the concerned agency. After *Nauka* module had latched onto the space station and had well settled, the mission controllers in Moscow commenced performing some post-docking "reconfiguration" procedures.[33]

It was then that, suddenly and inexplicably, the thruster jets of *nauka* module restarted and the mishap began. This malfunction resulted in the entire station to pitch out of its normal flight position compelling the US mission's flight director to declare a "spacecraft emergency."[34] The actual occurrence was that the space station spun one-and-a-half revolutions, i.e. about 540 degrees, before coming to a stop upside down, relative to its original position. The space station also lost altitude during this unexpected and unplanned manoeuvre. "The space station then did a 180-degree forward flip to get back to its original orientation."[35] This was achieved by the flight teams on the ground at the Johnson Space Centre in Houston, by activating thrusters on another module of the orbiting platform in corrective action. *Nauka* engines were ultimately switched off.

The correction activity to regain control of the space station was a "tug of war" between the two modules. Initially, however, the incident was underplayed by both Roscosmos as well as NASA. But with more information flowing on the causes and assessments of possible impact, the US specialists shudder to think of the event and accept that it was serious and could have caused a major mishap and consequent tragedy, human, and material. At that moment, there were seven astronauts on-board and at risk though escape module was available in readiness. Early reports inform that due to this glitch, the station was actually out of control for about two minutes while communication with all the seven members of the crew was lost or disrupted for several minutes.[36]

Russian space agency maintains and expects us to believe that the incident was caused "due to a short-term software failure and a command was mistakenly implemented" to fire the thruster engines. Inadvertence is possible, yet it would be naive to accept such a simplistic explanation for a goof-up of monumental dimension. In fact, who caused the malfunction, whether man or machine, is still to be determined with precision and finality. On the other hand, a preliminary inspection of the ISS,

---

[32] *Nauka* is Russian language word for 'science'.

[33] "Space Station did 540-degree flip, turned upside down: Mishap more serious than earlier reported", *India Today,* August 3, 2021.

[34] *India Today*, ibid, updated report.

[35] *The New York Times*, August 3, 2021. Based on a statement by Zebulon Scoville, Flight Director at NASA's Mission Control Centre in Houston.

[36] Reporting and writing by Steve Gorman in Los Angeles and Polina Ivanova in Moscow. Editing by Mark Heinrich, Leslie Adler and Raju Gopalakrishnan for *News SCIENCE*.

post-mishap, reports that the space station would have certainly suffered stress on the structure and equipment. More revelations are expected.[37]

Be that as it may, it can be maintained that negligence in space operations, from space or on ground, is tantamount to crime. Every activity in and for space deserves due diligence of the highest order and actions in *abundanti cautela*. There is no scope for casualness or even inadvertence, leaving aside sheer negligence or dereliction in duty. Space environment is potentially dangerous and highly hazardous; thus, it is unsparing in effect and rarely ever gives a second chance. In this instance of presumed malfunction, luck was in our favour and providentially, things fell in place and in time to ultimately turn out right in result. Defects so caused by the upheaval in the ISS may be set right in due course of time but such a saviour opportunity may not repeat itself. Hence, maximum care and caution are mandatory else the crime and the criminal, both may vanish with much more.

1.6 Conclusion

The illustrative narrations of different episodes point to one thing in common that there was alleged misfeasance. In the McClain case, she has been cleared of the allegations in a magnanimous gesture by NASA and may be further rewarded by another trip to space with a planned space-walk. Her exoneration may be officially complete as if no misconduct has occurred, but a minor blemish, nevertheless, remains. On the contrary, her complainant spouse (also a defence officer) has been charged on two counts of making false statement in formal investigations before authorities. This becomes a separate case, not related to outer space.

The second illustration of "near-mutiny" or at least serious disobedience relates to Skylab-4. The crew was overworked beyond planned work schedule and had foregone three off-days in succession. As a result, they were fatigued physically and mentally for continuous discharge of duties. Obviously, they needed well-deserved rest for a day which was inappropriately turned down by the authorities. This prompted the crew to self-observe a holiday without due sanction. Further, their action of being incommunicado could have been dangerous, if not disastrous. Admittedly, their need for rest was genuine and deserving, yet their modus operandi was contra to the military rules, discipline and ethics. This violation of haloed services tradition taints their action and makes them stand in the line of the guilty. Condonation for such acts is rarely granted.

The third illustration of a mysterious hole in Soyuz module docked to the ISS is more serious and patently a criminal act. It appears, *prima facie*, a handiwork of a human being: whether an astronaut or a ground technician. It also appears an intentional act and not sheer inadvertence. The incident becomes graver with the dangerous dimensions of leaking pressure on the ISS and the lurking human intent in committing the act. The culprit may not be found with certainty of evidence, yet

---

[37] *India Today*, updated version of August 4, 2021.

the criminal implications of the act, possibly committed in space, become no less serious.

The fourth serious incident of traumatic roll-over of the International Space Station due to misfire of the wrong thruster boosters of *Nauka,* the Russian research module docked to the ISS, is still worse in physical repercussions, material disturbance and psychological impact. Whether it was caused by a false command by the computer or a temporary software failure or possibly an inadvertent yet negligent act by the Roscosmos manoeuvre operators may not be known with certainty, at least for quite some time. Nevertheless, this failure of man or machine, either way, leads to an element of criminality in negligent behaviour or lack of due care and caution by the concerned, relating to critical acts in or for outer space.

In concluding comments; it is, however, a different matter that the McClain case turned topsy-turvy where alleging party became the accused and McClain was cleared of the charges. The second case related to near-mutiny and military disciple does not exonerate such behaviour, irrespective of the reasons. In the other two cases clinching evidence, beyond reasonable doubt, was not found to prove the identity of the alleged offenders. It is equally painful that the evidence collected was not fully and honestly shared with the affected parties, leaving aside revealing the true version in the public domain. And motivated political bickering for blame on the US astronaut in the "hole" case has marred the atmosphere of cooperation in outer space. Damage has been done to mutual trust and building bridges for restoration of confidence may take a long time.

Further, such cases may tend to get mired in jurisdictional wrangles as also face conflicting claims on extradition either for the reason of national affiliation or for the states to escape political embarrassment that may arise on revelations in the trial. Many more complications are imaginable on the international as well as domestic scene like collection of evidence or applicability of the national criminal codes. Therefore, the cases narrated posit a number of legal issues which would require *lex specialis* for regulatory purposes and a novel institutional solution, viz., an International Court of Space Crimes under the aegis of the UN, for proper justice that is perceived as just and fair.

Chapter 2
Past Instances of Near-Crimes in Space: The USA

Typically, so far, space-bound astronauts and ISS-stationed crew members, belonging to whichever country, have generally exhibited best model behaviour while in space. This exemplary conduct has been without any major dispute or mutual conflict in orbit or any actual crime per se despite zero-gravity inconvenience, claustrophobic conditions, and ergonomic handicaps. But after all, humans are human and may not behave any differently in the haloed domain of outer space. Their frailties may manifest anywhere, and they may err or misbehave, inadvertently or irrationally, prankish or even advertently. Therefore, their usual good conduct, disciplined behaviour, and exemplary deportment in the past are no guarantee for the future and may not be taken for granted every time and for all times.

Anyway, McClain incident, presently, is only an allegation and not a confirmed legal guilt without official pronouncement. Whatever be its outcome, it is not the first crime in space though so projected and blared by the Media. Yet this remains as the first investigated and litigated malfeasance committed in space. This indiscreet act so bounced into prominence partly because of her personal misconduct for self-interest and partly because of a formal complaint by the spouse to concerned authorities. Misconduct and indiscipline of more serious nature have occurred earlier, but these were either condoned or punished in other ways, even without any strictures or censure in public domain or recording in confidential dossiers.

It is thus pertinent to recount some known cases of state experiments gone bad and which have fouled up the outer space environment or have caused near-unpardonable pollution on the Moon. Second variety is the cases of misfeasance committed by the space crew collectively or in unison while in space. The third kind of act is the negligence by the astronauts individually while performing allocated tasks or for sheer pranks of indiscipline. An act contrary to norms and best practices observed by space agencies has been committed by a private space player. These are, therefore, "almost crimes" of more serious nature and concern in space, whether committed by the state, a private actor or the orbiting personnel, individually or collectively.

2.1 State Experiments Gone Bad

2.1.1 The Copper Needles Experiment

Let's start with the USA, and the example is copper needles project. This was called the Westford Needles project and was undertaken in 1961 and 1963 in experiment to allow long distance communications by bouncing radio waves off of a band/belt of small copper wires (passive dipoles) as a reflector. For the purpose, nearly 480 million dipole needles were spread in a radio-reflective ring around the Earth at a height of about 3500 km. The specification of each dipole was 1.78 cm in length and a diameter of 25.4 μm (West Ford 1) or 17.8 μm (West Ford 2). Tiny copper needles in total weighed about 48 kg.

The 1961 Westford experiment was intended to create an artificial ionosphere through levitated dipole needles but did not turn out to be successful when the needles failed to sufficiently disperse in a ring-like manner. These actually jumbled in seven clusters and are still somewhere in space as experimental debris. The second experiment in 1963 was no great success either because needles were sparsely populated. The testing failed in its mission and did not achieve the desired result as radio reflector for communications. The project was later abandoned, since made redundant by the modern communication applications with geo-sync satellite technology.[1]

The experiment was greatly criticised by astronomers who feared optical and radio pollution[2] would interfere with space activities, apart from causing space clutter. In disregard of the unsolicited advice so offered, the USA, in its technological arrogance, failed to consult specialists *in abundanti cautela*. The USA may argue that it had then no obligation to consult other states as Outer Space Treaty[3] (OST) was signed later. But wisdom does not come from treaties alone. Nevertheless, the USA also had a higher obligation *erga omnes* under international law that was ignored.

The loud protests from experts in the field from Russia, Britain, and others persisted.[4] Ultimately, the matter was taken up in the United Nations where the USA defended on unsupported journalistic reports and explained that sunlight pressure would cause the dipoles to only remain in orbit for a short period and the same will disappear in three years. The wires still exist in space after six decades and are regularly tracked. The lie gets proved but as a result of this censure, a suitable provision on consultation, when deemed necessary, was incorporated in Article IX of the OST.[5] Thus, under the circumstances, it may be difficult to pin direct blame,

---

[1] Butrica, Andrew J. (ed.), "*Beyond the Ionosphere: The Development of Satellite Communications*", history.nasa.gov, The NASA History Series, NASA.

[2] https://space.skyrocket.de/doc_sdat/westford.htm. Accessed on 13 April 2020.

[3] Treaty on Principles Governing the Activities of States in the Exploration and Use of Outer Space, including the Moon and other Celestial Bodies, 1967. (in short OST).

[4] *International Academy of Astronautics* (Edited Publication, October 15, 2005).

[5] Böckstiegel, Karl-Heinz, Benkö, Marietta, *Space Law: Basic Legal Documents (1990)*, ISBN 9780792300915.

2.1 State Experiments Gone Bad   21

yet the pollution caused shall persist for a long time[6] and cannot be ignored. Suitable lessons need to be learnt.

2.1.2 The Misadventure of Nuclear Testing in Space

The USA in its euphoria of newly assumed leadership of space activities attempted Starfish Prime detonation experiment in July 1962. The USA exploded a 1.4 megaton nuclear warhead at a height of 400 kms creating a massive electromagnetic wave which disturbed the operation of electricity and telephone lines in Hawaii and the dismal effects were felt as far away as New Zealand. It was the first of its kind and had demonstrated its powerful effects. The world was shocked at its occurrence and humanity in conscience. Any action in this direction had to end and could not be permitted in a competitive race between the two superpowers. Therefore, such tests had to cease forthwith. To put an end to the testing of nuclear weapons in space, the Partial Test Ban Treaty was signed in 1963 putting a stop to high-altitude nuclear testing. Soon thereafter, the Outer Space Treaty came into effect in 1967 that banned nuclear weapons from space under Article IV.[7]

2.1.3 Riskiest Missions of NASA

It is generally believed that the riskiest mission was Apollo 11 of Moon-landing and return. But this was not so. Almost all elements of the Apollo 11 mission had been checked and rehearsed before except for landing and walking on the Moon and returning back into lunar orbit. In fact, Apollo 11 would be the first time the lunar module's ascent stage would be called upon to lift off from the Moon, but both Apollo 9 and Apollo 10 ran tests of the ascent stage engine that simulated a lunar launch as closely as it could be. Perhaps, a better candidate for the riskiest NASA mission ever would be Apollo 8 because it was the first time humans were put on-board a Saturn V after the failure of Apollo 6 on Saturn IV. It was the also for the first time that human beings were being sent out of orbit and, most importantly, Apollo 8 had no lunar module to act as backup. If the fuel tank explosion of Apollo 13 had occurred on Apollo 8, the astronauts would have died within hours and there was no fail-safe alternative of saving them.[8]

By scientific standards, the riskiest mission was the final Challenger flight. The technicians involved knew that the O-ring was charring when the weather was cold.

---

[6] Other similar cases of space pollution relate to ASAT tests by China, the US and India. Discussed in the next chapter.

[7] https://celestrak.com/publications/AMOS/2007/AMOS-2007.pdf

[8] Adapted from an account by Kevin Parker, former JWST Test Engineer at NASA Goddard Space Flight Center (2011-2012). Answered in Quora Digest, July 13, 2019.

Originally, there was a standard that if there was charring on the ring, then that was no longer safe. Charring appeared and showed the attendant risks but it was decided that the safety limit of charring be raised to 25% of the ring. Then charring exceeded 25% and its limit was raised to 50%. Safety was compromised and one could see the clear pattern and what it will inevitably lead to. The range safety officer knew the risk and considered that launching was an unacceptable risk. As the final authority, he aborted the launch. But the executives at NASA did not like that. They raised the level of authority and informed that the engineer was being overly cautious. The OK was given and NASA executives authorised the launch. But with the knowledge of high probability of failure risk, this becomes the riskiest mission NASA ever undertook. However, no criminal charges for the safety compromise were ever initiated. Not even a censure for the unwise hasty launch.[9]

2.1.4 Garbage Left on the Moon

Moon is the most visited celestial body in space. So far, 24 astronauts have flown to the Moon, and 12 have landed there. Incidentally, all those who landed there were men.[10] Believably, due to weight restriction for lift-off from the Moon, astronauts have discarded dispensable items and have left a lot of garbage on the Moon. To begin with Apollo 11, Moon-walker astronauts, intending to save on weight when lifting off of the Moon and to make room allowance for stacking samples of Moon rock pieces and surface dust, left their unwanted items behind on Moon. This included but was not limited to food wrappers, used waterless bathing toiletries, small containers, jettison bags, lunar shoes, hammocks, and human-digested waste, almost everything not required for the return flight. The mass they left behind was replaced in the lunar module with samples of Moon rock pieces and dust they brought back for exploration and experimentation. The subsequent missions would have also shed similar items on the Moon and littered in different places depending upon the site of landing. Thus, the litter left behind by successive missions, in a way, has caused pollution and, possibly, contamination with scattered garbage.

Scientists assure that the Moon's surface is totally dead, dry, sterile, and airless; so, applying conventional biological wisdom, there ought to be absolutely no chance of any bacteria surviving, spreading, and eventually evolving on the Moon to cause contamination. But these assurances are not empirically tested and sites of garbage have not been revisited. There is, however, a contrary view that the Moon, presumably, has undersurface water and that while casualties in the excrement would have been very high, it is possible there were some microbes with mutations that could have made survival within the faeces possible or that spores would have grown over the

---

[9] Ibid.

[10] Sixty women have gone into space but none has landed on the Moon, the first Russian woman in space was Valentina Tereshkova in 1963; and the first American woman to fly in space was Sally Ride, in 1983.

faeces. Be that as it may, both surmises remain conjectures only. In comparison, any mark of footprints on the dusty surface of the Moon is certainly expected to last a long time, yet not forever. Thus, there is very little chance that the Moon's environment will efface any distinctive mark or disturb the garbage or scatter it. There is no air, no water, no atmosphere, and no tectonics on the Moon. There is only sunlight, heat, cold, wind and meteors. These effects will wear away a mark far more slowly than our atmosphere on the Earth.

Nevertheless, pollution and contamination of some sort have surely been caused and their effects may persist for inordinately long time or till scavenged. Thus, the pristine environment of the Moon has been disturbed and polluted. Astronauts are not to blame for this because they just obeyed orders from the ground control and higher command. So, the major part of responsibility attaches to the launching state for bad planning of the mission and a desire to cut costs. The acts tantamount to introduction of harmful interference into the Moon's environment which was violative of the Outer Space Treaty, Article IX. Further, these acts also constitute an infringement of the Moon Treaty (Article 7) by leaving contaminants on the surface of the Moon.

2.2 Collective Defiance by the Crew

2.2.1 A Near-Mutiny in Space

Apart from states, astronauts too, individually or collectively, have exhibited reprehensible behaviour of indiscipline or performed unauthorised acts bordering on criminality. Take for example the case of a near-mutiny in space that happened over fifty years ago. NASA launched the first crewed, Apollo 7 mission into space. The goal was to test the latest spaceship technology, ensuring humans could survive their long trip to the Moon, and the expedition also marked the first 3-person American space crew, as well as the first to broadcast a live television feed.[11]

The stakes were already high when Apollo 7 launched in 1968 because it was the first time NASA sent astronauts into space since a cabin fire that had killed the Apollo 1 crew. Apollo hardware had proven safe enough in space but this mission would be a crucial test of new spacecraft command and service modules functioning properly in space, long enough to carry man to the Moon and back. Overall, the crew never encountered any issues they could not handle. The Apollo spacecraft had about four times more room than its Gemini predecessors, but conditions were still cramped and uncomfortable. The crew were not always happy about it.

Worst of all, the astronauts got sick. Schirra came down with a severe head cold about 15 h into the flight, with the rest of the crew soon joining him. And as annoying as colds usually are, space-colds are even worse with no gravity to pull at and drain mucus from the head. As a result, the Apollo 7 crew had typical symptoms, stuffy

---

[11] Bill Andrews, "Apollo 7: NASA's first mini-mutiny in space", October 9, 2018. Accessed on 15 April 2020.

noses, dry nostrils, and congestion. On top of it, a demanding work environment on-board does not typically mix well with feeling awful. When Schirra wanted to delay that first time live TV broadcast so they could complete crucial mission tests, he met with resistance. The ground control insisted to squeeze in some camera time. Schirra would have none of it. "We do not have the equipment out; we have not had an opportunity to follow setting; we have not eaten…at this point, I have a cold. I refuse to foul up our time lines this way."[12] The crew defiance was clear though later, TV schedule went well.

An even bigger breach of protocol came towards the end of a highly successful mission and concerned reluctance to put on helmets. Every previous crewed re-entry and landing, Mercury and Gemini missions, required the astronauts to wear their helmets. But Schirra and his crew had been relieving sinus pressure by pinching their noses and blowing in a deliberate act. Their helmets, new model for the Apollo mission, had no visor openings, which would make this bodily act of relieving their noses near impossible in emergencies. They were particularly concerned that the changing pressures during re-entry would wreak havoc with their sinuses, possibly even bursting their ear drums. So, they simply refused to wear the helmets[13] despite protocol and orders from mission control. Fortunately, they landed safe and fine.

The defiance was obvious but in the interest of personal safety. The ground control was not happy, yet it did not trigger a formal inquiry. Nevertheless, the insubordination did not go unnoticed or unpunished. As a result, none of the three crew members ever flew in space again. And also, while every other Apollo mission crew almost immediately received Distinguished Service Medals, NASA's highest honour, Apollo 7 crew did not. They, however, did get this award some 40 years later, albeit posthumously in two cases. It sure was no consolation at that time.

2.2.2 Mini-Mutiny on Skylab-4

Another infamous tale for the same reason and of similar dimension occurred on the Skylab-4 mission. In 1973, Apollo programme was terminated. The US government and NASA were content with the accomplishments of lunar missions and the political gains derived therefrom. So, despite the availability of Saturn V rockets, exploratory launches to the Moon were suddenly called off. As a result, Skylab programme was born that continued for four missions undertaking different tests and trials for future roadmaps.

It was December 1973, and this was the last crewed Skylab programme with the longest stay in space. It seemed the flight was bugged with glitches. Three highly annoyed astronauts aboard the US space station Skylab stopped talking to ground control on Earth for an entire day of 28 December, rebelling against their apathetic

---

[12] NASA's special publication, *The Apollo Spacecraft–A Chronology*. Also refer page 115 of the official voice transcriptions.

[13] NASA, ibid. Based on voice script from p. 1169.

and inconsiderate NASA "overlords" after repeatedly complaining of being overworked and fatigued. They clarified later that NASA had been pushing them too hard on a tight work routine with too little time to them even for daily personal chores.

So, they unilaterally, on their own, took some desired respite without official permission from the Capsule Communicator or even informal information to ground control. They went so far as to switch their radio off to remain incommunicado so that the crew could not even be contacted.[14] They spent the unscheduled holiday leisurely and self-indulgently. On this day of "do-not-disturb," they all took an unhurried shower, listened to music, looked out of the window at Earth and suddenly observed Comet Kohoutek, snapped pictures, took some time to catch up on sleep, thus generally having a good time and much-wanted relaxation, both physical and mental.

It is conceded that as per the mission plan, the crew were to observe a holiday after ten days of work. But due to heavily packed work schedule, this was not to be and they missed on three free days with bickering on the next. Heavy routine was really telling on their physique and nerves; fatigue had mounted beyond forbearance. And they simply conspired to take a day off disregarding the mission's reluctance. It was mutiny; though it makes a very strong labelling of the act, there is no word like strike in military parlance. Howsoever dire was their need for rest under the peculiar predicament, their modus and action were patently unauthorised and "undisciplined" where condonation is rarely granted. Let us honestly accept that indiscretions are mistakes that turn into crimes by their sensitivity and tendency towards repetition as also "offensive gravity" under the military rules.

It may be argued on the contrary that the facts of the case reveal a much lesser gravity of offence than mutiny. But military justice works on its own strict doctrines of discipline and haloed concepts of authority, and respective weightings are skewed. Defence forces never really condone such conduct in itself and more importantly tend to create precedence in deterrence for future insubordination. In this case also, perhaps, the commanders did not take the act kindly and possibly the defiant crew members were branded, if not openly, at least in their confidential dossiers. No wonder, all the three crew members never got a space sortie again.

Whatever was the style of punishment or injustice caused to the crew, this incident did bring about a realisation among the authorities that long stay in outer space has its own typical stress–physical, mental, and emotional–of a different kind which is not easily comprehensible because it is not experienced on the Earth. Thus, longevity of this mission highlighted a new challenge. This was a revelation and NASA, thereafter, did appreciate the psychological constraints of the astronauts and introduced flexibility in future routines. The work schedules of the crew were humanised.

---

[14] Jonathan O'Callaghan, "The Bizarre Story Of The "Mutiny" On Board A Space Station", April 21, 2018. This story has also been repeated in Smithsonian Magazine, LA Times and Gizmodo.

2.3 Impermissible Acts by Astronauts

2.3.1 Throwing Away Vomit Bag into Space

Skylab-4 mission right from the launch itself had been afflicted with glitches and been mired in controversy. The crew annoyed the mission control with their indiscreet acts that resulted in misunderstandings and caused a deflection in the confidence threshold. The bridge of implicit trust between each other was badly damaged. The major cause of tension and discord was frequent loss of communication signals and their acquisition sometime later. This "involitional" silence by the crew due to technical failure of transmission of signals led to a misconceived impression of unresponsiveness and dereliction of duty. Such incidents created a trust deficit with control and the seeds of mutual resentment had been sown.

Another incident of distrust happened within hours of the launch of the *Skylab* spaceship. After the launch on 19 November 1973, one of the astronauts, Bill Pogue, became sick and vomited into a bag. The crew did not want to alert ground control for fear it would cause an infructuous fuss or unnecessary hassles with limited remedial action. So, they had a discussion between themselves and decided to throw the bag away[15] out of the spaceship. Unfortunately, they had left their radio on by mistake during their internal deliberation. NASA had thus overheard the whole plan for a cover-up. The mission control was surprised at an attempt to concealment of an occurrence on-board which could have grave consequences.

Procedurally, the commander was bound to inform of this incident to the ground control for record and remedy because Flight Mission Rules required such reporting. Based on this report, the Surgeon at the Mission Control Centre would have evaluated the problem to recommend early termination if corrective medical dispensation was not effective. In this incident, the Skylab commander failed in his official duty and participated in the conspiracy of hiding the fact. It was tantamount to an offence attracting criminality, though only procedural, yet its ramifications could be serious for the health of the crew, in general, and success of the mission, in particular. As per prescribed rules, health of every crew member was of paramount importance and this intended opacity by the crew and the commander was demonstrated. Alan Sheppard reprimanded the crew on the air for their utter indiscretion at hiding facts.[16] This was a rather mild reaction because the issue was not the wrong decision on procedure or the ill-planned physical act of disposal of the bag or participation in the conspiratorial act but the underlying "mal-intention" or *mens rea*.

---

[15] Jonathan O'Callaghan, "The Bizarre Story Of The "Mutiny" On Board A Space Station", April 21, 2018.

[16] Ibid.

2.3.2 Throwing Dirty Linen into Space

As per protocol, dirty linen of the crew is not to be washed on-board in order to conserve recyclable water on the ISS. Therefore, undergarments, personal clothing and linen of the crew, when dirty or worn out or unusable for any reason, are deposited bins, which are disposable cargo craft. The US crew have a separate capsule, Orbital Science's Cygnus craft. Eventually, the trash-filled spaceships, when filled, undock from the space station and are hurtled down for incineration in Earth's atmosphere. The rules and modalities are clear and explicit to be abided by all at the ISS.

Despite this laid down procedure, two incidents are rumoured as instances of dirty linen being physically thrown in space. The first relates to such garbage hurled into space by American crew of Gemini 10 spacecraft in an irresponsible conduct. Rather than condemning this indiscreet behaviour, NASA condoned this. The act deserves highest censure for senseless pollution of outer space.[17] It is important to realise that there is a difference between inadvertent mistake and advertent or deliberate misconduct; the latter approximates to crime and should attract punishment. Surprisingly, in an act of bravado and upmanship, the Soviet crew also threw dirty linen in space. More details about this incident relating to the Russian cosmonauts are contained in the next chapter.

2.3.3 Sandwich Smuggled into Space

NASA's Gemini 3 was the first two-man mission into space that was launched on 23 March 1965. The astronauts were Gus Grissom and John Young, and the flight was to last about five hours. Just about two hours into the mission, Astronaut Young put his hand into space suit pocket and pulled out a corned beef sandwich. Commander Grissom was surprised and enquired as to where it came from despite stringent checks on embarkation. Pilot Young, matter-of-factly replied, from Ramada Inn and suggested to taste and smell that. This was the first contraband sandwich smuggled into outer space by an astronaut.[18] In another unverified version with similarity, the sandwich was smuggled by Wally Schirra and offered to John Young. Whichever may be the true version of the occurrence, but it is certain that for once a corn-beef sandwich was smuggled into spacecraft Gemini 3.

Gus took a bite of the sandwich and it started breaking up in crumbs so he put it into his pocket to control its disintegration. Both wished if it would just hold together. Flying crumbs were the concern. In the weightless environment of space, they could find their way behind electrical panels or fly into a crewmember's eye. Had they held it in hand a little time more for the sandwich to crumble, it could have created

---

[17] G S Sachdeva, *Outer Space: Security and Legal Challenges*, New Delhi, KW Publishers, (2010), pp. 79–80.

[18] Robert Z. Pearlman, "First (Contraband) Corned Beef Sandwich in Space 50 Years Ago", SPACE.com, March 23, 2015.

an existential panic, if not crisis. NASA's Gemini 3 press kit had described how a gelatine layer was to be added to food items to avoid just such a problem. And this smuggled sandwich just did neither have that resin coating nor the right bite-size for eating. Pranks sometimes can have serious consequences.

The entire corned beef sandwich "taste test" lasted about 10 s but the disintegrated crumbs of rye bread floated around in the chamber for over two hours of the rest of the Gemini 3 flight. This crumby pollution at times irritated the eyes of the crew and could thus jeopardise the safety of the craft. The risk was ominous but fortunately, the mission with its manoeuvres and experiments was successful despite odds of floating crumbs. On second thought, Gus and Young were not really amused at the gross prank; they realised that it was no "*buenos*" act but were excited that it was a "real first in space flight."[19]

To their good luck, mission control and NASA took it kindly and no investigation was held into the aberrant conduct. In another version, post-flight, congressional investigation was held to no punishment. On the contrary, this irregular act has been celebrated. A corned beef sandwich, embedded in acrylic, is exhibited at the Grissom Memorial Museum in Mitchell, Indiana, to "memorialise the infamous sandwich" on Gemini 3.[20] And now NASA orders are strict on "no-bread," instead only burritos are allowed as food in space because flour tortillas do not crumble.

2.3.4 Indiscipline in Space is Also a Crime

Space is a hazardous environment and its utter cruelty gives no second chance. Hence while operating in outer space, astronauts have to devote the best of their faculties and highest abilities. Nothing less is acceptable and indiscipline can be disastrous. Because the spacecraft itself is made fail-safe in excess of six sigma assurances and its failure is a remote possibility, whereas negligent dereliction by an astronaut due to impaired abilities or distracted mental state may cause a "Man-Malfunction" and possible consequences could go to any extent. In space, failure is not an option while success anyway is the motto. This exactly happened in the case of Scott Carpenter's Aurora-7 flight, the Mercury-Atlas orbital mission which, by NASA experts, is considered a near disaster that came close to making the first US space fatality. The jeopardy was serious; but to good luck, that was not to be.

According to Mercury Flight Director Chris Kraft, a distracted and irresponsible astronaut Carpenter completely depleted his manoeuvring fuel while doing "sightseeing," fell dangerously behind on his checklists, neglected to give information about a possible attitude control malfunction until it was almost too late to correct, ignored questions and instructions from Mission Control, and screwed up his re-entry by being several seconds late manually firing the retrorockets and by being a huge 24° out of position in yaw. He nearly had a heart attack due to the resulting 12-G

---

[19] Ibid.
[20] Ibid.

acceleration he pulled from making his re-entry at too high a speed, and overshot his landing zone by some 250 miles, leaving him bobbing in a tiny life raft for three hours while the recovery ships steamed to his point of rescue.

The general assessment was it was a case of maladroit performance at subpar level coupled with attention deficit towards operation of the system that led to a near disaster. According to Chris Kraft's opinion, essentially, Carpenter's unprofessionalism nearly got him killed, which might well have resulted in termination of the Mercury programme. This is not a sole observation, other contemporaries and colleagues in their memoirs have chronicled similar views and apprehensions. Deke Slayton gives his opinion of the Aurora-7 mission in his book "Deke!," succinctly listing Carpenter's mistakes on the flight, and understatedly summarising that "it was kind of sloppy."[21] Even Carpenter knew that he had botched up the end part of the mission and was prepared for accepting *mea culpa*. He was dissuaded from holding such a press conference in the larger interest of NASA's image and the future of US space activities. He relented hesitatingly, yet in silent punishment, Carpenter was never sent on a space mission again.

2.3.5 Sex in Space Against the Rules

As per NASA regulations for the astronauts, sex in space is strictly forbidden and is against the mission rules. This rule was stipulated in abundant caution because even as per policy also NASA does not permit or roster married couples together on the same mission. The present policy is purely aimed to protect the health and well-being of the astronauts in view of the unknown risks and imponderables that may befall the astronaut or the developing embryo in the event of pregnancy under conditions of zero-gravity and chance radiation. As per existing knowledge on the subject, the act of sex itself might induce motion sickness, the contraception may not work, and reduced gravity might prevent erections. This apart, in case fertilisation was to find a way, attendant risks to the mother, the gestation of embryo or the developing foetus could be many and yet unproven.

Despite explicit NASA policy on the matter, the first married couple to go in to space together was Jan Davis and Mark Lee. They served a mission together on STS-47 in 1991. As per information with NASA, they were not married, not even in relationship, on joining the training as cadet-astronauts. However, Lee and Davis had met during training for the flight, developed a strong relationship, and married in secrecy, contrary to rules of the US service. By the time, NASA came to know of this event it was too late to train a substitute and the couple made the flight together.

NASA has since changed to stricter rules and will not allow married astronauts, in couples, on the same flight. On persistent media questioning, both Davis and Lee refused to answer any questions about the nature of their relationship during the

---

[21] For another opinion, see Alan Shepard, *Moon Shot: The Inside Story of America's Race to the Moon,* Turner Publishing, 1994.

mission. As the dictum goes, refusal to answer is tantamount to a confession of guilt. Later, Mark Lee was scheduled to fly another mission to the ISS in the year 2000 but was replaced for undisclosed reasons. When it became clear that he was not going into space again, conjectures zeroed onto presumably an undeclared punishment though they had divorced in 1996. Mark Lee later took voluntary retirement. Incidentally, the first experiment on sex was done on cockroach species by the Russians in 2007. A cockroach, named Hope, became pregnant during her 12-day sojourn in space and gave birth to 33 roach-babies.

2.3.6 A Near Disaster in Space

The event occurred with Gemini 8.[22] Command Pilot Armstrong had docked the Gemini 8 capsule to the Agena booster, which was a "docking target" for this mission. The same had been achieved, and it was working flawlessly for weeks. The next plan was for David Scott to perform an EVA after the docking as practice for later missions. During this operation by Scott, after docking and before the start of the EVA, Armstrong noticed a sudden change in the attitude of the combined craft. He immediately took control to stop the movement, but as soon as he ceased thrusting, the "roll" movement started up again.

Soon, the combined Gemini capsule and Agena booster started rotating. Armstrong tried to keep up and to null the motion back to zero. His initial thought was the manoeuvring system on the Agena booster had malfunctioned, so while he tried to control the tumble, David Scott hit the "undock" switch. The Gemini capsule spun free. Armstrong then noticed on the orbit manoeuvring system (OAMS) that fuel was still dwindling rapidly on the Gemini capsule. This made the emergency even direr, requiring the system to de-orbit and consider coming back to Earth!

In a corrective action, Armstrong shut down the OAMS system, finally understanding and concluding that the problem was a stuck thruster; and he used the de-orbit system to nullify their motion to zero. Then Armstrong powered the OAMS system back up with one thruster at a time and thus managed to isolate the one particular thruster that was stuck and managed to shut it down. By that time, they barely had 25% of the OAMS fuel left. It was a critical situation but NASA decided that Gemini 8 re-enter after one more orbit, which was still three days ahead of the time when the recovery ship was supposed to be on-station to pick and recover them.

It seems pertinent to explain the criticality of the situation because this flight came close to within seconds of killing the two astronauts.[23] During the process of correction, the Gemini Capsule was at the maximum rotation and moving at 296 degrees a second. This stress was very nearly beyond human capabilities and enough to render the two astronauts unconscious. Therefore, if Neil Armstrong had lost

---

[22] Paul Feist, April 10, 2019. < https:/www.quora.com/Other-than-Apollo-13-what-was-the-closest-NASA-came-to-a-disaster-in –outer-space >

[23] Feist, ibid.

consciousness from the rapid tumble, or been unable to quickly figure out which thruster was stuck "on" in time to have enough of saved fuel to de-orbit, history would have been different.

2.4 Acts of Individual Negligence in Space

The astronauts are generally well-trained and conditioned to be careful at every step of their activity in space. They are tested for quick reflexive responses and best judgment for solutions. Time is of essence and they are trained to withstand stress. Success anyway is the motto. And despite all the care taken and attention to the tasks in hand, a few instances of negligence and lack of due diligence by the crew have taken place on the ISS or in outer space. Experienced astronauts say that it is easy not to feel the object that one is holding due to zero-gravity conditions. A pair of pliers lost by the crew has been sighted floating in space. A couple of such instances are narrated here.

2.4.1 Loss of Tool Bag in Space

For example, In November 2009, NASA astronaut Heide Stefanyshyn-Piper was commissioned to undertake a space-walk for inspection on the International Space Station. During performance of this task, she lost her tool bag, which was vitally required for the subsequent missions. The handicap due to the loss would have compelled sharing of the remaining boxes available with the crew for the rest of the space-walks and repair trips on the ISS. Thus, the loss due to lack of due diligence or assiduous effort sure caused inconvenience later.[24]

The usefulness and economic value of this kit was significant. The cost of the tool bag was $100,000, and it contained special, professional multi-purpose tools like electric drill, two grease guns, debris bag, etc. This neglect in not ensuring due safekeeping and proper custody of the bag and consequently causing loss to the state was certainly dire negligence, howsoever inadvertent or despite care and caution. Amateur astronomers on Earth tracked and monitored the orbit of the shiny tool bag, which had magnitude of 6.4 lx brightness, until it burnt up in April 2010.[25]

---

[24] Information provided by John Zuwasti Curran, who works at the United Nations, at *Quora Digest* on December 8, 2018.

[25] Curran, ibid.

2.4.2 Loss of Bag Containing New Debris Shield

Another similar instance of loss of vital equipment in space occurred on 30 March 2017. US astronauts Peggy Whitson and ISS Commander Shane Kimbrough were on a space-walk mission to undertake repairs to the debris shields on the ISS. They had completed the job to replace three when they realised that the bag containing the fourth whipple shield required for replacement at the docking port end was missing. The loss was caused by negligence and lack of due diligence but they somehow improvised and covered the damaged debris shield as a stop-gap arrangement to help temporarily protect the station from stray impacts and provide reasonable thermal shielding. It was not a permanent repair or perfect fit and carried endemic risks till properly replaced by a new part.[26]

The lost bag containing the brand-new debris shield for fitment was of a size of 1.5 m (about 5 ft). This bag weighed nearly 8 lbs and had presumably slipped into the void of outer space when not held properly.[27] It was later spotted by amateur astronomers on the same day who confirmed the existence of the lost bag orbiting in space. However, given its low mass and wide surface area, its orbit was expected to decay rapidly, and with this fast descent, its attrition through incineration in Earth's atmosphere was certain and expected fairly soon. Nevertheless, negligence was serious and loss to NASA was significant.

2.4.3 Instances of Minor Lapses and Technical Failures

The crew of Gemini 4 was the first to venture a space-walk outside the ISS. During this trip outside the space station, a glove floated away and was lost in space. Again, Michael Collins lost his camera during Gemini 10 operations. At the same time, astronauts by dint of their abilities and courage have survived disasters. One such instance is narrated here.

The year was 1970 and these were the days of glory for the Apollo space programme and successful landings on the Moon. NASA blasted off Apollo 13 on 30 June 1971 with Jim Lovell as commander and two other astronauts. It was America's fifth mission to the Moon and third human landing. Things were going fine and success was expected as usual. But that was not to be. Fifty-five hours into flight, disaster struck the spacecraft. It was a mysterious explosion that rocked the spaceship.

It was an explosion in the oxygen tank that crippled the mission. As a result, power started draining away; Lovell and his crew helplessly watched the cockpit grow darker and the instruments winked out one by one. It thus seemed a perilous voyage that needed grit and wits. In the end, it turned into a tale of astonishing

---

[26] Curran, ibid.
[27] Curran, ibid.

courage, reflexive responses, brilliant improvisation, and thrilling adventure.[28] The Moon-landing was abandoned; the ship orbited the Moon and returned safely to the Earth without landing there as planned. No wonder, subpar performance is not acceptable in space environment.

2.5 Misfeasance by Private Player in Space Activity

2.5.1 Dereliction by Private Player in Space Activity

SpaceX, a private corporation, undertaking space activities, was to test maiden Falcon rocket launch, which could carry the heaviest payload of 37,000 pounds on-board. Normally, such load competence tests are carried out by properly placing steel or cement blocks as mass simulators. Elon Musk, CEO of SpaceX, however, deemed this standard method and long-established practice "boring and uninteresting." So, he decided to send his personal cherry-red Tesla Roadster car instead "as perfect payload."[29] This was an unusual decision selecting equally unusual ballast that was much lesser than the authorised or planned test weight. Nevertheless, this Falcon launch was considered a technological milestone, except that the payload was far less than the maximum to be tested.

However, Elon Musk deemed it interesting and "feelingful" payload for a maiden flight, which if successful could carry the red car to orbit the red planet and, probably, stay there for millions of years. The Roadster was carefully balanced inside the payload-carrying part of the rocket with carbon fibre fairings and side padding to avoid loosening of the load in flight that might cause an accident or explosion or crash. SpaceX had obtained due permission from FAA for launch of this cargo. Later, it was decided that the car will also be embellished with a "driver" dummy, a mannequin Starman, in driver's seat. But it was not a mere mock-up because it was wearing a SpaceX spacesuit complete with logo and other markings.[30]

The decision for sending red Roadster car as payload elicited diverse reactions and comments from different fraternities. Musk was lauded as a visionary and innovative marketer and brand manager, yet some considered this as a business gimmick or publicity stunt of a maverick in furtherance of his corporate public relations and market growth.[31] In a salutary reference, *The Verge* likened the Roadster to a "Readymade" work of art and others eulogised that "the red sports car symbolises

---

[28] Jim Lovell and Jeffrey Kluger, *Lost Moon: The Perilous Voyage of Apollo 13*, Boston, Houghton Mifflin, 1994.

[29] Kevin Loria, "Elon Musk Shares Picture of the Tesla Roadster Heading to Mars in SpaceX's Falcon Heavy Maiden Voyage", *Business Insider*, February 5, 2018.

[30] Kevin Loria, ibid.

[31] Kevin Loria, ibid. Also refer *Mark Matousek,* "Tesla created the world's best car commercial without spending a dime on advertising", *Business Insider, February 7, 2018.*

masculinity–power, wealth, and speed."[32] Despite the flattering compliments and all the firsts achieved by this test launch, in the ultimate, SpaceX committed dereliction in compliance of the good practices recommended in guidelines for Debris Mitigation[33] and defiance of the advisory for the Planetary Protection.[34]

Let us first take the planetary protection desideratum. The red car till loading on to the rocket was in service with Musk and could be expected to contain the normal dirtying elements of usage like dust and grease as also other earthly bacterial and biological contaminants settled from the atmosphere or picked up from the roads. Understandably, the car was loaded in "as is condition" when handed over. Even if presuming that it was serviced and cleaned before loading, there is a big difference in "cleaned" character and sterilised or sanitised for trip to outer space. It seems that Planetary Policy recommendations were hardly adhered to. In nutshell, the red Roadster seems to have carried a future potential bio-threat to a celestial body where it would crash in outer space.

Under the circumstances, risk of biological pollution or earthly contamination, if the Falcon rocket crashes on the Mars or elsewhere, is ominous and may pose a challenge to posterity in its scientific explorations. It could thus be a case of "reverse pan-spermia" causing depredation of outer space environment and project wrong biological history of the planet. This indiscreet action, though a *fait accompli* yet also violates the mandate of Article IX of the Outer Space Treaty[35] that casts an obligation on member states, and in particular space-faring states, to "…avoid their [celestial bodies] harmful contamination." Under this provision, responsibility attaches to the state of registry of the space object and state of nationality of the private actor undertaking the notified space activity. NASA has an Office of Planetary Protection to check chances of contamination and sustain the pristine environment of other planets. It should have rightly sprung into motion prior to the "strictured" launch. Here, all reasons concur to point at USA.

The second consideration relates to injecting unnecessary junk into outer space. The Mitigation Guidelines strongly urge to adopt good practices for management of space activities causing least debris in space. Therefore, launch of a car with endemic risks of explosion or implosion due to stored energy as also external solar radiation, cosmic radiation, or "micro-meteoroid" impacts making it crash depending upon ambient gravity. Besides, quality deterioration and "de-structuring" of carbon composites and other alloys with exposure to high heat and radiation in orbit could disturb the stable balance within the rocket to skew its ellipsis and possibly lead to a hazardous crash at an unpredicted time.

---

[32] Loria, Ibid.

[33] Space Debris Mitigation Guidelines of the Committee on the Peaceful Uses of Outer Space, 2007. UN Res 67/217, December 22, 2007.

[34] COSPAR Planetary Protection Policy, 2002, as amended in 2011.

[35] Treaty on Principles Governing the Activities of States in the Exploration and Use of Outer Space, including the Moon and other Celestial Bodies, 1967. (In short Outer Space Treaty or OST).

2.5 Misfeasance by Private Player in Space Activity

As of August 2019, Falcon rocket with Roadster and mannequin "Starman" has completed its first orbit around the Sun.[36] Scientists estimate that this "space-load," if it remains intact, may keep orbiting in space for over three million years.[37] In view of the numerous imponderables, it was not a judicious decision to send the car as cargo, even for ego-satisfaction or self-aggrandisement. Further, a doubt has been raised whether FAA permission was taken specifically for the driver-dummy that was placed later.

2.5.2 Disregard of Co-orbital Space Traffic

A case has come to notice where SpaceX satellites have come dangerously close to other functional space object in orbit. The instance concerns where China has accused the USA of irresponsible and unsafe conduct in space over two "close encounters" between the new Chinese space station, Tiangong,[38] and Starlink[39] satellites operated by SpaceX. The incidents occurred in July 2021 and in October 2021 when the Chinese space station had to manoeuvre to avoid colliding with Starlink satellites.[40] Thus, such close trespasses, both times, had posed serious threat to the lives of the astronauts on-board and jeopardised safety of the space station. The diplomatic demarche on the subject to the US Foreign Ministry remains unacknowledged and unanswered. No wonder, in the absence of an official clarification, conjectures are bound to abound.

On the basis of these untoward incidents of dangerous closeness that necessitated emergency drill by the crew, China has asserted that the USA has ignored its obligation and responsibility delegated under Outer Space Treaty (Article VI) for supervision over private entities engaging in space activities. The USA has thus, failed in its bounden duty under International Space Law. These incidents have evoked strong reaction and comments with nearly 90 million views on Chinese social media, Weibo platform, to boycott Tesla products. Even American scholars have adversely commented on the proliferation of satellites by SpaceX and escalating collision risks in space.[41]

---

[36] Mike Wall, "SpaceX's Starman and Elon Musk's Tesla Have Made a Lap Around the Sun", *space.com*, August 20, 2019.

[37] Kevin Loria, n. 29 ante.

[38] The Chinese language word Tiangong means "heavenly palace.".

[39] Starlink is a division of Space X that operates a constellation of about 2000 communication satellites with aim to provide internet access to most parts of the Earth.

[40] AFP report, "China slams US after space station's near misses with SpaceX satellites", *the Times of India* (Chandigarh edition), December 29, 2021, on Global Times page.

[41] Ibid.

Chapter 3
Past Instances of Near-Crimes in Space: The Others

3.1 Acts of Indiscretion by the Soviets

The discussion in the previous chapter is bound to create an impression of partisan agenda, discriminatory treatment, and a biased approach but that is not valid because as a researcher little relevant or authentic material relating to other space-faring countries on the subject has been found in space literature or in public domain. At the same time, let me not convey an unintended impression that Russian *cosmonauts* or Chinese *taikonauts* or astronauts of other countries are a better breed of the fraternity with more discipline in their blood and a regimented mindset; and thus, less prone to have committed such acts of indiscretion or worse in outer space. This may not be true.

Humans will be human, and it is only because Russia and China being closed societies with opaque governance, such incidents of even substantial breaches do not leak out to get reported in the press and the media for public information. Thus, authentic information is rare, and bits of salacious news or motivated part disclosures or inadvertent slip of half revelation may tend to be misinterpreted, bloated into imaginary descriptions, and believed as plausible stories. These when passed to the rumour mill and the public media, including experts, get gullibly accepted as veritable truths.

Apart from the abovementioned modus of dissemination of half-truths, a lot of hoaxes and fake reports tend to get irresponsibly floated without factual verification and yet with impunity. And many times, due to scant information available in public domain, lack of genuine sources for authentication or limited means of verification, even intentionally planted narratives are often accepted as true and believed to be official versions. With due reticence, a couple of such unofficial attributions and unverified incidents are mentioned and narrated, with possible citations, in succeeding paragraphs.

3.2 State Misadventures

3.2.1 The Mystery of Lost Cosmonauts

It is undeniable that the USSR, in race to the outer space, achieved many firsts in conquest of the final frontier and its exploration. Its first space mission breaching the space frontier in 1957 was a surprise and shock to the USA who was almost ready for a similar venture but did not launch for reasons of over-safety. Beaten to the post, the USA diverted its effort to reach the Moon first and succeeded in achieving this mission in 1969. It was a glory regained and the USA re-established its technological supremacy. The space race continued between the two superpowers for nearly two decades, and it was dotted with failures and successes for both. Nevertheless, the journey to space has indeed been eventful for humanity.

In general, all monumental human events of historical importance attract myths and tend to be shrouded in mysteries because the unsuccessful sacrifices made therefor are underrated initially. This has been more common to Russian space activities. Some unannounced sacrifices have been dug out. The first was from May 1960 of a manned spacecraft reportedly going off-course; the second in November that year of an SOS Morse code from a troubled spacecraft leaving Earth's orbit and, most chillingly, a third in 1961 of a cosmonaut apparently suffocating to death. Corroborative details are not available.

However, the story of Gagarin as the first space traveller or a test-subject or astronaut, has also courted controversy which has often been resounded and has remained only partly unravelled by declassified documents, later accounts, and mentions in biographies. However, one mystifying fact is that Gagarin died young at a psychiatric hospital and under mysterious circumstances. Nonetheless, despite all doubts, protestations, and allusions to the contrary, history records Gagarin as "the first human who went into space –and that will always be the truth."[1]

There are many unconfirmed reports and speculative theories that Soviet *cosmonauts* had gone into outer space before Yuri Gagarin also, but their factual occurrence and ultimate fate have never been made public or officially acknowledged by either the erstwhile Soviet or Russian space authorities. Proponents of the "lost cosmonauts" theory argue that the Soviet Union had attempted to launch two or even more human spaceflights before the much-vaunted successful flight of Gagarin which was publicly announced with flourish, and that too, after it had returned safely. And even this case is surrounded by a controversy whether Gagarin was a subject of experimentation or a pilot of the spaceship, as crooned by the Soviets.

According to Gagarin's biography, these rumours were likely to have been started as a result of two Vostok missions that were made just prior to his flight. These rockets were equipped with dummies and human voice tape recordings to test if the

---

[1] James Osberg, "Twenty Myths About Gagarin's Spaceflight", *SPACEFLIGHT,* April, 2011.

3.2 State Misadventures	39

radio worked.[2] Conjecturally, there were at least two cosmonauts who died in those earlier attempts and possible failures because of being hurriedly planned and half-baked projects.[3] Another such incident concerns Valentin Bondarenko, a would-be cosmonaut, whose death during training on the Earth facility was covered up by the Soviet government. This information has now been verified and confirmed from declassified archival records and secret documents. Records state that "a trainee-cosmonaut named Valentin Bondarenko suffered massive burns in a fire while he was in an oxygen-rich isolation chamber"[4] and later succumbed to his death.

Another interesting incident relates to Cosmonaut Vladimir Ilyushin. According to recently declassified documents, Ilyushin was placed in a capsule named Rossiya, and the secret flight took place in the early hours of the morning on Friday, 7th April 1961.[5] After a guidance malfunction, the cosmonaut is reported to have made an unguided crash landing off-course inside China instead of the planned spot. He, too, was critically injured and was rescued and held by the Chinese government. This was highly embarrassing and that too at the height of the Cold War. Thus, Ilyushin admittedly carries the honour of being the first man to go into space. But to save face, Government of the Soviet Union supposedly suppressed information about this failure in an alleged cover up to prevent bad publicity or the US taunts.

The evidence cited to support the theory of lost cosmonaut is generally unsupported and regarded as inconclusive. In the 1980s, however, an American journalist researched regarding space-related disasters of the Soviet Union and found no evidence of these. Moreover, since the fall of the Soviet Union in the early 1990s, much of previously restricted information has been declassified and brought into public domain. Even with the availability of authentic Soviet archival material as also from the memoirs of Russian space pioneers, no clear evidence has emerged to support the lost cosmonaut theory.[6]

According to a report published in 1988, Cosmonaut Nikolai Gogolansky died in his failed space suit. Another cosmonaut died when their capsule "exploded on impact as it was returning to Earth"; three cosmonauts were killed in 1981 when their spacesuits were pierced by space debris during space walks; and four cosmonauts died due to a faulty airlock in 1984.[7] This is the price humanity pays for scientific experimentation and technology trials. Or is it the cost of irrational haste! The official silence on this matter was nominal, yet many other tragic affairs in the history of space exploration have been allowed to fade away into confused memory and oblivion of history in connivance with bureaucratic bosses and blessings of clever politicians.

---

[2] Piers Bizony, *Starman: Truth Behind the Legend of Yuri Gagarin,* (1998), Bloomsbury. ISBN 0-7475-3688-0.

[3] Sourced from *Wikipedia*, the free encyclopaedia.

[4] James Osberg, n. 1 ante. Also refer < http://sectrum.ieee.org/aerospace/space-flight/twenty-myths-about-Gagarin's-spaceflight >

[5] Asif Siddiqi, *Sputnik and the Soviet Space Challenge,* (2000), p. 251.

[6] James Oberg, *Uncovering Soviet Disasters,* (1988), ISBN 0-394-56095-7.

[7] Mike Jones, "Lost in Space", US tabloid, *SUN*, September 21, 1993, p. 7.

3.2.2 The Shady Selection of Komarov as Cosmonaut

Vladimir Mikhaylovich Komarov was a Soviet test pilot, aerospace engineer, and cosmonaut. He was one of the most highly experienced and qualified candidates accepted into the first squad of cosmonauts selected in 1960. He was declared medically unfit for training or spaceflight twice while he was undergoing the training programme. The reason and the manner in which he was later cleared for spaceflights is a mystery. Nevertheless, he became the first Soviet cosmonaut to fly in space twice when he was selected as the solo pilot of Soyuz 1, its first crewed test flight. A parachute failure caused his Soyuz capsule to crash into the ground after re-entry on 24 April 1967, making him the first officially announced human to die in a space flight.[8]

It is generally believed that it was his perseverance, superior skills, engineering knowledge, and consequent contribution to space vehicle design, innovative cosmonaut training protocols, and evaluation process that allowed him to continue in an active role. With his steadfast dedication and illustrious contribution to the space programmes, he ultimately earned the assignments for space flights but his career ended in a tragic accident.

3.2.3 The Failed Moon-Shots

The Soviet Union lost the crewed Moon-landing phase of the space race to the USA. However, some sources claim that just before the historic Apollo 11 flight to the Moon, the Soviets undertook a hasty yet an adventurous attempt to beat the Americans to this goalpost. Despite the unsuccessful first test launch of the new Soviet N1 rocket on 20 January 1969, it is alleged that a decision was made to send a crewed mission in Soyuz 7K-L3 craft to the Moon again using an N1 rocket. This attempted misadventure is believed to have occurred on 3 July 1969, when it ended in a ground explosion, destroying the launch pad and killing the cosmonauts on-board.

Official sources state that the L3 was not yet ready for crewed missions. Its Lunar Lander, nicknamed the LK, had been tested a few times with good performance but its orbiter, the 7K-LOK, had not yet yielded successful results by the closing of the Moon-landing programme at the end of 1974. The abandoning and closure of the programme was officially denied, and this information was maintained top secret until 1990 when the government allowed the archives to be published under the policy of *glasnost*.

In another hasty Soviet venture to reach the Moon first, Andrei Mikoyan was reportedly killed together with a second crew member in an ill-prepared attempt to reach the Moon ahead of the Americans in early 1969. Due to system malfunction, they failed to get into lunar orbit and shot past the Moon. This may be a hoax foisted

---

[8] James Oberg, n. 6 ante, pp. 156–76.

on a failed Soviet effort undertaken in a hurry but the story appears plausible and believable.

3.3 Acts of Misconduct by *Cosmonauts*

In spite of rigorous training, instilled discipline, and drill-conscious mindset, there have been occasions of failure of good conduct and incidents of impermissible acts by the *cosmonauts*. Psychologists believe that zero-gravity environment cramped space, claustrophobic living in spaceship, and pressures of work routine, all add up to induce a mental condition under which fatigue, annoyance, and frustration creep in and the crew get besieged by moody tantrums, which at times burst into misbehaviour or misconduct that may border on crime. Few such incidents pertaining to the Soviet crew have spilled into public domain. Nevertheless, certain leaked rumours and biographical accounts have formed the basis of this study. Hence their veracity, at places, may be in doubt.

3.3.1 Sexual Misconduct in Space

Rules for the conduct of *cosmonauts* do not permit any, even remotely sexual activity while in outer space. Despite the strict instructions, a prohibited situation happened on Mir space station. Doctor Valeri Polyakov is the holder of the record for the longest single spaceflight in human history. He stayed aboard the Mir space station for more than 14 months (437 days 18 h) at a stretch in one trip. During his tenure on Mir, Elena Kondakova made her first trip into space on Soyuz TM-20 on 4 October 1994. She returned to Earth, along with Valeri Polyakov on 22 March 1995 after five-month stay at the Mir space station.

A little after their return from the space mission, rumours started circulating about the unorthodox cosiness between Elena and Valeri while in space. The alleged event took currency after a video got viral showing Valeri playfully splashing water on Elena in the washroom during the course of flight on Mir. No further details about this incident or the treatment meted out to the *cosmonauts* for the alleged act are known in public domain. In fact, space agencies as a matter of policy do not comment on personal and personnel matters of the staff, hence this silence on the issue.

3.3.2 Throwing Dirty Linen into Space

As per protocol, dirty and soiled linen of the crew is not to be washed on-board the ISS in order to conserve recyclable water. Therefore, personal undergarments and clothes of the crew, when dirty or worn out or unusable for whatever reason, are deposited separately in respective bins, which becomes disposable cargo to be ejected into atmosphere for incineration. The Russians have Progress capsule for the purpose. Eventually, the trash-filled bin-modules, when fully filled up, undock from the space station and are hurtled down to burn up in Earth's atmosphere. The rules and procedures are clear and explicit to abide by.

Despite this laid down procedure, an incident is rumoured when the Soviet crew of Salyut indulged in a condemnable act to throw their soiled clothes into outer space in an advertent show of bravado. It is believed that this misconduct was prompted and incited by a similar act by the American crew of Gemini 10 spacecraft hurling garbage into space. Both acts, if factually correct, constitute indiscreet behaviour, are highly irresponsible, and are against the mission rules that deserve highest censure for senseless pollution of outer space,[9] regardless of the condonation of the impugned acts and misdemeanour of the crew by Roscosmos and NASA. Because, it is wisely said that a condemnable activity if condoned repeatedly may become an undesirable norm.

It is important to realise that there is a difference between inadvertent mistake and advertent or deliberate misconduct; the latter approximates to crime to attract punishment. Moreover, outer space is not the same as ground on Earth where an item thrown lies till picked up and removal by scavenging is easy and mostly arranged at regular intervals. The case of space is different. Any item thrown in the void of space keeps moving at high speed and does not get destroyed or biologically degraded. Objects once injected in space tend to remain moving in space for long periods of time and constitute obstruction thus posing a possibility of collision risk to useful and functional space objects.

3.4 Abandoning Garbage on Celestial Bodies

The Soviet Space Agency has attempted several missions to the Moon, some have failed on the way, and many have landed on the Moon either in crashlanding or with successful landing. Successful missions, like Luna 16, have returned with dust and rock samples for investigation though in much smaller quantities and weight. In order to make room for the stacking of samples, as was done by the American astronauts, the *cosmonauts* would have also jettisoned some of the used and useless articles on the Moon. Not much details about their actions and the type of garbage littered on the Moon are available in public. Though silence is also an option, it can be stated with certainty that they would have also caused pollution on the Moon, similar to that by the Americans. And since each landing would have been at a different place, the garbage would be lying scattered over an area and not at one place alone. For example, Luna 15 crashed into a mountain in Sea of Crises and another one in Sea of Rains due to explosion of booster of the module. The debris still remains there.

---

[9] G S Sachdeva, *Outer Space: Security and Legal Challenges*, New Delhi, KW Publishers, (2010), pp. 79–80.

The Soviets predominantly resorted to robotic missions in preference to crewed ones in experimentation on Mars programme. This practice continued for over a decade (1960–73) and gave them an edge in technology and a niche in space missions. Most of these were fly-by or orbiter missions. The first landing on Mars happened in May 1971 by the Soviet Mars 2 lander. Hence, the quantum of debris left behind by the Soviets would be much lesser than the Americans on the Moon but much more on the Mars due to several mission modules that crashed and failed to achieve a soft-landing for survival to undertake rover drill.

The aspect of pollution by crashed modules and discarded garbage littered on the planetary bodies deserves consideration as a challenge in future. Firstly, because littered or crash sites become relatively risky for future landing due to ground having become uneven. Secondly, some of the thrown-out junk may be contaminated to need remedial measures, apart from basic scavenging of the place. It may be difficult to blame any of the parties under the then existing space laws, nevertheless, some of the actions were highly unethical like abandoning human poop and used articles and wrappers on the celestial bodies.

3.5 Acts of Indiscretion by Other States

3.5.1 Israel's Beresheet *Lunar Crash*

Beresheet was a privately funded initiative and Moon-landing experiment by Israeli non-profit organisation, "Space IL." It sponsored a mission that was partly successful for having reached the Moon orbit but met a tragic end when its lunar module, instead of soft-landing, crashed on the Moon on 11 April 2019. The austere project cost $100 million could not possibly cater to multiple failsafe systems even though the spacecraft was planned for a short lifespan of about two days, which was not to be. The purpose of this launch was to provide high-resolution imagery from the Moon surface as also to measure the magnetic field at its landing site in *Mare Serenitatis*, which had revealed magnetic anomalies during earlier probes. Possibly, this mission would have provided valuable scientific information about the life and history of the Moon through its magnetic variables from within rock formations.

Beresheet (בראשית) is a word from Hebrew language meaning "in the beginning," and its covert implication has now been revealed. It now transpires that the lunar module was carrying a cargo of dehydrated microscopic life forms known as tardigrades.[10] These are odd little creatures, yet strikingly distinctive, measuring up to about half a millimetre long with a rounded, sucker-like structure in the centre that can project outwards, have four pairs of stubby legs, and a front-end showing a set of dangerous-looking sharp teeth. These are often called "water bears" also, because

---

[10] Monica Grady, "Tardigrades: We're now polluting the moon with near indestructible little creatures" in *The Conversation*, August 9, 2019.

they get their living element, oxygen, from water and ingest algae as food. These can suck fluids from other creatures or even other tardigrades for survival.[11]

These are hardy creatures and could probably live on the Moon for a long time and can survive extremes of temperature and ambient pressure, including the frigid vacuum of space as also withstand heavy radiation. When dehydrated, they roll up into a spore-like state that slows down their metabolic rate by about a 100-fold, enabling them to survive for potentially over 100 years. The project, forsooth, is designed to act on the format of Noah's Ark, providing a repository from which plant and animal species could be regenerated to repopulate the Earth should a catastrophe akin to a flood of biblical proportions overtake the planet. Despite the best ostensible intentions, it was a deed ill-conceived, and the state cannot abdicate its national responsibility imposed under the Treaty Law and the UN Guidelines. This was a deliberated experiment with awareness that it could cause harmful contamination irrespective of the crash.[12] Thus, this may only be symbolic of what type of crimes may come in future by irresponsible activities of state agencies and private enterprise.

Believably in all possibility, as a result of the crash, the tardigrades, in whatever form, may have by now scattered and spread across the lunar surface. Whatever be the motive of sending this cargo, the primary concern, at present, is that these organisms with estimated long life may reactivate and cause biological pollution on the Moon. The state authorisation to send a private consignment of biological organism to the Moon seems an impermissible act and highly irresponsible that fouls with COSPAR guidelines.[13] The COSPAR policy, even if normative in approach, strictly prohibits causing harmful contamination to the environment in outer space, and it can be deemed to have substantive legal force as it has been formulated under the aegis of the UN.

The Israeli action also contravenes Article IX of the OST in many ways. First, activities of states in exploration and use of outer space and celestial bodies be so conducted "as to avoid their harmful contamination." Second, in case an experiment or activity "would cause potentially harmful interference…it shall undertake appropriate international consultation." Third, that states "shall conduct all their [space] activities with due regard to the corresponding interests of all other states…" Israel has failed on all the mentioned mandates of this provision and has been derelict on an affirmative duty. Irresponsibility attracts liability in many ways.

It is also relevant to allude to the germane provision of the Moon Agreement.[14] Article 7 of the Moon Treaty exhorts, "States Parties shall take measures to prevent the disruption of the existing balance of its [the Moon's] environment, whether by introducing adverse changes in that environment, by its harmful contamination through the introduction of extra-environmental matter or otherwise."[15] The concern of the

---

[11] Grady, Ibid.

[12] Article IX of the Outer Space Treaty.

[13] COSPAR Planetary Protection Policy, 2002.

[14] Agreement Governing the Activities of States on the Moon and Other Celestial Bodies, 1979. Also popularly called as The Moon Treaty.

[15] Words in parentheses added for clarity in understanding.

3.5 Acts of Indiscretion by Other States   45

international community is serious and has been vouchsafed through global assent in the United Nations. Arguably, Israel has not ratified this agreement but imbibing its wisdom need not wait till then.

Another experiment of similar nature by taking live insect to the space was conducted by the Soviets in 2007. Thus, Russian cockroach was the first creature to become pregnant in space. The female-roach was named Hope, and she conceived during her 12-day space sojourn. On completion of gestation period, she gave birth to 33 baby-roaches. The best part of this story is that the experimental subjects were brought back to the Earth, and the moral lies in responsible state activities in the outer space.

3.5.2 ASAT Experiments

In 2007, China conducted an ASAT experiment in space by destroying its own unwanted, Fengyun-IC weather satellite on its polar orbit at an altitude of 865 km. The destruction of the satellite caused a cloud of nearly 3200 particles in space at an orbit from where it may take centuries to fall down and incinerate in the atmosphere. There was great resentment and condemnation worldwide including that voiced by the USA. But just a year later, in 2008, in an ostentatious display of technological advancement, the USA also conducted a repeat experiment since 1985. This act also caused clouds of debris in space and was as reprehensible and detrimental to the space environment as the earlier one by China. Misdemeanour had occurred.

A decade later, on 27 March 2019, India conducted a similar, successful trial in a show of techno-prowess by engaging its own target-satellite at an altitude of 300 km for an ASAT experiment. This was "Mission Shakti" accomplished by Defence Research and Development Organisation (DRDO) of India in a series of testing of missile as a weapon but was India's first exo-atmosphere interceptor. This success put India in league with other three, the USA, Russia, and China. Despite the prestige gained, this experiment also caused space debris though on a much lesser scale and at a much lower altitude where the shattered pieces would reach the atmosphere and get burnt up within a decade. This should be no consolation nor justification. Nevertheless, an indiscreet act polluting the space environment had occurred, and it attracted even more vociferous condemnation.

Again, on 15 April 2020, Russia conducted the latest of their practice launches for the new anti-ballistic defence system A-235, popularly known as Nudol. It was launched from the Plesetsk Cosmodrome by a Russian military contractor Almaz Antey. The missile splashed down 3000 kms away in the prenotified area of the Laptev Sea, off the northern coast of Siberia. No objects were hit by the missile. The tried system is designed to protect Moscow city from enemy ballistic missiles by intercepting them at a high altitude, possibly even as high as low-earth orbit. The developed defence system though can legitimately be said to have attained the capability to operate as an anti-satellite system too. These are just the bald and unconfirmed facts available in public domain.[16]

However, the American Space Command[17] has been alarmed by this trial and has accused Russia of carrying out a so-called DA-ASAT test (anti-satellite test). The USA suspects it to be yet another example that threats from hostile acts in space to the space systems of the USA and its allies are real, serious, and growing. The USA is ready and committed to deterring aggression and defending the nation, our allies, and US interests.[18] Given the publicly announced circumstantial facts about the Russian test, this retort seems misplaced. Opinions may differ though perceived threats may turn out to be real and ominous. Nations often put masks on their covert experiments.

Be that as it may, Russia has now carried out a confirmed anti-satellite weapon test on 16 November 2021. The weapon targeted an old Russian spacecraft, Tselina-D, which was non-functional and was in orbit since 1982. Russia has accepted conducting this test which hit the target with "razor-sharp precision."[19] This in a way shows that Russia is developing new weapon systems but statedly, in an effort to neutralise the impact of a similar test by the USA in 2008 and also in response to its aggressive efforts in establishing an American Space Command in 2020. No wonder, the competitive race is still in progress.

On their part, Britain and NATO have accused Russia of generating a debris field of nearly 1500 pieces of different sizes in low-earth orbit which endangered the International Space Station and nearby satellites as also would pose a hazard to space activities for years. The US reaction is, however, sharper and has condemned that this test reveals reckless and irresponsible behaviour that may turn out to be a destabilising trigger. On the other hand, the Russian defence ministry has accepted the factum of creating debris by the test and that the ISS crew had temporarily moved into their respective quarters but has denied the accusation that the debris would pose any threat or concern to the ISS which remains in the green zone.[20]

The Soviet Space Authority, Roscosmos, has issued an official statement in its defence, "Ensuring crew safety has always been and remains our top priority. Commitment to this principle is an underlying condition both in the manufacturing of Russian space equipment and in the programme of its operation."[21] This notification in English, further adds, "We are convinced that only joint efforts by all spacefaring nations can ensure the safest possible coexistence and activities in outer

---

[16] Helen Ntabeni, "The curious tale of the ASAT Test that was'nt", published April 23, 2020 in Quora Digest. The author is LL.M., at Northumbria University.

[17] The US Space Command was established in December, 2019 by President Donald Trump.

[18] Helen at n. 16 ante.

[19] A report from Moscow, "'Razor-sharp precision': Russia hails anti-satellite weapon test", *The Times of India*, (Chandigarh edition), November 17, 2021, Chandigarh Times Supplement, p. 4.

[20] Ibid.

[21] Elizabeth Howell, "Russia defends anti-satellite test amid US criticism" Space.com, November 17, 2021.

space," Anyway, the debris cloud is being monitored by the Soviet warning system on space debris to prevent and counter all possible threats.[22]

Historically, the USA was the first to set the scene for ASAT tests, and the first attempt was made in June 1959 when the Bold Orion rocket was launched from a B-52 bomber that targeted the dead US Explorer-4 satellite. The rocket only got to within 4 miles of Explorer-4 proving that it was indeed difficult to strike an orbiting satellite. Future efforts were stalled in this direction. Concurrently, the Soviet Union had also tried to create ASAT capability through the sixties of the last century and was the first to succeed in an ASAT test in the destruction of an orbiting asset. It was in February 1970. But further trials were discontinued unilaterally on a realisation that, in the bargain, they had destroyed their own costly assets both ways and it was doubly expensive. Another justification to this stoppage was the unnecessary creation of unwanted debris in the outer space environment contrary to the then mandate under Article IX of the OST.

All these countries, in pursuit of their competitive experiments, have caused pollution in space environment by unwanted and unnecessary space debris that may pose hazards of collision to the operation of useful and functional space satellites for a long time to come. Time is ripe to consider and develop modalities to apply the principle of "proportional responsibility" and "polluter pays principle"[23] as these have crystallised in parleys on climate change. Consensus on these can be effectuated when the process of scavenging of outer space becomes technically a feasible operation and can be outsourced by the proposed Space Utilisation and Sustenance Regulatory Authority (SUSRA), once established.[24]

3.5.3 Negligence in Space Operations is a Crime

It was 2021AD. The *Nauka*,[25] a multi-purpose module, was to replace the recently discarded *Pirs* research module. *Nauka* was designed to serve as a research laboratory, storage unit, and airlock device to upgrade Russia's capabilities aboard the ISS. *Nauka* was ready for launch from Kazakhstan's Baikonur Cosmodrome after experiencing a series of glitches which were satisfactorily sorted out. Once launched, it docked on the underside of the ISS, though under tense operations. Anyway, docking was successfully achieved on 29 July 2021 and was so confirmed by the concerned agency. About three hours after *Nauka* module had latched onto the space station and had well settled, the mission controllers in Moscow commenced performing some post-docking "reconfiguration" procedures.[26]

---

[22] Ibid.

[23] Opinion on this principle has crystallised in Climate Change parleys.

[24] For more details refer Chapter on Appraisal and Solutions.

[25] *Nauka* is Russian language word for 'science'.

[26] "Space Station did 540-degree flip, turned upside down: Mishap more serious than earlier reported", *India Today*, August 3, 2021.

It was then that, suddenly and inexplicably, the thruster jets of *Nauka* module restarted and the mishap began. This malfunction resulted in the entire station to pitch out of its normal flight position, some 250 miles above the Earth, compelling the mission's flight director to declare a "spacecraft emergency," US space agency officials said.[27] The actual occurrence was that the flying outpost spun one-and-a-half revolutions, i.e. about 540°, before coming to a stop upside down, relative to its original position. The space station also lost altitude during this unexpected and involuntary manoeuvre. "The space station then did a 180° forward flip to get back to its original orientation."[28] This was achieved by the flight teams on the ground at the Johnson Space Centre in Houston, by activating thrusters on another module of the orbiting platform in corrective action. *Nauka* engines were ultimately switched off to stabilize ISS.

The correction activity was described as a struggle to regain control of the space station as a "tug of war" between the two modules. It is generally believed by experts that initially the incident was underplayed by both Roscosmos as well as NASA. But with more information flowing on the causes and assessments of possible impact, the US specialists shudder to think of the event and accept that it was serious and could have gone out of control to cause a major tragedy in micro-gravity, human, and material. At that moment, there were seven astronauts on-board and at risk of survival, though escape module was available in readiness. Early reports inform that due to this glitch, the station was actually out of control for about two minutes, while communication with all the seven members of the crew was lost or disrupted for several minutes.[29]

Russian space agency maintains and expects us to believe that the incident was caused "due to a short-term software failure and a command was mistakenly implemented" to misfire the thruster engines. Inadvertence is possible, yet it would be naive to accept such a simplistic explanation for a goof-up of monumental dimension. Even space-worthiness of this module at launch can be a suspect. In fact, who caused the malfunction, whether man or machine, is still to be determined with precision and finality. On the other hand, a preliminary inspection of the ISS, post-mishap, reports that as a consequence of the upheaval, the 900,000 lbs monolith space station would have suffered stress on the structure and equipment. More revelations are expected,[30] yet one cannot wink away such an occurrence. An old adage advises, never waste a crisis, convert it into an opportunity for learning and correction.

In conclusion, it can be maintained that negligence in space operations, from space or on ground, is tantamount to crime. Every activity in space and for results in space deserves due diligence of the highest order and actions in *abundanti cautela*. There is no scope for casualness or even inadvertence, leave aside sheer negligence or

---

[27] *India Today*, ibid, updated report.

[28] *The New York Times*, August 3, 2021. Based on a statement by Zebulon Scoville, Flight Director at NASA's Mission Control Centre in Houston.

[29] Reporting and writing by Steve Gorman in Los Angeles and Polina Ivanova in Moscow. Editing by Mark Heinrich, Leslie Adler and Raju Gopalakrishnan for *News SCIENCE*.

[30] *India Today*, updated version of August 4, 2021.

dereliction in duty. Space environment is potentially dangerous and highly hazardous; thus, it is unsparing in effect and rarely ever gives a second chance. In this instance of presumed malfunction, luck was in our favour and providentially, things fell in place and ultimately turned out right in result. Defects so caused by the upheaval can be set right but such a saviour opportunity may not repeat itself. Hence, maximum care and caution are mandatory else the crime and the criminal, both may vanish.

Chapter 4
Crimes and Space Crimes: A General Discussion

4.1 Introduction

Crimes, generally so understood, remain crimes irrespective of the domain where committed, whether on the Earth, on sea, under sea, in the air, in the outer space, or on the celestial bodies. The qualification, "generally so understood," has been added because human perception on crimes varies in different countries and communities due to historical factors, cultural legacies, religious injuncts, economic development, educational standards, constitutional guarantees, geographical compulsions, cultural beliefs, social influences, familial values or personal mindset, to mention only a few. Beset with such mental grooming, experienced predilections, and acquired fixations, different minds and at different times, may look at the same or similar event or action to evoke varied tolerance, different responses, and varying levels of reaction.

Such situations do confront us on the Earth also, even within the same country, province or community where our opinions may vary and views differ or conflict. These dissimilarities or points of dissent, however, would become more pronounced and manifest in internationally mixed groups in space stations, space resorts, working laboratories in orbit, excavation and processing units on celestial bodies or planetary habitations. Thus, individual perceptions would tend to differ, and so would responses, creating a predicament for dissension, dispute or conflict which may lead to any imaginable results within limits of human capacity for compromise, correction, condemnation, confrontation, or vengeance.

Humans, being human, tend to carry their inherited and acquired baggage of genetic personality, individual experience, basic disposition, nurtured habits, and personal eccentricities, wherever they venture out. Although these traits improve with conscious effort, training and experience yet original predilections, personal kinks of personality or repressed anger do wake-up from the subconscious mind under provocation or similarity of encounter. In fact, some typical reactions, oft-observed reflexes, and innate propensities are biologically and psychologically wired within the DNA. This is more so in certain identifiable communities or ethnic groups among which such stereotype responses recur with surprising frequency of repetition and uniformity of behaviour. These inherences, unwittingly, would surely follow to the outer space in some form or the other, to some degree or less.

Our dilemma in outer space would further increase due to pressures of specific influences of space environment, working hazards in unfamiliar milieu and associated mental anxiety for personal safety. It is to be expected that space passengers, hotel guests and planetary residents would constitute multi-nationality and multi-ethnicity groups with different habits, attitudinal mindset, living styles and cultural fixations. And space stations and space habitations would, perforce, provide cramped spaces, unergonomic workstations, not-too-comfortable living and scant privacy. Under such conditions, disputes, conflicts and crimes may result. In fact, humans are mentally wired with anger and pugnacity and resultant expressions under deprivation or frustration, stress or provocation could be near-crimes or actual ones.

Therefore, actions deemed innocuous or non-provocative on Earth may elicit surprising responses to precipitate dissent and may escalate to a crime. On the other hand, an act of crime, as on Earth, may reveal disparate contributory factors or proximate causation which may draw an unexpected retort, leading to divergent reactions and seemingly unnecessary provocation resulting in the commission of acts which could constitute patent crimes. This short general discussion should set the stage for the topic of crimes to be taken forward for analysis and adaptation to the domain of outer space with motley groupings.

4.2 Crimes: A General Discussion

Crimes and humanity have travelled together in history and humans have offended others on some cause or pretext to incur disapproval or reciprocal wrath. Possibly, norms were breached and such defiance was unacceptable to the community elders and the society at large. However, with passage of time, the then normative irritants and innocuous disputes have now grown into moulds of coded crimes. Generally, the crimes result from the innate human nature of aggression consequent to disagreement, deprivation, or refusal and reflect an element of volitional ill-will (*mens rea*) which is a peculiar characteristic of human beings alone.

Animals commit no crimes and behave by their genetic instincts and generic nature because they possess little thought-process and least of all *mens rea*. It is, thus, only humans who indulge in crimes with advertent volition, a malevolent mind, a guilty conscience, ill-will infecting the perpetrated action, full knowledge of repercussions, and an awareness of consequences thereof. And it frightens to imagine that despite the well-known empirical knowledge and an almost daily spectacle of life concerning sanctions for crimes, these are still committed, intentionally and knowingly, for own benefit of whatever kind or personal prestige or psychological ego.

In a way, perhaps the first crime was committed by Adam. He was ordained by the Lord that while living in Heaven, he should never, ever, eat the fruit of apple tree. He succumbed to his temptation, even though on seduction, to taste the forbidden fruit of apple and consequently indulged in the sin of fornication. This act was in utter disregard and defiance of the rules of the place and contra to the Lord's specific command and caveat. The Lord's ordainment had been disobeyed, a prohibition had been infringed, and as such a sin, or in other words, a crime had been committed. Consequently, Adam being the sinner or criminal under the circumstances was punished by summary expulsion from Heaven to the Earth.

In legal rephrasing, a crime had actually occurred, it was committed by a person, having been properly so cautioned of the rule, with due knowledge of the prohibition and possible awareness of the consequences. The other party, despite ostensible seduction, was deemed innocent, neither an accomplice nor contributor in guilt. In this regard, we still live in an era with a judicial system, where in this crime, men are deemed guilty till proven innocent and women are innocent till proven guilty. Apparently, the illicit act was not pardoned nor was the offence condoned for Adam by the competent authority. Accordingly, the criminal was duly punished and justice prevailed in his expulsion from Heaven. Simplistically, it is a crime and punishment sequence. And since then, the progeny of Adam, the humankind on Earth, has been committing crimes, of whatever kind and in whatever ways imaginable.

The character, modus, style, and complexion of crimes have been changing with cultural and social evolution as also economic development of societies through the ages. In the tribal or traditional communities, the crimes related more as retaliation on dispossession of things or chattel or other acts of deprivation by inadvertence or design. Individual prowess and supporting strength of community were the motivator and survival of the fittest was the law. Back then, the victor was deemed to commit no crime and the vanquished punished mostly for no fault. With economic evolution of societies and ushering in of industrial revolution, men remained at work for long hours and the character and predominance of crimes changed to sexual transgressions and disturbed family relations. Prosperity had its dark shades.

As some societies turned highly capitalistic and the institution of private property got entrenched, entrepreneurs and owners became more affluent and exploitative. With the acquired riches and available luxury, their ideas became more liberal and attitudes more permissive, yet they remained besotted with concerns of prestige and privacy. Insults and breaches were least tolerated and punished harshly; thus, a new genre of crimes gained currency with the growth of capitalism. This is just an illustration of the evolving structure of societies and the changing complexion of crimes through the times. However, there can be permutations and combinations of different elements of socio-economic change alloyed with cultural compulsions and political events. These, in turn, inducing varying dynamics that may lead to mutated results with diverse responses and emergence of new breeds of crimes.

4.2.1 Ingredients of Crime

In general, the essential ingredients of a crime are a deliberate misconduct with mental awareness of transgression, motivated by personal advantage, tangible or intangible, and with conscious awareness of possible results. But techno-legal connotation of a crime is that it is an antisocial act, so presumed and treated "by law to be harmful to society in general, even though its immediate victim is an individual. The notion of crime as a threat to whole community is the material counterpart of the formal rule that State alone is master of criminal prosecution."[1] A Latin phrase puts it more succinctly, *actum est de republica*. Therefore, no private person is deemed to have a direct, individual, or personal interest in a criminal proceeding, although exceptions may be made by the law or courts in certain cases of contractual offences or those of breach of trust, or frauds, etc. "It is common knowledge that a criminal prosecution is not intended for the private satisfaction of personal vendetta or revenge."[2]

However, an essential and substantive element of crime at law is *mens rea* or guilty intention or offensive state of mind to commit the crime. This mental condition of the criminal is well explained in a Latin Legal maxim, "*Actus non facit reum, nisi mens sit rea.*" This means that the overt act alone does not make the performer a criminal unless there is also felonious intention or criminal mindset, immediate or past. Therefore, *mens rea* is a unity of intent, motive, desire, and consciousness about consequences. This principle excludes ignorance or mistake or mere heedlessness unless it results in grievous injury or fatality. These exceptions to the rule duly caution that the maxim must be applied with consideration and circumspection because mere want of explicit intention does not always constitute sufficient defence.[3]

So, the emphasis on guilty mind deserves to be discussed a little more because *mens rea* is a mental process or a thought sequence that is not overtly visible and cannot be perceived by human faculties or easily comprehended by human intelligence. Therefore, it is often implied, imputed, inferred, or assumed and thus may be difficult to establish and prove beyond doubt. This illusory nature of *mens rea* merits elaboration because these are evil thoughts still in the mind processor that have not been expressed in verbal language or an overt act and humans understand only spoken word and physical actions. Hence, as long as a thought remains in the brain and does not find expression or activation in an evident criminal or antisocial act, it does not become a crime.

In law, a plausible criminal thought and a manifest criminal act should almost concur to constitute and culminate into an offence. But there could be instances where the investigating authority may fail to identify the material existence or even a perceivable illusion of an evil thought in premeditation of a criminal act or as a sponsor of impugned activity. In such cases, in the absence of or for unestablished *mens rea*, the gravity of the offence or the heinous nature of the committed crime can be material determinants and indicators towards premeditation and existence of the guilty mind prior to the indictable act. Anyway, courts remain the final arbiter.

---

[1] *KJ Aiyar's Judicial Dictionary*, (Twelfth Edition), revised by Satish Chandra Srivastava, (1998), Allahabad, The Law Book Company (P) Ltd., p. 346.

[2] *PSR Sadhanathan v. Arunachalam*, AIR 1980 SC 862–63: 1980 SCC (Cri.) 649.

[3] *Trayner's Latin Maxims*, Fourth Edition, 1993, Delhi, Universal Law Publishing Co. Pvt. Ltd., under special arrangement with Sweet & Maxwell Limited, UK. First published by W Green & Son in 1861. First Indian reprint,1997, pp. 33–5.

4.2 Crimes: A General Discussion

To reiterate the crux, a mere thought or sheer intention, not accompanied by a motivated attempt or without a correlated physical action, does not constitute a crime. Another Latin maxim, "*Cogitationis poenam nemo patitur,*" specifically upholds this viewpoint of law. The maxim lays down that no one suffers or is punished for simply thoughts or intention alone or even preparation for the act unless it is followed by an overt, active, physical implementation. Action cannot be assumed from mental resolution while a criminal intention can be judicially presumed from the occurrence and nature of a wicked act, even if the act is not successful in its aim, purpose or object and fails as an attempt or venture in that direction.[4]

Therefore, crimes are conscious and intentional commission of a prohibited activity under orders or in self-volition and in contra-distinction, a deliberate omission in performance of an obligatory incumbency. Thus, in common parlance these are illegal acts with consequences or negligent failures resulting in accidents causing damages thereby creating liability. Accordingly, crimes can be classified or categorised in diverse manner based on different criteria or model differentiations. For example, individual crimes, joint conspiracies or collective acts for law-and-order disturbance; bodily crimes, economic ones or those for honour or prestige; minor crimes, major or heinous; crimes as per national laws or international laws or those under Human Rights or Humanitarian laws; or at many other levels or in categories. This listing is surely not a conspectus view while criminals in this field may commit, as yet, unimaginable offences to wreak global destruction or cause apocalyptic havoc to humanity.

4.2.2 Analysis of Crime

To reiterate, in legal jurisprudence, mere *actus reus* or a physical action, howsoever prejudicial, does not sustain as a crime and may comfortably evoke the defence pleas of provocation, self-defence, contributory negligence, spontaneous response or temporary (emotional) insanity and other similar ones. As such a mere act may not be able to withstand the judicial rigour or legal soundness of commission of a crime and thus may be ill-founded in law. As a juris principle, a criminal act should be prompted or backed by motivation, if not prior planning or conspiracy. A Latin legal maxim states, "*actus non facit reum, nisi men sit rea*" meaning "The act does not make (the performer of it) a criminal, unless there be also criminal intention."[5]

To put it more explicitly, an act becomes a crime when the following parameters concur. Firstly, the act must be prohibited under the law in deference to the right of the others and yet committed or else required to be performed as a duty to ensure competencies under the law and yet failed in or not acted upon. Secondly, the person involved as accused should have the capacity and capability, physical and mental, to engage in the impugned criminal act, as alleged. And lastly, though not of least

---

[4] *Trayner's Latin Maxims*, ibid., pp. 81–2.

[5] *Trayner's Latin Maxims*, ibid., p. 23.

importance, is the intent or motivation or the subjective mental element of crime that is judicially summed up as "*mens rea.*" Thus, the essence of all crime is the felonious or criminal intention prompting or causing every such act so committed to constitute as a crime under law.

Most often, motive or intention is not apparent or clearly discernible and has to be investigated and then assumed, imputed or attributed to the alleged act, making it appear criminal in cognition and law. For example, a person attacks with a lethal weapon in utter disregard of consequences and death ensues, law may presume guilty intention and any defence on this plea would be entirely unavailing despite when the defence counsel "redargues" to confute the assumption. Such assertions, therefore, must carry the support of circumstantial proof of materiality of the guilty intention and the prosecutor be bound to prove its existence. Though this element is of essence in crimes yet there can be crimes without bad intention like culpable neglect where the cause is omitting or failing to ensure sufficient care and caution in dutiful performance of an obligatory or lawful act.

Similarly, acts committed under prohibitory Statutes like pertaining to drugs and psychotropic substances bear *prima facie* liability and automatically attract penalty on possession because in such cases, the very factum, and decision to infringe the law makes the individual guilty per se and as such no intention needs to be culled out or established for prosecution. The rule laid down in the maxim of *mens rea* is, however, applicable in generality and *in limine*. Even Trayner sounds a word of prudence that "This maxim must, however, be read and applied with caution, for the want of intention is not always a sufficient defence..."[6] nor equally enough to cause prosecution. It is for these reasons, other attendant uncertainties and convoluted behavioural imponderables that crimes in space become pertinent to deserve a separate and appropriate treatment in our discussion. *Mens rea*, howsoever, important element of crimes gets mutated and muted in the outer space and on celestial bodies due to changes in behaviour and psyche consequent to zero-gravity inconvenience, claustrophobic conditions and ergonomic constraints and other reasons peculiar to the domain.

4.3 Sociology of Crimes

Psychologists believe that there are several innate human traits that lead to crime. Such human proclivities could be acute anguish, repressed pugnacity, pent-up anger, uncontrolled emotions, deep distrust of others, intent for self-acquisition without due effort, urge for self-possession by trick or chouse, a desire for self-preservation and seeking undue ego-satisfaction or aggrandisement, to mention a few in illustration. Any clash of ideas or physical obstruction or ego-conflict caused in the process of

---

[6] *Trayner's Latin Maxims*, ibid., p. 24.

acquisition or possession would propel humans towards crime. The desires are deep-rooted and urge strong enough, where the weak-in-power or feeble-minded may become overly aggressive or in rebellion turn antisocial and commit criminal act.

A pertinent factor that makes this topic relevant to our consideration of crimes is that humans are instinctively aggressive for self-protection and self-survival. So, aggression as a technique of self-defence or self-perpetuation is normal, natural and almost reflexive. Thus, violence is preset and prewired in human mind and is a normal response that finds usual outlet in external behaviour. Similarly, humans are intrinsically self-centred and possessive, and this human propensity and innate thought-fixation encounter differences, disputes, conflicts and crimes. In primitive times, under these circumstances, justice and settlement of disputes was direct and instant with individual fights, may be, at times, aided by kinsmen or community violence, for recovery of "personality" or acquired possessions or family-owned property or redeem honour of the clan, in retribution or revenge.

On the contrary, some sociologists like Boulding believe that humans are neither innately aggressive nor genetically peaceful; this attitude is imbibed from community culture, in sympathetic learning from the social system and partly inherited from familial predilections. It can, therefore, be moulded and reshaped because "society contains in itself resources that can shift the balance from preoccupation with violence towards peaceful problem-solving behaviour."[7] Nonetheless, for centuries bygone, humans have committed acts offending others on some cause, excuse or pretext and have experienced reciprocal wrath, retaliation, and vengeance in return. However, with the dawn of civilisation and organised societal living, human actions and social conduct have come to bear a changed character and ordered behaviour through regulation by cultivated values, social norms, and state laws.

Ironically, with the industrial revolution and rise of affluence, there was concomitant growth in opportunities for generic theft and to commit associated crimes. Perhaps, crime became a lucrative habit for some, and for many others, a vocation. In India, the British government, towards the end of the nineteenth century, issued a notification listing certain wandering communities and nomadic tribes as "Criminal Tribes."[8] The law enforcement agencies and District administration were wary of their entry or presence in the urban areas, as it predictably led to rise in crimes. The irony of the situation was that the tribe was "as a whole" labelled with an insulting identity that caused alienation and socially forced their coming generations to be adept in crimes by sympathetic learning through observation, association, and participation.

Even in modern societies and countries worldwide, mafias for extortion, criminal gangs for killing[9] and drug cartels of smugglers operate with impunity and most operators of such organised crime have amassed wealth and wallow in luxury. These

---

[7] Elise Boulding and Randall Forsberg, *Cultures of Peace: The Hidden Side of History*, (Syracuse, Syracuse University Press), (1998), p.8.

[8] This notification was annulled after Independence of India, in the fifties of the last century and this label of notoriety was removed.

[9] In India, it is called *"supari killing"*.

Mafioso, possibly, operate in close connivance, mutual collusion, supporting intelligence and active support (for cover-up when apprehended), ranging from the police to the politicians. This may present a sorry state of affairs in governance yet is an unpalatable truth and its existence, in whatever form, gravity or rampancy, has to be faced and cannot be denied nor wished away.

This scenario fits into the Theory of Anomie, which theorises that criminality results from an offender's lofty ambitions and high aims; and at the same time, his incapacity to achieve his unrealistic goals by socially accepted means, methods or vocation. Disappointed and in desperation, the to-be-criminal resorts to easier and illegal avenues, even though risky. His satisfaction comes from the thrills and the glitter and the availability of promised money as also the bonus of bane pleasures. These operatives evolve their own subculture of criminality with an alternative set of moral values and social expectations which create a "differential association" in the mind, in self-rationalisation of their antisocial activities.

There is an old and wise saying that nobody is a born criminal, society makes one so. As a child grows up at home, gets preached with ideals while listens to lies and observes wrongdoings, and in its innocence, gets confused. Later, in school and at work he finds similar behaviour around and feels uncomfortable, but peeps at the advantage behind this misdemeanour and rationalises the same to either adopt or reject for himself. Thus, it is not as important what happens around you as is how you react to what happens. And this is where and how criminality breeds, and in nutshell, society, as a collective, is responsible for this dilemma. Moreover, when a raw criminal sees another one escape the clutches of law by crook, connivance or collusion, he has learnt the ropes of business for advancement. If such illicit escape from the process of law was not possible, or at least not easy, there would be fewer crimes. It is often said that the hands of law are long, but fingers do not catch the criminal.

Similar research by Albert Bandura becomes relevant to unravel the reason for normally respectable, moral and dutiful people to indulge in a behaviour that contradicts their religious beliefs, social standards, personal values, duty dictates and usual temperament. Thus, Bandura theorises that this occasional delinquency occurs because of a temporary cognitive reconstruction or a fleeting mental lapse that obscures or weakens the human cogitative control or sense of righteousness. The frailty in this mental process, induces momentary moral disengagement with reason to infuse an illusory sense of self-justification for the intended or actioned behaviour. The criminal also mistakenly harbours a misunderstanding that minimises the consequences of the act.[10]

Other sociologists like David Cressey, Gresham Sykes and David Matza have propounded Neutralisation theory to explicate the abovementioned scenario. They explain that such an occasional delinquent subscribes to the morals of society and wishes to live by the norms and laws yet sporadically descends into objectionable or derelict behaviour with a queer justification by a "process of neutralisation" to

---

[10] Albert Bandura, *Social Foundations of Thought and Action: A Social Cognitive Theory,* (N.J., Prentice Hall), 1986.

be redefined as morally and socially acceptable. This view compares well with Hirschi's theory of low self-control causing a remiss of logic and simulating compensatory self-vindication.[11] This self-induced semblance of justification creates delusion of a worthy and benign act which seemingly mitigates or obliterates personal responsibility therefor.

From another viewpoint, human beings are biologically wired to be clannish. We have an innate tendency to bond with "people like us" and have aversion to "people other than us." This primitive tribalist instinct, of course, imparted a sense of security and kept us safe in the jungles with spontaneous help in danger for collective survival. However, societies have progressed and this mental fixation, in present times, is a hindrance in the smooth running of a modern society, where populations have greater variety in ethnics, culture, language, religion, et al. Even financial disparities, economic inequities and educational differences have perpetuated. Therefore, no modern social group with democratic values and autonomous institutions of integrity can be governed based on the principles of exclusivity and preferences. Thus, call of the day for space crime management is to focus on what really matters: orderly societies with public tranquillity, good governance with transparency, police enforcement with impartiality, impetus to socio-economic development with equitable sharing of benefits and sustainable peace for humanity.

Biosocial criminology is another viewpoint to understand the causation of crimes that have recently found acceptance among criminologists and gained traction in the study of criminology. It is an emerging approach that highlights the interdependence between behaviour genetics and environmental factors in the aetiology of antisocial behaviours.[12] These factors have reciprocal impacts and interplay to mutate mental responses. Therefore, this approach maintains that there is a discernible connection between genetics and crime-like legendary male pugnacity, evolutionary psychology and crime-like minimisation of fear associated with such acts, and neuroscience and crime-like psycho-pathology. It would seem logical to assert that this theory and perspective would be equally valid for space crimes.

Some other sociologists break an important ground for a new thinking in the discipline of criminology. They tend to establish an interaction between physiological and environmental factors based on empirical research. This tentative hypothesis is also endorsed by Chris Gibson,[13] while Machado integrates forensic biology and sociological approaches to find an explanation for criminal behaviour.[14] He ascertained the causes through sociological inquiry to reach a conclusion that crimes are human responses to social circumstances. This finding would aptly apply to space crimes, too because of multi-ethnicity groupings in celestial habitations.

---

[11] This theory has been published in the journal "Criminology". Other details not available.

[12] Kevin Beaver and Anthony Walsh, eds., *Biosocial Theories of Crimes*, 2010. Also refer Anthony Walsh and Kevin Beaver, *Bio-Social Criminology: New Directions in Theory and Research*, Routledge, 2009; and Walsh and Beaver, *The Ashgate Research Companion to Bio-Social Theories of Crimes*, Routledge, 2011.

[13] Professor of Criminology at the University of Florida.

[14] H Machado, "Biological Explanations of Criminal Behaviour", 2020, *Springerlink*.

In the end, it seems pertinent to allude to another breed of criminals who happen to be afflicted with recidivism or are habitual criminals or possess crazy minds. Their plight can be explained under the Labelling theory. Generally, a convicted criminal, on return to society, gets labelled with criminal identity and his company is most often avoided or rejected by respectable, law-abiding people and even shunned by his erstwhile friends. This projected attitude often hurts as demeaning and frustrating and the person gets estranged from his former normal social circles. In reaction to this unsavoury treatment and to avenge the ostracism, the affected person starts socialising with other ex-criminals and their associates of dubious character and tainted reputation. The clique then coaxes him to understand "newer" crimes, as the last resort for his sustenance. Influenced by the company and to attend to his survival, he starts learning new tricks and chouses for his future and then starts to repeat the cycle of deviance and violence. Thus, breeds recidivism and unattachable fixation with crimes.

4.3.1 Considerations of Victimology

The contra-aspect of criminology is victimology. While most studies devote major time to study the psyche of the criminal, little attention is paid to the plight of the victim, his/her suffering from the crime and reaction to the criminal person and behaviour. This topic involves delicate issues to be discussed with anonymity, sensitivity, and empathy it deserves. The sufferer alone knows the pain and its severity or threshold of "bear-ability". Views can be widely different and reaction can vary from sympathetic condonation to award of capital punishment to public lynching. And none of them would be unreasonable or illogical. Suffering has its own analogues and syllogism.

Traditionally, jurisprudence has been obsessed with the crime, criminal, criminology or, at best or worst, penology. Thus, the emphasis has been to find the hidden criminal within the accused or attribute *mens rea* and application of codified punishment to balance the prescribed penalty to the legalistic gravity of the offence. Evidentiary proof of ingredients of the crime is more sacrosanct to the court than understanding the pain of the victim. And it has only been rare that the crime is related in its impact of the suffering undergone by the victim—physical, mental and psychical; least understanding that some offences leave life-long debasement of personality, dent on dignity and lowered self-esteem. Acceptance, compromise and amnesia of the unfortunate event may be prolonged and difficult but the victim generally has no other choice.

The courts, on the other hand, are obsessed with their duty to pronounce the verdict and sentencing of the guilty. In most successful trials, the criminal is incarcerated for a specific period and the case is deemed disposed of. Rarely, if ever, judges have thought about the economic plight and sustenance of, the direct and indirect, victims of the crime. This is because prosecution is taken up by the state and the victim becomes a forgotten soul in the process and its concerns and interests, howsoever vital, are not pleaded with relevance to the case. Thus, whereas the criminal is well assured of food, shelter and clothing in the prison, the victim, say the family of the murdered breadwinner, howsoever, deserving of economic succour and regular maintenance is often left to the mercy of God and support from the relatives, friends and good Samaritans. This dependence can be insulting and demeaning.

The considerations and principles of victimology are prominently and particularly applicable to cases of sexual offences and attempts thereat, marriage, divorce and custody, murders and abductions, cases of compensation claims and specific relief and a vast range of other offences. Criminal law, as a routine, does not consider award of reparations and restitution nor admit of monetary penalties except under specific laws like Terrorists and Disruptive Activities Act or Narcotics, Drugs and Psychotropic Substances Act which authorise confiscation of property and attachment of bank accounts, etc.

In a way, the accused is also a victim of the judicial system and the judges have shown scant regard towards reformation of the casual, incidental or circumstantial offender. In fact, a majority of such criminals are repentant of their impulsive action and are willing to make amends to return to the mainstream society as reformed persons and law-abiding citizen. But this is not to be and as long the breadwinner remains in prison, his dependents, too, are devoid of their sustenance and become destitute. Thus, crime is a bad business, both ways. That is why, it is wisely said, hate the crime and not the criminal. But the criminals lack a voice, even collective, that is heard in the right quarters and offers an alternative opportunity for the right purpose, may be in service to society. In fact, correctional counselling and reformative rehabilitation should be the right of every prisoner. No wonder, our prisons are overflowing their capacity and a person once a criminal sinks deep into recidivism.

In nutshell, the law enforcement machinery and the judicial system are all geared to apprehend and try an accused and if found guilty to serve a prison sentence. In the process, the travails of a victim of the crime are ignored and hardly ever come into consideration. Thus, our justice system is one-sided and alienated; oblivious to the plight of the victim, economic, social, or emotional, which also makes it partly unjust. It is conceded that law per se cannot penetrate minds yet law purports to justiciate social system and arbitrates conflicting claims which tend to remain fixated in mind though proved by facts and documents. Thus, the judicial system needs to reflect social consciousness and contemporary realities to provide social equity and humane justice. Thus, solution lies beyond the legalese and a purist attitude. May be, we need to reform and reshape the legal system to make it a viable instrument of distributive justice with humane enforcement process that assures legal protection to the contesting parties as per constitutional guarantees, staffed with judges of deliberative and perspicacious temperament and dispensation of a fair trial through judicial institutions of honour and majesty.

4.4 Space Crimes: An Introductory Discussion

The astronauts are generally highly disciplined, exceptionally proficient, thoroughly professional, and super-rated flyers. Despite such credentials, they are thoroughly re-tested for their aptitude, mental agility, and the speed of reflex actions. Thereafter, they are further trained in judgment techniques, conditioned for prompt and correct reflexes and drilled to be careful at every step of their activity in space. It has to be success at all efforts and costs; and failure is no option in outer space. Frankly, space environment rarely gives a second chance to amend a failure or even for survival. Thus, negligence would be a crime in outer space, as it may affect lives and hi-value machines. And despite all the care and attention devoted to the work schedules for in-station tasks and space-walks, a few instances of inadvertent negligence or lack of due diligence or want of abundant caution, by the crew, have taken place.[15]

Typically, so far, space-bound and ISS-stationed crew members, belonging to whichever country, have exhibited best model behaviour while in space, by instinct, training, and experience, despite zero-gravity inconvenience, claustrophobic conditions, and ergonomic constraints. Thus, there have not been any major dispute or mutual conflict among the crew. But after all, humans are human and may not behave any differently in the haloed domain of outer space when subjected to long periods of stay under stress and in separation from the family. They may err inadvertently or advertently or even irrationally, anywhere. Therefore, their usual good conduct and exemplary deportment in the past is no guarantee for extrapolation into the future and stable goodness may not be taken for granted every time and for all times.

Also, that space activities have so far been undertaken by officially controlled and state-funded agencies in almost all space-faring countries. And their focus has been on technological advancement for scientific exploration or for vindication and expansion of the knowledge-fund of humanity about the hitherto unexplored dimensions of outer space. There was thus an innocuous race to show technical superiority and for national aggrandisement. Apart from this, the emphasis over the last five decades has primarily been on peaceful exploration and public utility uses like communications, broadcasting, positioning systems and remote sensing applications for information dissemination, discovery of inland natural resources and other uses like weather forecasting, detection and surveillance of natural disasters and real-time management in their control and rehabilitation.

There have been, of course, cases of conflict of interest and disputes between states for different causes or grievances. For example, there were counterclaims and allegations of discrimination in the distribution of transmission frequencies or allocation of equatorial slots for placement of geo-synchronous satellites. But these were resolved by the good offices of international institutions like International Telecommunication Union, INMARSAT (before privatisation), and others. There have also been instances of damage caused on Earth by the falling debris of space objects like Soviet debris of nuclear-powered spacecraft on Canadian territory or American rocket parts falling on New Zealand. These have also been resolved by mutual

---

[15] A few such cases of items and tools being lost in space have been narrated in Chapters 2 and 3.

negotiations through diplomatic channels and agreed amounts of compensation duly paid and recovered parts of space objects returned. Thus, international disputes have hardly ever escalated and have generally followed the treaty wisdom and adopted diplomatic protocol for resolution. Therefore, any discussion on this aspect of crimes has been intentionally kept out of the scope of this book.

Till recently, dispute resolution was easy and fruitful due to the cooperative attitude of the states and of their desire not to defy the Space Treaty law or transgress the norms of space activities. This demeanour of cooperation transcended the political postures or ideological stances of the states and the result was friendly relations between nations, even among those with diametrically opposing mindsets and direct political rivalry. It was a golden period of thaw in strained relations after the Cold War, an era of voluntary cooperation rather than mere co-existence in international political microcosm and a time for realisation that space activities, hazardous by nature, need reciprocal help thereby infusing an attitude of willingness to reach out for mutual succour and spontaneous facilitation. Under this scenario, crimes were few and mostly that occurred were with individual onus and often condonable.

4.5 New Genre of Space Activities and Crimes

Be that as it may, the character and complexion of activities in outer space are going to be congestive, competitive, and conflictive. This is because states are gradually withdrawing from peaceful, exploratory activities and are tending to concentrate on strategic military objectives of defensive nature, ostensibly within the bounds of international space law. As a result of this reduced funding from state exchequers, private enterprise is making steady but rapid inroads into space activities, though their main interest is in commercial utilisation of outer space and profitable exploitation and appropriation of celestial resources. And the good of humanity is only incidental. Thus, the business focus would be on commercial space transportation, space hospitality, space laboratories for manufacturing, space logistics, commercial appropriation of celestial natural resources and building infrastructure for human habitations on celestial bodies.[16] All these business domains are highly competitive and intrusive, as such breaches of ethics and privacy may not be uncommon resulting in disputes and conflicts, which may be loosely termed as economic crimes.

Each of the mentioned commercial activities in space will create peculiar ground characteristics, societal imponderables and evolve new behavioural attitudes that would pose divergent challenges to need novel solutions. Because, the new environment will have different business compulsions, different operational strategies, different competitive playfield, different work norms, different ethical motivations, and different humanitarian considerations. Hence the nature, context and *mens rea* of new varieties of crimes in space will be of disparate identity and discrete causation.

---

[16] Bigelow Aerospace, Sierra Nevada Corporation, Lockheed Martin and Axiom have developed concepts for space habitats intended for space tourism and longer residence.

It may thus appear differently to different persons holding different beliefs, mindset, and legal understanding. Similarly, opinionated differences would arise relating to territorial and nationality linkages for jurisdictional claims on the offender or issues on national legal systems, with divergent national criminal codes and varying legal philosophies of jurisprudence. Thus, the trial of offenders in space crimes may be hassled with claims of extradition or procedural wrangles, tantamount to denying or delaying dispensation of justice. Therefore, space crimes need to be handled by jurisdictional certainty and definitive law so that to seek justice, an aggrieved space visitor or a victimised space inhabitant may not have to wade through onerous legal thickets and jurisprudential inconsistencies.

4.5.1 Commercialisation of the ISS and Private Space Stations

The US state budget is expected to cater for the maintenance and upkeep of its quarters at the ISS till 2030[17] and some of the partner states have also consented.[18] Thereafter, either these will be de-docked and incinerated in the atmosphere or leased to private entrepreneurs or rented for commercial uses to be self-sufficient for its sustenance and regular repairs. However, the legal visualisation or business plans for commercial uses and their legitimacy under the Outer Space Treaty may not be congruent. Both may concur to the extent of peaceful uses in the agreement but beyond that the freedom of commercial use by the lessee may progressively turn out to be unlimited and conflictive, unless amicably and reasonably circumscribed by mutual contract or multi-partite agreement.

In fact, a controversy has already arisen in another connection where SpaceX is assisting in plans to launch an "advertising billboard" into space. The project will consist of a tiny CubeSat-sized satellite with a pixelated screen on one side, which conceived and being executed by a Canadian start-up company, Geometric Energy Corporation. Tariff-paying followers will be able to see the commercial advertisement on the screen from the Earth. The satellite is expected to be launched in early 2022.[19] The legality of such a venture is being debated by law scholars. Ram Jakhu opines that the existing corpus of space law or even local laws of respective countries do not particularly prohibit such a space venture to term it as defiance. "Things may change later on".[20] However, the respective governments of the USA and Canada would have

---

[17] https://spacenews.com/other-iss-partners-start-planning-for-extension-to-2030/ DoA: 01 March, 2023.

[18] https://spacepolicyonline.com/news/japan-agrees-to-extending-iss-to-2030-reaffirms-artemis-contributions/#:~:text=Japan%20has%20formally%20agreed%20to,United%20States%20in%20that%20commitment DoA: 01 March, 2023.

[19] Mike Brown, "SpaceX to launch billboard into space: Is it Legal? Experts weigh in", *Shutterstock*, August 17, 2021. Also reported in *Business Insider*, August, 2021.

[20] Ibid.

to specifically accord authorisation for the activity and ensure continuing supervision for their responsibility under the Treaty.[21] At the same time, there are objections from the fraternity of astronomers that such an illuminated billboard orbiting in space may defile the beauty of sky-scape and disturb the serenity of night-sky.

Similarly, private space stations that are likely to come up in space as science laboratories or orbiting motels or for other commercial purposes will be inhabited by multi-nationality workforce, and so would be the tourist-guests. Situations are not unlikely where due to sheer misunderstanding verbal fights may erupt and compound into conflict and ultimately lead to a space crime. Crimes in such a milieu could be physical assault, verbal insult, "personalty" thefts, economic crimes, law and order disturbance or crimes relating to stealth of innovative ideas and appropriation of intellectual property. These certainly are terrestrial crimes which occur and are commonly observed on our planet and may equally commonly occur in outer space and on celestial bodies.

In simple cases with no jurisdictional dispute or counterclaims to extradition, provision of "jurisdiction and control" under the Outer Space Treaty (Article VIII) may be adequate and the link of nationality may not hold the key. However, for complicated space crimes involving multi-nationality, multi-territory or multi-domain, their handling, trial, and execution of judgment may pose unusual problems of jurisdiction, enforcement, legal procedures, trial system and legal codes. As a result, doubts may arise in the minds of both parties, the accuser and the accused, regarding the dispensation of justice. These aspects along with psycho-social issues in space have been discussed in later chapters.

4.5.2 The Nature of Space Crimes

In summary, the kinds and characteristics of space crimes will depend upon and be determined by the nature and type of oncoming space activities in the future. In the past, activities concentrated on space exploration and official transportation of astronauts and were undertaken by national space agencies controlled by the respective governments who abided by the provisions of Space Treaty law. Hence the situation was in conformance and peaceful, and a few derelictions or near-crimes that occurred were handled by the controlling agencies according to laws applicable to the delinquent personnel. However, no serious breaches of treaty law were reported or vocally protested for appropriate action.

The situation and the trend in the twenty-first century are likely to be different. The nature and motivation for space activities is tending to deflect towards economics and profit. This is natural because capital outlays for research in technology and construction of infrastructure are colossal and gestation period for break-even is long. Hence, business houses and corporates will not invest for only public good, welfare betterment, or sheer charity. Business fundamentals do not uphold altruistic

---

[21] The Outer Space Treaty, 1967, Article VI.

idioms and social responsibility as motivation by itself and sternly demand returns in profit. In the process, scientific exploration and social welfare are only incidental to the commercial space activities and not the core object of economic activity.

Commercial space activities are on the upswing and private corporations tempted by likely cumulative returns have already seized of this opportunity. The first occasion arose for the take-over of communications, broadcasting and remote sensing. It was enthusiastically grabbed by the private sector in different countries and the networks are running successfully and profitably. Subsequently, the space launch services for placing satellites of all sizes through independent launches or ride share mode to intended orbits in outer space, on commercial basis, has picked up. Known as "Commercial space launch services" is the order of the day, ventured into by many space agencies and private companies across the globe. SpaceX has launched multiple small satellites to supplement Starlink communication constellation and so has ISRO launched a record 103 satellites on a single launch vehicle.

The next opening has come for transportation of astronauts to the ISS and has been competitively accepted by SpaceX and others. And this experience of space transportation has facilitated a reach to commercial space travel which is fast blossoming into a public space travel service. Virgin Galactic and SpaceX lead the pack towards flourishing prospects that may touch a trillion $ target in a few years. Further this travel business is exfoliating into space tourism and hospitality industry offering a medley of interesting, novel and exciting experience of micro-gravity to honeymoon couples in space motels or an elitist walk on the Moon or even a short stay in the Moon village or at a resort on the Mars. Imaginable opportunities are endless and expanding.

Excavation of natural resources from asteroids and other bodies is another viable activity in the near future. In fact, celestial bodies offer an almost inexhaustible treasure trove of natural resources of precious metals that are of high utility to humanity having been almost depleted in the terrestrial mines or have become "in-excavation-able" due to low returns consequent to costs of deep mining and low-grade ore. Moon offers helium dust as a source of energy; some other planets contain siderophiles of iron and agnate concentrations; asteroids are rich in several precious metals and one such loose body is all diamond.[22] Thus, the value of celestial mineral reserves computes to an astronomical figure in economic values. And with growing prospecting, excavation of this celestial mineral is becoming technologically possible and economically viable. Hence, a boom in availability of certain minerals may be expected in a decade or two.

---

[22] G. S. Sachdeva, *Space Commercialisation: Prospects, Challenges and Way Forward,* New Delhi, Pentagon Publishers, 2019, pp. 53–56. There is, however, a creeping economic insecurity that precious metals mined from celestial bodies may, on Earth, cause a slump in their respective and sympathetic prices and thus, these may no longer remain precious metals and may disturb economies.

4.5.3 Cargo Transportation and Space Piracy

It needs no clairvoyance to expect that with burgeoning cargo transportation to space for hospitality services and from space, the excavated precious material would need space highways for transportation. Therefore, unguarded and vulnerable space capsules carrying vital and valuable materials may attract human crime of space piracy. In fact, with flourishing space economy in diverse ways, piracy in space, howsoever technical and risky, seems inevitable.[23] The expanding US activities in exploitation and appropriation of celestial mineral wealth and expansive mercantilism may tempt pirates to take advantage of the unprotected assets. And such crimes have an institutional precedence on Earth with tried and tested tactics to follow in their nefarious operations.

To begin with governments may not be able to assure or provide security to its corporate citizen or protect channels of trade or ensure continuity of supply chains due to governance vacuum and lack of police enforcement machinery in outer space. Given this situation, pirates may operate in touch and go manner and attack targets offering least resistance in an asymmetric war-like operation. In a way, the pirates also evaluate their own risk and reward parameters for every action and are no gritty fighters. So, lack of state protection could provide a perfect environment for space piracy to manifest itself and flourish in this domain. Further, an interesting aspect of piracy is that it may be government-sanctioned for several reasons. Competing for economic dominance may necessitate damaging the interests or performance of the competitor and what better method than to achieve it by proxy and in anonymity.

Piracy encourages ancillary crimes also. After all, looted goods and material seized have to be traded to finance piracy operations and reap profits too. This leads to proliferation of black markets and expansion of surreptitious trade which is most often covertly permitted by regulatory authorities with complicity of the state government. Howsoever condemnable, the governments on their part use, exploit, or encourage such operations as political or economic tools to beat their adversary and strengthen their posturing.

Humans are generally not a species with inclination for preventive measures or pro-active aptitude and normally respond in reaction when a problem truly stares in the face. For a problem of this character and magnitude, self-help in space guards or space mines around valuable assets[24] may be workable but would be an expensive proposition. Thus, individual self-reliance in the vast expanse of universe may not be the best option considering the low safety factor and high susceptibility to space risks and hazards. Survival quotient and existential threats would be pertinent. As an alternative, Moltz recommends space nationalism as cooperative, long-term relationship between space users and as a future structure of space defences.[25] As is wisely

---

[23] Matthew Schneider, "Space Piracy: A Condition of the Coming Age of Space Mercantilism", *ASTROPOLITICS*, Vol. 15, 2017.

[24] For details refer G S Sachdeva, *Outer Space: Security and Legal Challenges*, New Delhi, KW Publishers, 2010, pp. 187–206.

[25] James Moltz, *The Politics of Space Security*, Stanford University Press, 2011.

said, there is more to cumulated power in numbers; ergo collective, participative, and combined security set-up will be effective, protective, and economical.

As space traffic grows with diversity of space activities and exploitative economic market, the risks will increase and the criminal pirates when cornered and apprehended will have to be punished according to law. But terrestrial jurisdiction may pose obstacles[26] due to criminal's diverse affiliations and denominational biases and other reasons. Justice may be hindered and it points to a need for a universal effort to combat the scourge of space piracy. The obvious necessity is to counter jurisdictional hassles and declare piracy in space as a universal crime against humanity; and secondly, to "establish an international supervisory space agency"[27] to fight this common menace.

4.6 Complications Visualised in Space Scenario

The foregoing discussion highlights that the character and complexion of space crimes mainly depend on the nature and genre of the space activity and the human involvement in the processes of excavation and processing. Crimes emanate from disturbed human interaction while machines do not fight nor commit crimes. If at all, their failures and breakdowns are as a result of human failings in design, operation or maintenance. From another angle, human involvement and participation in space activities is bound to be multi-national and multi-ethnic which may create irritations and conflicts more conspicuous and irresolute than the machines. Hence space crimes will be more besotted with nationality issues and jurisdictional wrangles.

4.6.1 Jurisdictional Issues

The definition of launching state, despite clarification by a convention, is ambiguous and marred by duality. The complicating element could be the launching state as state of registry of the "humanned" space object in which a crime is committed. Normally, a launching state is the one that launches the object and on whose national registry it is entered and reported to the UN as its space object.[28] Further, launching state has *de jure* ownership of the object, permanent jurisdiction and full control over its operations and personnel within, whether crew or scientists or paying-passengers. This satisfies the territoriality criterion so long as all belong to the one launching country. But the scenario can be complex by varying nationality of every element at each step. It can be made further complicated by introducing possibility of a leased

---

[26] P J Blount, "Jurisdiction in Outer Space: Challenges of Private Individuals in Space", *Journal of Space Law*, 2007.

[27] Schneider at n. 23 ante.

[28] Convention on Registration of Objects Launched into Outer Space, 1975, as amended.

object or even on-orbit transfer and purchase. Such a transaction happened in the case of sale of non-functional Malaysian MEASAT satellite to the manufacturer, Boeing Satellite Systems, and its resale back to Malaysia for operations after making it functional by on-orbit servicing. This is where classical tests or established criteria of jurisdiction under international law will fail to offer clear-cut answers about *locus* of jurisdiction or point of transfer thereof.

The lack of a specific code governing such a state of imbroglio will be felt more acutely when a horde of private operators are involved in diverse commercial activities of space travel, logistics and tourism with service-personnel drawn from different nations and multi-national tourist configurations vacationing and enjoying stay at space hotels or resorts. One cannot deny the existence of dubious activities and profit mongering in this race, and possibility of crimes appears endemic to the situation. This is no oneiric vision nor the scenario seems too distant in time. In fact, such a predicament may be upon us sooner than imagined. The challenge is going to be formidable when actually confronted. Therefore, the military historians often advise in caution, with empirical wisdom, that to be forewarned is forearmed.

The nature of space crime and its impact on the victim can be another confusing factor that needs proper consideration. For example, a bodily injury or murder or one-to-one harm may be a simple case for jurisdiction settlement but cases of conspiracy or riots or law disorders will pose endless hassles of extradition and counterclaims for jurisdiction over offenders for obvious affinities like nationality, ideology, and religion. Take another case of theft of intellectual property and the search to pinpoint the actual culprit. This is not going to be easy either on the evidentiary burden or the jurisdictional clarity. And where does the *onus probandi* lie, whether on the defendant under French legal system or the complainant as under the British practice. Human Rights law, though suggests that a person is innocent till proved guilty.[29]

4.6.2 Commercialisation and Appropriation of Celestial Resources

Take another example from the OST. It mandates under Article I that "Outer space, including the Moon and other celestial bodies, shall be free for exploration and use by all States, without discrimination of any kind, on basis of equality and in accordance with international law and there shall be free access to all areas of celestial bodies." This guarantee, however, is circumscribed by the obligatory caveat of non-interference which is explicitly embodied in the Outer Space Treaty under Article IX that reads, "[Parties] shall conduct all their activities in outer space, including the Moon and other celestial bodies, with due regard to the corresponding interests of all other States Parties…" Ergo, conflict of interest cannot be ruled out and is endemic for advantages of being first to occupy or best accessible location or resources-rich site, et al.

---

[29] Universal Declaration of Human Rights, 1948, Article 11.

The above rider of corresponding obligation, however, is prudent and not unreasonable to obviate disputes, conflicts and crimes. Even jurisprudence proclaims that every right has a corresponding duty and demands reciprocity of enjoyment of common freedoms without breaching the domain of each other's legitimate right. But in experience, infringements are common and frequent resulting in irresolvable disputes, cognisable offences and consequent trials. This may not be much different in outer space either, where commercial activities demanding appropriation of resources will dictate primacy of self-interest, business strategy and profit considerations over cooperative existence, righteous adjustment and empathetic altruism. No wonder, conflict and crime reside hiding in this premise only to be unravelled by the regimen of commercialisation of outer space and private appropriation of celestial resources.

4.6.3 Different Legal Systems and National Codes

Different countries across the world have different legal systems which look at the crime and the criminal differently than other cognate systems. Further, apart from basic differences in the legal systems, there may be differences in the connotation of crimes and respective sentences. A couple of examples would vindicate this assertion. For example, the German legal system has no concept of contributory negligence while in legal systems that follow the British practices like India have an established doctrine of contributory negligence of the victim and quantum of compensation in liability cases is usually adjusted according to this factor. Another example could be negligence. In common legal parlance, it denotes neglect in performance of an assigned duty. The French equivalent of this is *"dols"*; but the connotation of *dols* is not mere negligence, it carries the meaning of gross negligence where the negligent person was aware of the consequences of the impugned conduct. Thus, simple negligence in France may not attract criminal accusation. Again, rape is a male-centred offence where man stands accused *prima facie* in much of the world. But in Saudi Arabia and some other Muslim countries there is no prima facie offence of rape by a man; on the contrary, the crime is loss of chastity or compromise on fidelity by the woman, who is punishable, even by stoning to death.

Similarly, the judicial systems for dispensation of justice also differ across the globe. The British tradition holds an accused not guilty till proved but it practices adversarial system of parties in the court. The French continental legal system, in a prima facie valid complaint, puts the burden of defence on the defendant. The American judicial system in many states operates by constituting juries for consideration of humane and social aspects of crime. And the Islamic penal codes bear the sanctity of the Quor'an and *qazis* act as judicial officers with authority. These variations in the legal systems are bound to create apprehensions in the minds of space dwellers about fair justice from different streams of law.

4.7 A Proposed Definition of Space Crimes

Earlier discussion has analysed the salient aspects of space crimes and challenges posed in the process of enforcement and their adjudication. The solutions thrown up in the discourse relate to the necessity for a *lex specialis* (specialised treaty law) for dealing with space crimes and a dedicated international court for trial of such cases. The evolved suggestion posits the need for a proper definition of space crimes to enable specifically determine and circumscribe the competence of the trial court and the expanse of law to seize jurisdiction over crimes committed or caused in the outer space or relating to the space domain and the alleged criminals. A rough-cut definition with proposed constituents of space crime is proffered that can be honed and refined by the space law fraternity for acceptance and usage.

At the very outset, exceptions to the proposed definition may be mentioned. First, there could be instances of space crimes involving an individual of only one country and the crime affecting the same country national or property with no international implication whatever for damage or loss. In such a reported or litigated case, the complainant person and the so accused may be dealt with by the parent country under its domestic jurisdiction and may not be deemed as a space crime. Perhaps, the best example of such a crime can be that committed by Anne McClain of USA, where under all kinds of jurisdictional considerations, this case lapsed back to the competence of the US courts or Federal authorities. Even in such "uncomplained" cases prosecution enforcement authorities may take *suo motu* cognition of the crime for reasons of national security or safety of space operations or for deterrence by precedent.

Second exception could relate to crimes where there are international involvements relating to the victim or the loss suffered but the case remains unreported for prosecution or remedial action for claims of liability. The case may thus remain uncontested either because of triviality of loss or damage, there being a minor injury not worth the fuss, lack of sufficient incriminating evidence or that adequate proof for a liability claim, according to strict judicial standards, cannot be adduced. Hence, a space crime even if not alleged for redressal at international level yet the country of the criminal national may pursue the incident for investigation under domestic jurisdiction, for corrective disciplinary action in the interest of national security, operational considerations, or social justice, per se.

Now coming to the definition, space crimes are those acts of commission by the resident/s of outer space or guests in a space resort/hotel or deployed in orbiting spaceships or working on celestial bodies in any capacity. And that should such a "space-person" cause injury (physical or mental or economic) to or death of another such person commits a space crime. Apart from familiar incriminating human acts, there would be crimes with economic overtones, business interests, monopolistic motives or property involvement, e.g., of illegal interference, unauthorised encroachment, theft of property items belonging to another, causing interruption in other's production facility, spying on or stealing of intellectual property secrets would be actionable. These could include harming or jeopardising the economic interests of another party from an orbiting station or while on a celestial body, by any device, in any manner of conduct or with whatever intention, shall be treated a space crime punishable under the space law regime and applicable international law.

In case a space-person advertently or negligently causes malfunction, damage to or destruction of any spaceship or space object in orbit or while stationed on a celestial body commits a crime. Further, if such person causes non-essential pollution with debris of any kind in outer space; scatter or clutter celestial bodies with unauthorised organic or inorganic material; causes contamination of outer space domain with terrestrial bio-organisms in any form or state of life, motility or reproduction; or introduction of any harmful botanical plant life, the impugned act would be deemed a crime. These clauses, as relevant, should also apply vice versa for introducing similar adverse effects on the Earth and its environment in any manner.

Similarly, obligatory omissions or advertent failure to take appropriate and necessary action or due safeguards in the outer space or on the celestial bodies to prevent abovementioned injury, death, malfunction, damage, destruction, pollution or contamination shall be treated as space crimes. In similar stance, causing an injury (physical or mental or economic) or death of a space resident; malfunction, damage or destruction of a space object in the space domain or space infrastructure by artificial intelligence, cyber technology, digital tools, laser emission, robots or any other means operated, controlled or directed from anywhere in the universe (including Earth) shall constitute a space crime. Further, causing such or similar damage to any object on the Earth, in the air and to the atmospheric environment of the Earth shall constitute a space crime.

The above clause relating to acts by robots becomes important because in future ventures of exploration into deep space or exploitation of celestial resources or other mundane operations for maintaining space infrastructure, robots may participate as human partners to multiply work-potential and augment synergy. Thus, robots are going to be substantial contributors and significant helpers in celestial infra-structure maintenance, future "humanned" visits to planets, scientific exploration in space, excavation of celestial natural resources, reconnaissance in hostile environment of certain planets and deep-space sojourns. But robots are not only as intelligent as programmed by human technologists but tend to learn by algorithms of experience and may over-step their programmed intelligence. As a result, these have in the past committed crimes, even murder of humans. This would be a patent crime and need legal expedients to handle such situations. It may have to be explained and faced by its creator in many aspects. Exceptions and immunities claimed may take effect only to a reasonable extent and may not fully exonerate the creators. Therefore, more elaborate rules need to regulate and control such operations.

There can be another category of crimes related to the violation of human rights by showing discrimination and bias in the event of emergency, accident or disaster. Outer Space Treaty mandates offering of shelter and all possible help to the sufferers under such circumstances and refusal by the authorities and state-agents to abide by this provision or causing unnecessary delay or bias of any kind, racial, nationality, gender or for any other reason would constitute an internationally wrongful act and punishable accordingly. Further, wherever such denial of safe facility or lack of help

4.7 A Proposed Definition of Space Crimes

inflicts torture to the victims of any mishap, the perpetrators may be held liable under International Humanitarian Law and its relevant protocols, which has since become Customary International Law.

In order to ensure peace, safety and security of the outer space domain, any weapon (kinetic, magnetic, directed energy, nuclear, chemical and biological, cyber, with artificial intelligence, or any other such device for mass destruction) positioned on a celestial body or placed in orbit or partial orbit anywhere in the outer space or the Earth would be a space crime. Similarly, such a weapon based on the Earth or from the air (atmosphere) is aimed at and fired at a space object in outer space or on a celestial body and, vice versa, i.e., from the outer space or from a celestial body targeting any place, area or point on the Earth shall constitute a space crime. Even a threat of use of such force is covered under this. Thus, the dictate of the Outer Space Treaty (Article IV) and the provision of the Moon Agreement (Article 3) remain sacrosanct and binding yet need amplification and a proper definition.

In furtherance of this subject, MILAMOS has defined military space activities, which are prohibited under the space law as, "…military space activities are space activities of a military character. In the determination of the military character of a space activity, the actors involved in the activity, the aim of the activity, and effects of the activity are to be taken into account, as appropriate."[30] But the text is cautious, skeletal and declaratory. The author feels that the ingredients should be more clearly defined and delineated in military terms. Thus, military space activities are those bearing military character and military objectives with military actors and desiring military effects.

Additionally, it could imply and tantamount to positioning of military potential and personnel in outer space or on celestial bodies in readiness to respond to any threat or attack in space, on space assets or on the Earth targets. This version still represents defensive posture, and solicits justification from the doctrine of retorsion under international law and Article 51 of the UN Charter which states, "Nothing…shall impair the inherent right of individual or collective self-defence if an armed attack occurs…" But overtly defensive posture may sustain covert military activities of offensive and aggressive character that may pose direct military threat of use of force. Be that as it may, such military activities are banned by treaty law through use of military equipment and personnel is not prohibited for scientific exploration and peaceful purposes.[31]

In nutshell, space crime is an act that is committed in outer space or on a celestial body or from any other domain to cause harm or damage or destruction in the outer space domain:

- an act that is prohibited but committed or is requisite under rules yet not performed with due diligence; or other crimes so defined in respective national codes and committed in outer space including celestial bodies;

---

[30] Ram Jakhu and Steven Freeland, eds., *Manual of International Law Applicable to Military Uses of Outer Space*, (MILAMOS), Montreal, McGill Centre for Research in Air and Space Law, 2022, Rule 103.

[31] Outer Space treaty, 1967, Article IV.

- an act inducing or causing detrimental effect into outer space or celestial body from anywhere in the universe, including the Earth and aircraft, which adversely affect or damagingly impact legitimate business interests, legal operation of a space object or damage/destroy infrastructure at a celestial body;
- an act caused by technological devices or gadgets or weapons to harm any legitimate interests or operations in outer space domain and committed from anywhere within the universe;
- an act to injure or kill person or personnel within any such space object or planetary structure, in any manner or by any device or action otherwise;
- an act that causes environmental pollution or contamination of space object or celestial body, and/or which affects their operation or sustainability;
- an act or any arbitrary or impermissible decision, during emergency or otherwise, that may jeopardise the safety or life of a person on a space object or a celestial body.

4.8 Solutions in Brief

These examples are merely illustrative and similar divergences of perception in legal systems can be adduced.[32] Many such comparative cases of behaviour and beliefs have been discussed in detail in Chap. 10. These thus, definitely flag the fact that persons brought up and who have lived in a particular legal system may vary of the unfamiliar system of other companions and compatriots in outer space and would be reluctant to accept and repose confidence in their systems. This mindset is natural and not easy to neutralise. Therefore, adjudication of crimes that are committed in outer space and on celestial bodies would need a revised law lexicon, new conciliatory procedures, modified system of justice and new space jurisprudence to elicit and command confidence in the system from both parties, the sufferer and the perpetrator. This may be called Social Justice that would show due regard to the parties involved and a harmonisation of the systems, when in conflict or objected to.

These objectives may also demand a new specialised treaty, mutatis mutandis, on the lines of the Hague Convention, 1970 for crimes in and from the aircraft. To put the system in place, timely initiative for crafting a suitable instrument may lie with the UN/COPUOS, though their drafting procedures are dilatory and time-consuming. Further, the new treaty would need an organisational institution for its execution, to ensure compliances, for competent governance of the domain and for professional management of non-traditional uses of outer space and natural resources on the celestial bodies. One suggestion can be to revive the UN Trusteeship Council, now defunct, to take charge of this duty that appears relatively akin to its previously assigned Charter. It may also need an independent judicial wing to effectively handle space crimes with promptness, objectivity transparency and universal acceptability.[33]

---

[32] A comparative analysis of such perceptions is contained in Chapters VIII and IX.

[33] This hypothesis has been discussed in detail in Chapter X on 'Appraisal and Conclusions'.

Chapter 5
Future Crimes in Space: A Visualisation

5.1 Introduction

It can now be asserted with confidence that human beings whether on Earth or in outer space or on a planetary body remain the same, physically, mentally, and genetically. Their reflexes do not change, their thought-process remains the same and their mindset also persists in fixations. In space, while living and interacting in multi-ethnic and multi-cultural environment, human mind may evolve through sympathetic learning in the new companionship and camaraderie. A person may thus acquire new or modified habits through revised social responses and frequent cultural mixing, but it may take a long time depending upon personal propensity: ability to change, capacity to imbibe, and acceptance of novelty. Till such a changed metamorphosis, there is likely to be a big churning in inter-relations when differences will come to fore, ideas will clash, disputes will occur, conflicts will arise and, in the process, unbecoming acts and crimes may be committed.

In fact, the situation can be worse because Earth is a familiar environment with accustomed living condition for humans, whereas in space orbits and on neighbouring planets human body and mind will be exposed to the effects of low gravity, unusual G-forces, unhealthy radiation, extreme variations in temperature, artificial atmosphere, cramped spaces, lack of privacy, unknown people for company, unfamiliar ambience and stress of concerns about safety and return to Earth. Overcoming trauma, acclimatisation and getting used to new fears take time. Therefore, the cumulative impact of these factors of angst and anxiety for personal safety would weigh heavily on the human mind in space and, for the weaker mortals, tension may burst into crimes, howsoever minor.

For space workers, the conditions may be still worse due to the fatigue of daily duty, stress of contracted work productivity, risks of injury, hazards of accident and emergency due to failure of infrastructure. All these imponderables do not make for peace of mind, effortless accustomed living, and comfortable life as on the Earth. The thrill of newness in heavenly scenario, gravity-free environment, and excitement of being out in space make for no compensatory bonus. Even professionally trained, mentally regimented, highly disciplined, and duty-bound astronauts have, in the past, committed unbecoming acts and near-patent crimes. It is, however, a different matter that most often these have been disregarded for considerations of unusual work-routine stress and gracefully condoned in view of success of the mission. Hence, crimes of whatever type and graveness are inevitable among all: the excited tourist eager to capture every sight and moment of the trip, the pressurised worker with mounting fatigue or the lonely resident of Mars Colony or the Moon Village rueing the decision to emigrate. Whatever be the context, content or gravity of the situation, these causes would prod space-farer towards acts that may escalate to space crimes on the slightest pretext or provocation.

5.2 Classification of Space Crimes

Crimes in space defy a neat categorisation based on conventional criteria. These tend to disperse over a spectrum much wider than the national codes for their range and causes and effects. These will also bear several other riders of lawful competencies, novel defence pleas, and disabilities due to inhospitable environment of outer space or other planetary bodies. Despite the diversity and specificities of the space crimes, these can be compressed under diverse classification in many ways, from different angles and on varied criteria. The most elementary classification can be on the basis of existing terrestrial crimes codified by different countries. It is, however, a different matter that their understanding and perception on the same crime and its ingredients, similar criminals and their culpability and methods of dispensation of justice may vary and even conflict.

Interestingly, the type of crimes in outer space and on celestial bodies will be tempered by four major factors: the stress of space environment, the emotional concern of family deprivation, a lurking angst for safety, and the nature of job in space. All these factors will exert their specific pressures and discernible tensions on humans in space. On the other side, it will depend on the capacity, tolerance, and resilience of the space-farer or space-dweller to withstand and neutralise such stresses and live a normal, amiable, conflict-less, and crime-free life in the new celestial surroundings, mixed groupings, and social environment of multi-nationality and multi-ethnicity. It seems a tall order in view of the innate human nature and attendant circumstances discussed later.

5.2.1 Classification Based on Terrestrial Legal Codes

Most common crimes among these are physical fights causing hurt or injury or battery as individual crimes in space stations and hospitality resorts. Collective or joint crimes like disorders of public law and conspiratorial or organised crimes like terrorist attacks in space may take place in the future. The main ingredient in such crimes would be the intention to cause harm, injury, or death, with excessive amount and application of certain force, choice and use of weapon and advantage in the hit. On the part of the victim quickness in reaction, counteraction in self-defence and manoeuvres of escape would be material for the safety. Such criminal behaviour, of whatever type, would involve a mental condition of ill-will and actual physical activity to harm, with or without premeditation or planning and may involve collaboration of other individuals as well into the actualisation of the intention and commission of the act.

More philosophically, a criminal act "means that unity of criminal behaviour which results in something, for which an individual would be punishable, if it were all done by himself alone, that is, in a criminal offence. [Thus,] the criminal act contemplated implies unity of criminal behaviour and the capacity of the individual to do the criminal act all by himself."[1] The existence of *mens rea* seems presumed and implied in this definitional statement of a criminal act in the "unity of criminal behaviour." The simplest crimes in this category would be verbal duel, battery, affray, theft or stealing, misappropriation or cheating, insulting or hurting sentiments and at worst causing death or committing a rape.

And now upcoming space residencies for permanent habitation, celestial hotels and resorts for space tourism, private space stations dedicated to commercial activities like advertising billboards or shooting of movies,[2] manufacturing activity of space-specific products like metal alloys, crystals, and vaccines as also exploitation and appropriation of celestial natural resources by private players, may spring up a new genre of crimes in space with different traits and implications. Policing and prevention, investigation and judicial enforcement of these criminal activities is an exacting task that throws up formidable challenges. Further, because of its administrative nuances and operational peculiarities, this duty is generally mired in criticism and distrust.

5.2.2 Agents of Crime

Crimes could be classified based on the character and status of the offender. Thus, crimes in space can be committed by states, space agencies, corporate operators, human beings, or robots. Robots, however, bear and display preprogrammed behaviour and as such their crimes would be program errors or digital bugs. Therefore, there are different rules of conduct and control for robots. Moreover, robots cannot be punished in the same way as humans while manufacturers and programmers escape liability under exceptions and exemptions. Certain rudimentary rules are, in place but their modification is under reconsideration. For our purpose, we

---

[1] *Rakesh Gunvantlal Gandhi v. State of Gujarat*, 1972 Guj. LR 717. Word in parenthesis is added.

[2] AFP report, "Russian crew returns to Earth after filming first movie in space", *Times of India* (Chandigarh edition), October 18, 2021.

will deal with crimes by humans only, in whatever capacity or authority, in whatever manner, with whatever devices or platform and from outer space or on celestial bodies.

For example, offender could be a state for a badly conceived and ill-planned experimentation, causing contamination like the Israeli crash of lunar module that possibly released micro-organisms, which are believed to be hardy with a life many centuries long, even on the Moon. Another example could be the USA causing space pollution by spreading of copper needles in outer space through an ill-conceived project. Both these projects were undertaken without international consultation as advised under the Outer Space Treaty. Or it could be negligence in regulatory responsibility of the state or unintended complicity in permitting unsanitised Tesla Roadster into space in a rocket testing experiment by a private enterprise, Space X. State lapses could as well relate to suppression of scientific revelation observed from space that should have been shared with scientific community or made public under the Treaty rules but were held back as undisclosed secrets. Similarly, non-registration of space objects launched or non-transmission of such information to the UN authorities in a reasonable time, all constitute dereliction of the Treaty mandate and could be deemed serious violations as near-offences under law.

The defaulter could as well be governmental space agencies for disregard of Outer Space Treaty or not following the best practices recommended by the UN committees, thus leaving garbage on the Moon as shedding of surpluses and wastes to make room for rock samples or creating unnecessary debris in space like with ASAT tests. The long-term impact and safety hazards caused can be deemed near-crimes, even if not specifically prohibited acts. It could also be a private sector space player defying the provisions of space law for not taking enough precautions as prescribed in Guidelines like loading of "unsanitised" Tesla Roadster car in a trial flight of rocket. Most of such actions have tended to cause some sort of pollution and/or contamination in outer space or on celestial bodies. In fact, all perpetrators, whether the state or governmental agency or private enterprise, are equally liable for disturbing, howsoever minimally, the "pristine-ity" and sustainability of space environment. Such space crimes have occurred with varying gravity and culpability and need to be stemmed.

Pollution and contamination in reverse are also true and factual. Take for example the landing of returning "humanned" modules or cargo capsules in the sea or the high seas which could be carrying some sort of space pollutants or contaminations from space or celestial bodies. These may get washed into the waters of the sea or may pollute the polar ice depending upon the area of fall. It happened when the debris of Russian spacecraft fell on the Canadian territory and presumably caused nuclear pollution. It could have been worse with space contaminations, the deleterious results of which may become apparent decades later.[3]

---

[3] More details on this topic under Nuclear Debris, discussed later.

5.2.3 Impact of Space Environment on Crimes by Humans

Space environment is different than what we are used to on the Earth. So, reaching outer space and living there have its own health encumbrances. Of course, human body starts to adapt in just a few days in space but not without adverse effects. Bones start to lose density and the muscles become smaller and weaker because they are not being used to stand up against gravity or to move around. While these changes may not pose much of a problem in the environment of microgravity, these can lead to increased risk of injury, back pain, or bone fracture on return to Earth. These changes are comparable to age-related degeneration affecting people on Earth, but happen much more quickly in outer space. Therefore, astronauts spend considerable time on exercising in space to minimise the effect of these unhealthy adaptations.

Another unhealthy influence of lack of gravity is that the position sensors in the ears (vestibular system) get confused and cannot tell if one is really moving or may not be able to sense which way is up or down. Thus, space travellers with vestibular impairments may be more susceptible to this propensity. The deterioration of this faculty may cause annoyance and irritation to create serious changes in behaviour, which may at times, be unacceptable to co-passengers or co-residents. This condition can also be a cause of space sickness and its allied consequences. Cumulatively, the consequences of this disposition may become cause of conflict or crime.

Also, going to space changes a person in brain and behaviour. Ever since NASA and the former Soviet Union started sending people into space in the mid-twentieth century such trips affect an astronaut's outlook[4] but changes are more pronounced in the body. Space physicians continually study astronauts to understand just what happens to them in space. The latest revelation is the effect of low gravity for long periods on the brain. In fact, the fluids in our bodies flow under the influence of gravity. Once a person goes into space the normal flow of fluids changes. This is particularly true for the cerebrospinal fluids and their spaces in the brain. We are all adapted to the force of gravity and accordingly, nature did not put our brains in our feet, it rather put them high up on the body. Once gravity is removed from the equation, changes happen to human physiology. Therefore, long-duration space flights alter the fluid-filled spaces along brain veins and arteries.[5]

Medical researchers decided to find out by measuring the perivascular spaces in astronaut brains. These are where cerebrospinal fluid flows in the brain. They are part of a system-wide brain cleansing that occurs during sleep called the "glymphatic system." Among other things, it clears metabolic proteins that would otherwise build up in the brain. Paradoxically, scientists assert that this system, almost comparable to space environment, seems to perform optimally during deep sleep.[6] Perhaps the catch could be in longer continued stay in space. To investigate further, space doctors mapped the brains of the astronauts preflight, during flight, and post-flight

---

[4] The case of William Shatner, discussed later.

[5] K. E. Hupfeld, et al. "Longitudinal MRI-visible perivascular space (PVS) changes with long-duration spaceflight". *Scientific Reports* **12** (2022): A7238.

[6] Hupfeld, ibid.

and compared with similar scans of those who had not gone into space. Changes were revealed but astronauts who had stayed long in space-tenures showed few changes, may be due to adaptation. Despite the noticed changes, the astronauts, in the study, had no problems with balance or visual memories nor did they show any other neurological deficits due to the changes in their perivascular spaces.[7] Nevertheless, the enigma remains to be unravelled and problems may resurface with the longer stay of Marsnauts.

However, the greatest risks to the health of space travellers and space residents are physical discomfort, biological changes, health indisposition and mental stress experienced during launch, zero-gravity situation, re-entry into Earth atmosphere, and splashed-landing. During launch, passengers would experience vibrations resulting from the extra-ordinary thrust generated as also experience an acceleration or the effect of G-forces. Space environment has near zero-gravity, even on the planets. As a result, during stay in outer space, human body starts losing red blood cells leading to the dangerous condition of anaemia. Unfortunately, this effect persists for long even after return to the Earth, though recoverable.[8]

During re-entry into the atmosphere, the G-force reaches a much higher threshold which can have profound effects on the human mind and body. G-factor is a tricky concept to explain, but simplistically, blood gets pulled away from the head which can starve the brain of oxygen which in turn can lead to visual changes including tunnel vision, loss of colour differentiation (grey-out), or complete loss of vision (blackout). In some cases, a G-force-induced loss of consciousness can also occur. Same way, at the end of take-off stage, when engines are switched off on completion of ascent, allowing it to slow down, the high G-forces abruptly disappear and the passenger feels weightless. This rapid entry into microgravity often leads to trauma and space sickness which may cause distressing reactions.

The discussed conditions of annoyance and irritation as also traumatic stress, secondary fatigue, and cumulated tension may exhibit a propensity towards abnormal and irrational behaviour leading to inane arguments, unreasonable disputes and unbecoming crimes, howsoever minimal. This may impact social living in space vessels and affect peace, tranquillity and public order in planetary residencies. In the end, it may be buttressed by a case study. William Shatner, an actor from the movie Star Trek, went into space as part of the Blue Origin team in October 2021. He was aged 90 years and is yet the oldest person having gone on a space trip. His comments on his feelings on and during the space odyssey are candid and revealing.[9] Shatner was confounded which induced "the ultimate catharsis." He was filled with sadness and cried in space. He honestly acknowledged that he found himself relieved when the spaceship landed and he stepped back on to the Earth.[10] Now let us accept that

---

[7] Carolyn Collins Petersen, "Astronauts' Brains Altered by Extended Trips to Space", *Universe Today*, May 10, 2022.

[8] *Space.com*, January 20 2022.

[9] Nick Caplan and Christopher Newman, "William Shatner oldest astronaut at 90—Here's how space tourism could affect older people", *Space.com*, October 15, 2021.

[10] Google search, accessed on December 6, 2022.

space travel is no bullock-cart ride and has its health travails including long-term adverse effects on human physiology, biological metabolism, psychological trauma, and mental state.

5.3 Economic Crimes in Space

The genre of economic crimes in space can have its own classification and criteria. Simple examples could be stealing of personal items or theft of valuable objects belonging to other person in space. At a higher level, it could be appropriation of secrets covered under proprietary rights of individuals or business houses or breach of intellectual property rights for innovations in space and so on. Economic offences of the future could also relate to cut-throat or unethical business competition in space travel and tourism, causing hindrance in operation of lease agreements for commercial exploitation of planetary mineral resources, unauthorised encroachment of astro-property or illegal interference in lawful economic ventures of mining, manufacturing, and others. Thus, untenable lease of or conflicting property rights, obtained for consideration, of real estate or infrastructure on a planet can be another reason for differences and disputes that may culminate in economic crimes in a competitive environment.

Another species of space crimes could relate to business or economic concerns involving interference in authorised activity on celestial realty, acts prejudicial to business interests, spying on secret research efforts or breaching intellectual property confidentiality and the like. Another activity that may lead to space crimes could be space transportation and space tourism due to profit mongering. Crimes of diverse nature could be committed by tourists and guests and on the other hand space carriers may also commit irregularities and compromises that may tantamount to crimes. One such aspect may relate to the responsibility for safety and security of the guests as also help and evacuation in an event of accident or disaster.

Further with progressing technological feasibility, private space companies may be tempted by the economics and profitability of the activity to control, excavate, and commercially appropriate celestial natural resources that constitute "the province of all mankind."[11] At present, international space law does not permit such free-enterprise of this exploitative space activity.[12] Nor does the germane law allow or create through occupancy, a right *in rem* on the unclaimed reality or ungoverned, non-sovereign territory on celestial bodies. Thus, to enjoy the entire profits of the mining activity *sans* stipulated modalities for sharing of benefits by all states and also not depositing the estimated quantum of such shareable profits in an escrow account for disbursement to entitled states later could be deemed an act of economic

---

[11] Treaty on Principles governing the Activities of States in the Exploration and Use of Outer Space, including the Moon and Other Celestial Bodies, 1967, also referred to as Outer Space treaty or the Treaty or OST. Refer Article I.

[12] The Treaty, ibid.

misappropriation.[13] Apart from a legal mandate, it turns out to be an obligation *erga omnes* for the benefit of all states.[14] Besides, it behoves as an element of corporate social responsibility (CSR) and a moral duty of the private sector to contribute towards betterment of humanity, collective, or discrete.

5.4 Crimes of International Wrongs

Another category of crimes committed in space may relate to deficiency in assurance of human rights and crimes under international humanitarian laws. Outer space environment is hazardous and not human-friendly. Therefore, when human beings visit hotels or resorts on celestial bodies, they may need and would deserve a special protection against atmospheric abnormalities, temperature variations, radiation hazards, or other possible catastrophes. Similarly, humans who migrate to the planets and live there in permanent residency need fail-safe infrastructure for their habitat and may need evacuation to Earth in emergencies and for failure of services. Again, with growing commercially exploitative activities and industrial manufacturing ventures on celestial bodies, a significant workforce would be positioned there which would need sensitive and empathetic treatment with human dignity and respect for life. Their needs in an event of distress, accident, disaster, or emergency would require alternate shelter for immediate safety or eventual evacuation to the Earth.

The OST ordains that "State parties…shall render…all possible assistance in the event of accident, distress or emergency…."[15] Though this provision relates to astronauts, who were deemed to be envoys of mankind, in space or on landing at sea or on land, it could "lawgically" extended and applied, though on a lower scale to human workers in commercial activities or industrial production, in space or on celestial bodies. The above article also creates an analogous legal responsibility when it states, "In carrying on activities in outer space and on celestial bodies, the astronauts of one state party shall render all possible assistance to the astronauts of other state parties."[16]

Overall, the state becomes internationally responsible for the legality and legitimacy of such space activities and a failure in this regard may constitute a crime in the negative sense. It can, thus, be validly interpreted and rightfully construed to treat astronauts as space workers or in converse consider space worker as para-astronauts, or at least as space personnel, so as to treat space workers eligible to entitled safeguards under the Treaty, without demur or discrimination. Further, by a logically valid inference, the state as sovereign authority of its nationals becomes responsible

---

[13] Gurbachan Singh Sachdeva, *Space Commercialisation: Prospects, Challenges and Way Forward*, New Delhi, Pentagon Press LLP, 2019, p. 37.

[14] Sachdeva, ibid, p. 213.

[15] Outer Space Treaty, Article V.

[16] Ibid.

5.4 Crimes of International Wrongs

for a bounden duty towards its nationals in outer space. This duty involves their safety and security in outer space domain as also safe return to the Earth on completion of tenure of contract (apart from contractual terms) or for the tragic reason of emergency evacuation due to distress, accident or disaster or any other cause. Tragedy does not need comparisons.

This mandated intention and a binding duty, as contained in the OST, is reiterated in the Moon Agreement where it asserts, "State Parties shall offer shelter in their stations, installations, vehicles and other facilities to persons in distress on the Moon."[17] The ordained obligation may be interpreted and amplified in content and spirit to imply that in an event involving a threat to human life, "States Parties shall adopt all practical measures to safeguard the life and health of the persons on the Moon. For this purpose, they would regard, as per Treaty-law mandates, any person on the Moon as an astronaut within the meaning of Article V of the Treaty on Principles Governing the Activities of States in the Exploration and Use of Outer Space, including the Moon and other Celestial Bodies and as part of the personnel of a spacecraft within the meaning of the Agreement on Rescue of Astronauts, the Return of Astronauts and the Return of Objects Launched into Outer Space."[18]

Accordingly, authorities in-charge of their work establishments in the space domain cannot forsake the interests of space residents and space inhabitants when they may need emergent help or evacuation. Therefore, the authorising state, government officials, or designated non-governmental personnel responsible for providing help and assistance in genuine need to others in space or celestial bodies would be liable in case they perpetrate discrimination or racial bias or arbitrariness in providing aid or evacuation. The relevant protocol of action must stipulate clear priorities and criteria to be followed in such an event. Else, it will tantamount to inflicting something comparable to mini-genocide by arbitrary orders, motivated action or prejudicial decision. Of course, a lot will depend upon how we view such an act or lapse, with legal objectivity or jaundiced eyes or a fixated mindset.

Nevertheless, the appropriate state and those in command of the predicament would be, *pro rata*, criminally liable for their indiscreet orders and arbitrary actions. They may, thus, be accused of appropriate offence to be tried in an international court or tribunal and punished according to international law. And where such an incriminating order has stranded persons on a planet or caused immeasurable trauma or torture to the victim by delay or default or has caused death, the derelict actions or inaction of the irresponsible person/s cannot be legally excused or politically condoned. Justice must prevail for the committed space crime, may be in tandem, under International Humanitarian Law.

Last, but not the least important, are the interests of researchers engaged in research in orbiting laboratories, workers engaged in hospitality industry, excavation of natural resources and other manufacturing activities on celestial surfaces. They may need local help for cover or shelter in the event of distress, accident, or disaster. Of course, such exigencies and attendant remedies would be part of the

---

[17] The Moon Agreement, 1979, Article 10 (2).

[18] Ibid, Article 10 (1).

employee's terms of contract and consciously agreed between the parties. Nevertheless, there are certain generic protections and safeguards provided for threat to human life under the Moon Agreement,[19] which cannot be vitiated or violated. These are international obligations that bind ratifying member-states and their resident agents to discharge, irrespective of the contractual conditions. And any violation of human rights and humanitarian considerations by authorities in-charge of affairs would make for culpable crimes under appropriate laws, national or international.

5.4.1 Dereliction in State Responsibility Imposed Under Space Law

The OST mandates under Article I that "Outer space, including the Moon and other celestial bodies, shall be free for exploration and use by all States, without discrimination of any kind, on basis of equality and in accordance with international law and there shall be free access to all areas of celestial bodies." This guarantee, however, is circumscribed by the obligatory caution of non-interference which is explicitly embodied in the Outer Space Treaty under Article IX that states, "[Parties] shall conduct all their activities in outer space, including the Moon and other celestial bodies, with due regard to the corresponding interests of all other States Parties...."

The above rider, however, is not unreasonable and is aimed to obviate conflicts and crimes. Even jurisprudence proclaims that every right has a corresponding duty and demands reciprocity of enjoyment of common freedoms without breaching the domain of each other's legitimate right. But in experience, infringements are common and frequent resulting in reportable offences and consequent trials. This may not be much different in outer space either, where commercial activities will dictate primacy of self-interest and profit consideration. No wonder, conflict, and crime reside hiding in this premise and in the regimen of commercialisation and exploitation of outer space. Participating state needs to create their own checks and balances according to their own business culture and legal ethos.

In amplification, Article VI, the Space Treaty commands that "State Parties…shall bear international responsibility for national activities in outer space, including the Moon and other celestial bodies, whether such activities are carried on by governmental agencies or by non-governmental agencies...." It further mandates, "The activities of non-governmental entities in outer space, including the Moon and other celestial bodies, shall require authorisation and continuing supervision by the appropriate State Party to the Treaty." This broad-spectrum responsibility is obligatory on the State Party by virtue of being designated as regulatory and supervising authority under the treaty, and non-governmental entities of the future are going to be from the private sector of space business and celestial industry.

Further, the Moon Agreement exhorts, "Any threat or use of force or any other hostile act or threat of hostile act on the Moon is prohibited. It is likewise prohibited

---

[19] Refer Articles 10 (2) and 12 (3).

to use the Moon in order to commit any such act or engage in any such threat in relation to the Earth, the Moon, spacecraft, and the personnel of spacecraft or manmade space objects."[20] Despite such ordainment, situations of crisis in defence strategy or military tactics, among superpowers like USA, China, and Russia, can be theoretically imagined. In certain eventualities of extreme desperation, such threats or attacks may actually materialise to deter the opponent or stall advance of operations or compel it in ultimate surrender. ASAT tests have just marked the possible beginning of this kind of space race. Creating such warlike situation by persons in authority, due to inadvertence, misunderstanding, or deliberation, on celestial bodies or on Earth could constitute internationally wrongful acts affecting persons present on the celestial bodies whether as workers or tourists or settlers. Such an action may be beset with dire implications under International Humanitarian Law which may lead to indictment.

Apart from the duties discussed under *lex specialis*, the state shoulders a corelative responsibility under international law to protect and safeguard its nationals in events of crisis, emergency, disaster, civil disturbance, racial unrest, or warlike situation in places of their domicile, temporary residence or place of authorised visit; and if imperative, even evacuate them to the mother country for safety and security. This international duty of the state should "lawgically" extend to outer space and celestial bodies wherever it has authorised its non-governmental entities, e.g. private companies to venture and operate as juridical nationals and permitted to employ its citizen as space workers. A person in dire need of help cannot be shut off or shut out from available safe facilities. Therefore, the moralistic and ethical nuance and humanitarian pertinence of such action can be ignored only at the cost of individual or collective culpability and to invite indictment under international law. Thus, the Treaty mandates constitute international obligations for which states are internationally accountable and this burden of responsibility cannot be negated or avoided.

From another angle of consideration, "space workers" should not be held hostage or under servitude by the employment agents and engaging corporations because of restricted work opportunities or for limited public transportation facility to return to the Earth on their own. This would foul with the Universal Declaration of Human Rights, 1948[21] because Article 4 forbids "slavery or servitude" of humans. Therefore, if a person from the labour force or any other employee is abandoned or forsaken in an eventuality of emergency or distress, it would tantamount to subjection "to torture, or to cruel, inhuman or degrading treatment...."[22] The essence of this right is to get safe evacuation to Earth in dire exigencies of distress or accident.

As per another instrument of international law also, refusal to provide mandated shelter or relief to ones in distress on the Moon or any other celestial body would

---

[20] The Agreement Governing the Activities of States on the Moon and Other Celestial Bodies, 1979, Article 3. Also referred to as the Moon Treaty.

[21] Adopted and proclaimed by UN General Assembly, Resolution 217 A (III) of December 10, 1948.

[22] Ibid, Article 5.

mean forsaking their safety interests and human needs in a "warlike situation." This abandonment thus could cause disrespect to the universally acknowledged principle of the dignity of the human person.[23] It could also, by extended analogy, constitute the offence of torture or "passive genocide" punishable under International Humanitarian Law.[24] I am conscious that some purist scholars would be uncomfortable with this liberal interpretation and at the constrained congruence of comparison but in a noble advance of law it maintains human dignity, promotes human safety, and meets the ends of justice.

In turn, this responsibility also attracts an attributable liability for any damage caused in terms of physical impairment to property and/or objects of another party or for causing harm or injury to or death of human beings. By same logic under the Outer Space Treaty, "Each state …that launches or procures the launching of an object into outer space, including the Moon and other celestial bodies, and each state from whose territory or facility an object is launched is internationally liable for damage to another State Party or its natural and juridical persons by such object or its component parts…."[25] The liability may be financially compensated and monetarily restituted but under certain circumstances, it may attract criminal culpability like gross negligence in action or deliberate inaction in management of emergencies, accidents, or disasters.

Based on the above assertions, under the OST and international law, non-compliance of established provisions or dereliction of duty by a state or its agencies or representative agents, albeit based on the gravity of consequences, could lead to criminal accusation. Similarly, non-discharge of this bounden duty and the devolved responsibility under conditions of accident, disaster, or distress, as per the Moon Agreement[26] could create a valid liability that may constitute a crime under domestic laws as well as international instruments. Thus, apart from allusions in the space law, there are several international law instruments supporting and upholding a right against torture.

Incidentally, the UN Charter particularly in Article 55 (3) espouses universal respect for human rights. Taking cue from this safeguard and empirical observation of worldwide violations, the first prohibition against this cruel act of torture was institutionalised in 1966, under Universal Declaration of Human Rights. Thereafter, this crime finds mention and assertion in Article 7 of International Covenant on Civil and Political Rights, 1966. The importance of this effort to eliminate such crimes is further buttressed by a UN General Assembly resolution passed on 9 December 1975.[27]

---

[23] The Fourth Geneva Convention Concerning Civilians.

[24] Ibid.

[25] The OST, Article VII.

[26] *Agreement Governing the Activities of States on the Moon and Other Celestial Bodies, 1979*, Article 10.

[27] *Declaration on Protection of All Persons from being Subjected to Torture and Other Inhumane or Degrading Treatment or Punishment, 1975.*

5.4 Crimes of International Wrongs

This right has since been embodied in the convention against torture, etc., 1984.[28] An individual tortured has a right to allege of having been subjected to torture and the authorities shall have to get the charges investigated promptly and impartially and shall provide protection to the accuser and witnesses.[29] The convention further assures that "The person tortured has an enforceable right to fair and adequate compensation, including the means for as full rehabilitation as possible."[30] The convention also urges states to enact suitable law to make torture a criminal offence. It thus becomes incumbent that relevant provisions be enforced in the best manner to assure and dispense due relief to the distressed, else, it will erode trust in law, treaties, and their redressal mechanisms. India, however, has signed but not yet ratified the convention.

Further, the private space operators may have to share responsibility to provide shelter and evacuation to humans, as necessary, in eventualities of accident, disaster, or distress. Failure or discrimination on any criterion or biased treatment in any manner would be breach of international law and may attract criminal action. Under certain circumstances, defaulting authorities may also become liable under Human Rights Law treaties. In view of the repeatedly stressed mandate, managers of space business, industry, and planetary infrastructure must have a constructive role in disaster management plans and standard operating procedures for systematic evacuation of working personnel, tourists, and planetary residents to Earth, in a certain predetermined order, in case of emergency.

Necessitated exit from space and safe return to Earth is a human right to life of all those deployed and then present on a celestial body or an orbiting resort. In such dilemma, it would be wise to think with our hearts, albeit within the legal framework. Arbitrary prioritisation of shelter facility or discriminatory evacuation of personnel can cause personal trauma to the victims and may be deemed comparable to torture under the International Human Rights Law with all applicable consequences. The parallel is not without lawful logic and inferential jurisprudence.

5.4.2 Misconduct by Astronauts in Outer Space

The alleged misconduct of astronaut Anne McClain has been treated as the first crime in space because this has caught the media attention to become newsworthy. Moreover, this misconduct, presumably motivated by personal gain, got reported to the federal authorities for investigation by the estranged spouse, Summer Worden. It thus became first case of malfeasance in space to be contested on Earth, hence its importance and notice-worthiness. Interestingly, this case has turned topsy-turvy

---

[28] *Convention Against Torture and Other Cruel, Inhumane or Degrading Treatment or Punishment*, 1984. It came into force in 1987.

[29] The Convention ibid, Article 13.

[30] The Convention ibid, Article 14.

and McClain has been found innocent by NASA while her spouse, Summer Worden, has been found guilty of making false statement in official investigation.

Anyway, this was not the first instance of crime by an astronaut in space except that this was formally reported and got spilled in the press. In fact, many more serious violations of laws, regulations, and military rules have occurred but have not been made public by the authorities as a matter of policy. For example, smuggling of banned item into space capsule, inexcusable negligence in operation during spacewalk and repairs, mini-mutiny by astronauts in space, and many such instances have taken place earlier. But these were enquired in-house and handled softly; either misconduct was condoned due to exemplary performance of the astronaut or offenders were punished non-traditionally.[31] Nevertheless, this tolerant leniency cannot be the new norm of discipline and reformation in dealing with culpable misconduct, unlawful acts or treating defiance of rules, committed intentionally and knowingly by the offenders.

5.4.3 Special Causations of Space Crimes

Certain space crimes would not appear as normal or usual action or wont of a person or compatible with one's habitual nature or usual temperament. These happen to be space-induced crimes by factors that do not influence humans on the Earth and are caused or take effect due to peculiar circumstances that occur only in outer space or on celestial bodies. Some such causations have been detected and analysed scientifically yet there may be many more which are as yet unknown or undetermined and will be unfolded with time and observation, and their full impact will be realised from the future research. Thus, reasons for certain space crimes may seem puzzling and remain unexplained. Importantly, this narration is not a plea in defence of the space offenders but a reality of attendant conditions and environmental factors that must be factored in and appreciated in search of justice.

Some such specific influences of space travel, long stay in space stations, forays in deep space or residence on celestial bodies for work or leisure can be surmised and empirically proved. These are consequent to unfamiliar environment, unaccustomed living conditions, and tensions for safety. A few factors with proven impact may be briefly listed for understanding. First, unusual G-forces exerted on take-off and during other manoeuvres in the mission cause an imbalance of blood in the body parts like the brain which may be temporarily blacked-out, impair thinking process and the faculty of judgment. Secondly, once a satellite goes beyond the pull of gravity of the Earth, another unusual condition of weightlessness prevails. Under this condition, a person does not walk on feet but floats in the openings of the module. Humans are unaccustomed to the walk-mode of traction for commuting and may feel uncomfortable or irritated despite short training and practice in prelaunch drills. Besides, there are a few other hazardous but natural, physical conditions to

---

[31] Some such cases have been discussed in Chapters II and III.

survive with, in such locales, for example, accidental exposure of a body part to even minimal radiation may damage its healthy and normalcy, extreme temperatures, and similar risks are bound to constantly tell on the mind.

In fact, the situation can be worse because Earth is a familiar environment for humans with accustomed living condition, whereas space capsules, celestial habitats and on neighbouring planets, human body and mind will be exposed to new conditions and hazards. Conditions of low gravity, unhealthy radiation, extreme variations in temperature and artificial atmosphere take time for adjustment and precautions. Further, spaces could be cramped with little elbow room, work environment could be unergonomic, company of unknown people, lack of privacy for rest or sleep, unfamiliar ambiance, and lurking concerns about safety and return to the Earth.

Therefore, overcoming trauma, slow acclimatisation and getting used to new fears take time. As a result, the cumulative impact of these factors of inconvenience, angst, and anxiety would weigh heavily on the human mind in space and, for the weaker ones, tension may burst into crime. For space workers, the conditions may be still worse due to the fatigue of duty, stress of work productivity, risks of injury, possibility of accident, and emergency due to failure of infrastructure. All these imponderables do not make for peaceful living and comfortable life despite the high of wages, thrill of newness in environment, and excitement of being out in space.

Even professionally trained, mentally regimented, highly disciplined, and duty-bound astronauts have committed unbecoming acts and patent crimes. It is however a different matter that most often these have been disregarded for reasons of unusual work stress and condoned in view of other glorious achievements during the mission. Hence, crimes of whatever type and graveness are inevitable among all, the excited tourists eager to capture every sight and moment of the trip, the pressurised workers with mounting fatigue or the lonely residents of Mars Colony or the Moon Village rueing the decision to emigrate. Whatever be the context or content, these would prod towards acts that may slide into lawlessness that constitute space crimes as per the definition proposed in earlier chapter.

5.5 Types of Space Offenders

The complexion or physiognomy of future crimes in outer space and on the celestial bodies is as yet hazy and indeterminate and partly depends upon the ingenuity of the criminal mind. Of course, minor crimes have been committed in space by astronauts but these have been magnanimously ignored or benignly condoned in the context of circumstances or the euphoria of achievements. Be that as it may in the past, future crimes in space may be committed by states in defiance of treaty provisions or as failed experiments. Examples could be, for causing environmental depredation by reckless experimentation like copper needles forming a dipole belt for communications; or satellite destruction trials by ASAT tests that created and scattered unnecessary debris that may keep dangerously orbiting in space for centuries; or by militarisation and weaponisation of space. Such acts may pose serious hazards to space operations evoking peer reaction and consequent international implications.

The other category of offenders could be private enterprise and business corporations operating in space. Their activities could comprise space travel, space tourism, manning space transit stations, mining of celestial natural resources, or supporting infrastructure dedicated to space habitats constructed for tourists and permanent settlers on planetary bodies. There may also be contractual legal infringements of diverse types or instances of unauthorised interference in legitimate activities of others, economic disputes or spying for intellectual property or business secrets, and so on.

Human psyche does not really change in outer space, and humans remain ingenious and the breadth of their imagination for crimes cannot be envisaged. Criminal acts by humans may be committed as an individual in several ways as causing grievous injury, murder, rape, or other heinous crimes. Humans can cause the above-mentioned or other crimes individually, conjointly, in consort or also as conspiracy or other collective unlawful acts. Further, humans, as social animals, may indulge in misdeeds with reasonable anonymity like riots or wrongdoings during law-and-order disturbances. Apart from these, there could be cases of contractual and economic offences like cheating, fraud, breach of contracts, infringement in intellectual property rights, and so on. And lastly, crimes with the use of technology like directed energy weapons, artificial intelligence, or cyber technology. These can be perpetrated from any domain to the intended targets. This listing is only illustrative and not comprehensive.

5.6 Future Activities in Outer Space

It must be accepted that crimes in space will depend upon the nature and spread of space activities. The era of space activities concerning scientific exploration and planetary discoveries for accretion to human fund of knowledge is almost over or tapered down to a great extent. Similarly, concentration on peaceful uses like communications, broadcasting, or remote sensing and their applications has achieved near-saturation. Thus, these activities would possibly continue traction on a slow pace with no significant developmental or phenomenal break-throughs or sensational applications. In fact, exploratory activities were funded by the States and their budgetary allocations have since drastically tapered down. Thus, the shift in emphasis is clearly discernible.

With shrinkage of exchequer expenditure, even existing infrastructures like facilities at the ISS are being disposed of for other commercial usages and private operations or will be de-orbited to be incinerated in the atmosphere. The Russian plans are not much different either and the ESA will not have much choice of independence. ISS seems doomed because the US budget for the operation and maintenance of the US quarters will end by 2025. However, to muster resources, efforts are afoot to lease out the facility for commercial opportunities or transfer to private sector in ownership.

5.6 Future Activities in Outer Space

Different possibilities of uses are being mulled, whether as a movie-shooting area or for display of bill-board facing the Earth or utilisation as space motel for hospitality services and a variety of entertainment. Options are diverse and still open.

Following the commercialisation of the ISS, there seem parallel plans to build more space stations. The Chinese effort in this direction to construct Tiangong Space Station[32] is progressing fast and taking shape. As per the current status in October 2022, Tianhe core module is in the middle, Wentian module on the starboard, Tianzhou on port, and Shenzhou at nadir. The space station will maintain an altitude between 350 and 450 km and is primarily meant for research and will be permanently manned for operations. Interestingly, China was goaded to work for and develop an independent space station by the refusal of NASA to permit participation in ISS facilities, in 2011.[33]

Further, hesitancy of states for public investment in commercial ventures and on the other hand, progressive development in space technologies, there grew a vacuum where private enterprise has been sucked into space activities. Technology has made commercial uses of outer space and exploitation of celestial natural resources viable and profitable. To illustrate, space transportation is fast becoming a safe reality and economical in tariff too. This mode of transportation, therefore, seems just round the corner. Space X and Virgin Galactic are front runners in this race to carry fare-paying-passengers to a zero-gravity experience in low-earth orbit. Their regular and commercial services may begin soon. Thus, scheduled services to spaceports on celestial bodies may start operating in the foreseeable future.

Space travel will, in turn, promote space hospitality industry. To begin with, there is a possibility of refurbishing of the US module at the ISS which is being offered for commercialisation under private ownership or lease agreement. The US administration has already taken a decision in this regard and intends to cut the budget for its operation and maintenance from 2028 AD. Therefore, NASA has planned to otherwise muster resources by a phased opening up of its ISS share to commercial opportunities and private usage. In fact, the Inter-Governmental-Agreement had originally envisaged such a contingency and under Article 1 permits generic activities like space transportation of personnel and cargo, space tourism, space advertising, and space commercial experiments. Therefore, NASA's plans to rent out American quarters at ISS appear legitimate and in consonance with the legal intent and spirit of intergovernmental agreement.

Nevertheless, this legitimate commercialisation of the US module at the ISS can pose several imponderables of governance and management and one of them could relate to discipline and law-and-order crimes. A lease of an ISS portion can be obtained by any country or commercial enterprise or private player on agreed rental. Thereafter, in the leased portion, its personnel or other-country hired specialists may work together. It could as well be a hotel for exotic thrills and imaginable pleasures.

---

[32] Tiangong means "Palace in the Sky".

[33] "What is driving China's race to build a space station", *Centre for Strategic and International Studies*, December 7, 2016. Also refer Namrata Goswami, "China Moves Towards a Permanent Space Presence", *The Diplomat*, May 01, 2021.

Foreseeable contingencies with potential criminality, beset with international ramifications of jurisdiction and extradition, should be visualised, comprehended, and legally catered for in the wider interest of individual security, societal harmony, and international peace.

The second set of new activities in space is expected to be commercial mining of mineral resources of asteroids and the Moon. Reliable sample testing has revealed that many asteroids are rich in rare minerals so direly wanted for use by humanity on the Earth. The mined ore could be processed in situ and extracted metals could be brought to the Earth. Today, economic viability of such transportation may be in doubt yet with advancing rocket technology, a distinct possibility of such a project can be envisaged in the future. Moreover, excavation is permitted under the Moon Treaty and modalities for sharing of benefits by all states could be put in place in due time. A beginning in this direction has been made by the Artemis Accords, 2020, and the remaining attendant legal issues can be settled amicably and cooperatively as the situation demands.

The last envisaged category of space activity relates to construction of the Moon Village, the Mars Colony and support maintenance of requisite infrastructure for hospitality resorts constructed for the tourists and liveable residence for settlers as permanent inhabitants of the celestial colonies. Blueprints for the constructions and support systems for the proposed habitats are on the drawing board.[34] Construction may be expected to begin within a decade or two. Residences and resorts with adapted living conditions may become available within two decades or so and may be inhabited shortly thereafter.

Having briefly discussed the nature of foreseeable space activities of legitimate commercialisation, the imponderables of governance, management, and enforcement become apparent. These could relate to maintenance of discipline, management of space workers, redressal of business disputes, enforcement of law and order to make life of all residents peaceful and tranquil. The space residents and workers would be multinational and multi-ethnic groups, and their living may not be congenial and amicable. Hence, foreseeable contingencies with potential criminality, beset with international ramifications, should be visualised, comprehended and legally catered for in wider interest of individual security, societal harmony, international cooperation, and celestial peace.

5.7 Crimes of the Future

Some space activities, incidentally alluded to in the discussion, relate to breaches of the Outer Space Treaty which are mentioned with concern but are not clearly defined nor their gravity amplified. As a result, the narrative contained in the Treaty remains more as an exhortation to refrain rather than codified prevention. Therefore, the looseness of prohibitions may permit concerned activities to expand and proliferate

---

[34] For example, Woerner's Moon Village Plan.

5.7 Crimes of the Future

making it difficult to pinpoint defiance for ensuring control by international comity or collective action by the UN. Select anomalies are militarisation and weaponisation, escalating quantum of space debris and contamination of outer space and celestial bodies. A violation in these, advertent or inadvertent, may cause an existential threat to humanity where it may not be able to recoup or correct the mistake. These may be treated as crimes *erga omnes* which need stricter controls ab initio. A few aberrations have happened in the past but in due course need may arise to convert the treaty provisions into imperatives of culpable ingredients of a binding law.

5.7.1 Militarisation and Weaponisation of Space Domain

Military strategists will certainly be tempted to militarise the space domain because it provides the advantage of high ground for intelligence and surveillance, to say the least. There is no definition of this activity in the OST but a devised definition treats military space activities as those bearing military character, military objectives with military actors, and desiring military effect.[35] On the other hand, prohibitory articles of the OST are weak and porous while permissive clauses, more or less, neutralise the prohibition.[36] The reiteration in the Moon Agreement (Article 3) is no stricter, either. Even the UN Charter concedes the Right of Retorsion. (Article 51). And to add to this, dual-use technologies are not banned in outer space and their covert and overt uses are unrestricted and rampant.

With regard to weaponisation also, the provision of the OST remains equally weak and impotent. It prohibits placement in orbit around the Earth any objects carrying nuclear weapons or any weapons of mass destruction.[37] A Russian experiment of fractional orbital bombing system (FOBS) circumvented this provision where each placement did a part of the orbit and not the whole orbit as proscribed under the treaty. The prohibition had been belied yet the treaty was abided by. However, it was later through negotiations that the Soviets submitted to the US remonstration and dropped this project from further development and perfection.

The Moon Agreement, too, in a bland statement prohibits to place a weapon in orbit of any celestial body or install any such weapon on the Moon or other celestial bodies or to station them in any other manner.[38] Even threat or use of force in a hostile act is not permitted. And international law bans testing of chemical, biological, or nuclear weapons in outer space and on celestial bodies. No doubt, prohibitions are in place yet the ambiguity in the text and lack of definitions make their abidance controvertible and rather suspect in acute eventualities. Hence, *lex lata* is incomplete

---

[35] Adapted from *Manual of International Law Applicable to Military Uses of Outer Space*, Rule 103. Also referred to as MILAMOS.

[36] The Outer Space Treaty, 1967, Article IV.

[37] The OST, ibid, Article IV.

[38] The Moon Agreement, 1979, Article 3.

and inadequate necessitating stronger legal prohibitions because even a casual faux pas by a political cabal may leave no constructive option for humanity.

5.7.2 Contamination of the Space Domain and *Vice Versa*

The framers of the Outer Space Treaty in a visionary stance had foreseen of the possibilities of contamination of the celestial bodies with contaminants from the Earth and bringing back space viruses on return to the Earth. This can be treated as forward and backward bio-contamination. Based on the obligations contained in the Treaty, space-faring states have evolved their own protocols of sanitisation and periods of quarantine for objects and personnel. Article IX of the Treaty reads, "States…shall pursue studies of outer space, including the Moon and other celestial bodies, and conduct exploration of them so as to avoid their harmful contamination and also adverse changes in the environment of the Earth resulting from the introduction of extra-terrestrial matter…and…shall undertake appropriate international consultations before proceeding with any such activity or experiment." But despite this futuristic advisory and procedural obligation, a few let ups and breaches have taken place. It needs to be understood that the damage so caused by a state in lapse of regulation or unsupervised misadventure cannot be completely undone and sustainability of the domain may be lost forever. Hence, such indiscreet acts without procedural safeguards should be designated as crimes *erga omnes*.

5.7.3 Israel's Lunar Crash of **Beresheet** Module

An Israeli non-profit organisation, "Space IL," funded a Moon-landing experiment, *Beresheet,* for high-resolution imagery of the Moon surface as also to measure the magnetic field at its landing site in *Mare Serenitatis.* The purpose of this mission was to provide valuable scientific information about the life and history of the Moon. But the launch instead carried a cargo of dehydrated microscopic life forms known as tardigrades[39] that are odd little creatures, yet strikingly distinctive. These are often called "water bears" also, because they get their living element, oxygen, from water and ingest algae as food. These can suck fluids from other creatures or even other tardigrades for survival.[40] The module carrying this life-form failed to soft-land and crashed on the Moon surface on 11 April 2019.

By now, these creatures would have scattered and spread out to cause contamination on the Moon. These can survive at extreme temperature, pressure, and vacuum conditions and live for over a century. It was an ill-conceived experiment carried out

---

[39] Monica Grady, "Tardigrades: We're now polluting the moon with near indestructible little creatures" in *The Conversation*, August 9, 2019.
[40] Grady, Ibid.

covertly which has presumably caused contamination on the Moon, the repercussions of which will become apparent centuries later. The State has defied the mandate of Article IX of the OST[41] and also not abided by the COSPAR guidelines.[42] Thus, Israel has failed in regulation and supervision of the space activity and has been derelict on an affirmative duty. Irresponsibility attracts liability in many ways but vigilance in the first instance is highly recommended.

5.7.4 Cockroach in Outer Space

Another experiment of taking live insect to the space was conducted by the Soviet Space Agency, *Roscosmos*, in 2007. In this mission, the Russian cockroach was the first creature to become pregnant in space. The female-roach was named Hope and she conceived during her 12-day space sojourn. On completion of gestation period, she gave birth to 33 baby-roaches. Astro-biology had made a breakthrough. The best part of this story is that the experimental subjects were dutifully brought back to the Earth, and the moral lies in responsible state activities in the outer space as per the Treaty law as also the soft law norms.

5.7.5 Dereliction by Private Player in Protection of Planetary Environment

SpaceX, a private corporation was to test maiden Falcon rocket launch, which could carry the heaviest payload of 37,000 pounds on board. Normally such load competence tests are carried out by properly placing steel or cement blocks as mass simulators. But Elon Musk, CEO of SpaceX decided to send his personal cherry-red Tesla Roadster car instead "as perfect payload"[43] that could stay in space for millions of years. This was an unusual decision but SpaceX had obtained due permission from FAA for launch of this cargo. Later, it was decided that the car will also be embellished with a "driver" dummy, a mannequin Starman, in driver's seat. But it was not a mere mock-up because it was wearing a SpaceX spacesuit complete with logo and other markings.[44] Many doubt whether FAA permission was taken specifically for the driver-dummy.

The decision for sending red Roadster car as payload elicited diverse reactions and comments from different fraternities. Musk was lauded as a visionary and innovative market doyen and brand manager yet some considered this as a business gimmick or

---

[41] Israel has not acceded to the Outer Space Treaty but the latter is since treated as customary law.
[42] COSPAR Planetary Protection Policy, 2002.
[43] Kevin Loria, "Elon Musk Shares Picture of the Tesla Roadster Heading to Mars in SpaceX's Falcon Heavy Maiden Voyage", *Business Insider*, February 5, 2018.
[44] Kevin Loria, ibid.

publicity stunt of a maverick.[45] For all the firsts achieved by this test launch, SpaceX committed dereliction in compliance of the good practices recommended for Debris Mitigation[46] and of the advisory for the Planetary Protection.[47] To explain the planetary protection desideratum, understandably, the car was loaded in "as is condition" while still in use and may be expected to contain the normal dirtying elements of usage like dust and grease as also other earthly bacterial and biological contaminants. There is a big difference in "cleaned" character and sterilised or sanitised for trip to outer space and the red Roadster seems to have carried a future potential bio-threat to where it would crash in outer space. It could thus be a case of "reverse pan-spermia" causing depredation of outer space environment. This indiscreet action, though a *fait accompli* also violates the mandate of Article IX of the Outer Space Treaty.[48]

As of August 2019, Falcon rocket with Roadster and mannequin "Starman" has completed its first orbit around the Sun.[49] Scientists estimate that this "space-load," if it remains intact and internally balanced, may keep orbiting in space for over three million years.[50] In view of the numerous imponderables, it was not a judicious decision to send the car as cargo, even for ego-satisfaction or self-aggrandisement. The US authorities have also erred on the duty for authorisation and supervision under Article VI of the OST.

5.7.6 Nuclear Pollution in Outer Space Domain

Of all the kinds of pollution in the outer space and on the celestial bodies, radiological pollution caused by radioactive material is the worst. This can be caused by space objects using or carrying radioactive fuel for propulsion or otherwise. Such a space object may pollute the space or celestial environment by accident, collision, explosion, or implosion due to natural reasons or even by an accidental leak in the object. The worst aspects of such pollution are: first, their radioactive cloud is so reactive that any other object or even debris passing through that toxic envelope will get ionised and pass the same infection to others in vulnerable proximity. Secondly, the active life of nuclear fission material runs into hundreds of millennia, and thus, this pollution once emitted by a source will remain live for long-long time. Thirdly, space law permits such usage of nuclear fuels to power space objects, albeit subject to specified

---

[45] Kevin Loria, ibid. Also refer *Mark Matousek,* "Tesla created the world's best car commercial without spending a dime on advertising", *Business Insider*, February 7, 2018.

[46] Space Debris Mitigation Guidelines of the Committee on the Peaceful Uses of Outer Space, 2007. UN Res 67/217, December 22, 2007.

[47] COSPAR Planetary Protection Policy, 2002, as amended in 2011.

[48] Treaty on Principles Governing the Activities of States in the Exploration and Use of Outer Space, including the Moon and other Celestial Bodies, 1967. (In short Outer Space Treaty or OST).

[49] Mike Wall, "SpaceX's Starman and Elon Musk's Tesla Have Made a Lap Around the Sun", *space.com,* August 20, 2019.

[50] Kevin Loria, n. 43 ante.

safeguards. But accidents or collisions of such space objects would be inevitable, howsoever, minimal. Ergo, the attendant dangers remain lurking and ominous.

There are generally three types of nuclear power sources which can be miniaturised for use in space objects. These are radioisotope power source, nuclear fission and nuclear thermal propulsion. However, most of the power sources have incorporated the use of radioisotopes as direct heat source. The devices are known as radioisotope heating units (RHUs) or electricity generators called radioisotope thermo-electric generators (RTGs). The latter use plutonium isotopes and convert the heat directly into electric power using thermos-couplings. Moreover, RTGs have no moving parts and half-life of their fuel is predictable; thus, these are reliable and safer.[51] In the nuclear fission technology, heat is generated in controlled reactor process, which is converted into electricity for on-board power utilisation. These are approved techniques as general-purpose heat sources (GPHS) under IAEA safety framework.[52] Approved techniques are safer and have been in use in space objects for decades, subject to safety considerations of size, mass, and other limitations, which are not the limiting constraints for terrestrial applications.

5.7.7 *The Misadventures of Nuclear Testing in Space*

Not to be left behind by the Soviet Union, the USA in a blatant display of superiority undertook the Project Argus in 1958. Under this project, conducted secretly though for non-military purposes, the USA carried out a series of high-altitude nuclear explosions over the South Atlantic Ocean.[53] The experiment was intended to create an artificial belt of trapped radiation which could be comparable to the newly discovered Van Allen Belts, which originated from solar winds and were held together around a planet by its magnetic field. These belts protect the Earth's atmosphere by warding off solar storms and deflecting solar flares.[54] The Argus experiment demonstrated the desired effect but it dissipated too rapidly to work as a permanent shield.

Again, the USA in its euphoria of newly assumed leadership of space activities attempted Starfish Prime detonation experiment in July 1962. The USA exploded a 1.4 megaton nuclear warhead at a height of 400 kms above Johnston Island in the Pacific Ocean.[55] The explosion created a massive electromagnetic wave which

---

[51] Melissa K Force, "The Legal Landscape for Nuclear Spacecraft: International Environmental Law and Space Law," in *Asian Journal of Air & Space Law*, Vol II, No 2, July-December 2012, p. 150.

[52] International Atomic Energy Agency, *The Role of Nuclear Power and Nuclear Propulsion in the Peaceful Exploration of Space*, 7, 2005.

[53] Philip C Jessup, et al., eds., *Controls for Outer Space and the Antarctic Analogy*, New York, 1959, pp. 224–5.

[54] Andrew G Hailey, *Space Law and Government*, New York, 1863, p. 267. Cited from Mani, Bhatt and Reddy, eds., *Recent Trends in International Space Law and Policy*, New Delhi, Lancers, 1997, p. 465.

[55] Gyula Gal, *Space Law*, New York, 1969, p. 149.

disturbed the operation of electricity and telephone services in Hawaii, and the dismal effects were felt as far away as New Zealand. It was the first of its kind and had demonstrated its powerful and adverse effects in widening of the Van Allen belts and altering the radiation situation of Earth's environment in a lasting manner.[56]

The world was shocked at such an immature experiment without any consultations with the scientific community. The humanity stirred in its conscience. Any further activity in this direction had to cease forthwith and could not be permitted in a competitive race between the two superpowers. To put an end to the testing of nuclear weapons, the Partial Test Ban Treaty was signed in 1963 putting a stop to high-altitude nuclear testing, among other bans. Soon thereafter, the Outer Space Treaty came into effect in 1967 that also banned nuclear weapons from outer space under Article IV. Similar prohibition has been provided in the Moon Agreement, 1979[57] to cover nuclear activities on the celestial bodies.

Despite such strict provisions in international space law, the year 2012 has been witness to a tragic event. The Russian Mars exploration object, Phobos-Grunt, powered by nuclear power source that contained 12-tonnes of radioactive fuel, failed to achieve the expected orbit, disintegrated and sped through the Earth orbit. It predominantly posed risk of radio contamination of atmosphere and the Earth, albeit discounted by Roscosmos. Scientists speculated that it would be incinerated on re-entry with lurking doubts that the unburnt portion of nuclear content, howsoever minimal, could spill on the Earth. And this happened on 15 January 2012 when, probably, twenty to thirty chunks of the debris fell in the southern Pacific Ocean between New Zealand and South America.[58]

The same year, the USA also landed a rover, named Curiosity, on the Mars. It carried radio-isotopes as power system to generate electricity from the heat of plutonium which was stored in rechargeable lithium batteries. The weight of the nuclear fuel was 10.6 lbs.[59] Thus, with successful landing, the Curiosity was the first nuclear power plant to land on the Red Planet. The mission of the Curiosity rover was to investigate and determine the existence of microbial life on the Mars. After ten years of useful and meaningful service, the Curiosity is still working towards its purpose. Scientists, in their Environmental Impact Assessment, assure of minimal risk and "probability of release" of radioactive material.[60] Nevertheless, nuclear power sources do inherently pose inevitable risks of pollution and contamination, sooner or later, due to accident, explosion or corrosion leak in their extra-long life. Therefore, the main worry should not be the isolated case of Curiosity on the Mars, but

---

[56] Declarations by Van Allen and J Warwick of August 22, 1962, cited in Gal ibid, n. 25 at p. 143. Cited from Mani, n. 44 ante.

[57] Article 7 (2).

[58] Gina Sunsiri, "Phobos-Grunt: Failed Russian Mars Probe Falls to Earth", *ABC News*, January 15, 2012.

[59] Melissa K Force, "The Legal Landscape for Nuclear Spacecraft: International Environmental Law and Space Law," in *Asian Journal of Air & Space Law*, Vol II, No 2, July-December 2012, p. 145.

[60] Melissa, ibid.

the dawning epoch of space activities for which nuclear power sources are permissible and shall pose cumulating hazards in the outer space domain.

5.7.8 Nuclear Debris in Outer Space

Despite the ban on placement of nuclear weapons and the prohibition on nuclear tests in outer space domain,[61] international space law permits the use of nuclear power sources for the power needs of satellites subject to certain enunciated principles and "in accordance with international law."[62] Thus, the law recognises and accepts the necessity "…that for some missions in outer space nuclear power sources are particularly suited or even essential owing to their compactness, long life and other attributes."[63] The usual risks, nevertheless, exist from the very nature of the material and the total quantum orbiting in space.

The US representative at the negotiations, suggested in the interest of better safety restrictions, that these Principles are safety goals and should not prescribe arbitrary dose limits, which have shown no relationship to accidents. However, in a gesture of magnanimity, the USA did not block the consensus in the Committee to forward the Principles to the General Assembly for adopting a resolution. But delegate expressed apprehension in the GA debate that the principles "do not yet contain the clarity and technical validity appropriate to guide safe use of nuclear power sources in outer space."[64] He also declared the USA, on the issues, has an approach that is technically clearer and more valid. It also "has a history of demonstrated safe and successful application of nuclear power sources. We will continue to apply that approach."[65] Whatever be the merit of this approach and manufacturing practices, the objective of the principles is safety all around and it can be best assured by defining the limits of use from all angles.

An empirical study in 1986 found that 48 satellites with nuclear power sources are in orbit. It also revealed that radioactive material contained therein weighed more than one ton of highly enriched uranium-235, plutonium-238 and assorted fission products which were expected to reach the quantum of three tonnes by the turn of the century.[66] And by a reasonable extrapolation, this level of nuclear fuel cores may exceed ten tonnes by the end of twenty-first century. These toxic fuels contained therein can cause ambient radiological pollution apart from structural damage to the satellites, functional, or defunct. This possibility arises from an estimation that

---

[61] Treaty Banning Nuclear Weapon Tests in Atmosphere, Outer Space and Under Water, 1963.

[62] Principles Relevant to the Use of Nuclear Power Sources in Outer Space, 1992, Principle 1.

[63] Principles, ibid, the Preamble.

[64] http://www.state.gov/documents/organization/65951.pdf Cited from Melissa K Force, "The Legal Landscape for Nuclear Spacecraft: International Environmental Law and Space Law" in Asian Journal of Air & Space Law, Vol II, No. 2, July-December, 2012, p. 155.

[65] Melissa, ibid.

[66] Howard A Baker, *Space Debris: Legal and Policy Implications*, Dordrecht, 1989, p. 14.

half-life of uranium-235 is over 700,000 years.[67] The extent and lifespan of possible damage to the environment in space and eventually on Earth can be well-imagined and seem scary.

To visualise the possibility of a malfunctioning nuclear-powered satellite losing its space orbit to enter the atmosphere of the Earth to get incinerated and remnants falling on the Earth, needs no clairvoyance. The wisdom of Murphy's law seems more relevant. In fact, the tragedy of the possibilities is that such incidents, major or minor, have occurred with detrimental effects and lasting damage. Some examples of the recorded falls of nuclear-powered sources are: the US Transit/SNAP-9A in 1964; Nimbus/SNAP-19 in 1968: Apollo 13/SNAP-27 in 1970; COSMOS 954 in 1978 and COSMOS-1402 in 1982.[68]

A pertinent event in this regard relates to the fall of the nuclear-powered Soviet Cosmos-954 on the northern Canadian territory on 24 June 1978. This satellite was launched on 18 September 1977 carrying a nuclear reactor enriched with isotopes of uranium-235. It suffered an uncontrolled fall from its space orbit, entered Earth's atmosphere, disintegrated, fell, and deposited the radioactive debris on Canadian soil. A claim for damages caused was preferred under the Liability Convention of 1972, it was negotiated between the parties and settled for C$ 3000,000 in 1981.

The point made here is not the value of the claim or modus of its settlement but to flag not-so-critical impact of the radioactive debris because it fell on uninhabited areas causing no death. And had the scatter of debris fallen in a densely populated country in the East, the extent of damage, possible deaths and isolation of radioactive debris would have posed serious issues in disaster management. Hence, it deserves a consideration that what should be the maximum permissible quantum of nuclear propulsion that a particular orbit can accept and its lateral separation before reaching the threshold of risky saturation and possible hazards.

Pollution and contamination in reverse are also true and factual. Take for example, the fall of nuclear-exposed debris is also pertinent and the risks attendant to such debris are well known. It was experienced on the Canadian territory from nuclear-exposed debris of Russian Cosmos satellite. Such falls could repeat anywhere, including the high seas or the polar glaciers. Though the exact nature, character and extent of space-induced pollution may not be known today, a possibility cannot be denied which may become apparent and real decades later.

Sensible regulation will be a better option than suicidal guarantees of freedom to every space-faring agency, under the Treaty, to launch and operate nuclear-powered satellites. Anyway, having put so much nuclear fuel into outer space domain, done so much potential damage and still continuing with affirmative support and permissive rules, it is time to realise the harm caused or its likely threat in the future. To undo this indiscretion, we may not be able to go back to change the beginning of the menace yet we can very well start anew to change the future into a safer time for posterity.

---

[67] N L Johnson, "Nuclear Power Supply in Orbit", *Space Policy,* vol 2 (1986), p. 230. For more details, refer V K Ahuja, "Space Activities and Environmental Pollution" in Mani, Bhatt and Reddy, eds., *Recent Trends in International Space Law and Policy,* New Delhi, Lancers, 1997, pp. 461–70.

[68] Ahuja, ibid, p. 463.

5.8 Debris Pollution of Outer Space Domain

5.8.1 The Copper Needles Experiment

The USA undertook an experiment called the Westford Needles Project in 1961 with a hope to allow long-distance communications by bouncing radio waves off of a belt of small copper wires (passive dipoles) as reflector. For the purpose, nearly 480 million copper needles were spread in a radio-reflective ring around the Earth at a height of about 3500 km. The experiment was intended to create an artificial ionosphere through levitated dipole needles but did not turn out to be successful. The needles failed to disperse and actually jumbled in seven clusters that are still somewhere in space as experimental debris. The second experiment in 1963 was no great success either because needles were sparsely populated. The mission did not achieve the desired result and was later abandoned, since made redundant by the modern communication applications with geo-sync satellite technology.[69]

The experiment was greatly criticised by astronomers who feared optical and radio pollution[70] apart from causing unwanted space clutter. In disregard of the unsolicited advice, the USA, in its technological arrogance, failed to consult specialists *in abundanti cautela*. The USA may argue that it had then no obligation to consult other states as Outer Space Treaty[71] was signed later. But wisdom does not come from treaties alone. Nonetheless, the USA also had a higher obligation *erga omnes* under international law that was ignored. The loud protests from experts in the field from Russia, Britain, and others persisted.[72] Ultimately, the matter was taken up in the United Nations where the USA defended that sunlight pressure would cause the dipoles to only remain in orbit for a short period of three years. The wires still exist in space after six decades and are regularly tracked. As a result of this censure, a provision on consultation between states was incorporated in Article IX of the OST.[73] Suitable lessons must be learnt.

5.8.2 Debris Scatter Through ASAT Experiments

In 2007, China conducted an ASAT experiment in space by destroying its own unwanted, Fengyun-IC weather satellite on its polar orbit at an altitude of 865 km. The destruction of the satellite caused a cloud of nearly 3200 particles in space at an

---

[69] Butrica, Andrew J. (ed.), *"Beyond the Ionosphere: The Development of Satellite Communications"*, history.nasa.gov, The NASA History Series, NASA.

[70] https://space.skyrocket.de/doc_sdat/westford.htm. Accessed on 13 April 2020.

[71] Treaty on Principles Governing the Activities of States in the Exploration and Use of Outer Space, including the Moon and other Celestial Bodies, 1967. (In short OST).

[72] *International Academy of Astronautics* (Edited Publication, October 15, 2005).

[73] Böckstiegel, Karl-Heinz, Benkö, Marietta, *Space Law: Basic Legal Documents. (1990)*, ISBN 9780792300915.

orbit from where it may take centuries to fall down and incinerate in the atmosphere. There was great resentment and condemnation worldwide including that voiced by the USA. But just a year later, in 2008, in an ostentatious display of technological advancement, the USA, also conducted a repeat experiment since 1985. This act also caused clouds of debris in space and was as reprehensible and detrimental to the space environment as the earlier one by China. Misdemeanour had occurred to breed reactions.

Over a decade later, on 27 March 2019, India conducted a similar, successful trial in a show of techno-prowess by engaging its own target-satellite at an altitude of 300 km for an ASAT experiment. This was "Mission Shakti" accomplished by Defence Research & Development Organisation (DRDO) of India in a series of testing of missile as a weapon but was India's first exo-atmosphere interceptor. This success put India in league with other three, the USA, Russia, and China. Despite the prestige gained, India had to defend that the space debris caused was on a much lesser scale and at a much lower altitude where these will get incinerated in atmosphere within a decade. But this should be no consolation nor justification.

Again, Russia carried out an anti-satellite weapon test on 16 November 2021. The weapon targeted an old Russian spacecraft, Tselina-D, which was non-functional and was in orbit since 1982. Russia has accepted conducting this test which hit the target with "razor-sharp precision."[74] This test has generated a debris field of nearly 1500 pieces of different sizes in low-earth orbit which may endanger the International Space Station and may pose risk to space activities for years. Anyway, the Russians have assured that the debris cloud is being monitored by the Soviet warning system to prevent and counter all possible threats.[75] No wonder, the competitive race is still in progress and the test was a Russian reaction against establishing of American Space Command in 2020.

Be that as it may, all ASAT-capable countries have caused pollution in space environment by unwanted and unnecessary space debris that may pose hazards of collision to the useful and functional space satellites for a long time to come. Time is ripe to consider and develop modalities to apply the principle of "proportional responsibility" and "polluter pays principle"[76] as these have crystallised in parleys on Climate Change. Consensus on these can be effectuated when the process of scavenging of outer space becomes technically, a feasible operation and can be outsourced by the proposed Space Utilisation and Sustenance Regulatory Authority (SUSRA), once established.[77] Concurrently, states may develop an instrument to declare ASAT tests as crimes *erga omnes*.

---

[74] A report from Moscow, "'Razor-sharp precision': Russia hails anti-satellite weapon test", *The Times of India*, (Chandigarh edition), November 17, 2021, Chandigarh Times Supplement, p. 4.
[75] Ibid.
[76] Opinion on this principle has crystallised in Climate Change parleys.
[77] For more details refer Chapter on Appraisal and Solutions.

5.9 An Appraisal

In nutshell, it seems established that humans will carry their propensities to outer space and celestial bodies and that crimes shall occur, of whatever variety or gravity. Preceding discussion has revealed that space crimes would posit a number of legal issues. One, jurisdiction over the accused. Two, considerations for extradition with or without such specific treaty between states. Three, the wrangles of procedural laws for prosecution. Four, competence of the domestic court to seize the case. Five, the decision to apply which laws as also the award of punishment on whose legal codes, of the accused or the victim. And finally, the perception of justice meted out to the parties.

The lack of a specific code governing such a state of imbroglio on space crimes will be felt more acutely when a horde of private operators are involved in multifarious commercial activities of space travel and tourism with multinational tourist configuration vacationing and enjoying stay at space hotels or resorts. Space mining could be another with space workers teeming celestial bodies. One cannot deny the existence of dubious activities in this competitive race and profit-mongering. This scenario does not seem too distant in time and such a situation may be upon us sooner than imagined. The challenge is going to be formidable when actually confronted. Therefore, the military sages often caution that to be forewarned is forearmed.

The USA, however, in order to meet its diverse treaty obligations has come up with a special provision in the US Code to address matters of criminal conduct that might arise in space, as well as other non-territorial areas. Known as the "special maritime and territorial jurisdiction of the USA,"[78] it covers procedures concerning how to handle criminal complaints outside of its national jurisdiction. In case, a US national was, to say, assault someone on a commercial space station, then this special type of jurisdiction would become relevant and can be invoked. Though as per Justice Department, this special jurisdictional provision mostly covers more heinous crimes, such as "murder, manslaughter, maiming, kidnapping, rape, assault, and robbery"[79] yet these can conveniently be used as guidelines.

However, for lesser offenses, such as hacking or identity theft, it is unclear if this would really apply. The law also becomes murkier if there is an incident that involves multiple people from multiple nations. For instance, if someone from the USA gets hurt on a private space hotel, along with other passengers from other nations, the situation would become confused and ambiguous. The obvious protocol would be consultation between concerned governments for an acceptable solution but if political or diplomatic bickering between nations exceeds three months, the aggrieved has an option to resort to his/her own national jurisdiction for remedies.[80]

---

[78] https://www.govinfo.gov/content/pkg/USCODE-2010-title18pdf/USCODE-2010-title18-partI-chap1-sec7.pdf.

[79] "The first alleged crime committed in space raises questions about jurisdiction in orbit", Loren Grush@lorengrush, August 27, 2019.

[80] Ibid.

Further, international treaties are generally state-centric and do not recognise individuals as subjects with legal capacity. The same is under space law. Therefore, liability, criminal or civil, for damage or injury caused by an individual does not attach directly and immediately. Under treaty law it rises to the state level and launching state and/or controlling state of that person or object in space are encumbered with such responsibility and liability, jointly or severally. The respective state accepting such responsibility and consequent liability can, without prejudice, reclaim liability share from the other state or take appropriate action against the offender under domestic jurisdiction.

On the other hand, having a framework based on the sovereign initiatives of the state does not make sense for the aggrieved individual and his resort to diplomatic solution yields no quick results and thus gives no solace either. Therefore, appropriate remedies with procedural clarities and jurisdictional simplification need to be devised because justice delayed is justice denied. The case of Allen McClain, widely reported in media, thus, becomes a wakeup call for the international community for timely action and requisite negotiations for such tricky predicament. We now have the opportunity and time to do this the right way and promote amity and peace among space-farers.

The international scenario concerning states considers "internationally wrongful acts" based on the definition accepted under "the Articles."[81] These are those acts that violate a substantive provision of an international treaty or convention and may thus be try-able under international courts like ICJ, ICC or a designated International Tribunal based on legal or contextual complexities. This template would certainly be helpful in the long run but does not instantly become applicable because no breach of international space law or any treaty provision has taken place.

The alleged act of misfeasance of Allen McClain reveals *mens rea,* it was voluntarily done, was an act with motive, intended to benefit the wrongdoer with knowledge of the consequences. Cumulatively, it establishes prima facie culpability that could be held try-able through due process of law in the USA. But investigation revealed that the complainant had committed more serious wrongs that diluted and condoned McClains culpability. Of course, this illustrative case of crime is simple and relates to only one state on all salient parameters. But the situation may not always be so simplistic in nationality or territoriality or the subject matter of offence or availability of evidence. Future crimes in space may be far varied and diverse and national courts may find it difficult to seize jurisdiction of the cases so easily.

Therefore, many more complications are imaginable on international as well as domestic scene. Even moot courts have evolved narratives with scenarios much more complex and intertwined with international implications and national compulsions. Permutations and combination can be imagined. One such contingency can be visualised concerning human rights violations in space and on celestial bodies where in an event of accident or emergency or distress, space operator or entities stationed nearby or on the same celestial body, shirk, or refuse to provide shelter or emergency aid or evacuation facilities. The Moon Agreement under Article 10 mandates such

---

[81] Refer Articles of Responsibility of States for Internationally Wrongful Acts.

an obligation. Incidents of denial or discrimination would tantamount to torture of the victim under germane conventions and hence perpetrators would be punishable under appropriate law, national or international. Such action would uphold the eternal principles of law and ensure respect of human personality and dignity.[82]

5.10 Conclusion

Be that as it may, the future complexion of activities in outer space is going to be different, competitive, and conflictive. This is because states are gradually withdrawing from peaceful space activities of commercial character and are tending to concentrate on strategic military objectives of defensive nature, ostensibly within the bounds of space law. As a result of this reduced funding from state exchequers, private enterprise is making steady but rapid inroads into space activities, but their main interest is in profitable commercial utilisation and exploitation of outer space. Thus, the focus of business would be on space transportation, space hospitality, space logistics, commercial appropriation of celestial natural resources, and habitation infrastructure for space residencies on celestial bodies. Each of the mentioned commercial activities in space will bear peculiar characteristics, pose divergent challenges and would need novel solutions. Because, these will have different business compulsions, different operational strategies, different competitive playfield, different work norms, different ethical motivations, and different humanitarian considerations. Hence the nature, context, and *mens rea* of new varieties of crimes will be of disparate identity with complex territorial and nationality linkages for jurisdictional considerations and conflicting claims on extradition of the culprit. Some aspects of such predicament are summarised below.

In the instant case of Allen McClain, no infringement of any international instrument seems to have occurred; and the provision of permanent jurisdiction over space objects under the OST also supports the position stated earlier. Therefore, international trial is neither mandated nor relevant. Accordingly, the trial venue rightfully shifts to domestic jurisdiction of the US courts. This decision can also be vindicated under the principle of nationality of the US astronaut; the principle of territoriality due to the US quarters of ISS being deemed US territory and the doctrine of *locus* that the indicted astronaut was stationed there. Thus, the alleged offender and the relevant subject matter require intervention by the US court. Ergo, the domestic jurisdiction of the appropriate US courts under the germane law becomes applicable and legitimate.

There can, however, be umpteen complications in future scenario of crimes. First, the complicating element could be the launching state of the "humanned" space object in which a crime is committed. Normally, a launching state is the one that launches the object and on whose national registry it is entered and reported to the UN as its

---

[82] Universal Declaration of Human Rights, 1948, Article 11.

space object.[83] This aspect is pertinent because launching state has *de jure* ownership of the object, with full control over its operations and personnel within, whether crew or scientists or paying-passengers. This satisfies the territoriality criterion so long as all belong to one country. But the scenario can be complex by varying nationality of every element at each step. It can be made further complicated by introducing possibility of leased objects or even on-orbit purchase, as happened in the purchase of a non-functional Malaysian satellite by the manufacturer and its resale back to Malaysia after on-orbit repairs. This is where simple tests of jurisdiction will fail to offer clear-cut answers.

Secondly a state of imbroglio will be felt more acutely in a space object/station where a horde of private operators are involved in diverse commercial activities like advertising, research, space travel, logistics and tourism with service-personnel drawn from different nations and multinational tourist configurations vacationing and enjoying stay as space resort. Further, one cannot deny the existence of dubious activities in this race and profit-mongering, and possibility of crimes appears endemic to the situation. This scenario should not seem too distant in time and such a predicament may be upon us sooner than imagined. The challenge is going to be formidable when actually confronted. Therefore, a pro-active approach to frame a suitable protocol to handle ensuing dilemma would be a sensible option.

Thirdly, the nature of crime and its impact on the victim can be another sensitive consideration in view of global variations in the judicial systems and legal codes. For example, a bodily injury or murder or one-to-one harm may be a simple case for jurisdiction settlement and appreciation of ingredients of crime. But cases of conspiracy or riots or public disorders will pose endless hassles and counterclaims for jurisdiction and extradition over offenders for obvious affinities like nationality, ideology, religion, etc. Take another case of theft of intellectual property rights and the need to pinpoint the true culprit. This is not going to be easy either on the interdomain scatter of evidence or the jurisdictional clarity. And where does the *onus probandi* lie, whether under French legal system on the complainant or British adversarial practice to satisfy competing claims. Human Rights law, though suggests that a person is innocent till proved guilty.[84]

With the broadening spectrum of space activities with diverse character and competition ethos, space crimes may wear a different complexion and bear varied causations. Future crimes in space may be initiated and executed with technology, cyber, digital, Internet and from any domain to any other domain. Legal conundrums would not be easy to solve with scant trail of evidence and anonymity of the perpetrator. Further permissive militarisation of celestial bodies and defensive weaponisation of space orbits may add another dimension of complexity. Therefore, it will be wise to cogitate on methods to minimise such incursive space crimes and plug the small leak now rather hopelessly handle a torrent later.

By and large, the flagged issues suggest the need for new definitions, new explanations, and new solutions in existing international instruments of space law. This

---

[83] Convention on Registration of Objects Launched into Outer Space, 1975, as amended.
[84] Universal Declaration of Human Rights, 1948, Article 11.

5.10 Conclusion

can be well achieved through a specific protocol to the Outer Space Treaty. An alternative could be to have a *lex specialis* for space crimes in a new treaty format devoted to the subject. This would contain revised jurisprudence for the space domain, new judicial processes and novel institutional solutions. But, the option of a new Treaty on Space Crimes may turn out to be difficult to negotiate and bring in force.

Prime necessity would be to have an institution for the governance of outer space and management of celestial resources. For this purpose, the defunct UN Trusteeship Council may be revived and tasked with the requisite functions, powers, and funds. The second necessity relates to redressal of specific disputes arising in the space domain and for dispensation of justice. This need can be met by the establishment of an International Court of Space Crimes, presently, as an adjunct or a special bench of the ICJ, providing for need-based expansion or independence. The flagged issues will be discussed in some detail in the following chapters.

Chapter 6
Space Crimes Through Technology: A New Trend

6.1 Introduction

In Chap. 4, in a general discussion, we have dwelled on the nature, character and ingredients of the crimes. The chapter also covered in brief, the sociology of crimes in relation to their motivation, the social learning for such acts, the personality of the criminal as also the reasons for the acts of recidivism. In the previous discussion in Chapter Five, there was an effort to visualise and identify the specific space crimes and their causation due to peculiar circumstances and the impact of the environmental forces of the space domain. Apart from crimes by humans, the genre of economic and business crimes in relation to growing commercialisation and privatisation of space activities were also considered at some length.

In the present chapter an effort will be made to describe the emerging trend towards use of technologies like artificial intelligence, cyber technology, directed energy devices and the use of rockets to disrupt the operation, disfunction the device, 'dis-control' the satellite to turn it zombie or in the ultimate to destroy a functional satellite. These are all supported by the digital triumvirate of computation, data and connectivity. A brief allusion will also be made to ballistic missiles as Anti-Satellite (ASAT) weapons, hyper-missiles and banal use of agnate devices in the outer space. All hostile acts, with the use of these technologies and devices, that may induce dysfunction, cause damage to or destruction of others' space assets would constitute crimes, in some sense and manner. And with adequate evidence and proved ingredients, the act would be patently criminal and duly punishable. This possibility of techno-crimes cannot be wished away and their oncoming seems an ominous reality.

Lately, technology has gone bold, and where it has yielded peaceful utilities like communications, broadcasting and remote-sensing as also commercialisation of space activities, there are lurking dual-uses of technology which pander for military applications. Some common non-aggressive benefits derived by the armed forces relate to intelligence, reconnaissance, surveillance, command and control with integration of digital technologies. Many of these facilities and utilities of defensive character can be converted and put to direct use in or to augment offensive roles. It is often rued by strategists that in modern day warfare, a person can cause more damage by pressing of a computer key than with a bomb. Hence, the risks from cyber, directed and digital technologies towards safety and security of operational space assets devoted to peaceful uses.

Fortunately, no significant or noticeable acts of threat or actual use of force in the space domain have come to notice so far but with the rising new space powers like China, India, European Space Agency and Japan, all with divergent ideologies, defence strategies, domestic compulsions and national postures, the situation may become volatile and unpredictable. Again, the prohibitions under the Outer Space Treaty on the militarisation of celestial bodies and weaponization of orbits around the Earth, the Moon and other celestial bodies are generalised, porous and weak. Despite this frequent lament and a consistent complaint, it is further generous on selective permissions for the use of military personnel and equipment for peaceful activities. Under this façade a lot of mischief is possible. So, a strong or head-heavy political leader, or others in retaliation, may use technology as a tool to cause militarisation and weaponization of the space domain for obvious geo-political motives.

It is equally pertinent to consider that the era of space activities directly under the state control or only by state-controlled agencies for scientific exploration and peaceful activities is almost over. There are, at present, an increasing number of private enterprise and corporate business taking over economically promising and highly profitable space activities like commercial space transportation for passengers and cargo, et al. Space tourism as hospitality service for the tourists is in the offing. The next activity in line is space exploitation covering excavation and appropriation of celestial mineral resources that appears round the corner. Celestial bodies are a treasure trove of precious metals and common-use minerals, the stocks of which have depleted in terrestrial mines. Such highly competitive industries may develop and bring forth their own technologies and attract *mens rea* for disruptive interference, technology thefts and related crimes.

The next futuristic visualisation relates to celestial habitations for permanent human residencies. Even at present, public surveys have revealed that a large number of Earth-dwellers are willing to buy one-ticket to the Moon and settle down there permanently, if facilities permit. In response to this demand and even to accommodate space workers employed by the hospitality, exploration and manufacturing industries, efforts are afoot to create compatible infra-structure for living of humans. The design of Woerner's[1] Moon Village is one such positive step in this direction. Such a settlement of multi-national, multi-ethnic population can be a breeding ground for conflicts and crimes. And the then evolved technologies would provide another criminal edge to such populace. And these are no oneiric visions but imaginations that may soon become real and dreams that may come live.

Lastly, space activities are diversifying in character and content, apart from the existing high density in the low-earth orbit and congestion in geo-synchronous orbit

---

[1] Dr. Woerner, a NASA scientist, has created a blue print of the Moon Village which will be live-able by human inhabitants.

6.1 Introduction

with dead and non-functional satellites. Further, the trend towards launching of hundreds of 'cube-sats' or 'pseudo-sats' as part of constellations comprising thousands of its type is scaring. In fact, most of our current space activities, whether commercial or military, are concentrated in the low-earth orbital ranges and have blurred the distinction between air-space and outer space. This is also because most space activities benefitting humankind primarily make use of the Earth orbit. No wonder, this orbit is highly congested.

Apart from the density of satellites, functional or dead, in the Earth orbit, there are deposits of 'sheddings' from different stages of launch rockets like shredded nuts and bolts, discarded fuel tanks, etc. The dumped fuel tanks that are not-so-empty further add to space debris through their explosion or implosion. This congestion is due to natural causes but as a consequence of our actions; and it is no small component either. Hence, the routes to outer space are getting progressively clogged where future generations may have to wait long for an opportunity window for a desired launch.[2] Such a situation may induce mass-harm and would be highly deplorable, thus, least acceptable to the millennials.

Today, we are becoming more aware and conscious of the problem of space debris and its repercussions on space activities in the future. For the mitigation of space debris in the future, the UN has issued guidelines.[3] But this is not enough and we need to atone for old sins of accumulated space debris. This needs measures for remediation in the overall context of debris management. Moreover, soft law recommendations are too soft for ensuring effective implementation and need a wider thrust at total space debris management. The menace is, nevertheless, growing and with escalating hazards so posed, the non-obligatory ethics of soft law may have to turn into binding rules of tomorrow and ultimately breaches may have to be treated as crime against humanity.

6.1.1 *A Brief Note on Crimes Against Humanity*

The concept of crimes against humanity traces its history long before the realisation of human rights and humanitarian laws as also their inclusion in international law. In fact, its roots can be traced to philosophical ethics of Socrates, Plato and Aristotle while theologians like St. Augustine and St. Aquinas espoused it as a notion of natural law and justice. Eventually, it came to be preached and taught as morality in international relation and was applied even to the wars to cause least harm to the enemy.[4] Alberico Gentili referred to this as common law of humanity while Pufendorf considered that human beings owed each other the duties if humanity. These ideas

---

[2] Take the case for the launch of Artemis 1, in September 2022, in which rectification of a glitch in the fuel system was fast but the launch had to wait for days for an opportune window. The status of the future can be imagined.

[3] UN Guidelines on Mitigation of Space debris, 2007. UN resolution 67/217 of December 22, 2007 based on COPUOS recommendations.

[4] Views of Francisco de Vitoria and Balthazar Ayala taken from *German Encyclopaedia of Law,* 1994, pp. 869–71.

evolved, hardened and were eventually codified in the Hague Conventions of 1899 and 1907 as laws and customs of war, also called as the laws of humanity and the dictates of the public conscience.

For a long time, this law remained in the books for teaching and pedantic discourses, and only by innuendoes was applied to piracy, slavery and similar serious crimes against humanity. It resurfaced after WWI and was actively applied after WWII through International Military Tribunals for trial of those who perpetrated massacres of the innocents. However, currently, it has been used to condemn and denounce genocide, terrorism, torture, warfare (nuclear, biological and chemical–NBC), environmental pollution, etc. Hence, this concept appears highly germane to the outer space domain where similar conditions and threats loom large to be noticeable.

Crimes against humanity may be divided into two categories. First category could cover such acts which are targeted towards innocent people not involved in war-like activities or stand in opposition to the perpetrators or resist their movement and yet become the target of such crimes. Here the criminal behaves indiscriminately and unconcerned about the results of the action intending only to obtain blitz-effect and news-splash for propaganda by attacking soft targets. Shedding blood of the unconnected and the unaware for sheer media attention appears atrocious and barbaric. Terrorism, NBC warfare and environmental pollution could easily come under this class.

The second category of such crimes could pertain to acts that cause an existential threat to the humanity that could be direct or indirect. Direct criminal acts with ideological motivation for intended results are obvious. Whereas, an indirect threat, for example, can be caused by an action that stirs or starts a chain reaction or initiates 'dildoe effect' where building-blocks of existence start crumbling to create a holocaust. Or another inadvertent or motivated act to cause an accident or inducing debris in a highly dense orbit where one deliberate accident leads to another collision and so on and on, beyond any control, to cause an apocalypse. It could be low-earth orbit or geo-synchronous orbit where density is high and separation distances are low. One cannot imagine the end result of such a deliberated mischief or lack of due diligence in space actions or an outright crime. Here mens rea, lack of *abundanti cautela* and knowledge of possible consequences of the action are important as ingredients of the crime.

The author is conscious that there is no universal agreement for a strict ban on all kinds of war or regarding all specific acts that may constitute crimes against humanity. Therefore, some positivist scholars may differ with this amplification of crimes against humanity because they consider that every action is licit if taken in pursuance of legitimate goals, even if it is a war. They may also argue that there is anyway a doctrine of just wars or *bellum justum*, if waged for a good cause or in pursuit of justice. Beliefs and practice of sovereign state, more so powerful ones, do not concur on this point and international law does not develop in a political vacuum.

Nevertheless, some precepts of international law seem to have through usage become peremptory norms that are considered binding and have gained the status of customary law. Same way, some concepts of international conduct and relations have been exalted as *jus cogens* and deserve the majesty of obligatory law. Striving for international cooperation with pacifist motives and efforts at avoidance of war belong to the tribe of customary law and *jus cogens* because these ideals seem "so basic, fundamental and natural to the legal regime"[5] of world peace and humanity's prosperity. Most states as a practice do negotiate for settlement of disputes and *opiniojuris* exalts this option to the status of *jus cogen*, though it still remains "part of a persistent evolutionary process reflecting the expanding social consciousness of the world community"[6] and collective will and inner conscience of humanity.

6.2 Cyber Technology

6.2.1 Space Crimes Through Digital Technologies

The digital triumvirate of computation, data and connectivity determine the trend of future living and killing. Digital technology was a great innovation and has opened flood gates of possibilities. Its applications have proliferated very fast and have come to be used globally with ease in usage and almost ubiquitous availability. Among its ramifications grew cyber techniques which created a new domain of cyber-space with electromagnetic spectrum. Further, this technology is neutral and the quality of action depends upon the user or perpetrator. Ironically, most of the crimes to be committed in space can also be triggered with digital technologies. These can be effectuated as Cross-Domain-Crimes, (CDCs) i.e., from any domain: land, water, air or space and committed in any domain. Thus, cyber is all-pervasive and overlaps other domains yet with its own distinctive existence and intangible characteristics. It provides capabilities of swiftness and repetition with decisive and precise effects. It is boundless in its reach and effect and it is for this reason that cyber-space is euphemistically called the fourth domain or dimension[7]; even though it is an human creation while other domains are the creations of God.

Cyber-space is not a visible domain but has virtual existence that pervades all domains through technology and information data. As a result, cyber-crimes are virtual crimes which may be technology-related, data-related, software-related and social media-related. More explicitly, these may be Voice-over-internet Protocol (VoIP) or electronic burglary, e-mail crimes or Web solicitation. These may also exploit technologies like Google lens, Cloud Computing and Internet-of Things (IoT).[8] Ironically, new areas and novel applications are expanding as well as

---

[5] G S Sachdeva, *Outer Space: Law, Policy and Governance*, New Delhi, KW Publishers Private Ltd., 2014, p. 2.

[6] *German Encyclopaedia of Law*, 1994, p. 871.

[7] Some scholars consider cyber-space as fifth dimension and treat water as a separate domain from land.

[8] For more details refer M K Nagaraj, "IoT of Crimes: Evaluation of Forensic Evidence" in CMR University Journal for Contemporary Legal Affairs, Vol. 2, Issue 1, August, 2020, pp. 133–57.

diversifying very fast and are equally prone to gross misuse and prostitution of purpose.

The cyber-domain, created in the internet, works as "common heritage of mankind". Its open and freely accessible use poses certain regulatory issues. Firstly, it evades jurisdiction because it has no boundaries and can exist anywhere. Cyber-actions may leave a trail but evidence may not be complete or convincing to establish jurisdiction over a crime. Secondly, there is a trend in transition for conversion of tangible assets to intangible assets e.g., crypto-currencies through cyber applications like blockchain which afford global reach and global power. This change-over has found acceptance or partial acceptance with certain governments. The crypto assets exist in cyber-domain and not in physical possession which lend security and anonymity albeit need independent global vigilance. Despite high protection and near fool-proof security, these economic transactions are vulnerable to crimes and had their nadir in a few cases. Thirdly, being neutral in use and open to all, it is susceptible to benign uses as well as crimes. This poses a moral question on its utility and it may take decades to evolve cyber-ethos.[9]

Due to the peculiarities of technology, cyber-crimes leave behind scant and fragile trail of evidentiary e-date spread over information systems, hardware peripherals, network system and other manifestations of internet. Hence, the task of forensic evidence here involves special procedures of identification, retrieval, preservation, collection, collation, processing and presentation of magnetically encoded data in acceptable legal formats. Cyber investigation, therefore, requires specialised knowledge, skills and expertise to trace digital footprints, forensic fragments and validation of computer hardware and network systems. Further because of its global reach and ubiquitous cross-domain operations, it would necessitate international protocol or agreement to enable digital detectives and forensic specialists to carry out search and seizure of computer hardware as also in virtual environment.

In fact, America programmed 'cyber-space', created it in the internet and fashioned it in its own liberal image and democratic values: free, open, accessible, decentralised, distributed, shared and self-governing. It also offered qualities of swift, decisive, precise and frequent-use effects. No wonder, this human innovation mesmerises net-addicts with the intoxication of freedom and reach. It has no boundaries and behaves porous to every domain. In fact, it can now be treated as common heritage of mankind and appears the last surviving "common" that has so far escaped proper and strict regulation. Lately, its misuse and dis-use, have deterred many states and seem to necessitate censorial restrictions and regulatory controls.

On the contrary, if internet had been created in Russia or China or North Korea, its architecture, characteristics and utilities would have been different: restricted, constricted and constrained. Authoritarian nations view the freedom of communication differently and accordingly, proliferation of cyber-space as a threatening utility. Hence, they would have needed to build firewalls to protect their systems and societies from such manifestations of freedom, openness and libertarianism. May be,

---

[9] K Prasanna Rani, "Space Law through the Lens of Cyber Law", in V Balakista Reddy and Rahul Nikam, eds., *Space Law and Contemporary Issues,* Hyderabad, Asia Law House, 2012, p. 436.

their perception is right in their own traditions and mindset. Possibly, they apprehend misuse of cyber possibilities within their controlled society as also threat to their space assets and systems.

Further, cyber-crimes can be committed incognito by a person, from any common platform and with a high degree of secrecy and anonymity with little tell-tale evidence. Thus, problems concerning probes for detection of the crime, establishing identity of the criminal, gathering evidence relating to the criminal act and even the relevance of applicable law may defy existing procedures of investigation, modalities of prosecution, posology of punishment or determination of sanctions. The dilemma is serious and may be aggravated by international implications of cyber-crimes. Hence, grave maladies need drastic remedies.

Unfortunately, the very openness, freedom and inclusivity of digital technologies have become its bane and a source of vulnerabilities. The situation is further compounded by its most attractive feature that its entrance threshold is so low that even a person not formally educated could use its ingenious facilities; and a slightly clever one, even self-taught person, could create new applications and new platforms, with any intention. Thus, it has become a utility being developed and used by the masses and its openness is expansive, almost endless and unrestricted. Hence, its easy access and 'freely' availability to everyone and anyone: the common user, the hacker, the scammer, the fraudster, the terrorist or the non-state actor, is showing up as its weak-link and drawback. No wonder, even good intentions can have a bad harvest.

6.2.2 Instances of Cyber-attacks

As pointed out earlier, cyber technology has the potential to inflict attacks on any digital assets in cross-domain scenario. A few instances of serious security breaches through cyber-attacks, worldwide, are narrated to highlight the dimensions of the ominous risks and dangers. For example, the US faced a cyber-attack on Colonial Pipeline, one of America's largest distributors of fuel on 7 May 2021. The supply system was disrupted and a demand for ransom was made. The criminal hacking was claimed to have been carried out by an affiliate of DarkSide, a cyber-hacker's group, and a ransom of 75 Bitcoins was paid in cryptocurrency which amounted to nearly $5 million.[10] Incidentally, the ransom paid could not be traced with the available technology because cryptocurrency is based on block-chain technique.

It is also believed that Chinese hackers have been accessing major US weapon system designs to modernise its military. In another instance some years back, a PLA unit located in Shanghai had "systematically stolen hundreds of terabytes of data" from (nearly a hundred) US corporations, organisations and government agencies. The data stolen related to "product blueprints, manufacturing plans, clinical

---

[10] Narain Batra, "Power's New Dimension" in *The Times of India*, (Chandigarh edition), May 21, 2021, Editorial page.

trial results, pricing documents, negotiation strategies and other proprietary information..."[11] Most of these affected units were clients of Mandiant, a US computer security company which traced the hackers and pinpointed the criminal. Thus, the US is under constant threat in relation to its most precious assets viz., intellectual property and strategic military secrets, existing and of the future.

Again, a recent incident struck Iran on 11 April 2021, which caused a black-out at its underground atomic facility at Natanz on Sunday early morning.[12] Iran has expressed outrage and this black-out and has condemned it as a despicable move. Though initially considered as a grid failure, it has been now attributed to a cyber-attack with the needle of suspicion pointing to Israel.[13] Many think-tanks have, however, dubbed it as cyber-warfare well suited for grey zones where offensive activities are carried out below the threshold of an all-out war or in asymmetric reactions. But the basic occurrence remains a cyber-attack and does not change in content or context. The episode amply reveals that cyber techniques bear endemic advantages, to need fewer resources and that acts can be carried out incognito and rather discreetly, which have, in turn, incentivised cyber-attacks.

In another attribute, cyber-security attacks are contactless, unobtrusive, stealthy and insidious. These activities are ungoverned and no rules or principles regulate or protect cyber-space, the domain where all the data relating to activities of strategy think-tanks, military secrets, political negotiations, economic plans, financial data, technological innovations, et al. are stored. The risks now are obvious. Thus, hackers or scammers belonging to hostile states or non-state actors acting alone or in collusion could disrupt operations of power grids, financial systems, defence networks and other vulnerable areas.

Nearer home, such disruptions have been caused in India. In October, 2020, a cyber-attack occurred on the electrical grid of Mumbai causing a complete shutdown plunging millions into darkness and in many ways disturbing the financial capital of India. It was a new experience and administration had to grope in the darkness to find solutions it had not catered for. The US had a different take on this. The New York Times speculated that it was a Chinese cyber-attack to show that China could not only fight India in the Himalayas and the North-East but also hit hard right in its very heart.[14] It is a future shock for India and a clarion call for protective steps and counter measures from wherever the threat may originate.

In another instance on 29 June 2011, three techies who alleged that they had been outsourced for programming but denied higher wages for the software development and networking of CUPPS (Common Use Passenger Processing System) at Terminal 3 of Delhi airport. In revenge, they used 'logic bombing', a cyber-attack technique, to disable the working and operation of check-in system. This crippled the system and

---

[11] Ibid.

[12] The event is remembered as Black Sunday, the 11th April, 2021.

[13] "Blackout at Natanz N-site, Iran calls it 'nuclear terrorism'" in *The Times of India*, (Chandigarh edition), April 12, 2021.

[14] Narain Batra, n. 10.

50 flights were delayed due to the domino-effect of the attack. On a report lodged by the Airport Authority of India, the scammers were arrested on 16 November 2011.[15]

Be that as it may, in the ultimate analysis, cyber-space is nothing but data and data is power, more so if the data is useful to the hackers' masters in some way or its theft harms the owner-victim in some other ways. The importance of data with galloping 5G technology and Internet of Things cannot be belittled. In fact, the development of these would tend to quantitatively expand data exponentially and turn everything into networked unitary object. Of course, the advantages of availability and freedom are exciting and tempting yet vulnerabilities are becoming equally obvious, threatening and detrimental.

Another primal characteristic of data is that it is "non-rival" in the sense that it can be used simultaneously and repeatedly by any number of users without diminution or destruction. In another sense, this very trait of being "non-rival" becomes its bane to confidentiality which can be almost openly used by rivals with chagrin and impunity. Such leaks can cause tremendous damage to economy, business, politics, military secrets, defence strategy and other sensitive national issues. The consequences and costs of such uncatered for competitive losses may be astronomical in terms money, waste of time and effort as also reputation in international arena.

Despite the isolated successes in identifying and apprehending the culprits, the cybercriminals, by and large, remain incognito, act extrusive to the locale of impact, operate from remote locations, can select their technique, choose their platform and thus, leave few traces of material evidence. The dilemma is serious and solicits urgent remedies and viable solutions. Technology is being developed to identify and locate perpetrators in several computer research hubs in the US,[16] Europe and even India. Believably, success has been achieved in parts but its advantages are being continuously eroded by the openness of technology and the ever-improving skills of the hackers.

Nevertheless, a guilty rider remains as to what can be achieved if hackers originate from Russia, China or North Korea. More so, when "China continues to be the largest origin of IP thefts today…"[17] and the criminals well know that they cannot be apprehended, prosecuted and punished. This attitude and behaviour call for stricter international laws for extradition and trial, along with fast development of reliable technology for fool-proof encryption to protect data from such temptation of stealth as also identify the perpetrators for punitive action. Further, most of the data-rich countries are switching to data-intelligent system to reduce the abundance of data and yet be able to make good use of it for analytics and for dynamic policy decisions.

May be, digital surveillance and protective encryption coupled with legal steps work as deterrent to effectively tame the errant techno-autocratic nations and crony hackers. Complementing these measures, humanity may still need a new digital world

---

[15] Updated report filed by Naveen Ammembala in *Hindustan Times*, New Delhi, November 21, 2011.

[16] Mandiant, a computer security company of the US, is prominent among developers of this technology.

[17] Narain Batra, n. 10.

order that would regulate the use of data-domain as well as the conduct of 'data-rich-nations' in their very own interest and for the betterment of humanity. Live and let live may, then, be the right motto to follow for common good of all, with inclusivity. However, sometimes slogans do not work for the desired effect.

6.3 Cyber-crimes in Space

Under the circumstances, one needs no skills of clairvoyance to envision the possibilities of cyber-attacks and digital interference in satellite operations, to say the least, render the satellites dysfunctional or take them out of control from the operator, even temporarily. The consequences of such rogue acts turning a satellite zombie could be seriously interfering, highly detrimental, possibly disastrous and could be even be 'techno-cidal'.[18] The extent of impact and the result could even be beyond imagination of the perpetrator. Hence, cyber-crimes in and from space is not just an oneiric vision but is tending to become a reality and a bane of the modern space operations. In fact, cyber-attacks have occurred in space on the US as also on Indian satellites, temporarily rendering them incommunicado or out of control of the operating agency.

Such crimes with cyber technology pose multi-dimension disadvantages in detection, apprehension, evidence collection and trial of the criminal-individual or the hacker organisation, or non-state actors or the rogue state. This is because cyber-attacks are unobtrusive, long-distance operations and extrusive to the locale impacted. Thus, anonymity engulfs the identity, platform and domain of the offender and as such rarely leave tell-tale signature material. In consequence, investigations are often beset with a difficult task of identifying the perpetrator on weak clues and scant evidence. Hence, it becomes a difficult task to investigate, apprehend the culprit and prove the cause for liability in respect of cyber-crimes in space.

At the same time, it would be pertinent to explicitly mention some of the adverse possibilities from cyber-attacks and attendant crimes. These could be aimed to disrupt the critical service of a satellite or to cause loss its control. Espionage of industrial intellectual property or business plans of competition or military strategy secrets are additional advantages. Lastly, it could be used for extortion or ransom by non-state actors or unattached hackers who could, with reasonable concealment and anonymity, demand payment for their criminal threats in bitcoins or any other crypto-currency. However, secrecy shrouds such missions and much information is not public.

6.3.1 Suspected Hacks by China

Presumably, cyber-attacks have already occurred on orbiting satellites and ground control systems. Though hard evidence pin-pointing the perpetrator has not been

---

[18] A term morphed from the word suicidal.

6.3 Cyber-crimes in Space

found, yet needle of suspicion points towards China wanting to obfuscate competing super-powers and sound a warning that superior technologies inimical to you. A US-based research institute, China Aerospace Studies Institute (CASI), in a 142-page report mentions that China carried out multiple cyber-attacks on the US agencies between 2012 and 2018. A notable one was conducted in 2012, when a Chinese network-based computer attacked NASA's Jet Propulsion Laboratory (JPL). The cyber-attack "allowed 'full functional control' over JPL networks," as per the report.[19] Such inimical cyber activities bear dangerous dimensions for tactical reasons and strategic impact.

In the case of LANDSAT, there is more than suspicion of China's involvement. In 2007/2008, the US geological, Earth-observation satellite had detected radio-signals from the ground that seemed an attempt to "lock-on" to it before commands can be received. The attempt, however, failed in its purpose to breach privacy and security. The matter was, nevertheless, reported to the Department of Defense for investigation as per protocol. A detailed investigation found that the prime suspect was Chinese Military and the attack came in via a ground station in Norway. It was feared that if the attacker had achieved command privileges, this could "deny or degrade as well as forge or otherwise manipulate the satellite transmission" and could damage or even destroy the satellite.[20] Thus, this was indeed, a particularly worrisome attack.

Again, China has long been accused of carrying out state-backed cyber-attacks and cyber espionage activities against numerous nations including, it's not-so-neighbourly neighbour, India. And People's Liberation Army (PLA), has also continued to acquire and commission newer technologies that are geared towards complete cyber-surveillance and cyber-warfare. These may include tools for cyber espionage, data manipulation, political interference and impact on infrastructure of critical sectors of supporting military strategy and national economy such as defence, oil and gas, energy, nuclear power generation, space and other cognate spheres.

US-based China Aerospace Studies Institute (CASI) has flagged numerous and persistent cyber-attacks made by China on India spanning over a decade. Believably, the most notable act among these, committed against India, was launched as a "computer attack" against Indian satellite communication in 2017. This was part of a range of proving experiments involving "counterspace-related testing and operations."[21] Surprisingly, India is not aware of such incidents of cyber-intrusions and remains in a denial mode regarding compromise of its data security or communication integrity.

ISRO chief, K. Sivan, has asserted that he has no direct knowledge of any instance of cyber-attacks impacting or compromising ISRO data or operations. He, however, acknowledged that cyber-attacks have consistently targeted ISRO over the past few

---

[19] Sarthak Dogra, "China Attacked Indian Satellite Systems, Several Times in the Past Decade, Says Report", *The Times of India*, September 24, 2020.

[20] Jim Wolf, "China key suspect in US satellite hacks: Commission", *US News*, updated October 28, 2011.

[21] Shouvik Das, "China targeted ISRO, Indian Communication Satellite with Constant Cyber Attacks", a report from US-based *China Aerospace Studies Institute* (CASI), September 23, 2020.

years, albeit without success.[22] A constant cyber threat still looms large and beckons caution, vigilance and alertness. In response, Sivan, again, assured that India has "an independent and isolated network which is not connected to the public domain, including the Internet", thus ISRO is keeping its systems safe.[23]

In an earlier case also, ISRO had received an alert of a possible cyber-attack on its systems early 2019, prior to the launch of Chandrayaan 2 mission. This attack, the analysts found was through phishing emails targeted at senior officials. An Indian Space Research Organisation official confirmed that an alert was received from the Computer Emergency Response Team, India (CERT-In), but the space agency was not affected. The source is generally difficult to trace and still remains unknown.[24]

There is also a rumoured case that an Indian functional satellite in orbit was interfered with to make it incommunicado with control headquarters for some minutes. The motivation and purpose of the attack seems to point the suspicion towards China, but with scant evidence. Maybe, because the mute-mode was insignificant at that time and the deficiency was not particularly noticed. Further, the source of threat or attack cannot be ascertained or confirmed with certainty, hence, are possibly, ignored after taking necessary action for protective security.

Nonetheless, it is pertinent to mention, the US study cautions that such attacks are particularly critical for any nation, as it can impact ground satellite and network stations, telemetry and command systems, affecting satellites placed in geosynchronous Earth orbit (GEO). All this and more can be achieved without launching physical warfare. This study further endorses the findings earlier made by Carnegie Endowment for International Peace in their report for 2019 and affirms that China already has sophisticated cyber infrastructure that is capable of intercepting and damaging spacecraft and satellite communication systems of most space-faring countries.[25]

6.3.2 Russian Intrusions with Cyber Technology

The Russian cyber challenge is not new. In fact, they were one of the pioneers in in this field of intrusions and interruptions. The first known cyber-attacks initiated by Moscow against the US military date from 1986 at least. At the time, the Soviet Union, working in collaboration with the East German secret services, acted through West German cyber proxies. Realising the benefits of the information thus obtained and the low cost of remotely-conducted cyber-intrusions, Moscow put in accelerated

---

[22] Ibid.

[23] Sarthak Dogra, at n. 19 ante.

[24] https://economictimes.indiatimes.com/tech/internet/isro-warned-of-A-possible-cyberattack-when-dtrack-came-calling/articleshow/71964232.cms?utm_source=contentofinterest&utm_medium=text&utm_campaign=cppst

[25] Shouvik Das at n. 21 ante.

6.3 Cyber-crimes in Space

and concerted efforts to overcome its 'cyber-laggard' status way back in the 1990s.[26] As a result, hacks and disruptions have become common and effective methods of breaching cyber-security.

Therefore, it may be inferred that Russia's strategic 'cyber holiday' is now over, and that cyber-active countries have entered a new, much more contested phase of cyber geopolitics where the great cyber powers will henceforth adopt a more aggressive, 'gloves-off' approach.[27] This attitude and advantage has permeated to the space domain because of the obvious ease in operation and advantage of sophistication because the perpetrator leaves little digital footprint or forensic fragment trail. Further, the finds and results of the inquiries also remain shrouded in opacity for valid reasons of non-disclosure.[28]

Another incident of intrusion by Russia relates to ROSAT. This exploratory satellite was a joint project of Germany, UK and the US launched on 1 June 1990. It was an Astro-physics explorer for X-ray imaging for the study of low-surface brightness and low- resolution spectroscopy. On 25 April 1998, failure of primary star tracker led to a pointing error which made it move towards the Sun causing solar overheating. ROSAT was made operational again but with performance deficiency in tracking and control. This satellite was once again severely damaged on 20 September 1998, when a reaction wheel attained maximum rotational speed and went beyond design parameters causing damage. Both instances happened due to inexplicable reasons.

Later, in 2008, NASA investigators in a study found that the ROSAT failure was linked to a cyber-intrusion. It was further reported that the cyber-attack was directed from Russia. The hostile intrusion compromised NASA computers that, directly or indirectly, affected "command and control codes".[29] Thus, security of the system was breached and the attack was successful in intended interference. It was further reported in the Blog that this was not an isolated or singular cyber-action but that NASA had been subjected to a series of such attacks, mostly with indiscernible impact.[30]

Ergo, given the versatility, reach and proliferation of cyber technology, its abuse is increasing as much as its friendly use. Permit me to add a caveat that this dream technology may not turn into a nightmare because tomorrow's terrorists may, possibly, be able to do more damage with a keyboard than a bomb; and in outer space, the possible disaster may embark on the Kessler effect to become an existential threat to humanity. Thus, 'the cyber-space' has become a global menace and circumstances necessitate global vigilance by all stakeholders in cyber-space viz., international community, state governments, business sector and the civil society.

---

[26] Nicu Popescu and Stanislav Secrieru, eds., *Hacks, Leaks and Disruptions: Russian Cyber Strategies*, (Chaillot Papers), European Union Institute for Security Studies, Paris, 2018.

[27] Ibid.

[28] Refer Meg King & Sophie Goguichvili, "Cybersecurity Threats in Space: A Roadmap for Future Policy", a Blog in *STIP & Cybersecurity*, October 8, 2020.

[29] Bruce Schneier, "Cyber-Attacks Against NASA", a Blog dated December 4, 2008.

[30] Ibid.

However, the zeal for vigilance should respect privacy, not cramp freedom nor compromise anonymity yet clamp its misuse and abuse in any form and by any or all. Cyber can be a multi-headed hydra requiring tight regulation and strict control. Freedom carries with it responsibility which cannot be abdicated under any circumstances. Therefore, this amiable compromise of contras and correlatives flags the need for an international protocol on Search and Seizure of hardware, software and the relevant data for a proper investigation that should be followed by judicial trial and punishment, duly resolving the hassles of legal procedures, jurisdiction and extradition. Deterrent punishment may yield better assurance of security and avoidance of recurrence.

6.4 Space Crimes with Directed Energy Technologies

The past 50 years have seen rapid technological change that has fundamentally shifted the boundaries of human possibility, enabling radical improvements in neo-productivity, novel scientific advances, and the advent of both new communities and new divisions within society. These changes have yielded a rapid inflow of information and knowledge and forced transformation of mental fixations, the operational structure of business and the core tenets of competitiveness thereby creating a host of new challenges and corresponding opportunities for research and development as also for consideration and cogitation by the strategists and policymakers.

One needs no spell of clairvoyance to envision the complexion of the next wave of space crimes. Over a period of time, other technologies that are dual in purpose or bear mischief-effect have been developed. These are fast gaining pin-point precision with digital support and can be used to commit crimes in outer space and on celestial bodies. The latest trend in research and development is towards Directed Energy technologies which have shown dual-use: for peaceful purposes as also for space weaponry. Thus, Directed Energy Weapons (DEW) have been developed for diverse purposes, range and targets. The earliest recorded use of a directed energy weapon, named ALKA, has been in Libya by Turkey in August 2019.[31] Such and other weapons of this genre are under development in the US,[32] Russian Federation, the UK[33] and India.[34]

A directed-energy weapon (DEW) is a ranged weapon that damages or kills its target with highly focused energy, including lasers (Light Amplification by Simulated

---

[31] From Wikipedia.

[32] Amy Thompson, "Atlas V rocket launches NASA laser communications prototype and Space Force experiments into orbit", *SPACE.com,* December 7, 2021. This experiment in long-range communications is a game-changer in scientific exploration on the moon and the Mars.

[33] From Wikipedia.

[34] P Raja, "DRDO plans Star Wars-style weapons for battles of future", *The Times of India,* September 14, 2020. (India News page).

Emission of Radiation),[35] microwaves (e.g., Active Denial System for personnel), magnetic plasma (e.g., MARAUDER), particle beam (bolt or stream of neutral or charged particles) for endo and exo-atmospheric uses, and acoustic or sound beams (e.g., LRAD). Potential applications of these technologies include weapons that target personnel, missiles, vehicles, optical devices and operational systems. Another line of technology under continued development aims to "blind and deafen" the enemy to gain advantage in action and war. Its application to the space domain may not be far behind.

This brief allusion to the directed energy weapons of space crime, as a generic reference, need elaboration on their modus and impact. Take for example, Microwave beams discharge heat and energy. This technology yields extensive peaceful uses. Plans are on the anvil to construct space electrical stations (SPS) in geosynchronous orbit to constantly tap Sun's energy and transmit the same to ground stations on the Earth to be fed into international grids for use as electrical power. It is likely to provide a cheap, competitive source of clean, green energy that will be conducive to global climate change. But micro-wave weaponry is primarily targeted to personnel with a reaction to heat up the body in order to dry up liquids in the blood streams. This stops circulation of blood leading to death.

Particle beams is another technology that can help rocket propulsion. In fact, rockets are momentum machines that get propulsion from the mass so ejected. In conventional rockets, fuel is chemically combined to provide energy and the exhaust is ash. Further, since rockets work on power-to-weight ratio, it will help if the function of energy is removed from the spacecraft and is beamed from a ground source. The beam transmitted could be either pulsed or continuous. The advantage is clear and peaceful. Yet this foliating technology can offer applications that may be devastating in effect and lethal in impact. In a malicious act, particle beams can be used to bore a hole in the hardware of a space object to cause leak in the internal pressure and penetrate further to damage the working systems. The dangers are real and minatory.

6.4.1 Applications of LASER Technology

Electronic and Directed Energy (LASER) emits high-energy beam that can cause burns and skin damage to humans, and a very intense one, may even cause death. If such beam is directed towards a satellite or an aircraft, it may damage, render dysfunctional or even cause a crash. Lasers are a cross-domain device with potential to operate from any domain to any other domain. With this versatility in use and ease in operation, if this technology freely remains in human hands, without proper control or strict regulation, it can play havoc and induce chaos with crimes in outer space domain.

---

[35] A project undertaken by the US under Strategic Defence Initiative (SDI) of 1980's involved space-based X-Ray Lasers. In all probability, development of this project has been shelved.

At the same time, laser devices and weapons yield several advantages over conventional weaponry. First, these devices can be used discreetly because radiation does not generate sound and can as well be in invisible spectrum. Secondly, light is unaffected by gravity, windage and other forces which trait imparts it an almost perfectly flat trajectory. Thirdly, Lasers travel at the speed of light and have long range, thus, have proved themselves useful in peaceful applications for communications as also other uses in the space domain. Fourthly, lasers potentially eliminate, or at least minimise, logistic problems of supply and carriage of requisite material or weaponry and therefore, are easier to operate and cheaper in transportation over extra-long distances. Lastly, lasers provide an in-built self-destruct technology for defunct, dysfunctional or damaged satellites that may be used discreetly. Considering the above-mentioned advantages and also exponential growth of allied technologies, radical disruptions in space activities are possible and seem likely to accelerate in the near future and almost seamlessly penetrate the space domain with its adverse bonding. This could be a daunting scenario of imponderables.

Nevertheless, Lasers can be specifically and usefully adapted for peaceful purposes. An initiative called, Peaceful Use of Lasers in Space (PULS) has caught fancy of the international community[36] and several proposals are floating to harness laser technology for advancement of human welfare as well as progress of the Sustainable Development Goals espoused by the UN.[37] Thus, PULS initiative will usefully aid in ensuring orbital safety of satellites on which we vitally depend for our daily communication activities, all types of navigation and traffic management, as also command and control actions, on and from the Earth. So, lasers can help dramatically improve intelligence gathering, surveillance and speed of communications. This technology can also be useful in observation of treaty compliances, benefit in debris removal from outer space and also act as an effective early warning instrument to protect the Earth from collision with dangerous asteroids by deflecting the latter's orbital path.[38]

Another commendable initiative has been taken by the science fraternity urging its members to undertake research for peaceful applications of lasers in space particularly stressing on scientific exploration, asteroid deflection and space debris removal. In this direction, scientists have passed and signed, "Declaration on Peaceful Use of Lasers in Space, 2018." The declaration acknowledges that lasers can be used to adversely affect critical assets in space which are so vital for our daily chores and interconnected lives. It also flags the trend towards constellations of mega satellites in numbers and micro in size while highlighting it as a cause for escalating debris which can be removed by lasers. The Declaration, therefore, addresses the problem and prods for pooling of scientific resources, knowledge-fund and research capabilities in cooperation as responsible stakeholders for the betterment of humanity.

---

[36] Conference Report of *Prague Laser SpaceApps Workshop,2019,* held from 25-27 September, 2019.

[37] Report to the UNSC on *Responsible Use of Lasers in Space*, published by the UN Office of Disarmament, May 2021.

[38] "Asteroid Deflection, Fact Not Fiction", *The Times of India*, December 4, 2021, p. 16.

6.4 Space Crimes with Directed Energy Technologies

Further, laser-induced remote-analysis of space resources can unlock cislunar economy and provide impetus to expansion of human commercial activities into space. Lasers can also help us reach relativistic speeds for extending the range of communications in deep space with the cleanest space engine i.e., light. Same way, lasers can shoot data to the Earth fast and almost in real-time. Also, it can be used to beam clean power to the Earth to supplement efforts towards reducing carbon emissions from power generation and thus stall climate change. This is the dire need of humanity, today.

However, all these visions to materialise and become real require transparent, benign and inclusive governance as also trusting and sincere cooperation of all stakeholders to harness synergy. On the other hand, to check misuse and abuse of such technologies, it would need three-tiers: regulation, control and supervision. At the base, business should behave responsible and ethical to develop and market peaceful applications to peaceful people; states should supervise space-worthiness of production, legitimacy of usage and transfer of technology; and at the international level a broad oversight by a Technology Commission co-opting scientists and technologists from different countries.

Consequent to dual-use applications, many of the susceptibilities of and consequences of the directed energy and electronic devices may be equated with war weaponry and rated as instruments of strategy or triggers of race for superiority in such capabilities. In this role, DEW is in principle or by inference prohibited by the various treaty provisions under Space Law[39] or specific international instruments.[40] Nevertheless, possibility of threats is apparent because specificities can be breached by specious arguments and legal loopholes that may be set up to escape criminality and liability unless suitably plugged and sealed with a *specialis* treaty.

The author is conscious of the travails connected with treaty negotiations, yet the dreaded impact of contingent possibilities solicit attention for resolution of weaknesses through a 'prohibitory' international treaty, in tandem, supported by an institutional governance and judicial mechanism to tackle breaches. The potential of serious threats with ominous consequences, in the future, can be discounted or ignored only at our own existential peril. Apparently, the suggestion for an international treaty may appear an extreme grandstanding proposal, so often proffered, but in reality, seems a realist and pragmatic solution to an ominous challenge.

Perhaps, another supporting option would be to find a viable solution to tackle such crimes at the national level by amending local legal codes. Advantages would be that evidence would be easy to find and investigate as also apprehend the criminal, seize of the competent jurisdiction and institute trial for punishment. Suitable national laws can help achieve this objective, yet it would need positive political will, cooperation of states and a sincere judicial process to deter potential offenders and punish the actual criminals. Space-faring nations would be able to appreciate this necessity in better perspective and would be voluntarily impelled to take adequate action. The US and Japan are already looking in this direction and have initiated legislative action.

---

[39] Outer Space Treaty, 1967, Article IV.

[40] For example, Comprehensive Test Ban Treaty, 1996.

6.5 Advances in Artificial Intelligence

The next wave of crimes in space domain, though would depend upon the nature, character and spread of space activities and space eco-system on the celestial bodies yet may involve technology beyond lasers and directed energy devices. Attacks from co-orbital satellites with digital, hacker and jammer capabilities may also appear on centre-stage of space conflicts and artificial intelligence makes such attacks precise and accurate. However, as yet there are no publicly documented record of satellite-to-satellite hostile techno-attacks.

In fact, artificial intelligence (AI) is the mother-science of all cyber technologies and robotic developments; while its own independence and freedom are non-negotiable and non-comprisable. Artificial intelligence relates to planning, vision, learning, reasoning, speech, language etc., by machines and to embed them with methods for good decision-making and solution-finding, evolve algorithms capable for making plans and for reasoning under uncertainty on complex problems. Thus, AI is becoming a ubiquitous tool in search engines, content recommendation, fraud detection, as digital assistants, smart speakers and in self-driving cars.[41] In fact, artificial intelligence visionaries predict a weird future where human beings will either become superfluous or "will need to add an artificial intelligence layer to the human brain itself. The future, it appears, is cyborg."[42]

Notably, future improvements in artificial intelligence will tend towards visual perception, understanding of language and machine translation. This technology has usefully entered space systems and is facilitating operations and ground control. Further, the necessity for and provision of AI in space applications, control of satellite systems and space robots are ever increasing and becoming almost indispensable. Robots as off-spring of AI have already established their presence, potential and utility. ISS has since deployed robots for routine work but their tasks could expand to more intelligent and risky duties with experience and learning.

Another branch of technology that could be of concern comprises cyber, laser and allied applications which may induce banal interruption in satellite systems or create dysfunction in space objects to defeat their mission-objective and thus hamper or sabotage space activities. The peculiar characteristic of cyber-attacks is that these can be launched from any platform or domain and the offending attacker may remain anonymous or hidden or at least difficult to track with certainty and enough legal proof. Such eventualities may evoke normative behaviour from all stakeholders. But soft law may not work well because the crime must be seen through the prism of positive and enforceable law.[43] Hence, the evil may be warded off by deterrence and

---

[41] An interview of Stuart Russel by Srijana Mitra Das, "AI can bring a golden age to humanity-but only if we have humble machines" in *The Times of India*, March 13, 2021, Times Evoke columns, p. 12.

[42] "The Weird Future", *The Times of India*, June 5, 2016, editorial column.

[43] Thomas Wischmeyer and Timo Rademacher, eds., *Regulating Artificial Intelligence*, Springer, 2020.

actualities well handled with the suggested solutions proffered. Thus, we can use today to script tomorrow that we want to hand over to posterity.

6.6 Crimes by Robots

Robots are an application of and development from artificial intelligence and thus, bear and display pre-programmed behaviour. And as such their behavioural crimes would be programme errors or digital bugs. Therefore, there are different rules of conduct and control for robots. Moreover, robots cannot be punished in the same way as humans while manufacturers and programmers escape liability under exceptions and exemptions. Certain rudimentary rules are, in place but their modification is under reconsideration. For our purpose, we will deal with crimes by humans only, in whatever capacity or authority, in whatever manner, with whatever devices or platform and from outer space or on celestial bodies.

Robots are a creation of human wisdom and modern technology and, at best, are humanoid mates. These are generally tasked to perform jobs that are dull and dirty or chores that are routine and repetitive. But these have also been effectively deployed in tasks that are dangerous in nature and action yet need precision in work. So, robots have been used in myriad applications in manufacturing spheres like automobiles, electronics, medicine and others. With progressive algorithmic learning, improvements and upgrades, training and experience, robots are expanding their territory and diversify their applications.

Another new area of 'deploy-bility' of robots is space-station for hazardous space-walks and on the celestial bodies for mechanical work and as space explorers. These can initially be put to do simple-motion jobs like wiping of railings and cleaning of switches, valves, knobs and other soft material inside the space-station, which is presently done by astronauts on every Saturday morning. This would, indeed, be a great help to save time and effort of the astronauts by working as their electronic surrogates. With time, familiarity and experience, these *Robonauts* can graduate the taskbars and undertake difficult and dangerous tasks relieving the astronauts from drudgery and hazards. This is one small step for a robot and a giant leap for the robotkind.

This option of humanoid mates in space and on celestial bodies offers several advantages. First, robots are highly dextrous, anthropometric machines. Their dexterity, mobility and control in task applications can even excel that of a suited and strapped astronaut. Secondly, robots are basically a machine whose requirements are fewer in terms of resources needed to sustain the. These do not need air, water, food nor do these require a narrow range of warm temperatures necessary for human astronauts or space workers. Thirdly, these do not need specialised and expensive space suits nor run the risk of hurt on exposures to the elements of space. Fourthly, robots accumulate no fatigue, except wear and tear, nor suffer pangs of separation from family and thus, are best suited for long duration space odysseys and protracted exploration. Fifthly, these can be remotely controlled and operated as required or work in autonomous pre-programmed mode for the mission. Lastly, robots in ultimate analysis, as machines costs $2.5 million apiece, are easily disposable or expendable and do not have to be brought back safely.[44] Thus, in comparison to human astronauts these would be cost-effective and life-saving, with least remorse in case of loss in dangerous operations or due to failure in recovery.

In fact, the first space robot, euphemistically called, Robonaut-2 (R2) has already visited ISS with astronaut Scott Kelly and has worked in the Destiny laboratory. At that time, President Obama had informed the ISS crew that you now have a new crew-mate to help in the Destiny Laboratory.[45] Thus, R2 is a pioneer of its kind like Gagarin for the historic flights for humans. But that is not to forget that dogs and chimps have preceded humans into the Earth orbit. R2 is a product from Oceaneering Space Systems, which is collaborating and working on the NASA project.[46] Research and development for the next generation of space robots is in progress which would enable optimised overlapping, dual arm dexterity, elastic joints and extended finger and thumb travel with miniaturised 6-axis load cells, hi-resolution cameras and infrared systems.[47] This would be a great improvement in precision task acceptance and higher accomplishments.

By their characteristics and capabilities, robots can also be deployed to commit crimes of almost any kind and anywhere as also in outer space and on the celestial bodies. But whatever be their acts of commission or omission, these shall remain pre-programmed robots, at best humanoid-bots, and can never become human or their equivalent thinkers or equally proficient workers. The reason is that man can think by himself to be prepared, anticipate moves and reactions better and visualise the scenario in total perspective. Anyway, a word of caution, let not technology race towards creating super-intelligent, super-human robots who can claim superiority or seniority over humans in some way. Instead, our endeavour should be towards creating humble machines that are uncertain about our orders or desires and modest enough to ask and clarify before executing.

There is, of course, a controversy that robots can become wiser than human beings because they learn from experience which remains an effective algorithm in their memory which may not have been experienced by the programmer or remembered in live-memory for coding. Even otherwise, though a peculiar looking electro-mechanical contraption yet many adore R2 for its cuteness and charisma as also it's being state of the art marvel. Some magnify its glory to deem it as replacement for the astronauts. This view seems disappointing and disillusioning because such comparisons are odious and unnatural thereby undermining the glorious achievements of the celebrated astronauts. More so, their undue exaltation may be dubbed a big psychological and existential let down for our species, the creators of robots.

---

[44] Refer Roger Launius and Howard McCurdy, *Robots in Space: Technology, Evolution and Interplanetary Travel,* (USA, 2008).

[45] Presidential Address to the ISS astronauts and Discovery crew members in 2009.

[46] News from BBC, published in *the Hindu,* April 26, 2011. http://www.thehindu.com/sci-tech/science/article1701981.ece?home.

[47] Ibid.

Nevertheless, R2 is tough, stoic and its relentless quest, into the deep outer space and forays as inquisitive space traveller on the celestial bodies, may exalt it as a hero of sorts.

Robots, however, broadly bear and display pre-programmed behaviour and as such their crimes would be programme errors or digital bugs. Therefore, there are different rules of conduct and control for robots. Moreover, robots cannot be punished in the same way as humans while manufacturers and programmers escape liability under exceptions and exemptions. Certain rudimentary rules are, in place but their revision is under consideration. For our purpose, we will deal with crimes by humans only, in whatever capacity or authority, in whatever manner or method, with whatever devices or platform, in and from outer space or on celestial bodies.

6.7 Rules of Conduct for Robots

Robots have been the creation of sci-fi movies and fiction writing but have to real existence with new technologies. By and large, these are pre-programmed to act and behave and thus are thus circumscribed in its activity by the intelligence and foresight of the programmer. Despite care and caution in software development, there have been instances where robots have harmed, injured and even killed humans, co-workers or others. And robots cannot be punished like humans while programmers escape liability or criminality under contractual exceptions and exemptions.

Nevertheless, certain general rules of robotics, to regulate the conduct of positronic robots, have been prescribed which are customarily accepted and almost universally abided by. These are the three fundamental rules of Isaac Asimov. First law, a robot may not injure a human being or, through inaction, allow a human being to come to harm. Second law, a robot must obey the orders given to it by human beings except where such orders would conflict with the First Law. Third law, a robot must protect its own existence as long as such protection does not conflict with the First Law or Second Law.[48] Over time, however, these have been found to be insufficient and Asimov added a Zeroth Law which states that a robot may not harm humanity, or, by inaction, allow humanity to come to harm.[49] This was primarily an ethical framework for sentient machines that were smarter than human beings, in a fictional setting and devised situations. No wonder, loopholes and contradictions were artificially created in the plot to demonstrate conflict. But this fiction revealed the spectre of singularities where machines become more intelligent than humans.

A few more additional laws for robotics are stated here for better understanding despite this subject being out of purview of this book. For example, Lyuben Dilov, in 1974, enunciated a new law of robotics which requires, "A robot must establish its

---

[48] Asimov, Isaac, "Introduction" to *The Rest of the Robots*, Doubleday, 1964. (ISBN 0-385-09041-2). Also refer *Handbook of Robotics, 2058 AD*, 56th edition.

[49] Asimov, Isaac, *In Memory Yet Green*. Doubleday, (1979). (ISBN 0-380-75432-0).

identity as a robot in all cases." His justification was that modern designer psycho-robots have human-like form and feel and this rule is necessary for identification and confirmation.[50] Another rule propounded by Nikolai Kesarovski demands, "A robot must know it is a robot". This was necessitated by a storyline in which a human victim was killed by a hug from a humaniform robot that did not identify itself as such.

Satya Nadella has propounded that artificial intelligence "must be designed to assist humanity, be transparent, maximise efficiency and protect privacy."[51] In addition to these main objectives, robots must respect human autonomy and privacy and must not carry any bias in their actions. Again, robots must maximise synergistic efficiencies without hurting the dignity of humans. So also, technology industry should not dictate the values and virtues of the future and must bear algorithmic accountability and functional flexibility so that "humans can undo unintended harm."[52]

There are, however, several ambiguities and loopholes in the programmed logic of robots and the rules so framed that one can get away with murder, literally. No wonder, these can be and have been deployed to commit crimes with the actual criminal hiding leagues away from the site and leaving hardly any traces of evidence for accusation. Defence and business strategists have also used these contraptions for espionage, intellectual piracy and business or industrial interruptions. So, there is a good and a bad side to this coin and intention determines the result. The same can be expected to permeate in relation to space activities and human habitations on celestial bodies. Thus, robots can be skilfully used in the outer space environment. Hence, space crimes with robots may not be far behind.

Nevertheless, software programmers believe that the intelligence of robots can be significantly improved by introducing algorithms of cultural perspectives and human values. These can impart them the capability for ethical evaluation of their own conduct or ensuing activity by ensuring differentiation of good and bad before the act.[53] In further advancement, software engineers of modern applications claim that machines can learn morals. And accordingly, researchers in artificial intelligence have designed a programme to make moral judgments. They call it Delphi, after the religious oracle that was consulted by the ancient Greeks.[54] As a programme, Delphi is a neural network which is a mathematical system loosely modelled on the web of neurons in the brain.

It is a first step towards making AI systems more ethically informed, socially aware and culturally inclusive", said Yejin Choi, the leader of the project at the University

---

[50] Introduced by Lyuben Dilov in his novel, *Icarus's Way* (a.k.a., The Trip of Icarus), 1974.
[51] "Satya Nadella sets rules for Artificial Intelligence", *Times of India,* July 5, 2016.
[52] Ibid.
[53] "Killer robots aren't science fiction. Push to ban them is growing", *The Times of India*, December 19, 2021, Sunday Supplement, p. 4 (Global Times).
[54] Cade Metz, "Can machines learn morals? Ask Delphi" in *The Times of India,* (Chandigarh edition), November 28, 2021, Sunday Times, p.8.

of Washington.[55] Researchers concede that Delphi is by turns fascinating, frustrating and disturbing because evaluation is on whose morality (Tribal, medieval or modern) or whose ethics (religious, business or scholarly). In fact, concept of morality is as knotty for a machine as it is for human beings. To neutralise the variations, Delphi learned its moral compass by analysing more than 1.7 million ethical judgments by real live humans. Despite the colossal effort, in the ultimate, it "can be as flawed as the people who create them."[56] Therefore, vibes about this software are not yet settled and some "found the system woefully inconsistent, illogical and offensive."[57] In the end, one can conclude with a wise thought and a valid lament from Isaac Asimov, "The saddest aspect of life right now is that science gathers knowledge faster than society gathers wisdom.

6.8 Space Crimes with Anti-Satellite Technology

So far, only a few countries have developed anti-satellite technology and have tested it in space to destroy their own satellites under the pretext of non-functional object that may hazard smooth and safe orbiting of functional satellites and other space activities. The logic is laudable but the truth behind the action may be different or loaded with secrecy. Same way, incidental consequences of the tests have caused and created considerable debris that may take a long time to descend and get incinerated in the atmosphere. Whatever be the explanations from each country, the threshold of sustainable space environment has been disturbed. Hence, international opinion should veer around that such action in the future be deemed as a near-crime as also crime against humanity.

Historically, the US was first to set the scene for ASAT tests and the first attempt was made in June 1959 when the Bold Orion rocket was launched from a B-52 bomber that targeted the dead US Explorer-4 satellite. The rocket only got to within 4 miles of Explorer-4 proving that it was indeed difficult to strike an orbiting satellite. Future efforts were stalled in this direction. Concurrently, the Soviet Union had also tried to create ASAT capability through the sixties of the last century and was the first to succeed in an ASAT test in the destruction of an orbiting asset. It was in February 1970. But further trials were discontinued unilaterally on a realisation that, in the bargain, they had destroyed their own costly assets both ways and it was doubly expensive. Another justification to this stoppage was the unnecessary creation of unwanted debris in the outer space environment contrary to the then mandate under Article IX of the OST.

China was the first to again start a chain reaction on ASAT tests. In 2007, China destroyed by an ASAT vehicle its own unwanted, Fengyun-IC weather satellite in polar orbit at an altitude of 865 km. The destruction of the satellite caused a cloud

---

[55] Ibid.
[56] Ibid.
[57] Ibid.

of nearly 3200 particles in space at an orbit from where it may take centuries to lose altitude and incinerate in the atmosphere. There was great resentment and condemnation worldwide including that voiced by the US. But just a year later, in 2008, in an ostentatious display of technological advancement, the US, also conducted a repeat experiment since 1985. This act also caused a cluster of debris in space; and was as reprehensible and detrimental to the space environment as the earlier one by China. Misdemeanour had occurred.

Over a decade later, in 2019, India conducted a similar, successful ASAT trial in a show of techno-prowess by engaging its own target-satellite at an altitude of 300 km. This was "Mission Shakti" accomplished by Defence Research & Development Organisation (DRDO) of India as its first exo-atmosphere interceptor. Prime Minister Modi defended the mission as one showcasing the wealth of Indian talent in space industry. This success put India in league with other three, the US, Russia and China. Despite the prestige gained, this experiment also caused space debris though on a much lesser scale and at a much lower altitude. This should be no consolation nor justification. Nevertheless, an indiscreet act polluting the space environment had occurred and it attracted even more vociferous condemnation. Russia even proposed a complete ban on ASAT tests in space but the proposal did not attract many votaries.[58] However, this was not the end of tests.

Again, not to be left behind, Russia in April 2020, conducted the latest of their practice launches for the new anti-ballistic defence system A-235, popularly known as Nudol. The missile splashed down 3000 kms away in the pre-notified area. No objects were hit by the interceptor missile.[59] Whatever be the intention, the developed defence system can legitimately be said to have attained the threshold and a capability to operate as an anti-satellite system too. These are just the bald and unconfirmed facts about the incident, available in public domain.[60]

Russia actually carried out an Anti-satellite weapon test on 16 November 2021. The weapon targeted an old Russian spacecraft, Tselina-D, which was non-functional and was in orbit since 1982. Russia has accepted conducting this test which hit the target with "razor-sharp precision".[61] This test has generated a debris field of nearly 1500 pieces of different sizes in low-earth orbit which may endanger the International Space Station and may pose risk to space activities for years. Anyway, the Russians have assured that the debris cloud is being monitored by the Soviet warning system to prevent and counter all possible threats.[62] Nevertheless, ASATs have proved their proficiency as a kinetic weapon of attack on satellites in the outer space and the achievement is portentous with threatening ramifications. No wonder,

---

[58] Helen Ntabeni, "The curious tale of the ASAT Test that was'nt", published April 23, 2020 in *Quora Digest*. The author is LL.M., presently at Northumbria University.

[59] Ibid.

[60] Ibid.

[61] A report from Moscow, "'Razor-sharp precision': Russia hails anti-satellite weapon test", *The Times of India*, (Chandigarh edition), November 17, 2021, Chandigarh Times Supplement, p. 4.

[62] Ibid.

the competitive race is still in progress and the latest test was a Russian reaction against establishing of American Space Command in 2020.

Kinetic-impactor technology has advanced great leaps and the US, in a demonstration of the power of engineering and science, has successfully impacted the orbit of a small asteroid by its Double Asteroid Redirection Test (DART) on 27 September 2022.[63] The impactor was aimed at 160-m-wide asteroid Dimorphos, which was orbiting a larger asteroid Didymos, both of which were circling the Sun, 11.2 million kilometres away from the Earth. DART was a test mission to see if this technique, known as kinetic impactor, would give the necessary 'nudge' to an asteroid and alter its course. After a study of its new deflected course for over ten days, it has been confirmed by NASA that the orbit of Dimorphos has indeed been altered as desired. It is not unlikely that intoxicated by the success and accuracy of this experiment, the US may attempt similar exercise nearer Earth that may go awry under the Murphy's law. Anyway, the U.S. is not alone striding in this direction. China also has a plan to deflect a 40 m wide, Earth-crossing asteroid named 2020PN1 by 2026.[64] Despite the proven technology and safe distances from the Earth, there exist imponderable risks.

Be that as it may, all these ASAT-capable countries have caused pollution in space environment by unwanted and unnecessary space debris that may pose hazards of collision to the operation of useful and functional space satellites for a long time to come. The use of this technology is asymmetric globally and limited to only a few countries who should be deemed responsible for this specific pollution. These states should also be held liable for its removal, if not specifically their own dispersion, it may be restricted to an estimate of equal quantum otherwise or monetary payment for their share of outsourced debris-removal services.

Time is ripe to consider and develop modalities to apply the principles of "proportional responsibility" and "polluter pays principle",[65] as these have already crystallised in parleys on Climate Change and have found acceptance. Consensus on these can be effectuated in space law when the process of scavenging of outer space becomes a technically feasible operation and can be outsourced by the proposed Space Utilisation and Sustenance Regulatory Authority (SUSRA), once established.[66] Concurrently, states may develop an international legal instrument to declare ASAT tests, threats of use and anti-satellite attacks in outer space domain as crimes *erga omnes* to minimise the scourge of escalating space debris and eliminate existential or collateral risks to other space objects.

---

[63] "Smash hit: On NASA's Double Asteroid Redirection Test" *The Hindu*, October 15, 2022, editorial page.

[64] *The Hindu*, ibid.

[65] Opinion on this principle has crystallised in Climate Change parleys.

[66] For more details refer Chapter on Appraisal and Solutions.

6.8.1 A Real-Check of Technologies

Having scripted the negative potential and the dark side of the latest and advancing technologies with potential for applications in or reach to outer space, it will be wise to attempt a real-check of their potential threats and dangers. Of course, many states are striving for digital leadership through digital strategy. Believably, most of the projects mentioned above are on the anvil and at different stages of completion and operationalisation. But some are still at a nascent stage of development or in experimental phase. Thus, it is as yet uncertain as to when and which ones of these will be ready for deployment as practical space systems, high performance tools of crimes or operational military weapons. Nonetheless, the mischief element of DEW and similar potential of other cognate beamed applications to cause destruction of or damage to space objects, their systems and facilities is becoming pronounced and menacing. As also operationalisation of robots and proving of ASATs pose respective dangers.

However, the assuring aspect is that not all of these technologies are attack-worthy and fit for committing crimes in the space domain. In fact, most of the technologies discussed are at diverse stages of design perfection, hardware development, practical demonstration and operational use. Apart from developmental asymmetry these have a lot of shortcomings yet to be tackled for perfect operational usage. Some of these weaknesses that need attention to detail are discussed below.

First, the outer space is so expansive that the practical distances involved are in millions of miles, if not astronomical for crimes to happen. This makes constant tracking of a desired target difficult. This problem is further accentuated because the object-target also moves at high speed in space, so its continued tracking and chasing are not easy and as a result necessary trajectory adjustment becomes difficult and inaccurate. This frailty needs devoted improvement with selective thrusts in research.

Secondly, most of the directed-energy or beam devices require a high-power source to cause the bursts and thereafter the source depletes its energy and needs recharging as a huge power-bank. With the existing metals and materials for such compacted storage in requisite power is as yet not possible. Nor is the technology for quick replenish-charge sufficiently advanced for reasonably sustained operations. Thus, compact and light-weight storage of power and concentrated fast-recharge facilities matching to the intended purpose show vulnerabilities and still need honing.

Thirdly, the use of kinetic devices aimed at a target in outer space, with criminal designs cannot be initiated at random or in immediacy. These need a window of opportunity for launch because of the hazards of space situational conditions. Even peaceful launches wait for an opportune time for safe transit to the host object. The persistent problem is the scatter and density of debris at certain orbits and the orbiting constellations of satellites which must provide safe clearance to penetrate in order to reach the target for damage or destruction. The imponderables are many in the way to commit a crime.

Despite the physical availability and operational readiness of the devices, the comforting feeling is that almost all these have grown out of peaceful technologies and only lend themselves to dual-uses. So, the criminal use of these is "bannable" with deterrence of punishment on commission by the criminal using such undesirable option. It needs to be educated that the application of these devices may lead to an existential threat to humanity where even the criminal may not survive. The scenario could be dismal and suicidal for all, at worst. Wisdom lies with us to choose our actions wisely and in service of humanity.

Chapter 7
Jurisdictional Issues: An Analysis

7.1 Jurisdiction: General Discussion

Jurisdiction is a multi-effect word used with different meaning or technical context and hence should be taken with utmost caution. A vague idea may tempt to misuse this word because it can acquire variable meaning that could be misleading. Sometimes, it simply connotes territory or jurisdiction of the court or of the country. But more specifically in our context, "jurisdiction refers to powers exercised by a state over persons, property, or events."[1] Further, powers of the state are trifurcated between legislature, executive, and judiciary with respective jurisdiction. And then states have extra-territorial jurisdictions like embassies, ships, aircrafts, or spaceships so registered in the country and launched, flying or sailing with its flag.

In this context and meaning, jurisdiction as universally recognised is "that states are competent, in general, to punish all crimes committed within its territory" and takes cognisance of "the place where the crime is consummated."[2] This sovereign right necessarily bestows absolute and exclusive territorial jurisdiction for the maintenance of law and order within the realm and the preservation of peace. And any limitation, if imposed, would prejudicially compromise the sovereignty of the state. "The same view [of unqualified acceptance of territorial competence] is held [and preached] by numerous distinguished commentators"[3] and law glossators.

International law mostly consists of prohibitions and denials and as such it imposes certain limitations on the jurisdiction of municipal courts from deciding cases contrary to the provisions of the ratified treaties. In general, though, it neither forbids nor requires municipal courts to hear particular cases yet aggrieved parties

---

[1] Michael Akehurst, *A Modern Introduction to International Law*, Third edition, London, George Allen & Unwin, 1977, p. 103.

[2] Satya Dev Bedi, *Extradition in International law and Practice*, Rotterdam, Bronder-Offset, 1966, p. 60.

[3] Bedi, ibid, p. 63. For example, refer G Schwarzenberger, *A Manual of International Law*, 4th edition, London, 1960, chapter 3. Also refer L Oppenheim, *International Law*, 8th edition, London, 1958, Vol. I, para 123, p. 286. Words in parentheses added for clarity and understanding.

to judgments ignoring established international law obligations can seek remedies through competent international institutions. In nutshell, international law imposes no restrictions on the jurisdiction of courts in civil matters, yet it places limited restraint on jurisdiction of municipal courts relating to criminal cases having international implications or those for prosecution under International Human Rights and Humanitarian laws.

However, in relation to outer space, the connotation of jurisdiction may have to be fine-tuned to adjust to *lex lata* pertaining to the space domain. Accordingly, a definition of the term jurisdiction provided by a Soviet scholar, Malkov put focus on the aspects of competence to assert and carry out legislative and judicial authority as also executive control over persons, and objects, which are in outer space and on the celestial bodies.[4] Here, the word control has limitation because persons and objects may not remain under control for all times while in space. There can be defiance of authority by personnel in space while space object may go rogue or zombie and thus out of control. Nevertheless, theoretically this definition may be acceptable because such control is a right of the state.

Incidentally, the topic of extradition is also related to jurisdiction but is not a substantive part of this topic. Extradition is more of a procedural remedy for obtaining justice and to bring the culprit under competent jurisdiction. Accordingly, this topic has been relegated for discussion in the next chapter on Legal Procedures.

7.2 Examples of Crimes with Jurisdictional Issues

7.2.1 Anne McClain Case

In order to analyse and determine jurisdiction in specific cases, the wrongdoing must first be tested on the dichotomy of domestic laws and international law to find the most appropriate forum. For example, the presumed offence, in the case of Anne McClain, had occurred in the registered American quarters of the ISS by an American astronaut making unauthorised use of American official equipment and privileged working system and against an American citizen.[5] Thus, it could tantamount to breach of ISS Crew Code of Conduct (CCoC) and violation of privacy laws of the US. Apparently, it looks a simplistic case of domestic jurisdiction and unreservedly, is the US concern, covered entirely by the US law. So, has opined Michelle Hanlon,

---

[4] Malkov, an article in Russian, 2002, cited from Aleksander S Milanov, International Legal Regulation of Space Debris and the Protection of Outer Space Environment, Thesis submitted to OP Jindal Global University, 2022, (unpublished), p. 88.

[5] Anne McClain, the astronaut, has been cleared of the charges by NASA after a lengthy investigation. Further, in a twist to the case, the accuser spouse, Summer Worden, has since been declared the accused and held guilty of making false statements in official investigations. Whatever be the outcome, this case serves as an illustration of crimes in outer space and compels us to identify the shortcomings of the germane law and the institutional system for dispensation of justice.

a space law expert, in an interview to *The Verge*.[6] But we certainly need to search for the relevant legal moorings even for such an obvious deductive answer.

In fact, governance of the respective ISS modules and control over astronauts and personnel within the ISS are regulated by an international treaty called the Intergovernmental Agreement (IGA) on Space Station Cooperation[7] that was signed on 29 January 1998.[8] The Agreement is between the governments of fifteen partners of space station, though major ones are USA, Russia (erstwhile USSR), European Space Agency, Canada, and Japan. The IGA is a fairly comprehensive document and is supported and supplemented by interagency bilateral Memorandum of Understanding between NASA as one party and Roscosmos (Russia), European Space Authority (ESA), Canadian Space Authority (CSA) and JAXA (Japan Exploration Authority) as the other parties, respectively.

The basic provision that permits a partner country "control and jurisdiction" over its nationals and equipment stationed in ISS in orbit would have to be based on a back-to-back agreement to recompense the repercussions under any treaty. Competent provision is articulated in Article 5 of the IGA. In amplification of this umbrella clause, this document includes a pertinent section on criminal jurisdiction under Article 22. The Agreement here concerns itself with this specific aspect and elaborates that the countries which are mentioned in the agreement may exercise criminal jurisdiction over their own assigned nationals in space, in the ISS or in flights, as long as their acts and actions do not adversely affect someone from another country. It is, however, silent on the prosecution of the alleged perpetrators in crimes involving other nationals, except, offering a valuable suggestion for consultation between concerned countries and responses under Mutual Legal Assistance through diplomatic channels for extradition or recovery of evidence.

In the instant case of McClain, which happened in the US module of the ISS, immediate relevance is drawn to the Agreement. The alleged crime was stated to have been committed by a US national in US quarters of the ISS, while handling US systems and using the US computer network. The complainant is also a US national with permanent residence in the USA and the cause of the grievance exists in the USA. The crime under consideration, therefore, directly evokes the provisions of the IGA for settlement of jurisdiction. The indictable cause accordingly falls within the domestic jurisdiction of the country and competent court in the USA may seize of the matter for adjudication.

Over the decades, with expanding space industry, launches are increasing in numbers and becoming capable of putting multiple satellites in orbit, space activities are becoming diverse in missions, gaining multiplicity of players with changing character towards commercial ventures whether for space tourism or commercial

---

[6] Mike Baker, "A divorce battle on Earth leads to 'first crime in space'", *The Times of India*, Chandigarh edition, August 24, 2019, pp. 1 and 14.

[7] https://www.gov/?wp-content/uploads/2019/02/12927-Multilateral-Space-Space-Station-1.29. 1998.pdf.

[8] The IGA was originally signed in 1988 and was re-signed with minor amendments and to include Russian Federation as a Party.

exploitation of celestial mineral resources. This escalating density and growing diversity due to technological advances can induce situations of dispute and crimes in space that could be more complicated and complex. At present, no specific rules are in place, internationally or nationally, in most space-faring countries, to handle offensive individual acts involving a matrix of multi-nationality offences and liability nuances.

The problems of this genre can aggravate due to privatisation of American quarters of the ISS. The US administration has already taken a decision in this regard and intends to cut the budget for its maintenance from 2024. Therefore, NASA has planned to muster resources by a phased opening of its ISS share to commercial opportunities and private usage. In fact, the IGA had envisaged such a contingency and under Article 1 that permits generic activities like space transportation of personnel and cargo, space tourism, space advertising, and commercial experiments. Therefore, NASA plans appear in consonance with the intent and spirit of IGA. Other aspects of applicable international law and relevance of treaty instruments relating to crimes in outer space have been discussed later in the chapter.

7.2.2 *Detection of Hole in Russian Module*

It was August 2018. The Russian vehicle, Soyuz MS-09, had flown three astronauts, Russian cosmonaut Sergey Prokopyev, European Space Agency astronaut Alexander Gerst, and NASA's Serena Auñón-Chancellor, to augment the existing crew strength at the ISS. Later, on 29 August 2018, ISS controllers at Johnson Space Centre, Houston, noticed a slight drop in pressure inside the orbiting laboratory. This variation was informed to the crew for investigation. The crew on internal inspection of the ISS traced the leak to a small hole in Russian Soyuz MS-09, which had docked to the station in June same year. The hole was patched up on 30 August 2018, with gauze and epoxy composite by astronaut Prokopyev, the then commander of the Soyuz. With this patch repair, the danger was averted.

Based on the inspection report from the ISS and repair procedure from the astronaut, the Russian authorities decided to investigate the reason for leak in the pressure and who could possibly have done the sabotage. An early report from Roscosmos announced that the breach in the Soyuz wall was a drill hole of the size 2 mm (0.08 inches), possibly made by a person with apparently "a faltering hand" because of the scuff marks nearby that likely resulted when the drill slipped. Russian officials "further insinuated that the unsteady hand was likely due to the culprit drilling in micro-gravity" implying that someone among the crew was to blame.[9] They also ruled out the suggested possibility of it happening at the assembly line or testing stages of the module prior to its launch.

---

[9] Amy Thompson, "Russian space officials try to blame NASA astronaut for Soyuz air leak in 2018: report", *Space.com*, August 14, 2021.

7.2 Examples of Crimes with Jurisdictional Issues

NASA, on the contrary, based on a video footage from the space station surveillance system, asserted that none of the US astronauts on the station were near the Russian segment where Soyuz vehicle was docked and the suggestive accusations are baseless. The Russians, however, did not accept this plea nor its basis and in reciprocal recrimination have brazenly claimed that the camera results could have been tampered with or doctored. The Russian official further alleged that they "were denied the chance to examine Russian tools and administer polygraphs, or lie detector tests, on the astronauts."[10]

The Russian media has gone far to pinpoint the suspicion on an American astronaut. The Russian news agency TASS reported that Serena Aunon-Chancellor had an emotional breakdown in space, and it was then that she caused the damage to the Russian spacecraft docked at the station so that she could return home to Earth ahead of schedule. NASA was upset at such personal attack on the astronaut and her medical history. Crewmates have strongly commented that the disclosures and accusations are not credible. They have lauded, "Serena is an extremely well-respected crew-member…and…we stand behind Serena and her professional conduct."[11]

In a latest statement, Roscosmos has confirmed that the investigation into "what or who" caused a hole has been completed. The possibility that a micro-meteoroid strike may have caused the hole is ruled out. Another possibility that it happened by error of a technician on the ground before the blast-off was also dismissed because that person would have tried to cover up the mistake by remedial measures. It is thus certain that the hole has been punctured with human effort and with the use of a drill machine which was in all likelihood available nearby. It also seems credible to assume that it was a work of shaking hands of an unstable mind in fear while doing the act. By elimination of motivation and evaluation of *mens rea*, the suspicion moves towards astronaut Serena who had "an acute psychological crisis" while onboard ISS "due to stress after an unsuccessful romantic relationship with another crew member."[12] As a result of this mental disturbance and disgruntled attitude, she possibly wanted to return home to the Earth earlier than scheduled and could have, in all probability, resorted to this unprofessional act. However, circumstantially derived assumptions may not turn out to be true, always.

The truth may not come out soon as NASA does not, as a matter of policy and privacy, make public comments on the professional conduct or personal life of the astronauts. In general, NASA has complimented her professional performance and defended her conduct. Mutual recrimination and diplomatic pressures, however, may go on as Roscosmos has threatened of criminal charges against a NASA astronaut. It is also stated that "All results of the investigation regarding the hole in the habitation module of the Soyuz MS-09 spacecraft [have been] transmitted to Law Enforcement

---

[10] Ibid.

[11] Ibid.

[12] Eric Berger, "Russia threatens criminal charges against a NASA astronaut", *Space.com*, November 30, 2021.

officials," who would "decide whether or not to initiate a criminal case which would be akin to issuing an indictment."[13]

Proven facts and presented circumstances proved the existence of a hole in Soyuz module where it should not be and posed danger. Thus, evidence makes it clear that an act equivalent to crime has been committed. Only the identity of the person who committed this act has not been established beyond reasonable doubt. Such a dilemma is often confronted in investigation of terrestrial crimes. But crimes in space should be less pardonable for their possible impact and accompanying consequences. Therefore, deterrent punishments are more important to instil fear to lessen the incidents of crimes. May be, because at times, the criminal may not survive the consequences of own act and jeopardise others.

This act of unprofessional conduct impacting safety of the ISS cannot be dismissed by impunity and for sheer lack of determinant evidence of the criminal. The matter seems serious and deserves fullest attention and efforts at investigation rather than ward off responsibility for vested reasons. This incident highlights possible aspects of space crime when the offender could be from one nationality, the locus falls in the jurisdiction of another state, and evidence is beyond the control of alleging state and is minimal to establish an indictment beyond reasonable doubt. Ergo, the problems for a fair trial become manifestly obvious.

The Russians have an option under "IGA for the ISS" and the relevant provision reads, "In a case involving misconduct [in] orbit that (a) affects the life or safety of a national of another Partner State or (b) occurs in or on or causes damage to the flight element of another Partner State, the Partner State whose national is the alleged perpetrator shall, at the request of any affected Partner State, consult with such State concerning their respective prosecutorial interests." Further, according to Article 22 (1) of IGA, states can invoke the nationality principle and can exercise criminal jurisdiction over its national, made out to be an offender, irrespective of the fact that the alleged offence has occurred in a module of the ISS controlled by another state. For amicable settlement, consultations with right mind and attitude can be fruitful. Besides, there could be further complexities in space crimes in future which should prod us to be prepared for eventualities rather than face an embarrassing predicament of *non-liquet*.

7.2.3 Negligence in the Nauka Case

The *Nauka*,[14] a multi-purpose module was designed to serve as a research laboratory, storage unit and airlock device to upgrade Russia's capabilities aboard the ISS. *Nauka* was launched, and it docked on the underside of the ISS, though under tense operations. Anyway, docking was successfully achieved on 29 July 2021 and was

---

[13] Refer https://arstechnica.com/science/2021/11/russia-threatens-criminal-charges-against-a-nasa-astronaut/. Verb in parentheses has been changed to suit context.

[14] *Nauka* is Russian language word for "science".

so confirmed by the concerned agency. After *Nauka* module had latched onto the space station and had well settled, the mission controllers in Moscow commenced performing some post-docking "reconfiguration" procedures[15] as per the protocol.

It was then that, suddenly and inexplicably, the thruster jets of *Nauka* module restarted and the mishap began. This malfunction resulted in the entire station to pitch out of its normal flight position compelling the US mission's flight director to declare a "spacecraft emergency."[16] The actual occurrence was that the space station spun one-and-a-half revolutions, i.e. about 540 degrees, before coming to a stop upside down, relative to its original position. The space station also lost altitude during this unexpected and unplanned manoeuvre. "The space station then did a 180-degree forward flip to get back to its original orientation."[17] This was achieved by the flight teams on the ground at the Johnson Space Centre in Houston, by activating thrusters on another module of the orbiting platform in corrective counteraction. *Nauka* engines were ultimately switched off.

The correction activity to regain control of the space station was a "tug of war" between the two modules. Initially, however, the incident was underplayed by both Roscosmos as well as NASA. But with more information flowing on the causes and assessments of possible impact, the US specialists fear to think of the event and accept that it was serious and could have caused a major mishap and consequent tragedy, human and material. At that moment there were seven astronauts on-board and at risk though escape module was available in readiness. Early reports inform that due to this glitch, the station was actually out of control for about two minutes while communication with all the seven members of the crew was lost or disrupted for several minutes.[18]

Russian space agency maintains and expects us to believe that the incident was caused "due to a short-term software failure and a command was mistakenly implemented" to fire the thruster engines. Inadvertence is possible, yet it would be naive to accept such a simplistic explanation for a goof-up of monumental dimension. In fact, who caused the malfunction, whether man or machine, is still to be determined with precision and finality. On the other hand, a preliminary inspection of the ISS, post-mishap, reports that in consequence, the space station would have certainly suffered undue stress on the structure and equipment. More revelations are expected.[19]

Be that as it may, it can be maintained that negligence in space operations, from space or on ground, is tantamount to crime. Every activity in and for space deserves due diligence of the highest order and actions in *abundanti cautela*. There is no scope for casualness or even inadvertence, leave aside sheer negligence or dereliction in

---

[15] "Space Station did 540-degree flip, turned upside down: Mishap more serious than earlier reported", *India Today*, August 3, 2021.

[16] *India Today*, ibid, updated report.

[17] *The New York Times*, August 3, 2021. Based on a statement by Zebulon Scoville, Flight Director at NASA's Mission Control Centre in Houston.

[18] Reporting and writing by Steve Gorman in Los Angeles and Polina Ivanova in Moscow. Editing by Mark Heinrich, Leslie Adler and Raju Gopalakrishnan for *News SCIENCE*.

[19] *India Today*, updated version of August 4, 2021.

duty. Space environment is potentially dangerous and highly hazardous; thus, it is unsparing in effect and rarely ever gives a second chance at survival. In this instance of presumed malfunction, luck was in our favour and providentially, things fell in place and in time to ultimately turn out right in action and result. Misconnections and defects so caused to the internal systems by the upheaval in the ISS may be set right in due course of time, but such a saviour opportunity may not repeat itself.

Hence, maximum care and caution are mandatory and imperative, else the crime and the criminal, both may vanish with much more at stake. The actual cause, whether by man or machine, may not be convincingly proved in this case or honestly accepted by the negligent party yet the dereliction tantamount to crime in space for its dimension and gravity. In *legito modo*, the *dolus,* in this instance, was of high magnitude, a gross fault equivalent to a bad intention or a patent crime. It, therefore, highlights the need for highest standards of due diligence and abundant caution in space activities. Saviour opportunities may not often repeat themselves in outer space because life is not always a matter of wishful choices.

Further, future crimes in space maybe more complicated and may bear intertwined complexities of survival; and attendant ramifications of jurisdiction which, at present, may be beyond our imagination and comprehension. With passage of time and greater experience in usage of outer space and celestial bodies, new genre of space crimes may open up. The causes may be diverse and indeterminate, yet, constituting ominous consequences with immeasurable risks causing threat to our survival. The situations may have to be diagnosed and prognosed. After all, as is wisely said, you cannot judge an injury from the size of the hole.

7.3 Jurisdiction Under Space Law

7.3.1 The Outer Space Treaty, 1967

Space Treaty also deals with the issue of jurisdiction though not directly from the angle of crimes in space. Their concern is more pertinent to the safety of astronauts and return of astronauts and space objects to the launching state or that of registered nationality. Thus, the principle of nationality is upheld and endorsed here for settlement of jurisdictional issues. However, their relevance to jurisdictional issues in space crimes can be validly invoked and legally applied to the extent of clarity or limitation.

Outer Space Treaty[20] (hereafter referred to as OST) offers a formula to decide on legal jurisdiction and executive control over the space object, space crew, and other personnel on-board spaceship, while in outer space, on a celestial body or return to the Earth. In concrete terms, the OST, as per Article VIII permits "A state…on whose registry an object launched into outer space is carried shall retain jurisdiction and

---

[20] Treaty on Principles Governing the Activities of States in the Exploration and Use of Outer Space, including the Moon and Other Celestial Bodies, 1967.

control over such object, and over any personnel thereof, while in outer space or on a celestial body." Further text of the clause of this article covers ownership of space objects and their components whether "in space or on a celestial body or by their return to the Earth." It, however, failed to provide national protective cover to the crew and other personnel on-board, on their return to the Earth. This specific lacuna in the treaty was soon realised and made up by an Agreement on Rescue and Return of Astronauts in 1968.[21]

The jurisprudence of ownership defines it as a bundle of rights *in rem*. Philosophically, it is not the property that is owned but the rights attached to it or accruing from its actuality.[22] And Austin emphasises the period of time and use related to a piece of property. The time-period covers indefinite in longevity that could last forever, and the use could be uninhibited in nature.[23] When unbundled, the rights comprise first, exclusive use of property in any manner or for any purpose in denial of the same to others; secondly, competence to discard the owned property or to destroy it. This right to ownership can be best illustrated by action of the states to destruct and destroy their own space object during anti-satellite test (ASAT). In this connection, we may allude to Cook who maintains that this right is not absolute and entails responsibilities, too.

An allied incident of ownership is the right to control its longevity in time-period and the nature of deployment or use of the property or a space object. It would seem rather simplistic and automatic that the authority for control and its manner of exercise vests in the owner. Thus, this aspect would need no positive law to enforce the right of control as an adjunct of property right because this position is an age-old practice of civilised societies and the two are co-terminus in hold and periodicity on legal transfer. The same precept should hold valid in international space law, too.

7.3.2 Agreement on Rescue and Return of Astronauts, *Etc.*, 1968

It is, therefore, pertinent to allude to the existence of another pertinent provision under another space law instrument, namely Agreement on the Rescue of Astronauts, etc.[24] (hereafter referred to as R&RA). It becomes vitally germane and adduces jurisdictional support to personnel on-board on the principle of nationality of the spacecraft. R&RA in clarification, caters to eventualities, "[i]f owing to accident, distress, emergency or unintended landing, the personnel of a spacecraft land in

---

[21] Agreement on the Rescue of Astronauts, the Return of Astronauts, and the Return of Objects Launched into Outer Space, 1968, (hereinafter referred to as R&RA).

[22] For this connotation, refer Patrick J Fitzgerald, ed., *Salmond on Jurisprudence*, Sweet & Maxwell, 1966.

[23] John Austin, "The Province of Jurisprudence determined", first part of lecture series on Jurisprudence in J Murray, *The Philosophy of Positive Law*, vol. 2, 1863.

[24] R&RA at n. 21 ante.

territory under the jurisdiction of a Contracting Party or have been found on the high seas or in any other place not under the jurisdiction of any other state, they shall be safely and promptly returned to representatives of the launching authority."[25]

The stated provision, "prompted by sentiments of humanity" and "to promote international cooperation,"[26] also binds and requires State Parties to render assistance and recover any astronaut in the event of accident, distress, emergency, or unintended landing to safety and return to the launching authority, which in most of the cases may turn out to be the state of nationality of the spacecraft. And once an astronaut, and by analogy an offender, is in custody of its own state, the disputes or competing claims to jurisdiction get minimised. And a competent domestic court can legitimately seize jurisdiction over the offender for the alleged offence for trial.

7.3.3 The Liability Convention, 1972

This convention[27] recognises and accepts that the space objects so launched into outer space may cause third-party damage to other space objects. This may result in economic and business disputes requiring adjudication, if not settled by diplomatic procedures. The Liability Convention, therefore, establishes the principle of *vinculum juris* for damages so caused and has endeavoured to stipulate "elaborate and effective international rules and procedures concerning liability for damage caused by space objects and to ensure,...full and equitable measure of compensation to victims of such damage."[28] This was intended to strengthen international cooperation and to ensure prompt payment for the damages caused.

However, the nature of liability prescribed varies geospatially. "If the damage has been caused to the third State on the surface of the Earth or to aircraft in flight, their liability to the third State shall be absolute."[29] The quanta for absolute liability have, however, been negotiated and settled diplomatically as in the case of Canadian claim against Russia for the fall of debris of nuclear-powered space object, Kosmos 954 in January, 1978. The claim, invoking Liability Convention, was preferred for over C$ six million but was negotiated reaching a full and final settlement of C$ 3 million in 1981.[30]

The damages so caused to other space objects in the outer space accrue differently. The principle applicable here is one of fault-liability, which means that the calculation of the quantum of damage is based on the element of fault, the party at fault, and

---

[25] Ibid, Article 4.

[26] The Preamble to R&RA.

[27] The Convention on International Liability for Damage Caused by Space Objects, 1972. Hereafter referred to as the Liability Convention.

[28] The Preamble to the Liability Convention,

[29] The Liability Convention, Article IV (1).

[30] For more discussion see, Edward G Lee & DW Sproule, "Liability for Damage Caused by Space Debris", published online by *Cambridge University Press*, May 9, 2016.

extent of its voidability.[31] Law professionals are well aware that it is an onerous task to prove fault-liability beyond doubt for a convincing claim to obtain a favourable verdict. No wonder that hardly any claims in this regard have been preferred despite apparent fault and attendant liability. For example, the in space collision between the US, privately owned, functional satellite, Iridium-33, and derelict Russian military satellite Kosmos-2251, on 10 February 2009, at an altitude of 789 km.[32] Kosmos was no longer actively controlled while Iridium was part of a constellation of 66 communication satellites. No claim for liability has been raised for the accidental collision.

7.3.4 Space Law Accepts and Absorbs International Law

OST accepts the established customs, principles, doctrines, and tenets of international law; and in a way, international law becomes an integral part of the space law. This assertion can be vindicated by allusion to a provision under the OST that exhorts, "States Parties to the treaty shall carry on activities in the exploration and use of outer space, including the Moon and other celestial bodies, in accordance with international law, including the Charter of the United Nations, in the interest of maintaining international peace and security and promoting international cooperation and understanding."[33]

Apart from this generic provision, it is equally important to refer to the Statute of the International Court of Justice, 1945, which expands the scope of the relevance of international law to the human activities in outer space and on the celestial bodies. The Statute requires the ICJ to apply international conventions, international customs as evidence of state practice, judicial decisions, and teachings of highly qualified publicists for determination of rules of law.[34] In other words, the Statute of ICJ accepts the force of Customary International Law and *Jus Cogens* in the form of *opinio juris* to adjudicate on contentious matters pertaining to the domain of outer space.[35] Therefore, there is no gainsaying in asserting that space law invokes, accepts, and absorbs international law within its gamut for judicial working.

---

[31] The Liability Convention, Article IV (1).

[32] Wolf Jim, "US, Russian satellites collide in space", Reuter report, February 11, 2009. Also refer, Brian Weeden, "Billiards in Space", *The Space Review*, February 23, 2009.

[33] Outer Space Treaty, 1967, Article III.

[34] The Statute of International Court of Justice, Article 38 (1).

[35] Refer G. S. Sachdeva, *Outer Space: Law, Policy and Governance*, New Delhi, KW Publishers, 2014, pp. 1–30.

7.4 Principles of Criminal Jurisdiction Under International Law

Customary international law under the doctrine of the sovereignty accords two indisputable characteristics to the state. First, a state must have territory to prove its sovereign existence and exercise of its supreme and exclusive authority over such spatial area on the surface of the Earth. Further, that the territorial limits of sovereign land extend to the control beneath the land, into territorial waters along coastline and into the sky *ad coelum* (up to the heavens). The second element of state sovereignty is its right to bestow nationality on its citizen and other permanent residents by its choice and authority. Thus, sovereignty accords jurisdiction over its territory as also its nationals, thereby creating a duty to protect the national territory and a right to try criminals for decreed offences of the land. Apart from incidents of sovereignty, there are other principles in seizing criminal jurisdiction in international context as also international conventions that confer jurisdiction on bilateral basis or universally for crimes against humanity, like acts of terrorism, in any relation or context. Nevertheless, these rules often lack congruence in iteration and commonality in approach and need to be interpreted for the object and in spirit.

7.4.1 The Territoriality Principle

Every state, by the doctrine of national sovereignty and equality of states, claims jurisdiction over crimes committed in its own territory and legitimate extensions under its control like territorial coastal belts. This principle has also been extended to honour extra-territoriality in notional territories like embassy premises or flag-bearing ships on sea or aircraft flying with national symbols or spacecraft held on national registry and accordingly all these moving assets bearing its nationality.[36]

Having decided on the extent of territorial jurisdiction, the law applicable under such jurisdictions would relate to *locus delicti* meaning "...[t]he place where the defendant did the act from which the harm ensues..."[37] This view concurs with the American Doctrine supported by Beale that states "...the place of wrong is the place where the person or thing harmed is situated at the time of the wrong..."[38] This follows the established principle of *lex loci delicti commissi*. The rule also ordains that "the place of performance governs the "mode" of performance"[39] and this is *lex loci solutionis*. By extended analogy, it becomes applicable here on all counts.

There can be circumstances where totality of the criminal act is not completed within a single jurisdiction. A criminal act may begin in one state and may be

---

[36] Ian Brownlie, *Principles of Public International Law*, Oxford, 5th Edition, 1998, pp. 299 et seq.
[37] G. C. Cheshire, *Private International Law*, Sixth Edition, Oxford, Clarendon Press, 1961, p. 292.
[38] Beale, *Cases on the Conflict of Laws,* ii, 514. Cited from Cheshire Ibid.
[39] Ernst Rabel, *The Conflict of Laws*, Vol. III, The University of Michigan Press, 1964, p. 42.

completed in another. For example, a person may shoot across the border and kill someone in the adjoining state. In this case, there can be competing claims to jurisdiction: the state where the crime begins in that the shooter was standing can seize jurisdiction under the "subjective territorial principle" while the state where act gets completed with consequences has valid jurisdiction under the permissive rule of "objective territorial principle." The predicament best fits *the Lotus Case*[40] between France and Turkey, though it was essentially ruled on grounds of state practice and *opinio juris.*

It is also pertinent to allude to the doctrine of double criminality which protects the liberty of the alleged offender. Therefore, the state requesting for extradition has to submit proper evidence of a prima facie judicial proceedings of an offence that was cognisable and punishable against the extraditable accused. And this criminal accusation has to stand valid and to concur the crime as per the criminal codes of the country where the fugitive offender has escaped or has been found. "Consequently, a state may decline to surrender the person claimed if he [/she] is charged with an act which is not punishable under the laws of the requested state."[41]

As a corollary to this doctrine, "it is a well settled that an English court will not lend its aid to the enforcement, either directly or indirectly, of a foreign penal law. The imposition of a penalty normally reflects the exercise by the State of its sovereign power, and it is an obvious principle that an act of sovereignty can have no effect in the territory of another State."[42] Cheshire cites cases to buttress above point of view that a plea for the enforcement of a penalty imposed in the supposed interest of a foreign sovereign would fail.[43]

7.4.2 The Nationality Principle

The second well-established rule for jurisdiction that stems from the doctrine of sovereignty of states is the nationality principle. In this connection, nationality is a connecting factor or a convenient attachment between the state and an individual and through link this principal derives the benefits of the Law of Nations.[44] The dictum goes, "Every man has the right to nationality…No one shall be arbitrarily deprived…nor denied the right to change his nationality."[45] But this nexus assumes a bond of allegiance and obedience by the citizen towards the state. Thus, nationality is *domaine reserve* of a sovereign state, and it has the competence to confer citizenship on its domiciled residents and by virtue of this conferment and the inherent rights so

---

[40] 1937, PCIJ, series A, no. 10, pp.28ff.

[41] Bedi, note 2 ante, p. 69. Words in parenthesis added to eliminate gender bias.

[42] GC Cheshire, *Private International Law,* 6th edition, Oxford, at the Clarendon Press, 1961, p. 138.

[43] Cheshire, ibid, p. 139.

[44] L Oppenheim, *International Law,* London, 1958 (8th edition), vol I, p. 645.

[45] UN Document A/811, Resolution 217 (III).

bestowed, the state in return acquires an intrusive power to try offenders of crimes to ensure public peace and stability as also law and order in society.

According to the above discussion, "the state may prosecute its nationals for crimes committed anywhere in the world."[46] This rule is almost universally accepted and customarily honoured by states globally, and there have been few challenges to its extensive applicability and use in state practice. This is mainly because of the natural justice embedded in this principle and reciprocal operation favouring interests of each state. Besides, it is the duty of the state to protect the interests of its citizens, even while temporarily resident outside the country, anywhere in the world. This obligation is the correlative of the rights bestowed with citizenship.

Historically, this principle finds acceptance under the tenet of sovereignty of the states. Apart from other ingredients of sovereignty, it accords immunity according to which accredited representatives of the state, e.g. heads of state, ambassadors, government officials and the like cannot be tried by another state. Extending the logic, the professional astronauts as members of the defence forces attract this immunity. Thus, sovereign immunity traces its basis to the equality of states and holding the status of official representation or performance of an assigned duty of the state.[47] International courtesy also gets factored in the application of *jus gentium*.

It may be pertinent here to distinguish a nuance in this principle. As active nationality principle, the state claims jurisdiction over crimes committed abroad by its citizens alleged as offenders, notwithstanding in whose module of space station such act has been committed. Closely associated with this is the passive nationality principle under which the national state of the victim may like to seize criminal jurisdiction over the culprit for trial in its domestic court. Under both subprinciples, the state of nationality acts as protector of the interests of its nationals to obtain due justice.

Let's not ignore another eventuality of practical situation where the offender has multiple nationality, and there is need to determine the jurisdiction. In case, the offender is national of the state of forum and is found or living there, then this state can legitimately seize jurisdiction and additional foreign nationality can be disregarded. Belgium, France, Switzerland, the UK, etc., have traditionally adopted this approach while China, Japan, Egypt, Germany, etc., have adopted this rule in domestic law.[48] However, in a case of a person possessing multiple nationalities but as offender is found in a third country, the law most consistently applied is of the state of domicile or habitual residence[49] and claim to extradition of the latter state will take precedence over others, if any.

Another contingency that may arise could relate to stateless persons who are also called *apatride* or *apolide* or *staatenlos*. Persons may become stateless for different

---

[46] Michael Akehurst, n. 1 ante, p. 104.

[47] Under this principle and by this logic, space tourists may not be able to avail themselves of this immunity.

[48] Ernst Rabel, *The Conflict of Law: A Comparative Study*, vol. one, Ann Arbor, University of Michigan Law School, 1958, (2nd edition), p. 129.

[49] Rabel, ibid, p. 130.

reasons, one of them could be political events and upheavals.[50] For other reasons, gypsies, practically all over, are treated as apatride.[51] Individuals lacking a definite nationality are generally subject to the law of their domicile or habitual residence; and in default thereof, the law of their temporary residence. Most countries, like Belgium, France etc., accede to this position.[52]

7.4.3 The Protective Principle

The protective principle is invoked in the interest of security and stability of the state, and the principle allows a state to punish acts prejudicial to its sustenance and integrity. This would cover crimes, e.g. conspiracy for spying or intelligence leaks, plotting to overthrow an established government, forging of currency, etc. This principle could be extended even to those crimes that have been committed by foreigners abroad, individually, in collusion or conspiracy, against the nation claiming jurisdiction. Thus, this rule extends to alien criminals who are abroad but culpable.

Many countries have validly invoked and applied this principle in apt cases and to the best advantage with the understanding and cooperation of the concerned states. The principle makes sense in the interest of justice, but has an endemic risk that some states may interpret "security and stability of the state" too widely and loosely to use this principle on flimsy grounds or for the purpose of harassment of opponents or vendetta with the past rivals. That will not be judicious application of the rule for eliciting a positive response from other states.

7.4.4 The Universality Principle

Some states, under this principle, claim jurisdiction over all crimes, including those committed by foreigners abroad. But such jurisdiction is not viewed kindly by international law as the PCIJ refrained from discussing the validity of such jurisdiction in *the Lotus Case*. The obvious logic of this stand was that it could lead to unjust decision if an individual was punished for doing an act which was right and lawful under the legal system of the place where it was done. But application of this principle is more acceptable and less objectionable when applied to serious crimes that are universally considered as offences against international community as a whole, e.g. terrorist acts, war crimes, and crimes against humanity, like genocide or torture (of space workers) that fall under International Human Rights and Humanitarian laws.

---

[50] Rabel, ibid, p. 131–2. For example, the Russians who fled after the fall of the Russian Empire were not accepted as its nationals by the successor state of the Soviet Union.

[51] For example, Poland: Law of 1926, art. I, par. I, or Yugoslavia: Law of April 25, 1955, art. 157.

[52] Rabel, n.48 ante, p. 132.

7.4.5 *Principle of Forum Conveniens*

There is, however, another option to elect the jurisdiction best suited to the victim. Under this principle, "the place of wrong is the place in which the law is most favourable to the person wronged. The plaintiff can, at will, fix the *locus delicti* in any country in which any of the operative facts occurred."[53] This is selection of *forum conveniens* as best suited to the complainant according to its convenience either in domicile or availability of evidentiary facts or for any other valid reason.

This option surely does procedural justice to the aggrieved party in affording a choice of forum that is easily approachable judicially or most convenient due to domicile or most helpful in investigation and prosecution due to availability of material evidence in that country. Some treaties enshrine this principle in their text but some scholars frown upon the option of jurisdiction being elected by the complainant according to personal ease and advantage.

7.5 National Laws with Extra-Territorial Jurisdiction in Outer Space

National laws of many countries as also some treaties permit "immunised" national jurisdiction to static assets and properties like embassy premises abroad. This enables exercise of quasi-territorial jurisdiction on reciprocal basis. Similar provisions extend the right to exercise national jurisdiction over its floating vessels in the seas or flying aircraft in the air or even its registered space objects in outer space and on celestial bodies. This is notionally called the flag jurisdiction.

Historically, it is a legal fiction that originated as a custom of sea-faring and navigation under which ships may bear flag of the nation to which these belong. But each ship can bear and fly only one national flag. With passage of time this became part of the Law of the Sea and has since been codified in the UN Convention on Law of the Sea (UNCLOS).[54] Today this state-patronised custom has since assumed the force of a customary law that makes it universally binding irrespective of the ascension to the convention.

Analogous provisions are contained in the Law of Aerial Navigation which conceptually claim flag jurisdiction and seem to have been borrowed from the Law of the Sea. For implementation of this concept, the Chicago Convention 1944 imposes an obligation on the states to register their aircraft and accordingly grant its nationality. Further, each aircraft is also allotted a call sign which identifies the country and the particular aircraft. Nevertheless, "one aircraft, one flag" doctrine remains inviolable to define and uphold the extra-territorial or flag jurisdiction of the country.

---

[53] Cheshire, n. 42 ante, p. 292.
[54] UNCLOS I, 1958, Article 6.

Space objects also require national registration, generally, from the launching state. Outer Space Treaty obligates this action at two levels: nationally, by entry in the national register of space objects launched and internationally, by submission of similar information about the launch to the Secretary-General of the UN. This rule legitimises ownership over the object and entitles the registering nation to "retain jurisdiction and control over such objects, and over any personnel thereof, while in outer space or on a celestial body."[55] This provision also vindicates the quasi-territorial jurisdiction of the states in law by upholding a customary notion.

Thus, in space law, entry of a space object in the national register of space objects has the same material effect and legal consequences as in case of a ship or an aircraft so registered, albeit with a difference. "In space law, inclusion in the national registry does not confer nationality de jure to the spacecraft, only jurisdiction and control thereon."[56] But one may differ with this view. National registration coupled with the certitude of ownership of the space object and its parts, wherever these exist or are found, allows for exercise of practical sovereign right to obtain return thereof and thus assures a jurisdiction of de jure nationality for all purposes. Further, though technically, the state of registry may possess primary jurisdiction in contra-distinction to exclusive jurisdiction over its satellites, capsules, modules or spacecraft and personnel therein. All these shall, in the first instance, be subject to its laws and authority, although this jurisdiction may be breached by the other principles of jurisdiction.

7.5.1 Extra-Territorial Reach of the US Domestic Law

The USA, however, in order to meet its diverse and multifarious treaty obligations has come up with a special provision in the US Code to address matters of criminal conduct that might arise in space, as well as other non-territorial areas like Global Commons or for extra-territorial eventualities. This provision is found in 18 U.S.C. Sec. 7, titled as "the Special Maritime and Territorial Jurisdiction of the United States".[57] It extends its federal jurisdiction to ships, aircraft, and space objects bearing its nationality and covers procedures concerning how to handle criminal complaints arising outside of its true national jurisdiction. But simplicity of this law and brevity of the skeletal definitions may not always be effective in claiming jurisdiction on "lawgical" grounds or for national interests or the availability of reliable evidence to ensure due process of law.

---

[55] Outer Space Treaty, 1967, Article VIII. This provision has since been amplified by Convention on Registration of Objects Launched into Outer Space, 1974, in particular Articles III & IV.

[56] Michael Chatzipanagiotis & Rafael Moro-Aguilar, "Criminal Jurisdiction in International Space Law: Future Challenges in View of the ISS IGA", Conference Paper at 57th IISL Colloquium on the Law of Outer Space, at Toronto, October 2014, p. 5.

[57] https://www.govinfo.gov/content/pkg/USCODE-2010-title18pdf/USCODE-2010-title18-partI-chap1-sec7.pdf.

In case, a US national was to, for example, assault someone on a commercial space station, in that case this special type of assumed jurisdiction would become live and relevant and can be invoked, if and when deemed necessary. However, as per Justice Department, this special jurisdictional provision mostly covers heinous crimes, such as "murder, manslaughter, maiming, kidnapping, rape, assault, and robbery."[58] Such eventualities are more likely to become real and incumbent with commercial space travel and space tourism becoming popular. The ensuing predicament may necessitate a new branch of space law on the lines of private international law to provide guidelines to handle disputed issues and competing claims of jurisdiction over offending personnel irrespective of complexity of the crime, the locus of commission, nationality ramifications, or political wrangles.

In respect of lesser offences, such as in the case of Anne McClain involving unauthorised use of official, privileged computer, network hacking or identity theft, it is unclear if this stringent jurisdictional law would really be deemed germane and become applicable. The simplistic application of the law also becomes murkier if there is an incident that involves multiple people from multiple nations. For instance, if someone from the USA gets hurt in a private space hotel, along with other guests from other nations, the situation would become confused and complex. The ambiguity will be compounded further if an American along with persons of other nations hurts persons from other countries. The obvious protocol would be consultation between concerned governments for an acceptable solution but if political or diplomatic bickering between nations exceeds three months, the aggrieved has an option to resort to his/her own national jurisdiction to seek remedies.[59]

7.5.2 Extra-Territorial Reach of Other Countries

On lines of the US Codes, many other countries have similar domestic laws establishing quasi-territorial criminal jurisdiction. Russian domestic space law has umbrella rules extending extra-territorial jurisdiction to space objects. In Spain the relevant rule, though only for ships and aircraft, is Article 23.1 of the Organic Law on Judicial Power (Law 6/85 of 1 July 1985). Germany has Para 4 of the German Criminal Code for this purpose. And in Greece, there is Article 5 of Greek Criminal Code; and so on.[60]

Canada, too, seems to have taken a pioneering lead in this direction with cues from NASA investigation of the reported first crime committed in space (McClain Case). This case brought about awareness about criminal issues that could arise with

---

[58] "The first alleged crime committed in space raises questions about jurisdiction in orbit", Loren Grush@lorengrush August 27, 2019.
[59] Ibid.
[60] Bernhard Schmidt-Ted & Stephen Mick in *Cologne Commentaries on Space Law*, Vol. I/ Article VIII OST, Cologne, 2009, pp146-168. Cited from Michael Chatzipanagiotis, n. 56 ante. Also refer Wilfred Jenks, *Space Law,* London 1965, pp. 238 & 294.

progressing space activities like space tourism or space exploitation and the like, in the near future, and how the existing corpus of space law was patently inadequate to effectively handle them. Canada was also prompted by the progress of human forays to the Moon, crewed visits to the Mars and space beyond.

Further, considering prospects of its own humans in space as part of the Artemis Program, the Lunar Gateway is vital to conducting regular missions to the lunar surface and establishing the Artemis Base Camp. It is also a key component of NASA's plan to send crewed missions to Mars in the next decade. The core elements of this modular space station, the Power and Propulsion Element (PPE) and the Habitation and Logistics Outpost (HALO), are currently scheduled to be launched to lunar orbit by 2024. Considering it as an incident of this partnership, Canada has extended its own criminal law to cis-lunar space and the lunar surface.[61] The amendment has been included in Part 5, Division 18 of the document, titled "*Civil Lunar Gateway Agreement Implementation Act.*"

However, the current Canadian Criminal Code already has a similar provision with the text that reads, "[A] Canadian crew member who, during a space flight, commits an act or omission outside Canada that if committed in Canada would constitute an indictable offence is deemed to have committed that act or omission in Canada if that act or omission is committed (a) on, or in relation to, a flight element of the space station; or (b) on any means of transportation to or from the space station." Thus, only its limitation of applicability to the ISS has been expanded for expedience of future projects.

7.6 Discipline On-Board Spaceships

Apart from treaty rules on jurisdiction, national laws on extra-territorial annexation of jurisdiction, intergovernmental agreements on delimitation of criminal jurisdictional, there is another category of rules and an institution to control crimes in space. These are the disciplinary powers of the commander to maintain discipline and order on-board the spaceship. As a corollary of jurisdictional rules, the commander of the spaceship is accepted as a constructive authority of the state of registry over the personnel aboard the spaceship and reinforces the nationality of the space object. In a way, commander is the "delegatee of national authority" devolved from the state of registry for ensuring discipline and law and order on-board the spaceship.

This concept and detail appear to have been influenced by and derived from similar powers of the commander of the aircraft contained in the Chicago Convention, 1944 (Articles 17 and 18) or customary powers of the captain of the sea vessel. On similar lines, this authority in relation to spaceship follows a command-and-control lineage, similar to the defence services and civil airliners, over the crew, space travellers, and

---

[61] Matt Williams, "Lunar law: Canada can now prosecute crimes committed on the Moon", *Universe Today*, May 14, 2022.

others on-board. References to such provisions can be found in the USA and Russian domestic space law.

As per the US law, the authority of the Space Shuttle Commander is defined under 14 CFR 1214.7. This provision empowers the commander to enforce order and discipline on-board during all phases of flight of the Shuttle and authorises the commander to take whatever action deemed necessary or found judicious as per his/her judgment for the safety of the Shuttle, well-being of all persons, and protection of equipment on-board the spaceship. This authority includes reasonable and necessary means, including the use of physical force to subject any person to such restraint as the circumstances require and till delivery to the authorities. Hence, everyone on-board is obliged to obey orders and directions from the commander.[62]

The Russian Law on Space Activities, under Article 20 (3), also empowers the spacecraft commander with similar powers and with responsibility to ensure safety of the spacecraft, welfare of all personnel and security of property on-board. Accordingly, the commander is vested with all due and necessary powers to conduct the flight operations safely, with due diligence and with the support of the crew members; as also exercising effective and constructive command and control over the persons on-board.[63] The purpose of these powers is also to maintain peace and public tranquillity within the spaceship.

In the end, it seems pertinent to allude to the ISS Crew Code of Conduct (CCoC) formulated by NASA.[64] The CCoC governs the conduct and behaviour of astronauts on-board the ISS, which includes change of duties and work schedules. The necessity for such a Code arises to establish the hierarchy of command and control for exercise of the authority to ensure conformance, obedience, and execution of orders within the spaceship. It also prescribes rules for compliance and obedience by all personnel for smooth flight of the spaceship, successful completion of the mission as also its safety and security from all angles. Insubordination, disobedience and defiance of rules could constitute culpability attracting imposition of sanctions. The code thus becomes a statutory set of ethical and public-duty rules of conduct and behaviour for the crew and the personnel on-board.

7.7 Jurisdictional Challenges from New Space Activities

Traditional space activities of scientific exploration and peaceful uses have by now settled down and their imponderables have been sorted out by the three subaltern treaties concerning rescue and return of astronauts, liability for damage by space

---

[62] Michael Chatzipanagiotis, n. 56 ante, p.6.

[63] Ibid.

[64] CCoC was formulated in consonance with Article 11 of the IGA. This code was prepared by NASA in negotiation with other partners. The Code applicability covers both, the already existing crew and the visiting members. Besides other matters, it delineates administrative command and control authority that is effective on-board the ISS. It was adopted in September, 2000.

objects, and registration of space objects. New challenges now arise from new-era space activities that are likely to become real and operational over the next decade or so. These activities may relate to private space stations for scientific research, recreation and advertisement; commercial space travel and private space hospitality and tourism; and commercial exploitation and private appropriation of celestial mineral resources. Some of the activities wanting huge financial resources, techno-scientific research and development with long gestation periods may come from corporate conglomerates positing multi-national nuances. Similar undertakings as manufacturing laboratories for high-quality vaccines, bubble-free crystals, D-3 printing, and cognate products requiring sterile and gravity-free environment may also come to be established by multi-national corporations. This mixed-nationality situation may call for jurisdictional adjustments through *compromis* or agreement or contract. Efforts in cooperative partnerships by space agencies are also afoot to soon launch manned expeditions to the Moon and the Mars. The US Artemis project is pioneer in this direction.[65] An IGA-like agreement may serve as model to evolve specific agreements.

Another genre of anticipable space activities that may become real and working in slightly distant future, or relatively longer time frame, would be humanned sojourns into deep space, positioning multi-purpose service stations en route for refuelling, change over, and other attendant facilities. The other kind of development could relate to the construction of the Moon Village or Mars Colony for permanent settlement of humanity who are willing and keen for such migration. This would require elaborate infrastructure of living facilities, residential quarters with regular logistics, till agro-cultivation and water harvesting, in situ, become feasible and practical. And another type of space crimes may be committed with technology devices and cyber-crimes which may be activated from anywhere or any domain and at the same time maintaining the anonymity of the perpetrator. Thus, the search for the suspected criminal and forensic evidence would turn a difficult task with innumerable jurisdictional complications.

For reaching up to this threshold, there are legal and regulatory implications. First, whatever facilities are to be set up on the celestial bodies, the entrepreneurs would need legal permission to establish such infrastructure on temporary or longer leasehold of the celestial real estate. This may first necessitate an international space organisation (ISO) as a governing body for regulating and managing commercial uses of outer space and term-leases on the real estate of celestial bodies. Secondly, the space facilities, so created by private enterprise, would have to be registered with the UN as activity by a registering state that shall bear the responsibility, liability and other consequential incidents of such activity. Further, Outer Space Treaty imposes international responsibility for national activities and mandates "authorisation and continuing supervision."[66] Thus, this duty of the state of registry automatically bestows

---

[65] Space.com, August 13, 2022.
[66] Outer Space Treaty Article VI.

certain incidents of jurisdiction over the enterprise of the activity. In case, such activities involve multi-national participation, then specific agreements may have to be arranged between the agency from the state of registry with the other partners.

Agreements with the state of registry or its operating agency may become imperative in joint ventures like this to define territorial control within the station modules, criminal jurisdiction over personnel, the nature of activities operated and the authority of the commander. In general, the authority of the commander is regulatory and administrative to maintain public order on-board; and control of misconduct in the interest of safety of personnel, security of equipment and integrity of the entire space station. This duty assumes significance because external help or timely intervention at the spaceship in orbit may not be possible due to distance and other attendant reasons. So, the commander and crew may have to devise and ensure judicious and effective measures to handle crimes under given circumstances.

Further, in such agreements, criminal jurisdiction becomes more pertinent as commercial activities may be susceptible to unauthorised business interference, covert spying intrusions or unhealthy competitive overtures. Parties can, of course, safeguard their respective interests while negotiating the agreement, at the same time, exuding good faith, mutual trust, and working confidence. Occasionally however, contracts may need additional and specific clauses to meet the special characteristics of a mission profile, project objective or to handle unexpected contingencies on-board.

7.8 Division of Territorial Jurisdiction of Outer Space and Air Space

Consideration of jurisdictional issues also reaches out to the principle of territoriality in handling crimes in international scenario, and this in turn brings to focus the territorial jurisdiction of outer space within which a crime so committed can be treated as space crime. For humanity inhabiting the Earth, it is demarcation of boundary between Earth and rest of the universe. This domain, today, stands divided between airspace and outer space. It is therefore, necessary to distinguish and recognise the two domains separately in order to apply the specific and germane legal regimen. Therefore, a scientifically established and universally accepted limit of the frontiers within contiguous spaces is necessary. It will also clarify that primarily, if not exclusively, space crimes are those that would generally occur within the bounds of outer space and on the celestial bodies. It would thus, dispel any doubts relating to territorial jurisdiction applicable to the offenders of crimes committed in outer space.

Of the many definitional, legal, and technical issues surrounding outer space activities, perhaps none is more persistently elusive than defining where outer space begins. More specifically, it is a question of demarcation of boundary or the delimitation where atmosphere ends and the lower end of outer space begins. The dilemma

7.8 Division of Territorial Jurisdiction of Outer Space and Air Space

relates to finding a salient criterion as to the highest level at which aircraft can fly or the minimum level of operation of spaceflight. This ticklish issue, apart from being a legal one, is also a matter with political dimension and concerns of national security that implicate sovereign rights and invite defence considerations of nations. Apprehensions may be genuine yet can aeroplanes practically fly at those atmospheric heights with thin air that may not support aerodynamic airlift.

The debate over the delimitation of outer space is still technically unresolved, while the advent of commercial spaceflight, in particular suborbital flights, may lend an impetus to clarify the ambiguity, if not in law at least in practice. This necessity and urgency would lead to the delineation of the lower limits of outer space and maximum altitude of airspace. It would possibly be a pragmatic decision, though not technically perfect and flawless or legally and universally accepted limit for reason of customary national sovereignty in the air, so traditionally accepted. Generally, repeated, consistent and sustained practice of states supported by *opinion juris* becomes customary international law and thus binding and obligatory. It applies to sovereignty in the air.

An established doctrine and a Roman legal maxim endorse private ownership appurtenant to the right in land, *ad coelum* ad infinitum. With the advent of aircraft, this private right got converted to national sovereignty in all columns of superincumbent air space. The logic was practical use of height over land, public utility of air services, and as a matter of public policy. Further however, lack of delimitation between airspace and outer space regions did not impede or impair development in any field. This contention may be valid only thus far but the status may not remain so in the near future when commercial suborbital flights become operational, regular, and popular. Possibly, disputes may arise among travellers or with the carriers; or crimes may be committed on such flight may fail determination of criminal jurisdiction. Hence, the necessity for separate demarcation of outer space domain bearing a differentiated legal regime may become real and pertinent.[67]

Till the conquest of the third frontier, an axiomatic definition of airspace up to unlimited altitude based on total and exclusive sovereignty of the subjacent state was normatively and customarily acceptable for practical purposes as per conventional air law.[68] State practice also abided by this customary norm of airspace up to unlimited height (*coelum* ad infinitum). Pursuing this state practice, the USA also recognised no upper limit to national sovereignty in the air. The Soviets also zealously defended this customary limit as a policy statement but later modified its stance with the launch of Sputnik-1. Its revised stand was that it did not violate the sovereign right of other nations in the airspace with the launch of Sputnik because it had flown at fast speed and at a high-altitude towards its mission when foreign territories just passed underneath. Thus, it was not considered an unauthorised overflight like aircraft or

---

[67] The US has since enacted, Commercial Space Launch Amendment Act, 2004. It is tailored to suit the needs of commercial space flights and puts a limit on airspace at 100–112 km from spatial point of view.

[68] A McNair, *The Law of the Air*, (London: Steven & Sons, 1964), pp. 394–5. Also refer DHN Johnson, *Rights in Air Space*, (Manchester: Manchester University Press, 1965), p. 12.

trespass into the sovereign airspace. Besides, in the euphoria of humanity breaching the third frontier, no country protested the trespass of Sputnik into their sovereign aerial space. Nor did any nation take an official position to object or prohibit the trespass by a space object. In this universal acquiescence to innocent flight of space objects, a new practice of states was born. Space objects do not violate the sovereign air space so long there are no repeat passes through it.

Encouraged by the almost universal silence on the Sputnik's trespass, the USA also found this pretence and specious Soviet argument favourable, in the first instance, and deemed it a wise policy paradigm in the long run. It thus, eminently suited the US space activities in future. So, the USA also subscribed to the theory of the division of atmosphere into two separate and independent regions of airspace and outer space.[69] And ultimately both domains came to be governed by varying legal regimes and differing legal tenets. Airspace was governed by the Chicago Convention, 1944, while outer space and celestial bodies were regulated by the Outer Space Treaty, 1967.

However, commonality of opinion, facade of congruent logic and mutually condoned practice of states was not enough for the Soviet and Chinese hardliners. They insisted that the issue be redressed and resolved on the criterion of effective and useful operations as also through a legally binding treaty. The USA hedged this commitment but compromised to regulate the limit based on the nature of effectiveness and usefulness of the "mediums" in the domain for respective activities in relation to the distance from the Earth. In a way, this was a call for functional approach seeking dichotomisation into two domains with particularised range of operations or nature of activities with respective controlling legal regimes comprising segmental sets of international regulations.[70]

To support the above contention, it was categorically stated in the Outer Space Treaty, 1967 (or the treaty) that with a different and differentiated legal regime "…use of outer space, …shall be the province of all mankind."[71] Thus, state sovereignty vanished from the outer space regime. Again, Article II of the treaty asserts, "Outer space, including the Moon and other celestial bodies, is not subject to national appropriation by claim of sovereignty, by means of use or occupation, or by any other means." It again makes amply clear that state sovereignty ends where outer space begins. Yet this notional beginning of outer space may appear a misnomer or illusive because Earth being part of the universe is itself situated in the outer space. Ironically, however, the treaty uses the term "outer space" 37 times in its text but does not provide a definition for this oft-repeated word.[72]

Now the dilemma is to find that particular level or altitude that separates the two and makes specific legal regimes operative and effective within respective domain. Towards this intent, UN General Assembly had entrusted the task of formulation

---

[69] Michael Listner, "Could commercial space help define and delimitate the boundaries of Outer Space?", *NSRC,* nsrc.swri.org October 29, 2012.

[70] G. S. Sachdeva, "Sovereignty in the Air", IJIL, vol. 22, nos. 3&4, Jul-Dec 1982, p. 418ff.

[71] Outer Space Treaty, Article I.

[72] Sachdeva, n. 70 ante, p. 416.

7.8 Division of Territorial Jurisdiction of Outer Space and Air Space

of such a definition and demarcation to the Scientific and Technical Committee of the COPUOS in 1966.[73] Various operational operatives, environmental parameters, terrestrial characteristics, technical criteria, jurisprudential logic, and scientific fundamentals were discussed. The consensus emerged that none of these could establish a uniform, constant and sustained line of spatial demarcation around the globe with technical finesse and uniformity for universal acceptance. Nevertheless, let us consider a few desiderata to evaluate the above assertion.

Airspace is an envelope around the Earth and comprises gaseous fluid that is transparent, perfectly elastic and highly compressible in which aircraft gain lift to fly. But the density of air in the atmosphere progressively decreases with altitude and at a certain height aircraft can no longer obtain lift to fly with their aerodynamic characteristics. The traditional property law yields the ownership right in airspace to the owner of land underneath. A Roman maxim of *cujus est solum, ejus debet esse usque ad coelum* supports this stance. With the advent of aeroplanes, the US courts truncated this common law doctrine under the principles of eminent domain of the state and in the interest of public policy. The Chicago Convention 1944 made states sovereign in their respective airspace.[74] But the vertical limit of this airspace remained legally undefined and un-demarcated, perhaps because it was neither relevant nor necessary with the then budding air forces and struggling commercial aviation. But with space activities and formulation of space law, the situation has changed, highlighting the necessity such a demarcation to separate each other's jurisdiction for operative laws. A few recommendations by scientists and jurists as possible parameters for division of the air are briefly mentioned below.

(a) Joseph Kroell has advocated that the limit of airspace be settled at the altitude at which gravity of Earth ceases to exist and weight loses its manifestation. This criterion seems objective and rational but gravitational variations at different parts of Earth like the poles or deep oceans make this altitude variable.

(b) Another proposal is based on the theory of perigee of satellites where projectiles move by their own force of inertia and aerodynamic displacement ceases to exist. Though logical for operations of space objects, yet this height tends to be variable as affected by the rotation of Earth and unequal distribution of the masses of water and land. This may as well be affected by changes in solar activity and occasional solar flares which may expand or contract the atmosphere and the demarcation line may not remain consistently valid.

(c) Cooper recommends the altitude of effective capability of control to patrol and monitor its airspace by the subjacent sovereign state. This criterion though pragmatic yet appears ambiguous and discriminatory because nations will always differ in technological competence on this parameter.

(d) In a similar vein, the Soviet scholar, Zhukov favours the vertical air boundary be fixed on the basis of defence and security imperatives. In a way, this consideration would best satisfy the inclusive and exclusive interests of the states. But

---

[73] UN General Assembly Resolution 2222 (XXI) of 19 December 1966.

[74] For a detailed discussion on the subject, refer Sachdeva, n. 70 ante, pp. 396–421.

with technology advancement, this line would keep advancing and would need frequent and periodical refixation. Hence, not the best option.

(e) Von Karman has attempted to work out a primary jurisdiction line based on Kepler's Laws. He has suggested an altitude of 100 km, which though still practically imprecise and technically variable yet well compromises the scientific calculations and security apprehensions of states and has, in general, found wide acceptance.

At present, for all practical purposes, the boundary of airspace has been deemed to be at 100 km, even if the top layers of airspace have no aerodynamic use for commercial aviation. This evolved trend that has crystallised into an accepted practice is yet to get the final seal of authority in treaty law. Therefore, launches into outer space follow this very criterion of 100 km limit that generally demarcates the boundary between airspace and outer space.[75] This altitude has found practical advantages and good acceptance internationally. The states have, thus, conceded to permit one pass by a launching rocket and its payload through their sovereign airspace and treat it as permissible and innocent passage. Therefore, space launches passing through airspace controlled by different countries are not deemed as violation of respective air sovereignty. For our purpose, this essentially determines the domain from where space crimes can be committed though there may be other possibilities also based on the definition and scope of space crimes.

7.9 Conclusion

International space law enshrined in the Outer Space Treaty accords to the state of registry a bundle of rights; it acknowledges its ownership of the spaceship, irrespective of its geospatial location and enables the state of registry to exercise the right to "jurisdiction and control over such object and over any personnel thereof."[76] This means that a spaceship whether in outer space, on a celestial body or on seas or the Earth, simplistically, belongs to the country of registry. Under the same rule, should any person on-board commit a criminal offence, that person would be arraigned for judicial trial before a competent court as per quasi-territorial jurisdiction permitted under the treaty. This remains the general law of jurisdiction in the domain of outer space.

There are, however, some exceptions, though not widely dissimilar, yet agreed between states. These are contained in the Intergovernmental Agreement (IGA) between the states participating in the ISS project for scientific experimentation, exploration of outer space and training of astronauts. This being one of the first multi-nationality cooperative venture, it sure needed some adjustments for mutual

---

[75] However, the US has fixed it at 100–112 km under Commercial Space Launch Amendment Act 2004.

[76] Article VIII.

7.9 Conclusion

confidence-building. Therefore, this Agreement chose to include the active nationality principle, to enable participating states to exercise jurisdiction over its nationals, in case of any crime/s committed by them, on-board the spaceship.[77] However, despite this clear and uncontentious articulation, the IGA also concedes the passive nationality principle to cater for jurisdiction as per the nationality of the victim; this concession though is permitted yet under certain limited conditionalities.[78]

Further, to fine-tune certain clauses, clarify certain aspects or to add specific legal mandates from national laws, IGA is supplemented by separate back-to-back Memorandum of Understanding between NASA and other partner agencies to include desired exceptions, special considerations, and reciprocal benefits. Prof Jakhu, however, in a recent interview has proposed that it would be logical and imperative that such rules are the same for all space-faring humans, irrespective of the fact that they hold different earthly nationality. But the anathema is that the earthly beings, even on the Earth, are being treated differently according to own judicial systems as also legal codes. The author apprehends genuine fears that such universal treatment with near-alien laws may lead to apparent injustice and cause tyranny of universalism. Adjustment and understanding of differences through an *amicus curia* would be a more humane approach to social justice than sheer legalistic verdicts.

The IGA model though evolved and developed for the first time to meet the exigencies of multi-national participation yet has proved its acceptance and resilience under difficult situations. It has been found convenient, workable, and cooperative in practice and experience. Opinions verge to praise it as an excellent international instrument for similar future ventures with international cooperation.[79] In the anticipable future, activities relating to private space stations for scientific research, recreation and advertisement, commercial space travel, private space hospitality and tourism, and commercial exploitation of celestial mineral resources may come up from corporate conglomerates positing multi-national nuances. Similar undertakings as manufacturing laboratories for high-quality vaccines, bubble-free crystals and similar products requiring sterile and gravity-free environment may also come up as multi-national and jointly managed corporations. Efforts by state agencies in cooperative partnership are also afoot to soon launch manned expeditions to the Moon and the Mars. The US Artemis-1 project (in 2022) is pioneer in this direction.

It is pertinent here to recall the responsibility of the state that authorises such space operation by private entities under the Outer Space Treaty. Article VI of the treaty makes it incumbent on the appropriate state to ensure "authorisation and continuing supervision…" The treaty also mandates that national space activities should be according to its provisions and the rules of international law, for peaceful purposes and scientific exploration. But activities of SpaceEra-2 have gone beyond

---

[77] Inter-Governmental Agreement, 1998, Article 22 (1).

[78] Ibid, Article 22 (2).

[79] For example, during discussions of the Legal Sub-Committee of the UNCOPUOS on "Review of international mechanisms for cooperation in the peaceful exploration and use of outer space." At http://www.unoosa.org/pdf/pres/lsc2013/tech-02E.pdf. Last visited in February 2015.

these tenets and are further heading in uncharted directions, for example, excavation and private appropriation of celestial natural resources or progress towards use of celestial real estate for commercial purposes and planetary human residencies, without legal permissibility. Thus, confusion remains in law whether jurisdictions are advancing, expanding, or breaking out. Besides, the complexities and the complexion of space crimes also cannot be clearly visualised at this stage.

However, to sort out matters, a simplistic dichotomised submission is offered. To reiterate, first, for private space ventures, whether jointly by state agencies and/or private corporates, the treaty provision under Article VIII, authorising jurisdiction of the state of registry, under extra-territorial jurisdiction, would be highly suitable and more apt. The state agencies/private entities may like to supplement the treaty provision with memoranda for reciprocal adjustments and disciplinary authority. Secondly, for interplanetary missions where participation of states or their controlled space agencies would be more likely, a flexible and cooperative arrangement without compromising sovereignty as an adaptation of IGA, embodying national sovereignty principle, may be more relevant and appropriate. Other supporting arrangements like powers of the commander and Crew Code of Conduct may be sustained in tandem for better enforcement of law and order and disciplined conduct.[80]

In view of the above appraisal, we sure need an articulate, holistic, and futuristic treaty or *specialis* protocols for comprehensive usage and applicability on jurisdictional and related aspects. This could embody the pertinent provisions of the IGA and supporting instruments for better acceptance and regulatory force wherever found applicable in space jurisdictions. It could be passed as a Resolution by the UN for umbrella authority and customary acceptance. However, despite the majesty of the UN resolution and universal endorsement by the states, these instruments remain only declaratory and regulatory, bearing no executive authority.

Therefore, in view of the above handicap and to ensure compliance and conformance by all stakeholders to the international space law, there is need for an international space organisation with due Charter, adequate powers, professional staffing, and financial stability. For this purpose and task, the erstwhile and now defunct, Trusteeship Council seems eminently suitable for the new objectives with the legacy of past experience and distinction of achievements. Further, it will be easier to resuscitate this Council to life than muster international consensus for establishing a new organisation. Wisdom and opportunity lie with us to choose our option wisely, in the best interest of present humanity as also the posterity.

---

[80] Also refer Michael Chatzipanagiotis, n. 56 ante, Abstract and p. 12.

Chapter 8
Legal Procedures Under International Law: A Cumbrous Process

8.1 An Analysis of Legal Procedures

8.1.1 Introduction to Procedural Law

Substantive laws, at national level, are generally declaratory of crimes and punishments to be announced by the courts. These are positivist in approach and clear on sanctions. They, rarely, if ever, contain procedures and protocols to reach the court for remedy or relief. Thus, these laws remain in limbo till procedural and other supporting laws ensure apprehension and prosecution. So, this distance between the crime and the alleged criminal reaching the court for trial is facilitated by the procedural laws: police, criminal, and civil. Hence, in a way, it is the legal procedures that guide and determine what the law is and what may possibly be enforced.

The topic of legal procedures supporting implementation of international law is not much discussed in academic curriculum, and hence, its importance is not fully appreciated in making *specialis* law real and meaningful. Therefore, the procedural perspective merits closer attention to better deal with the often-inchoate nature of international law, both in practice and doctrine. Generally, most international laws are toothless, with few inbuilt remedies for breach, and tend to depend mostly on voluntary compliance by the states and the morality of *pacta sunt servanda*. And where cooperation fails, diplomacy may not always succeed.

Thus, without procedures, a law remains abstract, illusory, and in limbo for want of means for ensuring abidance of the treaty provisions or execution of judgments of international courts or tribunals. The most obvious procedural efforts lie in diplomatic means, national initiatives, political postures, and foreign policy expediencies, but their success may not always be certain, leaving recourse to alternative redressal procedures which may have to be resorted to and invoked. These may be constitutional provisions or national statutes or domestic court procedures. A brief discourse on legal procedures will enlighten on its importance and highlight its utility.

Therefore, a discussion on the subject may well start with a broad generalisation which, though true, is least understood in its concept, little realised for its importance and rarely acknowledged in its purpose. This relates to the fact that most of the substantive law by itself has no traction of its own and is lame in the legs. It needs crutches of procedural law to proceed to the courts and address for dispensation of justice. Substantive law, howsoever ideal or favourable, has to work according to certain court rules, evidentiary norms and comply with statutory procedures thereof. The law practitioners, in particular Advocates on Record of the Supreme Court, know the utility and pertinence of this underrated procedural law the best and the most.

To put it more candidly, it is the legal procedures that facilitate, determine, enable, and realise the content of law, its applicability, the *onus probandi*, expanse of the judgment, method of its execution, and the means of its actual enforcement. On the contrary, police regulations and judicial procedures tend to get overshadowed by the glitter and promises of substantive law and get relegated to the rear ranks and tend to be merged with grey zones of law that rarely come in focus of limelight. It may be honestly accepted that there is a possibility that a case may fail for procedural lapses and missed details while being good at law. Therefore, procedural law deserves a better deal on its own merit and contribution to the success of any case.

A few examples would put the issue in right perspective. Penal code in every country is a celebrated law for luminaries in criminal practice, yet Criminal Procedure Code, the supporting rules of procedure, called by whatever name, is scarcely known to the public and least appreciated for its legal import in judicial proceedings. The main distinctive feature of the domestic criminal procedures is the compulsory jurisdiction over the accused by the state and that his assent or acquiesce for the trial is not necessary. State has a right and command over its nationals to prosecute for commission of decreed and codified offences.

Again, Code of Civil Procedure is an excellent set of auxiliaries and supporting rules which if skilfully and professionally applied can tilt the tables in a plea. Correspondingly, international private law or the conflict of laws has probably rendered the greatest service to an understanding of legal procedures as opposed to substantive treaty law due to the precedence on the *lex loci proceduralis* over any foreign *lex causae*.[1] Similarly, good professional use of the evidentiary rules in criminal or civil proceedings can bolster the chances of success of a case, while bad handling or poor selection of the same admissibility rules can mar the chances of a favourable judgment or a decree. This highlights the significance of procedural law and the attention it worthily deserves in any legal proceedings.

From the above perspective, substantive laws and procedural laws bear unique companionship and a peculiar relationship in augmenting and promoting each other in its avowed purpose. Substantive laws are ideal promises and lofty commandments that offer sustained hope to the aggrieved but are sterile and ineffective by themselves. It is the procedural laws that find the path through the judicial labyrinth to reach tangible and desirable results by enabling a court to seize of the matter and arraign the accused. Therefore, it is the legal procedures that contribute to decision-making whether a case has merit to succeed or bears limitations to fail. Thus, procedures make Statute law real and fruitful. Importantly enough, domestically, procedures

---

[1] Gernot Biehler, *Procedures in International Law*, Springer, 2008, Preface, p. V.

8.1 An Analysis of Legal Procedures

are mostly laid down and codified to be strictly followed and implemented by the prosecuting agencies supporting the court of competence.

The stated milieu can be expressed in a maxim that where there is a wrong, there is remedy. And it is a prime fundamental that injustice must be undone, or in the alternative the wrongdoer punished. Therefore, there has to be remedy for each wrong and sanction for each crime. This vindicates the doctrine of *bonafide*. But there has to be a committed and consistent method to achieve it. This could get effect and enforcement through courts, and to arrive at that stage of activity, one has to follow stipulated procedures and abide by the rules of the domestic court that is adjudicating on the matter.

Conversely also, it is a well-established legal maxim that a right without a remedy, for its infringement or total violation, is like a command without sanction or "*a brutum fulman*" meaning no law at all. Civilised societies normally do not indulge in empty promises and do not enact legislation that offers a right but has no embedded remedy, present or future. Therefore, in order to undo an inflicted wrong, there is an allusion to a procedure that would possibly help the wronged one to get the wrong undone, legally and judicially. This justifies an impressive role to the procedural law and vindicates a genuine procedural perspective. At the same time, it establishes a pertinent and fundamental need to study germane rules of the court, including those relating to jurisdiction.

Procedural law also determines and regulates the competence and hierarchical structure of the courts and informs of the apex court of final appeal. Apart from duty of the court to adjudicate and pass judgment, more importantly, there are laid down procedures for enforcement of court decisions and execution of decrees so awarded. In the domestic courts, this perspective is generally taken for granted and is rarely invoked to conscious attention for prudent consideration. Generally speaking, the essential contents of procedural law in national Statutes deal with imprisonment procedure in criminal codes and civil codes cover non-enforceable obligations like specific performance, calculation of damages for restitution, equitable remedies, injunctions, limitation periods, and exceptions due to public policy and political considerations. It is also this law that defines and informs of the relationship between the lower courts and the narrowing rise in apex in competence of appellate authorities.

In nutshell, substantive laws are philosophical reasoning, abstract statements, and decreed assumptions that delve more in the realms of morality, logic, ethics, and theology. Thus, these are texted principles, doctrines, and positive statements defining ingredients of the crime and punishment therefor; while procedural laws are professional tools in search of truth that makes substantive, tangible commandments realisable and implementable in delivering justice to the litigant. Thus, procedural laws are purposed to create harmony in the judicial system and facilitate vindication of rights and dispensation of equity and should not become a negative asset in the process of justice. It is, therefore, worth recalling a wise refrain that law cannot exist without procedures which furnish it the means to give effect and become real; contrarily, procedures have no utility without the existence of substantive law which uses these as handy crutches to tread to the altar of justice.

Undoubtedly, substantive law is fundamental and everlasting with accumulated experience of precedents under the doctrine of *stare decisis* to apply and distribute chronicled reasoned wisdom. But law is perceived and achieved through procedure and may be upset in a subsequent appeal or review again through applicable procedures. Law and procedures, therefore, must exist in harmony and walk together in step; else conflict can be damaging both ways. Ergo, procedural laws make for a unique bridge to create a beneficial nexus betwixt art and profession or skill and acumen. These abilities are inherently procedural in content and spirit and are acquired by lawyers through devoted study and professional practice.

8.1.2 Procedures in International Law

For centuries, nations have lived in amity by treaties and customs of international relations collectively called Laws of Nations. This branch of legal regulations and the collective corpus of bilateral and multilateral treaties, and conventions are presently called international law. Generally, treaties enshrine substantive law or principal doctrines agreed to between the parties, but the negotiated treaties are not so simple or easy to interpret. These may have hidden intent, deliberate ambiguities, and covert compromises and with no resolution avenues. It is only occasionally that mention of methods of dispute settlement or conflict resolution is embedded in convention or treaty. In treaty negotiations, it is indeed difficult to satisfy all the parties on all points at all times. Thus, discussion on procedural rules, rarely ever take place under the euphoria of the success of treaty negotiations where both or all parties deem themselves as victors. Procedural law and jurisdictional issues may be ignored or deferred; only to be fully appreciated when international law, both public and private, gets breached to the detriment of a state party or comes in conflict for causing damage or injury. The need for remedial procedures suddenly raises its head at that point and a quest starts for relevant rules to seize the matter, both nationally and internationally.

Empirically, in the past nations have tended to resolve their disputes by diplomatic negotiations, good offices and mediation, conciliation or arbitration, as possible; and it was rare that nations waged a war to settle differences that were reconcilable through mutual dialogue or minor ideological compromises. The international scenario has since changed; the world is, of course, turning towards enhanced globalisation but with gated nationalism, eroding confidence, and verification protocols. This shows escalating trust deficit that hampers dispute resolution. On the other hand, nations are coming together and closer in many ways and accepting the supranational position of international institutions[2] in a sensible compact of their national or economic or other aspects of sovereignty. Such compromises have paid widespread dividends and benefitted nations in maintaining international peace, ensuring global security and fostering global prosperity.

---

[2] For example, the United Nations, International Telecommunication Union, World Trade Organisation, etc.

8.1 An Analysis of Legal Procedures

Despite the international conviviality due to this trend, yet there have been isolated cases of aggravated human and humanitarian rights violations and mutually unsettled disputes leading to reference, trial or litigation in international courts and tribunals, despite handicaps of jurisdiction. The results, nevertheless, have been encouraging with increasing number of courts with expanding adjudicatory powers and ever diverse purposes. The majesty of international law has been upheld and International Court of Justice; judicial tribunals and other international institutions have been accorded the highest esteem. Despite due cooperation by all involved, one problem survives. It is the lack of uniform procedures of the international courts. This aspect will be discussed in succeeding paragraphs.

Consequent to the emancipation of territories ruled by the European empires and grant of independence, the mushrooming nations are becoming too conscious in obtrusive exercise and ostensive display of new-gained sovereignty around with their neighbours and narrowing the window of mutual diplomatic negotiations. This has created irritants with an orientation towards international disputes and litigation proceedings at international institutions. Most of such institutions have no procedural rules in place and perforce have to evolve their own special facilitating rules for the purpose depending upon the nature of dispute and the proclivities of the parties.

The above necessity puts in focus the procedural perspective as an auxiliary area of public international law that primarily dwells on practice and tenets as also concentrates on principles of agreement and doctrines for abidance. Treaties, seldom, if ever handle such nitty–gritty because consensus becomes difficult to achieve. In this connection, private international law also called conflict of laws has probably rendered greatest service to an understanding of procedural aspects in contradistinction to the substantive laws within the gamut of public international law. And this has been possible due to precedence given to "*lex loci proceduralis*" over any foreign '*lex causae*."[3] Another similar and favoured doctrine in settlement of jurisdiction is to apply *lex patriae* that is law of the country of domicile of the culprit.

The importance of procedural law, hitherto known but less appreciated, comes in sharp relief in relation to the implementation of judgments of international courts and tribunals where domestic law may also come into play. To illustrate, a treaty may permit or prohibit a certain action or activity, but its violation can be cured only by a diplomatic agreement, competent judgment or authoritative order which can be realised or implemented through procedures so framed or methods approved for execution of the judgment or decision. In contrast, jurisdiction in domestic courts is compulsory and vertical in appeals and binding for judgments denying the defendant any options whatsoever.

Interestingly, procedures in different courts instituted under international law or treaties have tended to adopt specific and individualised rules for their working and court proceedings. Minor differences and specificities due to *lex causae* can be conceded yet broad sweep of court procedures should be similar, if not exactly congruent. Peculiarities can be articulated in additional rules, if highly essential,

---

[3] For a more detailed discussion, refer Gernot Biehler, *Procedures in International Law*, Springer, 2008.

but uncoordinated and multiple sets of rules devised by each international court or tribunal for its purpose and period is lamentable. Accepted that international courts lack compulsory jurisdiction, yet there is need for general and standardised court procedures and these could, possibly, be the same as exist for the International Court of Justice.

However, due to lack of compulsory procedures under international law, support is sought from the procedural provisions in international instruments. But this is too often wanting and, perforce, a variety of procedures have to be evolved like general character procedures or to meet specific contingencies on matters relating to non-state parties.[4] Additional rules have been adduced by specialised courts and tribunals keeping in mind the aim of inquiry or by empirical approach, thereby catering to the peculiarities of the case, to facilitate adjudication and dispensation of justice. But international courts do not subscribe to the binding force of the doctrine of stare decisis, which may make judicial pronouncements fickle and even variable, if not outright conflicting.

However, locus standi of the individual before international courts is a matter of great concern and sensitivity because such cases belong to the political realm and are beset with enforcement issues. The individuals may be indicted for political crimes, economic interests, violation of human, or humanitarian rights or for torts or torture. Despite the criminal prosecution, individuals are still entitled to diplomatic protection and enjoy exceptions under the extradition proceedings like the political offence, rule of double jeopardy, the rule of speciality, and so on.[5] All these considerations encounter hassles of extradition, apprehension, and presentation before the appropriate forum. Nevertheless, the floating and variable nature of international procedures often cast doubts on the objective efficacy and undermine confidence in proceedings.[6]

8.2 International Court of Justice

The United Nations Organisation was born, like phoenix out of the devastation World War II and ashes of the League of Nations, in 1945. Its avowed objectives were to save future generations from the scourge of war, assure equality to all and basic human rights with "conditions under which justice and respect for the obligations arising from treaties and other sources of international law can be maintained."[7] To achieve these ends and realise the promises, a few organs were created for implementation

---

[4] Biehler, ibid, pp.46 and 59.

[5] Biehler, ibid, pp. 252–61.

[6] Biehler, ibid, pp. 186–8.

[7] Preambulatory Remarks to the Charter of the United Nations. It was signed at San Francisco on 26 June 1945, and amended from time to time. Also referred to as the Charter.

of programmes. One of the organs was International Court of Justice (ICJ) which was established under the Charter to "be the principal judicial organ of the United Nations."[8]

8.2.1 Support of Procedural Law

The Charter provisions in relation to its creation are brief and skeletal.[9] These are more regulatory on membership, descriptive of its functions, emphatic on enforcement of its decisions rather than judicial in intent. This directional and regulatory tone of the text has been amplified in the Statute of the ICJ (in short "the Statute"), which is reasonably comprehensive on the organisational structure, working methodology, jurisdictional competence, procedures for court proceedings, and rules of the court. The provisions to cover all these are spread over 70 articles.

Despite such detailed and comprehensive coverage of procedural aspects, a need was still felt for holistic elaboration of rules of internal judicial practice of the court as also procedural provisions. These were formulated and promulgated under the powers granted by Article 30 of the Statute and were adapted in 1976 and again in 1978, respectively. This explains the necessity to keep the rules revised and updated. It also vindicates the importance of procedural law to support functioning and smooth operation of any court and for judicial administration of substantive law for dispensation of justice in any field.

A reference may be made to the fact that over the years, courts, tribunals, commissions, and panels to handle diverse disputes or international crimes so committed have been constituted under the treaty provisions or as sanctioned by the UN. Thus, there has been proliferation of judicial bodies for different purposes. Almost each one has devised its own procedures of the court for its own judicial convenience leading to a situation of multiplicity, conflicting, and overlapping of rules. This has been partly wasteful and thus avoidable in effort and expense.

However, there could be economy of effort and saving of judicial time if a compendium of general and standardised rules and procedures for international courts and judicial institutions could be formalised and made available to the international judicial bodies so formed. In that case, only unavoidable specificities would need to be considered, handled, and rules evolved by a specialist court. Such an approach of basic commonality has been suggested by scholars, which seems appealing, tempting, and workable for its universality, certainty, clarity, and simplicity.[10]

It is pertinent to mention that "Only states may be parties in cases before the Court."[11] This stance is again reiterated, "The Court shall be open to the States

---

[8] The Charter, Article 92.

[9] Articles 92–96 of the Charter.

[10] Brown, Chester, *A Common Law of International Adjudication*, OUP, 2007.

[11] The Statute, Article 34(1).

parties to the present Statute."[12] The court will also entertain disputes, on certain conditions, from other States who are not members of the UN. By implication, this means that the court debars individual, non-governmental organisations, and non-state actors, among other such categories, as competent complainants to refer or contest a dispute for adjudication before it.[13] This exclusion is prejudicial in certain contingencies.

In such eventualities, the subaltern causes of international disputes or sponsored by individuals or organisations, respectively, shall, perforce of law, have to solely depend upon state support, sponsorship, or espousal to obtain resolution of the case, restitution of loss or dispensation of justice at the ICJ. In consequence, the promotion of such causes, even genuine and just, may be foiled by political compulsions or diplomatic tangles or interfered by state ideology or affected by strategic postures of the concerned country. It would be failure of justice, anyway.

8.2.2 Competence of the ICJ

To repeat, ICJ is the judicial organ of the UN and thus becomes a world court with global jurisdiction; and that its decisions shall be binding on the concerned parties and in relation to the dispute.[14] Additionally, it may be treated as ultimate court of last resort in international affairs and for the interpretation of international law and treaties. ICJ's "judgment is final and without appeal."[15] With this status, standing, reach, where even non-members of the UN can and have acquiesced into its jurisdiction, in eventuality, to get an international dispute settled respectably.[16] One would have expected that, likewise in domestic courts, ICJ would also have possessed binding and compulsory jurisdiction in international disputes between nations. This is not to be so.[17]

A brief discussion on the nature of ICJ judgments will be illuminating. First, Article 59 of the Statute reads, "The decision of the Court has no binding force except between the parties and in respect of that particular case." This negative formulation circumscribes the relevance and operation of the judgment to intimate concerns. It is doubtful if past judgments can be used as precedents or under the doctrine of *stare decisis*. It is equally suspect whether such decisions would be implemented in toto by the domestic courts. Thus, not only the binding nature of ICJ judgment but also

---

[12] The Statute, Article 35(1).

[13] This handicap will be discussed under the section for Solutions later.

[14] The Statute, Article 59.

[15] The Statute, Article 60.

[16] As of the end of 2019, 73 UN member states have accepted the compulsory jurisdiction of the ICJ. It implies that any contentious proceedings in international law or treaty interpretation may be submitted to the court, provided all states party to the dispute accept the jurisdiction of the ICJ in writing.

[17] The Statute, Article 36(1).

8.2 International Court of Justice

the finality granted under Article 60 of the Statute that makes "the judgment...final and without appeal" comes under the penumbra of doubt.

A confident belief in the esteem of the court and respect for its decision and a fervent hope for their adherence comes naturally. But in reality, and practice, it is belied when implementation of its decision gets thwarted or mutated by the domestic courts. Thus both, Articles 59 and 60, may appear illusory and fictional for lack of enforcement. This opinion is shared by other scholars also.[18] An example will illustrate this weakness rather vividly. The ICJ decision in *the Madelin case* was held unimplementable by the US Supreme Court for the reason of national self-interest.[19] Other instances of such subordination of ICJ decisions can also be cited like Corfu Channel judgment (1949).[20]

Thus, the jurisdiction of the court over international disputes between states is neither total nor automatic nor compulsory. In actual practice of States, none of these options are an automatic consequence or a binding resort. The notion of sovereignty of states seems a big spoilsport in this game, and, as result of this, documentary assent of the defendant to be sued in the ICJ was made mandatory. In other words, international adjudication is consensual between equal and sovereign nations; it is not adversarial like in the domestic courts. This attribute differentiates resolution of international disputes from the mechanics of domestic litigation. Therefore, defendant's reluctance or withdrawal can render the court's decision moot and a nullity. This is pity of the situation; perhaps, for a better cause of justice between equals.

However, the fundamental provision concerning jurisdiction of the ICJ is contained in Article 95 of the UN Charter. The text reads, "Nothing in the present Charter shall prevent members of the United Nations from entrusting the solution of their differences to other tribunals by virtue of agreements already in existence or which may be concluded in the future."[21] Thus by interpretation, ICJ is not the only and mandatory resort of dispute adjudication between states or even substate entities on international issues. Even by implication, the Charter offers alternative options of jurisdiction to adjudicate differences, and more importantly, other forums for dispute resolution are open and available to the parties.

In a way, it may be argued that the Charter does not claustrophobically restrict nor bind states into a single and unavoidable option, but on the contrary offers alternative choices and affords sufficient flexibility thus showing due respect to the sovereign dignity of the states. Thus, the jurisdiction is optional, consensual, horizontal, and non-hierarchical. These parametric bases of ICJ's jurisdiction could lead to motivated selection of a forum based on covert influences or ulterior motives apart from pressing, valid, and *bonafide* judicial considerations. The assumed flexibility and discretion in determination of forum may be prejudicial to the interests of the aggrieved and justice may be at risk.

---

[18] F A Mann, "The Doctrine of Jurisdiction in International Law", in (1964) *Recueil des Cours*, p. 73. Cited from Gernot Biehler, *Procedures in International Law*, Springer, 2008.

[19] Madelin v. Dretke, (544US660), (2005), see also Madelin v. Texas, 128 S Ct 1346 (2008).

[20] UK v. Albania, Judgment of 9 April, 1949 on Corfu Channel case.

[21] The Charter, Article 95.

The matter of jurisdiction of ICJ has been elaborated in greater detail in the Statute. Article 36 (1) reads, "The jurisdiction of the Court comprises all cases which the parties refer to it and all matters specially provided in the Charter of the United Nations or in treaties and conventions in force." Thus, the states have neither obligation nor compulsion to refer their international disputes for resolution to the ICJ. State may hunt for politically convenient forum or an economical option in costs or a pliable method for settlement of the dispute. Secondly, both or all parties involved in the dispute must concur in a written agreement to refer to and abide by the ICJ. This becomes a tall order and makes ICJ as resort for the elite who can afford its costs and the civilised states who deem it a norm.

There is, however, a consolatory proviso in Article 36 (2) which states, "The States parties to the present Statute may, at any time, declare that they recognise as compulsory, ipso facto and without special agreement, in relation to any other State accepting the same obligation, the jurisdiction of the Court in all legal disputes...." But this has a rider, "The declaration referred to above may be made unconditionally or on condition of reciprocity on the part of several or certain States or for a certain time."[22] This open-ended freedom of choice to the States weakens the jurisdictional strength of the court and makes States as sole arbiters of this discretion.

Apart from the freedom to elect a forum, there could be instances of competing jurisdictions claiming to seize the case. The conflict could be with domestic jurisdiction of a state or between national and international law. In such overlaps of jurisdiction or double litigation, the case *in prelim* should be decided on the doctrine of *lis alibi pendens* and then only court proceedings be commenced. Generally, international jurisdiction is governed by customs of international law or the treaty provisions, and the national jurisdiction is determined independently by the *lex fori proceduralis*. Nevertheless, in such context, courts resort to the notion of judicial restraint to eschew conflict, and thus comity between courts should be the espoused policy.

Notwithstanding the almost absolute freedom to the States to elect or reject the compulsory jurisdiction of the ICJ, there is, however, a redeeming possibility where a state in a voluntary gesture may remit and exempt its jurisdiction through an executive fiat to refrain from creating a conflictive situation and thus save embarrassment to the courts.[23] Further strengthening the pedestal of the ICJ, the Statute has an empowering clause for the court, which asserts, "In the event of a dispute as to whether the court has jurisdiction, the matter shall be settled by the decision of the Court."[24] Thus, finality and ultimacy of the court's decision in matters of contentious acrimony between parties regarding its competence and jurisdiction are vindicated and upheld.

---

[22] The Statute, Article 36(3).

[23] Lotus case between France and Turkey (1927) may be a good example. Refer PCIJ reports, Series A, No. 10.

[24] The Statute, Article 36(6).

And the nature and kinds of disputes that may be accepted for compulsory jurisdiction are listed as follows:

(a) The interpretation of a treaty, convention or agreement;
(b) Any question of international law;
(c) A breach of an international obligation;
(d) The nature or extent of the reparation for the breach.[25]

Another jurisdiction conferred on the ICJ relates to rendering of "an advisory opinion on any legal question" to the General Assembly or the Security Council, whenever asked for.[26] The ICJ has also been made responsible to provide advisory opinion to other organs of the United Nations and specialised agencies on legal questions arising within the scope of their activities, subject to authorisation by the General Assembly.[27] In other words, the opinions are advisory to help consideration in or appraisal of a dispute and are by no means binding on the requesting institution.

However, an article of special importance that reinforces this capacity and competence may be cited here. "The Court may give an advisory opinion on any legal question at the request of whatever body may be authorised by or in accordance with the Charter of the United Nations to make such a request."[28] Other amplifications on working modalities of the ICJ, from all aspects of jurisdiction and procedures and related determinants, are contained in the Statute of International Court of Justice, 1945 (in short "the Statute"). This is a respected and haloed document in international judicial circles.

It deserves mention that occasions may arise where the court, in dispensation of justice, may require an on-the-spot study to verify ground reality in a State or need special interpretation or construction of a domestic law implementing the treaty in dispute or as a sort of *amicus curiae*. It has thus powers to appoint an individual or a commission to investigate the situation in relation to historical background of the dispute, cultural moorings of the parties, or jurisprudential philosophy of the judicial system of the country and advise the court accordingly. This power to appoint is articulated in the Statute at Article 50 which reads, "The Court may, at any time, entrust any individual, body, bureau, commission, or other organisation that it may select, with the task of carrying out an enquiry or giving an expert opinion."[29]

In this connection, it seems pertinent to allude to some new and recent developments in the field of criminal law and supporting fields like principles of criminology, importance of forensics, empathy in victimology, and necessity for procedures. The same values ought to apply to space crimes and their adjudication. To amplify, the principles of criminology are becoming more reformative than strictly demanding like "shylokian" attitude. The science of forensic is gaining importance because it is becoming exact and scientific, more so with advancing technology and digitisation.

---

[25] The Statute, Article 36 (2).
[26] The Charter, Article 95.
[27] The Charter, Article 96.
[28] The Statute, Article 65.
[29] The Statute, Article 50.

The crimes are evoking greater empathy towards the victim and the causation, and judges are becoming more considerate to his plight and incumbent harassment. And lastly, legal procedures are being better defined and simplified for ease in prosecution, yet irregularities in compliance of procedures can vitiate the very proceedings in the court.

A brief appraisal would make an understanding of this discussion easier. There is international law comprising customs and treaties. Breaches by states as contracting or abiding parties are justiciable at ICJ or any other special court or tribunal with competent jurisdiction. The substantive law of the treaties and customs is made realisable in effect by procedural law and rules of the court. These also help in implementation of the judgments and decisions. Despite all the elaboration, an aggrieved individual has no direct remedy or procedure. Accordingly, an individual for infringement has to depend upon the conscious willingness and diplomatic machinery of the state. This could be a difficult proposition.

And particularly under space law, individuals may often be victims and sufferers of contractual breaches or violation of basic human rights on celestial bodies as entrepreneurs or workers, respectively. This thus appears an unresolved imponderable beset with doubts, overwhelming uncertainties, and unknown conditionality. There may be different perceptions of the problem, yet all would possibly suggest the need for a *specialis* treaty or a modification in procedural rules where individuals can seek judicial redress in local courts with intercountry enforcement of judgments, decisions, and decrees subject to local judicial review in a specified time frame. Existing provisions in this regard are not universal and are only partially effective with suspect outcomes fouled by dilatory formalities. And international courts have been eliminated as option for reasons of lack of ease in access and exorbitant costs of adjudication.

8.3 Extradition as a Procedural Remedy

An allied subject of importance relates to the extradition of an offender, as necessary or requested by a state. Based on the principles of jurisdiction, discussed earlier, there may be situations requiring consideration for extradition for varied reasons. There can be occasions where a culprit of a space crime enters the jurisdiction of the state of nationality and escapes trial for offence, for some reasons, whatsoever. The reasons for non-trial could be nationalistic, political, jurisdictional, legal, or a combination of these. Nevertheless, the victim has been denied justice for the grievance. This would appear utterly unfair. Again, there is also a possibility that an offender in space may take sanctuary, refuge or asylum in or absconds to a country that treats the crime kindly on grounds of lenient laws, affinity of race or religious preference, denominational affiliation, or any other bias. Thus, the criminal may for any such consideration or justification may escape trial and consequent punishment. This situation would also be equally unfair and unjust to the sufferer.

8.3 Extradition as a Procedural Remedy

Techno-legal connotation of "Extradition is the surrender [or handing over] by one State to another of a person desired to be dealt with for crimes of which he has been accused or convicted [or even suspected of commission of crime] and which are justiciable in the Courts of the other State."[30] But howsoever, serious be the offence or justifiable be the process by the requesting State, the surrender of a fugitive person present within the territory of another State, whether apprehended or not, depends upon a government fiat. Therefore, extradition of "a citizen or an alien is a political act done in pursuance of a treaty or an arrangement ad hoc"[31] or under the Consular Agreement on legal aid.

However, under international law, the doctrine of extradition "is founded on the broad principle that it is in the interest of civilised communities that crimes should not go unpunished as a part of the comity of nations that one State should ordinarily afford to another State assistance towards bringing offenders to justice."[32] This law, soliciting the cooperation of independent sovereign States, depends upon concluded bilateral treaties, abidance of incumbent obligations thereunder, and commitment of the State to handle the procedure objectively and diligently. In fact, States have "no duty to extradite in the absence of a treaty."[33] It is, thus, a prerogative of a sovereign state. Nevertheless, asylum ends when extradition begins, though a state has the power and competence to grant asylum or refuge to a fugitive criminal from another state. On the contrary, an individual has no right to claim asylum.[34]

The Soviet view on the subject is, "Legal relations associated with the effecting of legal aid (diplomatic assistance) on criminal matters is governed either by the norms of multilateral international conventions related to control of crimes of an international character, or by special treaties concerning legal cooperation."[35] Further, the Soviet understanding of extradition of criminals "represents an act of legal assistance by one State (the requestee) to another State (the requester) with the aim of carrying out a criminal prosecution, finding and arresting a suspected criminal in order to bring him (or her) to court or for executing the sentence."[36] This, however, relates only to extraditable offences mentioned in the specific treaties, though acts of legal assistance can be of diverse character like searches and seizures, forensic examination, supplying material evidence or authenticated documents, etc.

There is, however, a rider to these general provisions accepted and practised by most countries. The exception provides that such a provision would not apply to one's

---

[30] KJ Aiyar's Judicial Dictionary, (Twelfth edition), 1998, Allahabad, The Law Book Company (P) Ltd., p. 493. Words in parenthesis added.

[31] Aiyar's Ibid.

[32] Aiyar's at n. 84 ante, p. 494.

[33] Michael Akehurst, *A Modern Introduction to International Law*, London, George Allen & Unwin, 1977, p. 105.

[34] Incidentally, even Article 14 of the Universal Declaration of Human Rights grants an individual a right of political asylum only.

[35] G I Tunkin, *International Law*, Moscow, Progress Publishers, 1986, p. 368.

[36] Tunkin, ibid, p. 369.

own citizens[37] and certain other categories of fugitives. Thus, "The countries which most uncompromisingly refuse to extradite their nationals are those in whose legal system the Roman heritage is most apparent."[38] These sovereignties have proclaimed national policies enshrined in national codes, laws, and rules that are uniformly opposed to such a concept and action.[39] There are just a few small countries where surrender of nationals in extradition is either not prohibited or is discretionary in support of human justice and international morality.[40]

On the contrary, countries that practise common law subscribe to the view that the fugitive offender should be restored to the appropriate jurisdiction for proper trial in the interest of justice. These sovereignties consider administration of justice more important than national affinity and would prefer jurisdiction most suited to the purpose of justice regarding availability of evidence or competence of the court. These treat refusal to extradite as "nothing but absurdity and travesty of the law."[41] Therefore countries like Australia, Canada, India, Israel, the UK, and the USA among others tend to be ready to facilitate surrender of own national, found fugitive and if accused, charged or convicted of a crime, even in foreign land under their legal code.[42]

During the decades of sixties, seventies, and eighties of the last century, terrorism was at its peak and it often found aircraft services and aviation facilities as attractive target for the weaknesses in the security system and the advantage of blitz for sensational news which would make the public more aware of the ostensible cause and perceived grievance of the terrorist group. India had its share of suffering at the hands of the terrorists in hijackings, blasts, and killings. But the attack on twin towers of New York in the USA, (9/11) on 11 September 2001 was barbarous and horrific which killed hundreds of innocent people and destroyed property worth billions of dollars. This was the first time, where aircraft were used as missiles and the perpetrators had also perished. One wonders at the strength of indoctrination, deep faith in belief, and the courage of conviction in the cause by the pilots. Whatever be the reason, their act perpetrated gross brutality and caused horrific killings that shocked the human conscience. Reprisals cannot be an answer to perceived grievances.

The terrorists may have, at times, used only threats and toy pistols to instil fear among crew and passengers rather than threatened blast or dreaded killings yet successfully achieved their purpose of hijacking the aircraft[43] and make it force-land in a country sympathetic to the terrorists or their objective for reasons of ethnic

---

[37] Tunkin, ibid. Also refer Article 7 of *the Citizenship Law of the USSR*, 1978.

[38] Satya Dev Bedi, *Extradition in International Law and Practice*, Rotterdam, Bronder-Offset, 1966, p. 95.

[39] For example, states of France, Sweden, Switzerland, Turkey, the USSR, Argentina, Uruguay and others. Cited from Bedi at n. 38 ante, p. 95.

[40] For example, Hungary, Italy, El Salvador, Mexico, Chile, etc. Ibid.

[41] Bedi, ibid, p. 97.

[42] For a more detailed treatment of the subject, refer Bedi, n. 38 ante.

[43] The first recorded hijacking occurred in Peru in 1930 and in Cuba in the fifties and sixties of the last century.

8.3 Extradition as a Procedural Remedy

affinity or religious similarity or political vengeance. And after reaching the country of refuge, the terrorists often roamed freely and publicly, duly supported, and at times pampered and honoured by the host country. In most cases, they were not arrested and prosecuted and incarcerated for the alleged crimes as per the law but were only overtly imprisoned with enough facilities and wide freedom in the jail.

This was travesty of justice and equally unfair to the sufferers and victims who lost lives, sustained injuries, or suffered damage. Terrorism came to be treated a crime against humanity, but it not only went unpunished but also was, in a way, encouraged within the safe-haven countries. This was judicially repugnant and politically frustrating. Coupled with this situation was the lack of bilateral treaties for extradition of criminals. In fact, after the World War II, the newly emancipated colonies had not yet renovated or formalised the old inherited treaties or negotiated fresh ones on the subject. This resulted in stumping of the request for extradition of the criminals. As such, diplomatic efforts failed and the predicament compelled for a viable solution.

Aviation services and airport facilities being the easiest and choicest targets, the resultant situation led to the negotiation of international instruments to tackle the problem of offences against aviation, as then confronted. Accordingly, a series of conventions were negotiated to tackle the problems as these emerged and aggravated, but the most relevant one for our purpose is the Hague Convention, 1970[44] which tackled the malaise of hijacking by enhancing the powers of the commander. But the best bargain from this convention was that the offenders and their accomplices shall be extradited under respective bilateral treaties and where these did not exist, extradition could be invoked and claimed under this convention. A similar convention can be considered and concluded in space law to extradite space criminals to competent countries for trial, between whom bilateral treaties do not exist.

By definition, the doctrine of extradition constitutes an act of approaching another state to apprehend and hand over a suspected or convicted criminal who has fled the *forum delicti commissi* to another country and in whom the soliciting state has interest or nexus of crime.[45] This process is not new to the modern international order, and this instrument of cooperation between states has been known to ancient civilised societies in mutual interest and security.[46] Earlier, in international law, it was known as "extra-tradition,"[47] which word has now been popularised as extradition in diplomatic circles. However, Oppenheim asserts that prior to the nineteenth century, there was hardly any extradition treaty for surrender of alleged criminals.[48] Nevertheless, cooperation between states could have existed without formal treaties,

---

[44] The Convention for the Suppression of Unlawful Seizure of Aircraft, The Hague, 1970.

[45] Bin Cheng, *Studies in International Space Law*, London, 1997, p. 387.

[46] E Vattel, *The Law of Nations or the Principles of Natural Law*, New York, 1916, (edited by JB Scott) in Introduction at p. 3.

[47] T Twiss, *The Law of Nations*, London, 1861, p. 343. Citation obtained from SD Bedi, *Extradition in International Law and Practice*, Rotterdam, Bronder-Offset, 1966, p. 15.

[48] L Oppenheim, *International Law*, vol. I, London, 1958, (8th edition), pp. 696 and 704.

and suspected culprits may have been surrendered in good faith or for maintenance of peaceful relations.[49]

As stated above, this process is currently regulated by bilateral treaties espousing reciprocity between the states.[50] But apart from bilateral treaties, many multinational treaties on certain specific crimes also bear such a clause to effectively ensure extradition on its own strength even in the absence of a bilateral treaty. Most of these extraditable offences relate to acts of terrorism and its illicit funding, taking hostages and torture, murder, rape, etc., which are universally considered as heinous crimes or crimes against humanity. In dealing with space crimes also, a provision of this nature, content and effect, in any Space Treaty or a protocol or an IGA, would be necessary and pertinent because such a predicament would keep recurring once space tourism becomes popular or commercial exploitation of celestial resources becomes the norm or planetary residencies get inhabited.

Despite international concern and existing bilateral treaty regime between sovereign states, the operation of this process has national moorings and political overtones. The decision that whether an offender should be handed over pursuant to a requisition is determined under national law and by a competent domestic court. On the other hand, the person to be extradited should have been accused or convicted of a criminal offence committed against the laws of the requesting State. It is necessary to prove the competence of the State making a demand or solicitation to try the alleged offender.[51] Be that as it may, "[i]n treaty practice and in the legislation of many countries there is a provision for the non-extradition of their national"[52] or where the perpetrator may be awarded death penalty by the trial court or the government of domicile may be disinclined or has granted political asylum.

However, the government of the victim, as an alternative, can resort to diplomatic pressure for a trial of the criminal in the country of refuge. But such an exercise or pressure tactic may not always be successful. It may meet with inaction, lame excuses, protracted delays, or even stark resistance. Then the next step would be to initiate a diplomatic process to seek extradition of the offender to the country of the victim. But the success of this alternative depends upon whether the two countries, one in possession of the offender and the other espousing the case of the victim, have concluded a bilateral extradition treaty under which transfer of the criminal can take place. In the absence of such a treaty, the request for extradition may be outright refused. Thus, we again reach a dead end where justice fails and this does not appear to be a satisfactory solution.

---

[49] There is a difference between extradition and deportation. While extradition is on request, the latter action can be taken by a state for refusal of entry on the bases of sovereign jurisdiction and territorial supremacy. The reception of a foreigner is a matter of discretion of the receiving state and *suo motu* deportation can be ordered for various reasons and causes.

[50] Even without professed reciprocity also, a criminal may be extradited in the interest of world order. Refer Charlton v. Kelly, 229 U.S. 447.

[51] *Rosaline George v. Union of India,* 1994 SCC (Cr) 304 at 315.

[52] *A Dictionary of International Law,* Moscow, Progress Publishers, 1986, p. 81.

8.3 Extradition as a Procedural Remedy

Under these circumstances, states can solicit good help from time-tested maxims of international law to counter the moves of the offender. Because, apart from pre-selecting the country of refuge, the offender may become a fugitive to escape a trial and even evade death penalty. To fight such impunity of an international delict and as state obligation towards extradition, Hugo Grotius had postulated a principle of "*aut dedere, aut punire*" which means either extradite or punish.[53] This principle has found acceptance in the legal fraternity and has become an obligation of states under the established law of extradition.

However, purist law scholars may raise an objection that this maxim prejudges guilt and obligates for punishment which seems contra to the natural justice and rights of an alleged offender. As a result, the International Law Commission, to combat the possibility of escape from extradition, has enunciated a more sober and rational version of the earlier Latin principle "*aut dedere, aut judicare*," which means either extradite or prosecute. Thus, it acknowledges the possibility that the offender may be found "not guilty" on trial. Further, it exhorts cooperation of the states for a common cause of curbing crimes against humanity. In fact, this doctrine was developed to facilitate regulatory necessities and combat political resistance from the states towards extradition on flimsy grounds. Hence, this doctrine was refined to impose a clear obligation on the states that approximates a *jus cogen* of international law.[54]

Transnational crimes are a different class altogether and throw up variable scenario regarding locus of crime, availability of evidence, nationalities of the offender, and the victim as also the claim of the state seeking extradition for trial of the alleged offender. The instant obligation was considered by the International Court of Justice in Belgium v. Senegal case, 2012.[55] In the Lockerbie case also, it was discussed and held that the obligation arises regardless of the extraterritorial nature of the crime and irrespective of the fact that the perpetrator and the victim may be of alien nationality.[56] Thus, the obligation to extradite is almost complete and binding except for the riders of own nationality, possibility of death sentence, and for political considerations, as mentioned earlier. Further, the discussed principle is embodied in several multinational treaties.[57]

---

[53] Hugo Grotius, *De Jure Belli ac Pacis*, Book II, chapter XXI, section IV (English translation by Francis W. Kelsey (Oxford/London: Clarendon Press/Humphrey Milford, 1925), pp. 527–529 at 527). Cited from Final Report of the International Law Commission (ILC Report) on "The Obligation to Extradite or Prosecute (*aut dedere, aut judicare*), UN, 2014, p. 2.

[54] Michael Kelly, "Cheating Justice by Cheating Death: The Doctrinal Collision for Prosecuting Foreign Terrorists—Passage of *Aut Dedere Aut Judicare* into Customary Law & Refusal to Extradite Based on the Death Penalty", 20 Ariz. J. Int'l & Comp. L. (2003), p. 491 and 496–497.

[55] ILC Report, n. 53 ante, p. 4.

[56] Stephen Hall, *International Law*, Butterworths Tutorial Series, LexisNexis Butterworths, 2nd ed., 2006.

[57] For example, aviation offences (1970), crimes against internationally protected persons like diplomats (1973), taking of hostages (1979), terrorist bombings (1997), financing of terrorism (1999), against corruption (2003), and many others.

Lately, however, "[E]xtradition is of declining importance throughout the world. Many extradition treaties were terminated by the outbreak of the First or Second World Wars and have not been renewed subsequently."[58] Moreover, on collapse of the British Empire, few erstwhile colonies have revived or concluded fresh extradition treaties. And new treaties have started including riders like nature of offences or the locus of crime, etc., to narrow the scope of extradition. At the same time, responsible governments have started resorting more to the modern statutory powers for deportation of aliens as disguised extradition, if the case merits action, rather than wait for elongated and time-consuming extradition processes and judicial verdicts. Diplomacy is known to be a slow marcher. But, so are the court proceedings.

8.4 Conclusion

The expanse and limits of the domain of outer space, including celestial bodies, have been defined earlier, and the character and complexion of space crimes have also been tentatively visualised. But space crimes are a different genre and may happen in an entirely different domain or concurrently violate more than one domain, with unforeseen possibilities attracting diverse implications of legalities due to varying codes and differing social values. Thus, seizing jurisdiction over a criminal for trial in a court, domestic or international, may be beset with hassles and imponderables. The variance in national laws and differences in social mores or cultural fixations would tend to make dispensation of justice rather uncertain in verdict and perception of the parties.

Even to arrive at this stage of trial is not easy because treaties rarely contain procedural expedients and substantive provisions need clutches of procedures to reach the portals of a competent court. Thus, difficulties countenanced to get the offender and reach the trial stage are many and diverse. A fairly detailed discussion on this aspect has preceded in the chapter to flag the importance of legal procedures and processes. In this regard, the majesty of judicial institutions and, in particular, the competence of the International Court of Justice has been elaborated because certain categories of space crimes, like crimes by states or crimes against humanity may fall within its jurisdiction.

Further, extradition has been treated as a procedural remedy and has been discussed from different aspects. This tenet may have to be invoked when the offender may not be within territorial jurisdiction of the state competent and desirous to try, whereas the state of domicile may not extradite the offender for vested interests or parochial reasons. This is because the law of extradition first requires a bilateral treaty between states, and secondly, a political will to extradite the offender. To overcome these bottlenecks, the alternative could be to invoke a relevant multinational treaty like the Hague Treaty, 1970, for offences against aviation, where a specific provision under the treaty deems it as an agreement authorising extradition of an alleged

---

[58] Akehurst, n. 33 ante, p. 107.

8.4 Conclusion

terrorist or offender. Similar clauses exist in many other multinational treaties that make extradition or a proper trial an obligation of the states under the doctrine of *aut didere, aut judicare*. As a result, extradition in such cases becomes claimable and easier even without a bilateral treaty between respective states.

Chapter 9
Diverse Legal Systems: A Global Review

As discussed earlier, outer space stations, orbiting space laboratories, orbiting hotels, celestial resorts, and planetary habitats are all going to be multi-nationality, multiracial, multicultural, and multi-ethnicity collective habitation or group living or work environment. This will bring in contact, and possibly in long togetherness, people with different background, mindset, and beliefs. Their divergent perceptions on personal etiquette, behavioural patterns, and living styles may not all be similar, acceptable, or tolerable. Even methods of interaction, body language, choice of words, verbal slangs, and dialectical expression may be different and at times, not too agreeable, apparently. These divergences can throw up differences in opinion, cause annoyance, or initiate disputes that may lead to conflicts and eventual crimes, physical or mental or both. Moreover, since guests, workers, and residents would be drawn from different countries with different background and different upbringing, their perception and responses to the same action or similar situations or comparable occurrences may not be matching or identical; reactions may vary widely, disputes may arise, conflicts may culminate, and as a result, even crimes may be committed.

Diverse legal systems have evolved in different countries across the globe, and each system has imbibed its own culture, social norms, and perceptions of public order. In fact, each country has "evolutionised" and developed its own legal system based on its societal needs, cultural practices, community values, geographical compulsions, and local peculiarities. All these factors cumulatively interact, mutate each other, and amalgamate into national legislation. Thus, each country has a specific legal code based on its cultural perceptions, social norms, political ideology, and geonecessities. And it seems pertinent to draw an analogy and lessons for the pluralistic, multi-ethnic, motley space societies, and planetary habitations where members would be drawn from different countries with distinct religions and diverse ethnicities. They would also be habituated to own legal system, cultural peculiarities, social specificities, individual conduct, and behavioural patterns which may not be amiable or compatible for cordial living. Some, with high tolerance threshold, may ignore such divergences, while others, more conservative, may take a strong objection and even cause disruption to create a conflict situation that may lead to unforeseen developments and unintended consequences resulting in crime. Thus, there is a need for understanding and appreciation of underlying causes for crimes in space communities and attendant problems of policing, procedures, jurisdiction, court trial, and dispensation of justice.

Generally, an important component in any legal system is a procedure for prosecuting criminals and a method of resolving disputes that may exist under the rules and codes of that particular legal system. This educates and enables the parties, within a given legal context, to observe their own obligations and respect the rights of others thus causing least overstepping on others toes or create irritable interference. On the contrary, they could assert their own rights in correlation of duties imposed within that system.[1] But this simplistic situation may not always operate for individuals in outer space or on celestial bodies or work environment or in orbital stations. The working groups or resident population may be drawn from different countries with different legal systems and accordingly with dissimilar expectations, different mindset and norms of discipline. Thus, conflict becomes endemic to the situation and its occurrence a possibility, while existing *lex specialis* for outer space is acutely inadequate for administration of criminal justice relating to space crimes, because of its scant existence of germane rules and its functioning in a fragmented manner, though in tandem with international law. This seems no desirable predicament.

At the same time, national criminal codes across the globe are also not likely to be congruent or uniform and may reflect mild to wide variance. These may differ in cognition, text, content, or ingredients of crime due to differences in social values, local ethos, cultural moorings, living habits, geographical compulsions, personal styles, or for other reason. These variations can result in not too compatible beliefs or cause disparity in personal behaviour or different expressions of conversation, which though remain only normatively variant, yet may appear disrespectful or insulting. Thus, what one considers mundane or innocuous may seem to another utter profanity or indecency to the extent of an unacceptable normalcy, offensive response, or even a criminal act.

Even inadvertence with decent intentions may be misconstrued to elicit unexpected resentment or a sharp reaction to the level of criminality. Ergo, in a demographic mix of space dwellers, whether temporary or permanent in time, such divergence of national laws, societal norms, and customary behaviour of people may create inconvenient circumstances, querulous retorts, and physical conflicts leading to accusations of varying degrees of criminality. The situations can unduly aggravate due to sheer misunderstanding of spoken language or apprehensions arising from unfamiliar body language. Further, there is no uniformity in the definition of crimes, their ingredients for proof, credence for evidence, or the quantum of respective punishments that may prejudice dispensation of seemingly true justice.

Therefore, internationally heterogeneous communities in space need to be tolerant and mutually appeasing rather than aggressive and accusative. But the outcome may

---

[1] Mahulena Hoffman, PJ Blount, "Space Law Disputes" in *Max Planck Encyclopaedia of International Law,* (MPIL). Article updated in October 2019.

not always be of ignoring or condoning the unsavoury act, while hardened attitudes or fanatic mindset may create ugly incidents. Thus, even a minor frustration may possibly get transformed into nihilistic anger prompting patently criminal acts even when the offending person as a hotel guest or a neighbour in habitation may not be conscious or aware of the sensitivities and sensibilities of the of the aggrieved person. The motivating *mens rea* may as such be absent from the act and may fail to impart it a criminal refrain, while the ground situation may escalate for no reason at all culminating in acts that may constitute a patent crime in another's consideration.

Such variations in perception and acceptance of deviations and tolerance of others behaviour are caused by sympathetic learning and social grooming of local law and legal systems. In turn, legal systems and legal codes also differ due to society's espoused values, cultural customs, geographical compulsions, and specific needs. Each parameter has its impact to cause variation. So a person accustomed to a particular legal code and system may find adjustment difficult and at times, near impossible leading to acts or reactions that may not be condonable but outright culpable. Such situations can be envisaged in an international environment of space stations, work milieu on celestial bodies, or living conditions of planetary habitats. This predicament compels us to make a detour of major legal systems prevalent across the globe and appreciate their differences, in our search of a legal system as a common denominator with maximum acceptability in the space domain.

9.1 Divergent Legal Systems: A Global Review

Legal systems comprise and facilitate dispensation of criminal justice and civil disputes redressal system. For our discussion, criminal justice system includes crime investigation, all the interdependent components of the court, and various stages of a trial procedure leading to sentencing or declaration of acquittal and setting the accused free. There are, however, different types of criminal justice systems with differing trial procedure for exposing and evaluating evidence in courts, yet the objective is same to investigate crime and punish the criminals. Thus, the criminal justice system is the process by which offenders are arrested, followed by stages of investigation to cull out and determine proof for prosecution after which charges are framed, then a defence is raised, trial conducted, and sentencing rendered if found guilty or acquitted if found innocent. And the trial is a judicial examination of the issues between the parties, whether these are points of law or factual evidence, presented in court before a jury or judge so as to determine guilt in the criminal proceedings.

Different countries across the world have different legal systems which look at the crime, the criminal, and criminality differently than other cognates. Their variations are clear and discernible. These systems can be broadly classified into four categories. The first category can be adversarial legal system which generally operates in the USA and most of the erstwhile British Colonies. The second category is inquisitorial judicial system followed in France, Italy, and some other civil law states. The third category can be jury system which is a successor to the ancient courts in Greece and ecclesiastical courts in Europe. Some remnants of this judicial system prevail in the UK, the USA, and some erstwhile colonies of the British empire. The last category has sway in Muslim countries following Islamic law based on Shariah. The legal codes here are primarily derived from the religious scriptures of Quran, and religious injunctions govern social life as well as regulate personal living.

9.1.1 Adversarial System of Common Law Countries

According to Black's Law Dictionary, "Adversary system is the court system where a judge decides on a case argued by a prosecutor who is suing the plaintiff and the defence attorney who defends their plaintiff." In other words, in adversarial system, judges do not play any role in the investigation mainly evaluate evidence presented, statements of witnesses, and arguments of the counsels to reach the verdict. The judges are, however, guided by the precedents and earlier decisions by the higher courts which are considered to have a binding effect. Thus, under this system, there are two parties to the case: the complainant and the defendant. The complainant has to present the case with available evidence to justify the alleged accusation or preferred claim.

Under this system, to begin with only allegations are made by the victim through a statement against the offender and case taken over for prosecution. However, in other cases of cognisable offences like serious, grave and heinous crimes of murder, rape, dacoity, corruption, etc., state authorities can take cognisance of offences *suo motu* and initiate investigation on its own through the police department. This responsibility involves investigation of the case, apprehension of alleged offender, preferring of charge sheet in the competent court, and prosecution of the accused till sentencing or acquittal.

However, under the practice of "plea bargaining," which is common in the USA, the accused pleads guilty or offers "no-contest" in exchange for a reduced sentence.[2] This, adversarial legal system is popular worldwide but is particularly prevalent in common law countries. In India also, for accepting and disposal of confession of crime or plea of guilty of an offence, a High Court has framed norms and guidelines that may obviate miscarriage of justice, particularly in respect of the uneducated masses, those ignoramus on law or cases of confession under greed, threat, or cocrcion.[3]

Importantly, in all cases of crimes, the accused is assumed to be and held innocent till proven guilty in a court of law. It is thus the responsibility of the state and its law-enforcing machinery to arrest the culprit, collect the evidence on the allegations, and put the accused in the dock for trial by the competent court. Here also there

---

[2] Glendon, Carozza, & Picker, *Comparative Legal Traditions*, (Thomson-West, 2008).
[3] Times News Network, "Kerala HC frames norms for handling guilty pleas", *Times of India* (Chandigarh edition), June 9, 2021, p. 11.

are two parties, viz. the State Prosecution and the defendant accused. It is the duty of the investigation agency to lead a tight case beyond any element of doubt on all ingredients of the crime to ensure prosecution and punishment of the offender. But the accused cannot be forced or even suggestively trapped into making a self-incriminating statement and has an inalienable right to a fair trial.[4] Further, adherence to the doctrines of protection of individual's right to liberty, presumption of innocence of the offender, and benefit of doubt to the accused may unduly aid the release of the criminal.

In other civil cases also, there are two or more parties to the dispute and the *onus probandi* is on the petitioner/s, while the defendant can cleverly prick holes in the presented evidence, prove it unreliable, present contradictory or counter evidence, and get away, irrespective of whether facts pleaded by either party are true or not. The judicial system operates on the judicial principles of admissibility, validity, and coherence of the evidence tested on the touchstone substantive law. And in this purist process, truth, at times, may be the victim. Further, the articulation of arguments, suave presentation, judicial acumen, and court management of the respective attorneys do matter for the success of the case. On the other hand, a single judge court with restraints on direct examination of witnesses and if the judge is not too clever in the job may not be able to see through the guiles of a smart lawyer and may, at times, err in the judgment. Thus, adversarial system has its weaknesses, despite popularity, and prevalence.[5]

9.1.2 Inquisitorial System of Justice

The second category of judicial system is inquisitorial that generally operates in France and its erstwhile colonies as also in Italy and some other countries. Under this legal system, the victim or the complainant makes a statement of the allegations with supporting proof, and thereafter prosecution takes over till culmination of the case. Under inquisitorial system, the defendant is held guilty till innocence is proved in a court of law. Thus, the major evidentiary burden of refuting allegations, presenting contra-evidence and offering defence pleas shifts to the one held guilty, who has to establish own innocence or prove the accuser as presenter of false or forged or fake evidence. Two points of difference get highlighted; first, the accused becomes guilty immediately on "cognisation" of complaint rendered by the plaintiff and remains so till proven innocent. Second, the *onus probandi* to prove one's innocence shifts to the defendant, who is on a weaker evidential threshold and disadvantaged to harness

---

[4] For more details, refer Christopher E. Smith, *Courts and Trials: A Reference Handbook*, (ABC-CLIO, 2003).

[5] Pat Schroeder, "The Adversarial Legal System: Is Justice Served?" (2010). Available at: http://www.thelawinsider.com/insider-news/the-adversarial-legal-system-is-justice-served/ Last accessed in February, 2014.

effective defence. Thus, in this legal system, judicial doctrine of presumption of innocence is disregarded and a person is deemed "guilty till proven innocent"; and accordingly, the principle of benefit of doubt to the accused degrades its primacy and relevance.

According to Black's Law Dictionary, the inquisitorial system is, "proof taking used in civil law, whereby the judge conducts the trial, determines what questions to ask, and defines the scope and extent of the inquiry." Thus, this system attaches less importance to the rigmaroles of court procedures, unnecessary wrangles relating to the rights of the defendant, and time-consuming sifting of hearsay evidence from eye witnesses. It is, therefore, structured to focus on truth-seeking by the judge without risking confusing diversions. In this system, as the judges investigate and raise questions,[6] recording of evidence is undertaken before the trial; therefore, there is usually no recall of witnesses for cross-examination or re-examination. This investigative function is usually overseen by *"juges d'instruction"* (magistrate judges) in France, and the same is often vested in the office of the public procurator, particularly in civil cases, in China, Japan, and Germany.

The effectiveness of the inquisitorial process depends on the legal ability and judicial acumen of the prosecuting judge or the investigating magistrate to thoroughly sift out valid, pertinent, and revealing evidence and thus be just and fair to the one on trial. This assumes importance because this legal system does not permit parties to the case, to be represented by attorneys or experts to bare and unravel the intricacies or nuances of the case. Thus, an inquisitorial system[7] is a legal system in which the court, or a part of the court, is actively involved in investigating the evidentiary facts about the case and thereafter the court delivers a considered judgment after trial.

According to French law, the presumption of innocence is obliquely acknowledged and a person accused of a crime is considered innocent until found guilty by a judge. This ordains that an accused cannot be deprived of guaranteed liberties during legal proceedings and detention is only in exceptional cases where certain prescribed conditions concur. But despite this presumption, the onus of defence rests on the accused, who needs to prove innocence beyond reasonable doubt because the plea of "benefit of doubt" is not available to accused.

On the other hand, even a confession of guilt or loud allocution of acceptance of crime by an offender would not be regarded as sufficient ground for a verdict of guilty. In fact, the doctrine of *"audi alteram partem"* dictates that nobody should be condemned unheard. It is for this reason that if an accused is not represented by a lawyer, the state provides one for this purpose. The prosecutor (magistrate judge) is still required to thoroughly search out relevant evidence and duly furnish the same to support a guilty verdict at the proper trial in the court.[8]

---

[6] In France, there is an examining magistrate and Chief Magistrate.

[7] Lately, there is a growing preference to call this system "non-adversarial" instead of inquisitorial.

[8] This requirement, however, is not unique or exclusive to inquisitorial systems, as many adversarial systems also impose a similar requirement under the maxim of *corpus delicti*.

9.1.3 The Jury System for Dispensing Justice

The third category is the jury system, which has a long and celebrated history that may be alluded to briefly, leaving minutia out. Ancient judicial regimes initially patronised Catholic Medieval Inquisition system by applying Canon Law of the Catholic Church, which was practised in Europe in the twelfth century. Inquisitions, then, basically relied on adversarial system in the courts for trial. But evidence was difficult to come by, and witnesses were hesitant, even scared, and refrained from participation because penalties for false accusation were high and there was also a risk of self-recrimination under certain circumstances. Besides, several non-rational modes of trial or extra-judicial procedures such as trial-by-ordeal with tortures or duel/combat-between-parties were also prevalent and outcomes of these were commonly accepted as judgmental verdict. No wonder, at times, justice dispensed could have been far from truth.

Beginning in 1198, Pope Innocent III issued a series of decretals that reformed the ecclesiastical court system. Under the new *processus per inquisitionem* (inquisitional procedure), an ecclesiastical magistrate no longer required a formal accusation for issuing summons. In continued reforms, later in 1215, the Fourth Council of the Lateran affirmed the use of the inquisitional system. The council then forbade clergy from conducting trials by ordeal or combat. Meanwhile in England, King Henry II had established separate secular common law courts that adopted the adversarial system. The adversarial principle upheld was that a person could not be tried until formally accused in a criminal case. In 1215, this principle became enshrined as article 38 of the Magna Carta.[9]

The first territory to wholly adopt the inquisitional system was the Holy Roman Empire, and the new German legal process was introduced. It was not until Napoleon introduced the *code d'instruction criminelle* (French code of criminal procedure) on November 16, 1808, that the classical procedures of inquisition were ended in all German territories. In a later development of modern legal institutions that took place in the nineteenth century, most countries codified their private law and criminal law as well as reviewed the rules and procedures. It was through this development that the role of an inquisitorial system became enshrined in most European civilian legal systems. As a result, eighteenth-century *ancien régime* courts were replaced by the nineteenth-century modern courts with new judicial procedures and codified laws, and in many countries jury system came to be officially resuscitated or newly established.

The origin of the jury is disputed. It may have been indigenous to England or have been taken there by the Norman invaders in 1066. But once established, two forces extended the jury outside England. The expansion of the British Empire brought the jury to Asia, Africa, and the American continent[10]; and the French Revolution and

---

[9] The article reads, "No bailiff for the future shall, upon his own unsupported complaint, put anyone to his law, without credible witnesses brought for this purposes."

[10] Kalven & Zeisel, *The American Jury,* (Boston: Little Brown, 1966). In the US, Army Court Martial Juries are also in practice.

its aftermath brought the jury, as a symbol of popular government, to the European continent. Juries were first established in France itself, and later the system was adopted in Germany, Russia, Austria, Switzerland, Luxembourg, and other countries. The USSR dropped this system on the defeat of Napoleon (only temporarily) and many others on his death. Lately, however, British jury system has lost its appeal as a legal model and its erstwhile colonies are weaning off from this system or are modifying its essential nuances.

There is also another view that the jury system developed out of an ancient custom of Germanic tribes under which a group of men of good character and reputation would investigate the crime locally and judge the accused. This custom evolved into "Vehomic Courts" of Medieval Germany. In this system, the jurors were mostly self-informed of the crime and were generally having personal knowledge about the parties involved, therefore, to reach the root of the crime was easy and possibility of mistrial was minimal. Nevertheless, this system has been criticised by some scholars.[11]

Over its history, jury has often changed its format, character, and jurisdiction. Nevertheless, a jury is a sworn body of people, called the jurors, who were generally eminent persons from the area or aware of the case. It was convened to render an impartial verdict on a question officially submitted to them by a court, or decide on a judgment, or to set a penalty. Juries developed in England during the Middle Ages and assumed different shapes with varying powers. Nevertheless, these remain a hallmark of the Anglo common law legal system. They are still commonly used, even today, in Great Britain, the USA,[12,13] Canada, Australia, and many other countries whose legal systems are descended from British judicial traditions. Most trial juries are "petit juries" that usually consist of twelve people or lesser numbers. A larger jury also known as a "grand jury" is convened only under special circumstances to investigate potential crimes, political atrocities, and to render indictments against suspects. This usually calls for a much larger bench of jurors.

This legal system involves judgment by a jury where the judge conducts legal proceeding to elaborate on the ingredients of the crime and elicits evidence for and against the impugned matter, evaluates its admissibility and efficacy, highlights important issues in the matter for consideration, and then dissociates himself unless any clarification is requested by the jury. Thereafter, the members of jury consider the evidence on commission of crime, deliberate on the verdict, and decide on the sentence. This system still prevails in the UK, Austria, Belgium, Norway, Australia, New Zealand, Brazil, Canada, and certain states in the USA,[14] among many others. Russian Constitution also provides for jury trials in criminal cases.

---

[11] Gerhard Casper & Hans Zeisel, "Lay Judges in the German Criminal Courts", *Journal of Legal Studies,* (January 1972), 1:1, pp. 135–191.

[12] Only in certain states and for certain minor crimes like misdemeanour or infraction.

[13] King NJ, "The American Criminal Jury". *Law and Contemporary Problems,* (1999), **62** (2): 41–67.

[14] Harry A. Bigelow & Other, *The American Jury,* (Chicago, University of Chicago).

9.1 Divergent Legal Systems: A Global Review

This system operated even in India also for over a century. The last important jury trial was of a love triangle where Naval Commander KM Nanavati murdered Prem Ahuja, who was in illicit sexual relation with his wife. The murder took place on 27 April 1959, and Nanavati surrendered himself before the police the same day. A nine-member jury was convened which returned an 8-1 verdict of acquittal. The judge dismissed the verdict as perverse in law and overturned it to guilty. The judge considered that jury was emotionally influenced and misled by the media that widely covered this case as a principled fight between a wronged husband with middle-class values against playboy image of the accused and sleaze of the bourgeois society. The case went in appeals up to the Honourable Supreme Court, which also upheld the pronouncement of guilty and imprisonment for life.[15] As an aftermath of this case, the jury system was abolished in India[16] under the revised Code of Criminal Procedure, 1973.

This system of judicial proceedings obviates the subjective bias of a single judge and vindicates the maxim that many heads are wiser than one. It also inducts fresh perception of many and minimises the possibility of animus or prejudice of a single judge. Juries also avoid the rigidity and technicality of the court to abide by the spirit of the law. Another advantage of the jury system is that it can consider and weigh in extraneous non-legalities like reformation of the criminal given his educational and economic background, reputation, and standing in society and is thus influenced by emotive issues of humanitarian considerations to remit, mollify, commute, or suspend the sentence. Although, these different legal options may adversely affect the perception of the victim towards the pronounced verdict yet the overall purpose in search of justice is, perhaps, better achieved in this system as it instils confidence in *vox populi*, inculcates self-discipline in the society, and urges people to refrain from committing premeditated crimes, culpable felony, or inadvertent indiscretions to avoid blot on personal reputation and social ignominy.

Basically, the principal demerit of this system lies in its co-opting laypersons at random from the population as jurors, who are unfamiliar with the nuances of trial and foul the principle of *stare decisis*, ignore precedence in past verdicts, allow them to deliberate in secrecy, to reach a decision by vote, and to hand over a "nonspeaking" indictment or a bare presentment without giving supporting reasons. The sheer wisdom of many can also not overcome jurors' own personal prejudices or ingrained family values or their well-known dislike for law. Apart from this, the jury is prone to extraneous influences like normative, informational, or even interpersonal as a result of which decision-making may be compromised. Therefore, this system can replace the expertise of specialists only to everyone's peril. It, thus, appears a mockery of law and lawyers, judiciary and justice; even if in isolated cases, the jury verdict has been right and judicious. Interestingly, the integrity of the juries has

---

[15] The Supreme Court judgment (1961) in the famous Nanavati Murder case. Nanavati was later pardoned by the Governor of Maharashtra in 1963 and released from jail.

[16] James Jaffe, "After Nanavati: The Last Jury Trial in India?"

rarely been questioned, and there have been equally few cases of hung juries, though at times these have been enmeshed in superfluous collateral aspects. Anyway, few sparrows do not herald spring.

Throughout its history, this legal system has perhaps been both overpraised as a Charter of liberty and sensitivity towards human values as well as overcriticised for undue reliance on legal ignoramus and incompetent amateurs with risk of mistrial in the highly technical and sensitive administration of justice. The fate of precious lives cannot be risked on an altar managed by novices when viable and credible alternative exists in trial by judges. Importantly, judges are knowledgeable by education, intelligent by selection, skilled by training, disciplined by service, honed by experience, security in job, and with memory of past precedents by dint of continuity to be able to apply in germane cases. The choice, indeed, should be obvious.

9.1.4 The Codes of Sharia

There is yet a fourth category of legal system where the legal code applicable to a religious denomination is contained in its scriptures and is believed to have divine origins. The faith accepts that the *Ayats* of the *Quran* were inspired by the God and naturally came to the mind of Prophet Mohammed and were scribed. This code is *Sharia* and is contained in the Holy Quran for abidance by the Muslims.[17] Sharia is an Arabic word which literally means "the clear, well-trodden path to water." However, in our context, it is a holistic law forming part of the Islamic tradition. It is derived from the religious precepts of Islam, particularly the Quran and the *hadith*. Generally, the term *sharīʿah* refers to God's immutable divine law and is contrasted with *fiqh* which refers to its human scholarly interpretations.[18] The authenticity and manner of its application in modern times have been a subject of dispute between Muslim fundamentalists and liberal modernists of the community.

Sharia is a non-legislated, non-sovereign code in the political sense yet normative adherence to it by the believers is exemplary and stricter than obedience to or abidance of the man-made rules. It is also an orthodox and closed system of religious observances, social commandments, political guidelines, and legal rules, which are not open to evolution in society or alteration by humans because of being injunctions proclaimed by the Allah. The tone of *Sharia* is, generally, moralistic, ethical, and altruistic; and it regulates an adherent conservative society with stern mandates and strict commands. It ordains legal dispensation of justice which is righteous in the eyes of the God.

It is believed that the Quranic holistic system was devised with divine inspiration and revelation for a certain society of converts and to meet their incumbent problems

---

[17] Mohammad Hashim Kamali, *Shari'ah Law: An Introduction,* Oneworld Publications, (2008). pp. 2, 14.

[18] Schneider, Irene (2014). "Fiqh", in Emad El-Din Shahin (ed.), *The Oxford Encyclopedia of Islam and Politics,* Oxford: Oxford University Press.

9.1 Divergent Legal Systems: A Global Review

of war-ridden Middle East, yet emendation is unthinkable despite intruding changes all-round, rise of new values, and the evolution of new humane principles. Sharia law acts as a code of conduct for all aspects of the life and living of a Muslim. Sharia law is also Islam's legal system and is derived from both the Quran, Islam's Holy Scriptures, and fatwas that are the rulings of Islamic scholars. New interpretations have been, however, offered by the learned Muslims through *hadith* taken from the lifetime actions and practices adopted by the Prophet and his favourite disciples. In some cases, the suggested changes have been accepted by the practising clerics, yet controversies persist.

However, traditional theory of Islamic jurisprudence recognises four sources of Sharia: the Quran, *sunnah; hadith*, the corpus of authentic traditions, and practices set by Prophet Mohammed and his loyal disciples; *qiyas,* meaning analogical reasoning; and *ijma* implying juridical consensus.[19] Different legal schools, of which the most prominent are Hanafi, Maliki, Shafi'i, Hanbali, and Jafari, developed methodologies for deriving Sharia rulings from scriptural sources using a process known as *ijtihad*. Traditional principles of jurisprudence (*usul al-fiqh*) distinguish two principal branches of law, ʿ*ibādāt* (rituals) and *muʿāmalāt* (social relations), which together comprise a wide range of topics.[20] Its rulings are concerned with cherished values and ethical standards as much as with legal norms, assigning actions of a devout to one of five categories: mandatory, recommended, neutral, abhorred, and prohibited. Thus, some areas of Sharia are peculiar and unique to living a life in accordance with God's will, while a few aspects overlap with the popular Western notions of law.

In general, the Muslim legal system prompts an injuncted, righteous society imbued with altruistic attitude and a desire for help of the needy. Sharia urges for *Zakah* or *Zakaat*, i.e. charity, alms-giving, and donations, to the needy or for the needy, particularly on festive occasions and during the month of *Ramazan*.[21] It is a religious impost for the help of the poor and gets profuse voluntary response from the devout.[22] Also, for example, the Islamic Economic Law[23] *(Shariah)* prohibits interest (*Riba*) on borrowings and lending,[24] speculative transactions or gambling (*Maysir*), selling something with uncertain outcome or subject matter or indefinite date of delivery (*Gharar*), and investments in businesses which deal in alcohol, drugs, pornography, gambling, weapons, among other restrictions.[25] After all, the purpose and function of law are to serve the society in all aspects of cordial living, social

---

[19] Schacht, Joseph, *An Introduction to Islamic Law*. Oxford: Clarendon, 1964.

[20] Ziadeh, Farhat J. (2009), "Uṣūl al-fiqh" in John L. Esposito (ed.), *The Oxford Encyclopedia of the Islamic World,* (Oxford: Oxford University Press).

[21] Hakeem Abdul Hameed, ed., *Islam at A Glance,* New Delhi, Vikas Publishing House, 1981, p. 40.

[22] Diwan Chand, *Fundamentals of Religion,* Kanpur, Nanakchand-Wazirdevi Trust, 1953, p. 66.

[23] Mahmoud El-Gamal, *Islamic Finance: Law, Economics, and Practice.* Cambridge University Press, (2006), p. 16.

[24] Dubai Investment Finance Centre (DIFC), however, in a liberalised attitude, permits interest on loans and deposits and even unconscionable profits on investments.

[25] For more details, refer Hakeem Abdul Hameed at n. 21 ante. Also refer Imtiyaz Hussain, *Muslim Law and Customs,* Srinagar, Srinagar Law Journal Publications, 1989.

progress, economic activity, and overall development. Thus, among the Muslims, law is, by no means, an end in itself.

It also provides for retributive justice for deterrence, reparative justice for the welfare of victims and sanctions on criminals for non-restorative crimes. Many Western legal experts believe that this system is strict, harsh, and brutal and lacks humanitarian sensitivities because the punishment for theft is chopping off of the hand of the accused. A story goes that the American president on his visit to the Saudi Arabia had made similar remarks before King Faisal, who retorted that there is only one person with chopped hand in my kingdom and there are no thefts in this country. This sacrifice in punishment by one man for his mistake is no inhumanity in the interest and security of the society. Deterrent punishments act as an example to the potential criminals and help to curb recidivism.[26] Interestingly, in Europe there is a growing trend towards "punitivism." For example, in France in a latest legislation, child abuse attracts up to 20 years of imprisonment.[27] In evaluation, the purpose of justice is not equalisation of crime or perpetration of same or similar decapacitation on the criminal but a judicious pronouncement of a sentence to reform the criminal in repentance or to cause repair to the loss of the victim in some manner and leave a feeling of a victor to both parties. The motto should be to hate the crime and "reformate" the criminal so as to enable such a person to return to the society as a useful and peaceful member after repentance.

The Islamic judicial system has evolved over time. In early days of Muslim domination, Sharia was traditionally interpreted by Muftis, who were learned religio-legal scholars, and they issued fatwas or legal opinion on matters of disputes. Fatwas were normally issued free; but later, Muslim rulers appointed salaried Muftis as state legal advisors. With the evolution of the system and increase in the number of disputes, *Mahkama* or courts came to be appointed for adjudication. Each *mahkama* was presided over by a *Kadi* or *Qazi*, who acted as the judge to administer the court and would issue verdicts in dispensation of justice. The system admitted of a possibility of making appeals, first to the King's Council and finally a *faryaad* or a prayer to the king himself, who issued *farman* that was final and binding. With passage of time, there was institutional degeneration of this system and Qazis succumbed to uphold the will of the king, right or wrong.

This judicial system, however, had distinctive differences compared to modern administration of justice. One such difference pertained to the evidentiary tenets which apparently were discriminatory against women. Accordingly, the evidentiary value of and credence on a female witness was half of that of a male one, which means that to contradict or negate a male assertion there would need to be two or more female witnesses deposing the same or similar affirmative statements in

---

[26] Weiss, Bernard G. *The Spirit of Islamic Law,* Athens, Georgia: University of Georgia Press,1998, p. 17.
[27] "France outlaws sex with kids under 15", *Times of India*, Chandigarh edition, April 17, 2021, Times Global, p. 13.

9.1 Divergent Legal Systems: A Global Review

contradiction of the male deposition.[28] Again, rape is treated as religious crime and *prima facie*, the woman is held guilty of losing chastity or compromising fidelity. This male superiority still continues to violate the principle of gender equality and natural justice and does not acknowledge the reality of life.

The Mohammedan Criminal and Personal Law prevailed in India also, during the rule of the Mughal kings but primarily applied to the Muslims. This law continued till 1773 AD when the English-style courts were established by the British rulers. Later common criminal code came to be applied to all communities in India under Indian Penal Code, 1860 for secular law enforcement and maintenance of public order. In this reformist movement, Lord Warren Hastings, Governor General of Bengal, played a sterling role. However, in matters of personal status relating to marriage, divorce, and succession, the community continues to be governed by Muslim Personal Law. Some peculiarities and differing perceptions of Muslim law on crimes have also persisted for long and are highlighted and discussed in the next chapter, in context and as relevant.

In recent times, traditional laws in the Muslim world have been widely replaced by statutes inspired by European models. Nevertheless, constitutions of many Muslim-majority states have accepted duality of legal system and contain references to Sharia as well as retained their foundations in traditional jurisprudence. Accordingly, in many countries, like Qatar, the legislated laws co-exist with Sharia's classical rules relating to personal status (family and succession) cannons. Some non-Muslim countries also recognise the use of Sharia-based family laws for the concerned minority populations. Nevertheless, human-legislated codification based on modern values has been opposed from many conservative quarters.

The Islamic revival of the late twentieth century has brought along calls by Islamism movement for full implementation of Sharia, including *hudud,* i.e. corporal punishments, such as stoning.[29] Brunei has implemented Sharia law.[30] But such moves have been resisted by progressive Muslim scholars and religious reformers across the globe.[31] Thus, the role and acceptance of Sharia have become a contested topic around the world and has also sparked intercommunal violence in Nigeria and possibly contributed to the break-up of Sudan. There are also ongoing debates as to whether Sharia is compatible with democracy, human rights, freedom of thought, women's rights, gender equality, LGBT rights, same-sex marriages, banking, etc.; and consensus is awaited.[32]

---

[28] Fadel, Mohammad "Two Women, One Man: Knowledge, Power, and Gender in Medieval Sunni Legal Thought", *International Journal of Middle East Studies.* (2009), **29** (2): 185–204.

[29] Kamali, Mohammad Hashim (1998). "Punishment in Islamic Law: A Critique of the Hudud Bill of Kelantan, Malaysia". *Arab Law Quarterly.* **13** (3): pp. 203–34.

[30] Brunei implements sharia law—UNAA (United Nations).

[31] Some jurisdictions in North America have passed bans on use of Sharia law and have framed restrictions on religious or foreign laws.

[32] Bernard Weiss, *The Spirit of Islamic Law,* Athens, Georgia: University of Georgia Press, 1998.

9.1.5 A Brief Appraisal

The diverse legal systems often impose implicit restrictions on judicial discretion; create a tendency towards inflexibility; cause discrepancy that can develop between theory and law in practice; and the potential difficulty of a criminal code fitting into a country's domestic socio-legal culture and understanding of the people. This aspect comes into focus, where wholesale codification is accepted and transplanted into another legal system. This phenomenon is more commonly visible in the continental law traditions. But such simplistic transplants from a different legal tradition can result in systemic frictions and other anomalies which may offend domestic culture and the believers. Thus, there is need for better understanding between the common law and civil law divide. And to consciously neutralise such variations, experiences of different countries can be compared and contrasted in an attempt to arrange segregation, stratification, and a common codification of space crimes on the basis of commonality and empirical occurrences. These aspects deserve proper attention and due considerations while adjudicating on space crimes.

In the end, it may be conceded that there would be countries across the world, where there will be yet many more different systems of judicial administration which reflect distinct and discernible modifications or mutations of the basic mother systems discussed above. The systems with minor variations have been excluded from this discussion, lest this digression leads us astray and loses focus on handling of space crimes in international milieu and the impact of diverse legal systems prevalent in different countries. The object of this discourse, *albeit* brief, was to flag likely apprehensions in the minds of multinational space-farers and allay their doubts in and angst concerning divergent legal systems because the goal of each one is to dispense justice, and they have succeeded in this purpose for centuries.

Despite broad knowledge, understanding with acceptance and convincing arguments, it may still be difficult for a person accustomed to a particular legal system to repose same faith and confidence in another system. To harbour doubts about others' efficacy, competence and speed to deliver justice are natural and valid. Yet it is the perception that erodes confidence and not truly the ground reality. This sort of confidence-deficit is likely to be encountered in international groups at private stations in outer space and planetary habitations on celestial bodies. This cleft of trust needs to be smoothened with exchanged awareness, better understanding, and an assurance that law would not fail in its prime purpose or to achieve its avowed ends. Therefore, a confidence-building measure could be a holistic space law that exudes legal certainty for the protection of individual liberty and personal freedom and successfully bridges extant gaps to legitimise diversity, so that apprehensions or misconceptions do not lapse into protracted problems of many dimensions, juridical, political, or diplomatic.

Chapter 10
Legal Codes and Social Norms: Divergent Perceptions

10.1 Divergent Perception of Crimes

The assertions made in the previous chapter now need validation and vindication. These also deserve to be buttressed with illustrations to become real, substantive, and understandable. Because, apart from the basic differences in legal systems for according justice described earlier, there may be differences in the connotation, interpretation, comprehension, or cognition of crimes and respective sentences prescribed therefor. Thus, what may be treated as crime as per the criminal code of one country may turn out to be an innocuous or permissible act in another country. In mixed societies, casual behaviour and unintended acts may be viewed and reacted to differently. Therefore, perception of crimes may differ according to community's moral norms, societal taboos, cultural practices, social values, and habitual verbal expressions which may be ingrained in their legal codes or unwritten laws. And these assume importance in mixed cosmopolitan groupings and societies in space environment. Some examples in illustration would justify this assertion.

10.1.1 Varied Understanding of Law

There is a doctrine of *"in pari delicto"* in criminal jurisprudence where parties could equally share blame or liability in the fault. Compared to this, the German legal system has no concept of contributory negligence under which even a partial fault of the complainant in the incident can afford a reprieve to the defendant, while many other legal systems that follow the British tradition and practices, like India and other erstwhile colonial countries, have an established doctrine of contributory negligence of the victim. Nevertheless, cautelous actions are important to avoid accidents, although the defendant can raise a plea of defence that negligence on the part of the plaintiff was the proximate and decisive cause of the injury. Thus, based on proportional contribution to negligence in the event, the quantum of compensation or recoverable damages in liability cases is usually adjusted according to this factor.[1]

It is pertinent to mention of Soviet Union and other communist countries where there is a peculiar dynamic relationship between politics and law. The legal culture of these states bears testimony to the socialist philosophy that again is based on a different understanding of economy and doctrinal interpretation of economics. Therefore, these countries have no concept of pecuniary compensation for loss or damage. This is because among the communist countries where everyone used to work according to his capacity and in return got everything according to the need from the state, such restitution was deemed an unearned profit.

Thus, there was no concept of bread-earner for the family or loss of recurring income with his death. The state doled out for every need of everyone for survival. Hence, there was no general law of compensation for loss or death by accident. The situation may have slightly changed with steady introduction of *perestroika* in the Soviet Union and gradual relaxation in trade and inclination towards free economy in other communist states. In due course, this legal requirement for monetary compensation for loss or damage may now find pertinence as a matter of eventual necessity in the Soviet jurisprudence.

However, in the West and others capitalist countries following common legal traditions, compensation is computed as per the doctrine of *restitutio in integrum* in order to make up for the damage or loss suffered by the affected party in terms of monetary valuation. This axiomatic formula is applicable even in respect of a snuffed out human life, as if the economic loss never occurred. For a death in a road or air accident, compensation is computed based on the earning capacity of the decedent, expected balance of average life span, social status and living standard of the family of the deceased, subject to the limit or ceiling prescribed in law, if any.

Another example could be our diverse understanding and connotation of negligence in different legal systems. In common legal parlance, it denotes neglect in performance of an assigned duty or improper completion of a task. However, judicial rigour puts it as "an omission to do something which a reasonable man guided upon these considerations which ordinarily regulate conduct of human affairs would do… [as] prudent and reasonable man…"[2] On the contrary, "Negligence would mean careless conduct in commission or omission…signifying want of proper [prudent and reasonable] care [as] demanded by circumstances…"[3] Thus, negligence is lack of due diligence or cautelous actions. Hence, the evidentiary rule of *res ipsa loquitur* applies in cases of human negligence and human failure to act prudently in *abundanti cautela*.

The French equivalent to the notion of negligence is *"dols"*; but the connotation of *dols* is not mere negligence as commonly understood but carries a specific meaning as

---

[1] *Wharton's Law Lexicon,* 1976 (reprint), p. 251. Also refer *K.J. Aiyar's Judicial Dictionary,* 1998, (twelfth edition), Allahabad, The Law Book Company (P) Ltd, pp. 321–22.

[2] *K.J. Aiyar, Judicial Dictionary*, Twelfth Edition, 1998, Allahabad, The Law Book Company (P) Ltd, p. 847. Word in parenthesis has been added.

[3] Ibid. Words in parenthesis have been added.

10.1 Divergent Perception of Crimes

"gross negligence." In French jurisprudence, it is construed that the negligent person was aware of the consequences of the impugned conduct and yet failed to perform it carefully and correctly. In a way, it may imply lack of due diligence in discharge of an activity or duty. Thus, in France, simple negligence, patent inadvertence, or sheer carelessness would be a condonable act and may not attract criminal accusation, while it may be treated as near-crime or a substantive crime in many other countries.

In China, motor vehicle accidents attract anomalous laws. In case, a person hits someone while driving the car and injures, he/she must pay to the victim/s for the medical care and support of the injured for rest of the life. However, if the same driver happens to kill someone in accident with the car, he/she only pays a one-time fee as punishment. For this very reason, it seems fairly common for accident-offenders to go back to the accident site to possibly kill the person who was accidentally hit and was only hurt by his/her car, with fair chances of survival. The law provides a bad escape window for acts of inhumanity, whereas in Germany, if one sees an injured person anywhere, accident or otherwise, and even if one cannot provide personal help or first aid, yet one is duty-bound to take emergency action to inform authorities at 112. Else, ignoring an injured person and walking away after noticing such incident is an offence and one would be liable for prosecution. The legal positions of the two countries on similar situation seem diametrically opposite and mutually inconsistent. Thus, this is where values and reflexes would differ.

Again, in Germany, it is permissible and legal to break out of jail in defiance of the court verdict and no punishment is prescribed for such an act. In fact, the German Legal Code commands, "No punishment without a law."[4] Presumably, the omission to include this act as a crime in the Code is a considered and deliberate decision based on the innate human instinct to be free and unfettered. The human urge for freedom is natural and universal and has been duly respected. In similar gesture, in Bolivia, a prisoner can reduce the jail-time by reading books under the programme "Books behind bars." Though Bolivia does not have life sentence or death penalty, yet it is a progressive reformative measure. This follows the initiative of Brazil to encourage literacy. In Bolivia also, prisoners have taken this assurance seriously and are improving their reading and writing skills.[5] Hope never dies. Further, individual liberty and human dignity are closely linked in modern democracies, as such citizens cannot be treated as subservient subjects of the state, even in prisons, or be ill-treated by any authority, and deserve all avenues and heartening impetus at self-reformation and reintegration into the social system.

Another interesting fact from the German Code is that a criminal offence lapses after 20 years, if the accused is not apprehended or prosecuted within this timeframe. This presumably approximates to the modern trend of "right to be forgotten" which implies deletion or erasure of data or information from the files, even criminal

---

[4] *German Penal Code,* First Chapter, Section I.

[5] "Pages for Pardons? In Bolivia, inmates can cut jail time by reading", *the Times of India,* May 4, 2022, Times Global page.

records.[6] However, such a law does not exist in India and a criminal offender can be apprehended and prosecuted anytime till deceased.[7] Because, in general context, crimes do not die, only criminals die. Despite such unusual relaxations, Germans are sticklers for law and would cross the road only at pedestrian crossing for the obvious fear of being hailed by the police for breach for cutting across at any other point.

Another type of example could be of Uganda which was the first country of the world to totally ban the use of plastics in 2007. It was an initiative par excellence. Now compare the Ugandan attitude towards plastics with that of Americans, where single-use plastics are in vogue and are rampantly and callously discarded thereafter. Or take the habit of Indians, who indiscreetly and carelessly throw away used plastic containers anywhere and everywhere. As a result of this attitude, non-bio-degradable plastic garbage mounts to millions of tons annually, including equally callous disposal in the hills which poses difficulty in scavenging and adds to environmental pollution. Understandably, perceptions are bound to differ widely, imparting different people a different mindset and attitudinal fixations.

10.1.2 Incomprehension of Religious Taboos and Symbols of Faith

Scant information about the religious taboos of others and lack of awareness about symbols of faith and regard owed to them has been the cause of much unrest and turmoil worldwide. Sacrilege in societies and offending haloed beliefs hurt popular sentiments and arouse strong passions to avenge. Hence, fanatic believers tend to commit serious crimes, though sacrilege for one may appear a frivolous misdemeanour for the other.[8] Reaction of a person would vary depending upon the degree of faith and reverence for the symbol. Anyway, it is not easy to unravel and explain this labyrinthine phenomenon which is highly sensitive, causes tremendous pain, trauma, and conflict.

Customs of faith is a complicated terrain and intrinsic to the mind of each person. Same way, desecration of a religious symbol is an abominable act yet evoking widely different reactions even within the believers of same religion or sect. Thus, the symbol is revered not because of its intrinsic value or material of which it is made, but the belief it represents. Accordingly, the cross is not a few pieces of wood jointed together nor is the idol of Durga just the lumps of mud embellished for worship.

---

[6] This law, in a different context of privacy, exists in certain countries of Europe, South America, and even Asia.

[7] For example, culprits of killing Sikhs in 1984 anti-Sikh riots are still being identified and prosecuted almost four decades later, and this hunt may continue on political will. Refer "Anti-Sikh riots: SIT identifies 67 accused in 11 cases in Kanpur", *The Times of India* (Chandigarh edition), December 3, 2021, p. 3.

[8] For example, the recent incident of sacrilege committed at Sri Harmandir Sahib (Golden Temple) at Amritsar in which the criminal was lynched to death. Comments by Dipankar Gupta, "Sacrilege and Societies", *The Times of India* (Chandigarh Edition), December 25, 2021.

In fact, the lower the intrinsic material value of the symbol or the tribal totem, the easier it is to imbue the same with potential to arouse sentiments and passions or live with dangerous delusions that are self-enforcing.[9] The dilemma seems real, and overall picture is more complicated and mixed with divergent intrinsic moorings and extraneous reactions. Thus, this subject seeks sensitivity in treatment and discourse so as not to offend individual sensibilities, popular beliefs, cherished values, and sentimental fixations.

Modern jurisprudence recognises respect for religious faiths and customs of communities, but only so long as these do not violate basic fundamental rights of non-believers. Therefore, crowd behaviour and mob immunity may be a threat, and if allowed free rein, it may undermine democratic traditions in the guise of popular will and cherished creeds. Such situations and eventualities, in any form of attitude or behaviour, are likely in the motley crowds of space groupings and planetary societies. Misunderstandings may arise from sheer ignorance and not necessarily from advertent or motivated disrespect to the sacrosanct yet leading to corrosive reactions that may be disproportionate to the meaning of misdemeanour or the gravity of cause.

10.1.3 *A Needy Hungry Commits No Crime in Stealing Food*

In Italy, it is not a crime to steal food, if one is hungry and, provided that, one has no other source of nourishment or sustenance to satiate the hunger. This urge is natural and irrepressible, and at times, its pain is so strong and unbearable that a desperately hungry one could go to any extent, even violently snatching food from another person. Hence, a personal act to satisfy the pangs of a basic human urge for survival would be no crime against society. Human rights activists may also construe it to favour the hungry one.

In an altruistic tradition, in Norway, when people have a bumper fruit crop of apples on trees grown on their private residential estates and have a surplus fund of fruit over their own requirement, they, in an act of kindness and altruism, hang small bags filled with apples outside their perimeter wall facing the public road. These are for anyone to pick and take away for personal or family consumption. This is an act of generosity and at the same time avoids waste or to let the delectable fruit, surplus to their needs, rot in storage in refrigerators at home.

In a similar vein, the Sikh tradition of *Langar* or free meal is based on a philosophical observation, *"bhooke khawat laaj naa aavey."*[10] Thus the hungry and poor and needy must be fed a free meal. Even, the Sikh scriptures accept, *"bhooke bhagath naa keejai."*[11] The gist of this recitation is that the pain of hunger is so intense that a hungry disciple will not be able to recite Thy name on a rosary. It thus implies that one must first have the wherewithal to satiate the hunger of the stomach before

---

[9] Dipankar Gupta, ibid.

[10] *Sri Guru Granth Sahib, Raag Sorath, Mohalla* 5 (Fifth Guru), *Ang* (page) 629.

[11] *Sri Guru Granth Sahib, Raag Sorath, Bani Bhagatan Ki, Ang* (page) 656.

taking up meditation. The emphasis is on the basic need of a hungry person and acknowledgement of a natural and irrepressible urge.

10.1.4 Harsh Punishments in Islamic Arabian Countries

In Arabian countries with Shariah law derived from the Quran, punishments are harsh, severe, and strict. In Saudi Arabia in 2015, on an average, one person has been executed for every day of the year. This may appear brutal but is effective in impact. For the crime of stealing, the punishment is chopping off of the hand/arm. The national belief is that crime is a crime and stealing of whatever item, for whatever purpose, under whatever circumstances, or personal compulsion connotes as theft. The logic for such severe punishment is deterrence from crime, to instil fear in the members of the society to abstain from such criminal acts and to obviate lapses into recidivism.

In this connection, a retort to an accusation of inhuman punishments in the country by a visiting US President, the King of Saudi Arabia boasted before the US dignitary that in his country there is only one of his subjects with chopped hands and this crime does not exist here. In consequence, shopkeepers do not lock up their shops and keep the display of wares when they go, a few times during the day, for *namaaz* prayers and no thefts occur.[12] Thus, sacrifice of one hand for virtual confidence, public security, and practical safety of the society is no inhuman retribution. It is equally commendable to note that in Saudi Arabia, apart from theft, even heinous crimes like robbery, rape, mass shooting, etc., are almost non-existent and inhabitants, even women, feel safe, and secure to venture out, even alone, at night.

10.1.5 Varied Views on Sex and Prostitution

Take another illustration of variance in views and values in different countries. An antithetical view prevails in Canada. According to current law passed in 2014, sexual services for money are illegal. It is equally against the law to live on the material benefits derived from sex work; there is prohibition on solicitation or to purchase or advertise sexual services. In contrast, prostitution is legally permitted in Germany. Possibly, because sex is considered a human urge and a basic innate need that will find a way to satisfaction in a manner, howsoever morally aberrant, socially condemnable, or legally prohibited. If compulsion of human nature demands so, then why not

---

[12] Lately, however, in a major shift, a Sharia ruled country, United Arab Emirates have eased many Islamic personal laws and punishments for certain crimes through a Governmental Decree. These generally relate to cohabitation between unmarried couples or alcohol consumption, etc., mainly aimed to attract tourists and promote tourism. Refer WAM report from Dubai, "In a major shift, UAE eases Islamic personal laws", *The Times of India*, (Chandigarh edition), November 8, 2020, p. 7.

legalise, regulate, and cleanse the profession of its known detriments and ills. And Germany has elected this pragmatic and realist option.

The Netherlands has gone a step further to view the need for sex as a licit and legitimate biological necessity and recognise it as a "basic human right." As a result, a legal right has authorised disabled citizens to receive government funds to pay for the use of prostitutes up to 12 times a year. Thus, voluntary sex between two consenting adults, for whatever reason was not a crime and the audacity and tolerance towards sex in Amsterdam, is indeed of a different genre. After 2000 AD, by law, it became legal to run a business in which sex workers could be hired. The rationale of this state-regulated business was to fight human trafficking and protect the sex workers against exploitation and clients from transmissible diseases. Other European countries also have similar attitude towards sex and prostitution, but their laws differ in content and degree of liberalism.

Possibly for a different reason, in Philippines, Singapore, Thailand, and a few other tourist-attraction countries around the world, prostitution is permitted and propped as quality service and brand value. Therefore, sex industry is reasonably organised, well-regulated, and mildly encouraged. Voluntary and consensual sex service is legal for women above the age of 18 years, though solicitation for sex work is legally prohibited.[13] Perhaps, the compulsion to permit such a relaxed system is because their national economies primarily depend upon tourism, and tourists mostly pander for such pleasures and pastimes.

Afghanistan is different with strange traditions and rituals. One of them is a centuries-old custom of *Bacha Baazi*, with which powerful men, warlords, commanders, and wealthy men entertain their guests. This is a play, where young boys, who have not yet grown beard, are dressed like girls. They are trained and experienced, wear trinkets, and dance to entertain the guests. Sexual offers are made by the host and enjoyed by the guests. There is lot of fun and merry-making in the party with no inhibitions. In fact, there is a popular dictum among such communities, "Women for progeny, boys for pleasure and melons for delight." The *Bachas'* are generally well rewarded and nurtured, but once they start growing moustaches and beard, they are cast away and abandoned. Thus, their post-bacha life is miserable and marginalised on the fringes of the society.

Apropos prostitution, it is morally reprehensible and socially unacceptable in most eastern and other conservative countries where such a profession is frowned upon by society and prohibited in law. Even in multi-denomination countries like India, practice of prostitution is illegal but enforcement is lax and selective. Thus, compulsions exist and devious means are deployed to evade or overpower the governmental system of policing and prosecution. For example, in Saudi Arabia, despite operative legislation, religious injunction, and social condemnation, prostitution is loosely patrolled and laws lightly enforced by the police though its existence is vehemently denied, whereas in some other orthodox Muslim countries, legal code and religious prohibition in this regard are strictly enforced and violations harshly punished. Disparities in law, norms of living styles and social customs become obvious.

---

[13] Quora Digest (31) at quora.com.

These variations in national laws: legislative, injunctive or normative, and enforcement practices of the police force become relevant and pertinent to our study because these laws evolve from the living etiquette, social values, cultural customs, and national prejudices of the concerned society which create perceptions on personal life and daily behaviour. Thus, inhabitants also imbibe a mindset of living standards, family proprieties, and local practices that mould their psyche, mindset, and attitudes accordingly. And those living in internationally mixed societies may, therefore, view and treat the same act with different mental evaluation, habitual understanding, legal inhibition, or gravity of seriousness and thus accord varying levels of criminality, only if, the dereliction is deemed so serious and impacting.

10.1.6 Differential Treatment of Women

In Imperial China, a not too vintage custom that had wide acceptance and social tolerance was an unwritten law. It required the women, at a certain age, to make a choice whether to marry and live as housewife or work as maid and be economically independent or be a concubine to the King or the nobles and enjoy the status or lastly, if still unbound, resort to prostitution. The status of women was graded in this order and those remaining unattached had no other option than to work as prostitutes. The women by themselves had no independent standing in society and gained their status on attachment to a man, whether permanent, terminable or temporary.[14]

Worse than China, Balinese culture had a dark streak regarding treatment of women, not so long ago. In the case of Bali, the position of women was discriminated and degraded until recently. Unlike other parts of Indonesia, Balinese Hindu women did not have the legal right to own their property. Even though they conducted a lot of the trade and business on the island, the property legally belonged to their husband or nearest male relative. Thus, the Balinese women worked hard in the fields, in construction, in trade, and in many areas of society earning for the family, while the husbands often spent their time gambling to squander away their hard-earned money. Even while at home, her hours were often taken up by an endless stream of preparations of customary offerings and other religious ceremonies. Further, when a Balinese woman became a widow, she was expected to sacrifice herself on the funeral pyre of the husband. Some accounts also mention of widows being buried alive. This status, though, is undergoing a change yet is not complete and liberated.[15]

The separation of women in residential quarters as also in outside gatherings is quite common among Muslim societies. But Qatar is a shade ahead in orthodoxy where wedding celebration functions are separately organised for men and women at different venues and no intermixing is allowed. Even children, babies and maids are not permitted to attend the functions. In a way, it enables women to enjoy the

---

[14] China has, of course, socially evolved under the new communist regime and gender equations are changing.

[15] Quora Digest (9).

festivity off guard with freedom, without having to don restrictive clothing and with feminine looseness in verbosity and gestures.

In Kyrgyzstan, there is a custom of bride-kidnapping and forced marriage, if not voluntarily accepted by the kidnapped. Most marriages, here, happen like this. A law enacted in 2013 prohibited such marriages, but its enforcement is weak. Even today, after ten years of the law, it is believed that such a kidnapping takes place every thirty minutes, in Kyrgystan.[16] Be that as it may, people "culturised" in such society may find treatment of women by westerners and others as unacceptable, may be, grossly appalling and vice versa.

Iran is equally orthodox and conservative, and hard-line Islamic leaders are dogmatic about morality and chastity of women. Recently, an Iranian boxer Ahmad Shirazi took an informal photo with his family in which his wife is not wearing hijab, which is a kind of head cover for a woman. This family photograph came to the notice of clerics who objected to this as shameless display of immodesty. In consequence, they both were sentenced to 16 years of prison for debauchery and prostitution, apart from 74 lashes[17] reflecting that 1000-year-old Islamic laws are still valid in the twenty-first-century liberalism. A westerner would be shocked and imagine their living together in space societies.

In another recent commercial advertisement by Dominos chain of restaurants in Iran, a woman is depicted with loose headscarf (hijab) while licking or biting "suggestively" into a Magfury ice cream. Clerics have demanded that the company be sued for the offensive portrayal. However, commercial adverts often are suggestive with innuendoes, but Iran authorities consider this representation against public decency and an insult to women's morals. Therefore, in an effort to strengthen Hijab and Chastity laws, women have been barred from appearing in commercials and advertisements.[18] The clash of views with Western culture comes in sharp focus.

Conversely, the social order in the Mexican town of *Juchitan de Zaragoza* where women have ruled for centuries and men play a second fiddle in all aspects of life.[19] The town is inhabited by people from the Baputak racial stock of aboriginal Indians. The women here are highly respected, rated superior to men, dominate the social order, enjoy total freedom, and are the virtual rulers. Even in matters of sexual indulgence, women decide the time, mood, and place. Of course, Mexico has a traditional *Manual of Conduct,* but its implementation is relaxed in most parts of the state, while in the town of *Juchitan*, the Manual is meticulously followed and governance is strict.[20] Though men comprise the workforce and work as artisans and labourers, yet they hand over their entire earnings to the respective wives and seek

---

[16] Quora Digest (11).

[17] Quora Suggested (9), January 30, 2021.

[18] "Suggestive advert of ice cream prompts Iran to ban women in commercial: Report", in *the Times of India*, Chandigarh Times Supplement, August 7, 2022, p. 6.

[19] G S Sachdeva, *Sacred and Profane: Unusual Customs and Strange Rituals,* New Delhi, SAGE Publications, 2020, pp. 47–48.

[20] Translated from a report by Chris Fuller published in *Hind Samachar*, an Urdu Daily, September 8, 1993.

doles as pocket money. Women have the prerogative to divorce the husband and who accordingly on divorce lose economic identity and social status, thus, to be deprived of all relations with the family and denial of liberty for work and earning in the trade market.[21] Thus, the acceptance of this regulated conduct remains traditional and unchallenged. Accordingly, dependence on and subservience to women is complete and absolute in this society.

10.1.7 Views on the Crime of Rape

In the westernised world, despite their permissive behaviour and libertine attitudes, in a crime of rape of a woman by man or men, the latter is/are *prima facie* held guilty, stand accused of the offence, and punished accordingly, unless there be strong evidence to the contrary. The woman is the innocent party in the proceedings despite her silent willingness, contributory actions, gestural faults, lack of due caution, or absence of resistance. Whatever be the circumstances of the case, the act of rape demeans her self-will, violates her dignity, breaches her privacy, and defiles the soul of the victim.

Following the league of other European countries like Sweden, UK, and others, Spain has accepted and adopted the same legal definition of rape where all non-consensual intercourse or non-consenting sex has been defined as crime of rape, while perpetrators of gang-rape will be condemned to a jail sentence of up to 15 years. This may soon become the law.[22] Therefore, unfamiliarity with other cultures or lack of knowledge of non-native laws may create an awkward situation while living in mixed societies.

Paradoxically, in Saudi Arabia and some other Muslim countries, with conservative attitudes and having *Sharia* laws, there is no such offence of rape by a man; on the contrary, the crime so committed is deemed as loss of chastity or compromise of fidelity by the woman and she stands punishable, even by stoning to death. Thus, rape is cast as a matter of women's own safety and care and not treated as an act of male violence and intrusion into her bodily privacy, thus a prima facie crime. Such orthodox views are undergoing a change in affluent Muslim countries[23], and women are gradually gaining more freedom and equal treatment.[24] Yet the Sharia laws remain sacrosanct. A real-life case from Iran will prove the point.

It is the story of a 16-years-old Iranian girl Atefeh Rajabi Sahaaleh, who was arrested after being raped by a 51-year-old man. According to Islamic Sharia law, she was convicted on charge of adulty and for crimes against chastity that pertained

---

[21] For more details, refer G S Sachdeva, n. 19 ante.

[22] Reuter report, "Spain says non-consensual sex is rape, toughens laws", *Times of India*, July 7, 2021, p. 10.

[23] Till recently, women were banned from driving motor vehicles in Saudi Arabia.

[24] For example, United Arab Emirate plans to send Noura al Matroushi as first woman into space. Refer *Sunday Times,* (Chandigarh edition), April 10, 2021, p. 16.

10.1 Divergent Perception of Crimes

to sexual behaviour. During her alleged torture, she admitted to having had sex repeatedly with the 51-year-old ex-revolutionary guard turned taxi-driver, Ali Darabi, who was a married man with children at the time. The crime continued for over a period of 3 years without her family being aware of the same. While in prison, she was, allegedly, further tortured and raped by prison guards. She confided this to her grandmother who visited her, saying that afterwards she could only walk on all fours because of the pain due to lacerations.

The trial judge in her case was Haji Rezai. When Atefah realised that she was losing her case, she removed her hijab, an act seen as a severe contempt of the court, and argued that Ali Darabi, the rapist, should be punished, not her. In empathy to her predicament, one arguably wonders, if any women can resist or thwart a rape without ignominy or public accusation. In a burst of anger at the ensuing injustice, she even removed her shoes and threw them at the judge. The Iranian Court, instead of convicting the culprit-rapist, sentenced the hapless surviving victim to death by public hanging. And she was publicly hanged from a crane in Neka town of Iran, on 15 August 2004.[25] There were, however, worldwide protests, including by Amnesty International; but justice is not only proverbially blindfolded, even laws are blind and insensitive and law-bound courts still worse on most counts.

Another Muslim country, Pakistan, considers women's security from sexual assaults as an important state responsibility and treats male rapists differently. A recently enacted law by Pakistan Parliament[26] introduces chemical castration[27] as a possible punishment for serial rapists.[28] There are, however, muted protests which term this punishment as un-Islamic and against the Sharia, while "Amnesty International has called for investigations into the causes for sexual assaults instead of opting for harsher punishments."[29] May be, deterrence is the answer to recidivism of rapes or that wisdom will dawn to remedy social causes.

In Soviet Russia, the act of rape is viewed with disdain and deemed as an invasion of privacy and a violation of human body and its dignity. Therefore, the law allows women to violently resist an attempt to rape and, if necessary, even kill the rapist in self-defence. It will not be treated as a crime amounting to murder. For the same purpose, in Israel, it is legal for women to move freely with a gun in self-protection. Such differences in connotation of crime, methods to deter and fight back the criminal act, and consequent sanctions assume valid salience to our discourse on crimes in multinational space hospitality resorts, space conglomerations, and celestial habitations for residency.

---

[25] "Execution of a teenage girl", *BBC*, online documentary, 2006. Also, "Execution of a teenage girl", on Four Corners, *ABC TV*, August 7, 2006.

[26] The Criminal Law (Amendment) Bill, 2021 which replaces the Anti-Rape Ordinance.

[27] Chemical castration is a process whereby a person is rendered incapable of performing sexual intercourse for any period of his life, as determined by the court. Incidentally, reversible chemical castration by use of drugs is practised in Poland, South Korea, the Czech Republic, and some US states.

[28] "New Pak law allows chemical castration of serial rapists", *The Times of India*, (Chandigarh Times Supplement), November 19, 2021, p. 8 (Global Times).

[29] Ibid.

10.1.8 Views on Virginity

In line with the Islamic thinking and Hindu orthodoxy, most people around the world see virginity as a treasured virtue and a coveted status for an unmarried girl, but not all. Compare this customary norm with the people of a tribe from Tibet who have an absolutely opposite social belief and a compatible custom. They hold the view that the sole purpose of a man getting a wife is to nurture the gene, beget progeny, and extend his family; hence, not a novice virgin but an experienced mate is better for the purpose. To strengthen this supposition, the community holds a superstitious notion that if a man marries a virgin, it could bring bad luck for the family.

Accordingly, they consider that a girl before getting married has to look for and sleep with at least twenty different men to accumulate enough sexual experience for a successful married life to bear many children. Thus, a tradition goes that any young girl has to be experienced in bed before getting married and after each night spent with a man, the woman will ask for a gift or souvenir such as earrings or bracelet to prove to the village patriarchs that she has done "it" so many times. A collection of 20 such souvenirs confirm her capability to be a good wife and ready to be married within the tribe.[30]

Take another example, there is a progressive trend in the developed and developing societies to protect children from sexual abuse and exploitation of any kind and in furtherance of this objective, France, like many other countries, has adopted a legislation that "characterises sex with a child under the age of 15 as rape and punishable by up to 20 years in jail, bringing its penal code closer in line with many other Western nations."[31] While spearheading this law in the French Parliament, Justice Minister, Eric Dupont-Moretti proclaimed, "This is an historic law for our children and society."[32]

Not surprisingly, there are men, with medieval mindset, among certain orthodox societies, who relish to believe in the old dictum, "Women for progeny, children for pleasure and melons for delight." At the same time, Muslim communities abhorrently shun same-sex marriages which Islamic law does not permit. In Muslim countries, such liaisons are not only a social taboo but a legally punishable crime, whereas same-sex marriages are legally permitted in some countries in Europe and no social stigma nor any popular prejudice attaches to the couple. This exemplifies different socio-legal notions and varying perceptions of people about the same event.

---

[30] Quora Digest (26).

[31] "France outlaws sex with kids under 15", *Times of India*, Chandigarh edition, April 17, 2021, Times Global, p. 13.

[32] Ibid.

10.1.9 Varied Opinions on Nudity

Nudity in many European countries is no taboo whether on beaches or locker rooms. People are uninhibited, and even in male locker room a female cleaner may scavenge or scrub the floor unconcerned and non-challantly in male-naked presence. There are no prying eyes or side glances or shyly avoiding eye contact common in many orthodox and conservative countries. With this cultural background, an explicit sexual advance or minor act of touching of a woman or even an objectionable gesture, which in the eastern world or Indian subcontinent may be treated as outrageous, atrocious, and reportable, may seem casual behaviour or an innocuous overture to the Western youth. For him, such a suggestive advance, even if repulsed, carries no derogatory imputation or offensive tenor attaching to the act and no crime exists unless there is explicit outrage of modesty, inappropriate contact, or bodily molestation that occurs forcibly and with intention.

With similar European attitudes, Finnish people, in particular Scandinavians, are very casual about and feel no shame in nudity. Finland has no doors to wash cabins and shower almost open and exposed. It is the same in gymnasiums and saunas. People here are really fond of sauna baths and prefer it fully naked; and to stretch it further, they do not mind its use among mixed bathers of both sexes. In fact, for them nudity is normal, familiar, and asexual; and "uni-sex" use is often the norm for health and relaxation in public saunas. Rich people have private saunas at home, and even there, it is believed, the entire family enjoys in the nude with no embarrassment whatsoever, no blushes nor are any awkward questions asked.[33]

Again, dwelling on varying perceptions, I may cite a public norm from Sweden where for taking a splash in an indoor swimming pool, one is required, by regulation, to strip naked and have a full body wash in public showers before entering the pool. Further, no underpants or underwear are allowed under the swimming gear, and if noticed, one can be turned out of the pool. The logic of such strict rule is to ensure better personal hygiene and keep the germs level low and thereby reduce infections and the need for higher concentration of chlorination to kill extra germs. Therefore, it is often jocularly and even sarcastically remarked that in case a person is too shy for a naked bath, in the presence of others of the same sex, he may better go and swim in a lake.

10.1.10 Acceptance of Nudism in Europe

Nudity is normal in most European countries and in designated places like beaches and public gardens. In Germany, Finland and France, however, locals feel just as comfortable without clothes as within them. But no one stares and people are casual

---

[33] From Quora Digest (26) at quora.com.

about it. Also, many families have no such taboo in their homes and feel no embarrassment in such domestic environment. It clearly shows that nudism is a socially acceptable norm across Europe and as a public custom on a wide scale.

France was an early liberalist in this regard and the first to open one of the biggest nudist resorts in Cap d'Agde, in southern France, in the 1960s. And even here, Germans were among the first to hit its beaches. On their own in Germany, a nudism organisation known as FKK maintains dedicated nude beaches where it is compulsory to shed clothes on arrival. The slogan is, "Park the bikes, then park the clothes." Along the German coastline, such a beach maintained by FKK exists at Kampen, on the vacation island of Sylt. It was, believably, established in 1920 and is popular with the rich and famous. Again, Germany's largest Baltic Island, Ruegen, has no fewer than five FKK beaches. Even during the Cold War, when Germany was divided by the Iron Curtain, it was united by its love of nudism. It is estimated that there are about 600,000 Germans registered in more than 300 private nudist/FKK clubs. Nakedness is permitted on all Berlin public bathing beaches, like the Mueggelsee and Mauerpark.

Besides, there are nudist zones in many public parks and gardens. Even the famous Tiergarten in Berlin has designated areas to go nude. However, it is not possible to strip bare everywhere in Germany or elsewhere in Europe without breaking the law. For example, strolling or walking around naked in public areas where most other people are dressed counts as a minor breach or a venial offence, if other people are offended. Most people would normally ignore or look askance though few may take offence at such an indecent behaviour.

Gender-neutral or uni-sex attitude is taking over in Germany. In a recent dispute involving gender identity and discrimination in which "ostensibly a female swimmer was asked to cover up at the pool…," the city administration of Göttingen has ruled on this complaint that from 1 May 2022, it "will allow women and men alike to bathe topless…to enable female swimmers to go bare-breasted in the pool…."[34] In a clear recommendation, the committee has allowed that in "the city's indoor and outdoor pools…all swimmers be allowed to bathe "*oben-ohne*" (without top) at weekends…." Thus, Göttingen, in central Germany, will be the first city to permit such gender equality.

It may seem almost unbelievable because public nudity is illegal in India, but the earliest known naturist club in the world existed in British India. It was called the Fellowship of the Naked Trust and was founded in 1891 in Thane, by Charles Edward Gordon Crawford, District and Session Judge of Bombay. The commune had its beginnings in Matheran and Tulsi Lake with just three members, viz. Crawford and two sons of an Anglican missionary. The club required members to go stark naked, but accessories like rings, eyeglasses, and false teeth were permitted. The club grew in patronage but ended when its founding father died in 1894. In the meanwhile, nudist fun had caught fancy and spread to other cosmopolitan towns like Calcutta, Bangalore, Bombay, and in Assam and Kerala. Even to date, nudist meetings are

---

[34] "German city allows women to bathe topless in pools", *The Times of India*, (Chandigarh edition), April 29, 2022, Global Times page.

10.1 Divergent Perception of Crimes 213

held as per "nudist calendar," and Nakations (nudist vacations) are planned. The gender ratio is, however, slightly skewed.[35] These are, in no way, sex rave parties, and decorum is maintained.

10.1.11 Dignity of the Royalty is Inviolable

Thais are very patriotic people and highly respectful to their monarchical system and hold their King and Royalty in great esteem and high reverence. Use of abusive or insulting language or uttering even disrespectful words in relation to the King and the Royal family in Thailand can make even a foreigner liable for arrest and prosecution for treason. It happened to an Indian snob travelling in business class on Thai Airline, who indiscreetly used cuss words to snub actions of the members of the Royal family, on-board at that time. He was politely advised by the hostess to please restrain, but in a burst of his ego and anger, he continued condemnation with greater loudness and irreverence. To his chagrin and surprise, he was arrested on landing at Bangkok airport.[36] Reverence for Royalty in Thailand is more than skin-deep, while law has long arms and ego has its dark manifestations, too. Democrats may argue that this tilts towards hyper-nationalism but codified culpability cannot be condoned. Many situations in joint living on planetary residencies could be similar in effect, import, and impact. But such situations call for understanding and harmony in dispensing social justice to unaware foreigners.

In a recent case, a Thai woman has been sentenced by a court to 43 years in jail for insulting monarchy by sharing online posts criticising the Royal family. The punishment was awarded in accordance with the law known as *lese majeste* under which each violation carries a sentence of 15 years of imprisonment.[37] In another case, Chamoy Thipyaso was running a pyramid scheme in which she defrauded the members of the Thai Royal family. She was awarded a total imprisonment for 141,078 years on various counts, and Thai prisons are far worse than one can imagine. This, incidentally, remains as the longest prison sentence ever handed out to a criminal in the global judicial history.[38]

In another example, the Queen (now the King) of England has many privileges and umpteen duties. First, the Queen of England needs no passport to travel abroad. It is a unique privilege not accorded to other heads of state. Secondly, in a tradition from yore and under the customary law dating back, possibly, to the twelfth century, the reigning ruler owns all the sturgeons and swans to be found in the territory of England and all ducks in the Thames. Messing with them or molesting or torturing them, by anyone, in any manner, is a serious offence and is punishable. There is

---

[35] *Chandigarh Times of India*, Sunday supplement, July 17, 2022, p. 3.

[36] Narration by a friend who was an eye witness on-board.

[37] *The Times of India*, (Chandigarh edition), January 20, 2021, p. 9.

[38] Ibid.

also a royal tradition of an annual census of these birds called, Swan Upping.[39] One particular duty performed by the King is to head the British Church, and for this reason, the ruler cannot change his religion.

10.1.12 Varied Notions and Supporting Laws

In North Korea, as an attitude in vendetta, wearing of blue jeans is banned because it is seen to be a symbol of American imperialism or as a loathed Western attire. In a further conservative attitude, North Korea has issued a decree to enforce this dress code. Women wearing "tight leggings and dyeing their hair" are filmed in the streets and dubbed as "capitalist delinquents with…an impure ideology."[40] This ban betrays an attitude of disrespect towards the West. Similarly, a North Korean will be surprised at the effusiveness and affability with which Mothers' Day is celebrated with love, hugs, and gifts in the Western world. This impression arises because in 2017, observance of Mothers' Day was banned in North Korea. The main reason being that it was distracting citizens from offering their professed love for the dear supreme leader, Kim Jong Un. It may also surprise many law scholars that in North Korea, a crime committed by one person may lead the entire, apparently innocent, family of the convicted criminal to jail. Thus, varying codes and rules, and their underlying perceptions can be surprising and embarrassing and may elicit different views or exhibit different reactions which may culminate into serious disputes or crimes.

Take another example, the Muslim countries that dispense justice according to Shariah, e.g. the Middle East and some African countries, the crime of murder of a person can be compounded by mutual consent and payment of "blood money" which is deemed as reparatory compensation by the convicted accused for loss of the deceased to the family. This "theo-legal" custom is called *Diya."* Thus, a mutually agreed compensatory payment can get the sentence duly condoned, revoked, and the convict can be set free with the approval of the court. In fact, there is a wide array of clemency options bearing different considerations, like political appeasement, humanitarian purposes, and other legal expedients. These options are available to the sentenced offender for some of the crimes in different countries following sharia laws.

In Japan, sleeping in a short nap while on duty is deemed acceptable and treated as legal. It is seen that the Japanese people can dose off in a minute and soon enough get up fresh and alert after a wink of relaxation. This, for them, is an involuntarily induced physical condition, which is a human need and is generally considered to have been caused by accumulation of fatigue or exhaustion due to hard work.

---

[39] G S Sachdeva, *Sacred and Profane: Unusual Customs and Strange Rituals*, New Delhi, Sage Select, 2020, p. 250-1.

[40] North Korea bans tight pants in crackdown on indecent fashion" in *the Times of India*, Chandigarh edition, July 7, 2022, p. 7, (Global Times).

10.1 Divergent Perception of Crimes   215

This *bonafide* impression and the resultant concession arise out of the ingrained traditions, sincere attitude, and honest work habits that are integral to the psyche of the Japanese labour. In many other countries, such an occurrence of sleeping while on the job during duty hours would be treated as unauthorised absence from work or dereliction of duty condigned for punishment. And in Sweden, there are no dress code to work in offices except where uniform is necessary like for police force. The cited examples are merely illustrative of the point, and further similar divergences of perception in customary traditions, legal systems, and judicial codes will also be adduced to highlight disparities.

10.1.13 Impact of Societal Ethos and Cultural Values

Besides the hold of national legal system, the cultural background, socially instilled values, and persistent fixations in psyche make an equal contribution to our perception of unfamiliar ethos or unknown norms which may lead to resultant crimes in multi-ethnic society in space. Such diversity in attitudes can make or mar our relations leading to disputes and conflicts which remain endemic to live situations in such composite, yet heterogeneous, societal system. For example, Singaporeans are different from other South Asians in wealth, happiness, and discipline. They are law abiding and highly regimented in life, while outsiders can be disruptive of their system and may unintentionally land themselves in legal problems. Singaporeans are particularly obsessed with cleanliness and hygiene in public places. For forgetting to flush out after use of a public toilet may incur a fine of S$ 8000 or suffer a jail term. "Keep Singapore Clean" is a popular slogan and was launched in October 1966, as a campaign against littering and spitting in public places, which has succeeded remarkably as a value system. As a result, many foreigners are uncomfortable in keeping the clutter to themselves till they find a proper bin for disposal.

Similarly, Singaporeans also abide by the rules and dictates of public order in helping and ensuring smooth flow of road traffic. They also avoid honking of vehicles to avoid irritation to other drivers and reduce unnecessary noise pollution. Such discipline is not seen in many neighbouring Asian countries like Thailand or India. Take for example, China where traffic rules are scarcely followed and vehicles zip past from all directions to the dismay of the foreigners while traffic police, on duty, rarely ever reacts to take control of the situation and regulate the movement of erratic traffic. Even pedestrian crossings are disregarded by the drivers which may seem be a culture shock to an American or other westerners.

At another level, it may be a common sight in India or Singapore or Japan, to see clothes lines with washed family clothes and even undergarments hanging in the "*verandahs*" of houses or balconies of plush flats for drying. In Australia also, drying clothes outside in public view is no taboo nor defiance of any law, whereas such an act, even though a matter of necessity yet, is frowned upon in a few Arabian towns. For example, according to rules issued by Dubai Municipality, hanging washed linen, particularly undergarments, for drying outside buildings or in open balconies in public view is not legally permitted and is socially abominated under Islamic traditions. Violation of this municipal *dictat* can lead to a hefty fine as penalty and may even render the habitual offender liable for prosecution.

In the Kingdom of Saudi Arabia, death penalty is prescribed for import, display, or consumption of alcohol or drugs (NDPS). So also, pornography is strictly prohibited and attracts death penalty under apostasy laws. Further, under blasphemy laws, any religious activity or loud recitation (other than Islamic scriptures) in public places would be profanity that is least tolerated and breaches may attract up to capital punishment under *hadud* sentences. In the USA, however, such a ban would be of no consequence under their constitution of liberal values with secular freedom and may be jeered at with contempt because of Americans' non-challance towards religion as also sporting other democratic values and socially libertine attitudes. Thus, social contours, cultural norms, and religious beliefs may differ and manifest in disputes, conflicts, and crimes in mixed and composite living in planetary residencies.

In the liberal USA, it may seem a weird restriction to an American tattooed-nigger, but in Japan, one cannot display or even inadvertently show a tattoo in public places. Even while visiting the gymnasium or wearing clothes exposing the marks, it has to be covered with a sticky patch or a cloth covering. Thus, customs accepted by the community and prevailing social norms do wear the garb of law and tend to get enforced. On the contrary, the Americans are fairly liberal and casual about personal display but are touchy about their personal rights. They also detest invasion of their privacy by any means or methods. For example, they resent interference by loud talking or intrusion by untimely or unusual noises in the vicinity.

In this regard, Swiss though polite and affable yet bear a fetish for punctuality in life and working systems. For example, Swiss trains are remarkably punctual with strict disciple and intense maintenance. A joke goes that if a train is to depart at 8 and the clock shows 8.05, then either the train is not Swiss or the clock is not Swiss. Another interesting feature of this country foxes about the capital town of Switzerland. It truly does not have a de jure declared capital city, but Berne is the seat of the Government which becomes de facto capital by necessity of the term and sovereign practice.

The Swiss is also a step ahead in sensitivity to disturbance by others and regard for personal comfort. For example, in Geneva, in residential flats people do not flush their toilet after 10 p.m. Of course, it is not a law but a customary practice which is, by and large, adhered to in peaceful collective living of society. Neighbours may even remonstrate at the neglect to abide by this social norm, and police may visit to issue a warning to the defaulter. Incidentally, such warnings are taken rather seriously. This narrative unfolds an unusual sensitivity and shows how entrenched prejudices, preconceptions, and attitudes can make for disaster in combined living and interaction. Agreed, adjustments, and change may seep in gradually yet mutual acceptance will take time, perhaps generational, while animus would be instant and deplorable.

Again, in the USA, taking camera pictures or recording of even exteriors of a private property, without proper permission, can land anyone in serious legal problem if not a patent crime, whereas in the UK, reaction is not so serious. In fact, there is

10.1 Divergent Perception of Crimes   217

a joke that the USA and the UK are divided by the same language. Comics of the joke might offend some yet the truth remains. On the same restriction and sensitivity, Swedes are different and enjoy what they call as Everyman's Right. In Sweden, one has an unconditional right to cross private property, provided it is not in the yard of the house or has crops growing on it. A person also has the right to camp for three nights anywhere, even outside someone's yard, without seeking permission of the landowner and for one night against the express refusal of the landowner also.[41] However, littering is strictly prohibited and one may pick up the trash on departure from there.

10.1.14 The Japanese Customs and Laws

In Japan, the almost universal Western custom of "Ladies first" is negated and it is men who embark or alight or enter first followed by ladies. Ergo, the customary precedence to the ladies is denied in etiquette, yet it shows true Asia and Asian-ness. While on another aspect, Japan has accepted marriage equality ahead of many Asian countries. Tokyo has started recognising same-sex relationship and LGBTQ partnerships in a step to fight discrimination. Authorities have started issuing partnership certificate to such couples to be treated equal to married ones and become eligible to a range of public services such as housing, medical, and welfare.[42] Thus, variations in deep prejudices, ingrained attitudes, reflexive verbality, diehard habits, superstitious beliefs, and fixated conformism, indeed, acquire salience in collective and joint living in spatial groupings and celestial societies. Therefore, psycho-social differences highlight causes and flag issues of conflicts that seem pertinent and assume good relevance to our study of space crimes.

The Japanese are also highly disciplined, peace-loving, polite, and accommodative. It is well known that some Japanese couples, who cannot afford separate living after legal divorce, due to scarce availability and exorbitantly high rentals, mutually share the same predivorce accommodation and facilities, on agreed, decent and dignified terms without much trouble or interference, and incidents of unwanted advances, and breach of privacy. Instances of forced intrusion are scarcely encountered and rarely ever reported. However, they do have a tradition of love hotels for convenience with privacy. These hotels are on the lines of motels in the USA and provide accommodation with bare skeletal facilities, like shower, condoms, and tissues, with reasonable anonymity. Similar hotels exist in Taiwan, Thailand, and some other countries. In Thailand, these are called curtain hotels and are not easily spottable.[43]

---

[41] Mats Andersson in Quora Digest (6).

[42] "Tokyo recognises same-sex relationships", *the Times of India*, (Chandigarh edition), November 2, 2022, p. 14.

[43] Hara Shidho, (5) Quora Digest.

However, such cooperative relationship and amicable joint living, after divorce, under the same roof, as practised and accepted in Japan would be considered by the foreigners as profane in concept, "unadjustable" mutually, viewed suspiciously by neighbours, unacceptable as a social practice and thus, would be a near-impossible arrangement in post-conjugal life. No wonder, sometimes, realities of life and economic compulsions do ordain cultural adjustment, impact conformist behaviour, and break mental fixations to bring about social acceptance of new norms. Accordingly, this shared arrangement has become the new normal of society in Japan.

10.1.15 *A Miscellany*

Again, take the Canadian they are so used to saying sorry at any or every point that government passed a law in 2009 declaring that casual or conversational apology cannot be used as evidence of admission of guilt or for remission of crime. In Italy, one opens an umbrella only outside as protection from rain because there is a superstition that if one does open an umbrella inside the house, as it may bring ill luck. Further, in Europe, public display of affections by hugging and kissing in public is permitted almost everywhere. So is in France where this practice is equally compulsive and socially acceptable to say bye on the railway stations. Interestingly, this familial "effusivity" and friendly intimacy is an acceptable norm before the train reaches there, but once the train arrives on the platform, from then on kissing is illegal on that specific premises.

It is believed that the Chinese are one of the cleanest civilisations. Their personal hygiene habits are equally good, and they are habituated to take shower before going to bed, whereas kissing is not permitted in public places in China. It is believed that they invented the tooth brush and their bath soap was called "bathing bean." They also found plant-based solutions to wash clothes and used plant ash to remove grease stains. With lineage of such cleanliness in habits, Chinese may find some space travel companions offensively smelly and unbearable.

Carrying the fetish of cleanliness forward, in Russia, one cannot enter canteens and restaurants wearing an overcoat despite the chilling and freezing cold of the season and snowfall. Perforce, overcoats have to be removed and left in the wardrobe at the entrance. Many places bear a public notice to this effect which is obeyed, but imagine the inconvenience of this tradition. Ironically, though overcoats are forbidden inside yet snow-covered dirty shoes are permitted in the same premises.

It is almost a universal custom to wear black attire or sober colours while attending a funeral or a prayer meeting on demise. But this may not be so on Jewish occasions. That is because Jewish tradition for Israelis ordains that they bury the dead on the same day, as far as practical. This norm creates situations where Jews have to rush to the funeral at any time, and they indeed rush to the procession in whatever clothes they are wearing because they may not find enough time to rush home for an appropriate change of dress. Thus, they could be seen at a funeral procession in office uniform or a formal dress or casual wear or even party dress with colours not decorous to

10.1 Divergent Perception of Crimes

the solemnity of the occasion. Dress decorum or clothing propriety may not have been observed, but urgency of occasion and sentiments for the departed are more important than a formality of dress code.

Sri Lankans, too, have an obsession for cleanliness and in particular for clean hands. Whenever they enter a resort, super store, restaurant, or a public place, they wash their hands as wash basins are provided outside the premises for this purpose. In contrast, Germans may blow their blocked nose, rather noisily, in public and one may not be able to object to the unpleasantness so caused as it is socially accepted and legally permitted in Germany. Thus, persons belonging to different nationalities, living in different countries, groomed in different cultures, schooled in different societies, and with overpowering individual predilections, yet living together, are bound to have differences, conflicts and crimes, and varying perceptions on others' law and dispensation of justice.

In Germany, wastage of food items is viewed with dismay. Germans leave no meal unfinished to be wasted, and this habit is taught and inculcated right from childhood. At hotels, you have to eat what you ordered, irrespective of its taste or aroma. The fact that you have paid for it and its disposal is none of the hotel business, is not an acceptable argument. The waitresses can tick you off sternly or call the police. The moral compass points that food cannot be thrown as waste. Sri Lankans share this trait with equal strictness, and the food ordered in a hotel has to be finished because mere payment is not enough remit. At places, you have to pay twice the bill amount for the leftover food item as deterrent penalty.

Habits do die hard and tend to be involuntary reflex actions. Such situations, if repeated or prolonged, may lead to remonstration, insults, and strife, and, may be, a near-crime. Perceptions do matter, and a person groomed under own national rules, cultural values, and social ethos may work oneself up to inadvertently annoy or offend unaccustomed others, in a heterogeneous group. Thus, even normal innocuous behaviour or usual innocent gestures or unintended reflexive actions may disturb or offend the unfamiliar companions. Ergo, it seems pertinent to highlight that most legal systems are a mirror image of civilisational values, cultural fixations, social ethos, and behavioural norms which tend to perpetuate their differences and identity rather possessively. Hence, diversity exists, differences perpetuate, and traditions continue which may be disruptive to motley groups of collective living in space and on planets.

In the end, please permit me reiterate and emphasise, even at the cost of repetition, that the essence and purpose of this chapter have been to explain and illustrate the global diversity in behaviour and beliefs, fixations, and mindset of people which may lead to differences, annoyances, unacceptance, disputes, conflicts, and even crimes, minor or major. After all, it will be from among these people who will, one day, be the tourists, workers, or residents of space colonies and would live in cosmopolis celestial societies. They are bound to carry their baggage of mental fixations and behavioural attitude to such collective living in outer space that may compel compromises in necessities and conveniences, comforts, and privacy. In such constrained and mixed groupings, differences, disputes, and conflicts are inevitable.

The preceding discussion has highlighted how attitudes can differ, reactions can vary, acceptance can wear thin in composite, diverse and heterogenous social groupings in space, and in habitations on celestial bodies to erupt in disruption of personal relations and disturbance of public order. Therefore, in space societies, we need to build social bridges of acceptance, encourage tolerance, induce compromises, create affability, and build harmony. This seems imperative for space inhabitants and other perpetrators because the cost of disharmony, disorder, and disruption could be unacceptably high. The risk could even be existential for the humanity up there in outer space as well as for the mankind below on the Earth. Wisdom for the right actions lies with us, else the history of tomorrow may be different.

10.2 In Search of Justice

These situations are likely to become relevant, rather pertinent, in space residencies, celestial habitations, tourism resorts or at international space stations, harbouring heterogeneous gatherings and composite groups, which though small may have disparate composition. These may consist of people from different countries, ethnicities, cultures, social background, educational levels, mental fixations, and behavioural patterns who may perceive and comprehend the same behaviour, expression, or occurrence differently. Therefore, an apparently innocuous or insignificant variation in national laws or societal values, cultural mores, or family practices may be cognised or treated as significant and substantial divergence or an offensive breach meriting serious condemnation or accusation. And the aggrieved party may be appalled at the muted protest, non-challant or cavalier response, or indifferent reaction of the others. There may thus be imperceptible angst, suppressed frustration or bursting anger among some which may, at times, unintentionally, inadvertently or involuntarily erupt into uncontrollable rage leading to crime in retribution.

Once the crime is committed in an international jurisdiction, the perpetrator and the victim, both remain apprehensive whether they will get justice according to their national laws, native norms, respective mindset, and usual expectation. Their apprehensions are understandable due to several uncertainties and imponderables. For example, an incidental culprit with impeccable background and high credentials may be afraid of victimisation or vengeance or character assassination and the victim may feel apprehensive whether due justice will prevail to ensure due incarceration of the offender or that reparation will be fair and reasonable.

The most prominent reasons for variables are intercultural differences, transnational law code disparities, incongruence of civilisational values, varying national ethos, admissibility or maintainability of specific defence pleas, variations in sanctions or punishments in diverse legal systems, and attitudes towards reformation or disciplining of the criminal. It is, therefore, natural that a criminal will grope for the most favourable jurisdiction and forum. And different lawful routes may be supported or even encouraged by ideological selection, sectarian affiliations and denominational affinity overshadowing purpose and objectivity that may blur the logic of the occurrence or lend a twist to the event. This undue influence may inordinately delay the legal process, thereby vindicating the maxim that justice delayed is justice denied.

The purpose of law is to solve societal problems, cultural non-conformism, community conflicts, and even individual disputes with due justice to all parties. Thus law, whether codified, unscripted, or normative, is not an end in itself; it is a means to create personal safety in the community, establish security in society, and to end a social evil by intended deterrence or actual punishment. Different countries with different cultural background, social values, and "psyched" mindset may arrive at different solutions to grapple with the same and common problem. The primitive societies had "norm-atised" tribal behaviour or "sympathetically" acquired social customs which progressively evolved into laws for good reasons of safety, security, morality, identity, and uniformity in the particular society, conforming to their beliefs and values, traditions, and practices. These in turn and with time developed into legal doctrines which were applied and used as precedent for uniformity in punishment.

However, these laws, mostly unwritten and uncodified, could slip from memory at the right time and may cause injustice. Hence, laws came to be codified and legislated as referential record, for public information wider acceptance and greater credibility. Space societies on different celestial bodies may also undergo a similar process of evolution, though faster, for their own specific and suitable legal system, policing methods, prosecution modalities, judicial enforcement measures, level of sanctions, and standards of common justice reconciling the jurisprudential diversity of space inhabitants, temporary or permanent. This would be in accord with their acquired adjustments, multi-ethnicity compromises, and native thought-process to develop new syllogistic paradigm and legal idioms for adjudication of local crimes committed in space.

Every evolving society and era of time is judged by its adaptability to change and its capacity to imbibe its past practices and experience and carry it forward to the future for harmonious adaptation. Therefore, the power of this traction should be wielded impartially and exercised judicially, lest it shows potentially dangerous outcomes. Further, it needs emphasis that the social enemy is not an individual offender or small mafia group operating at the fringes of the social order but those in power and authority, political, bureaucratic, or official, who cause greater damage and wreak havoc on the social system, from within and with impunity. And there is a dire need for human ability and sharp intelligence to distinguish between illusion and reality. May be there are covert compulsions which make us political eunuchs, ineffective bureaucrats, and impotent jurists who cannot hail the desired change.

In conclusion, individuals residing together in multi-ethnicity, multi-communal, and multinational societies will have reasons to differ on lingual expressions, behavioural gestures, cultural practices, social digressions, and living styles because of incongruence in understanding, diversity in mind fixations and lack of universal comprehension. These differences, howsoever, innocuous or unintended may give cause for misunderstanding resulting in individual crime that may be a physical act, an insulting slur, a provoked response, a vengeful reaction, or a planned vendetta.

Such crimes could as well be committed collectively in league, law, and order disturbance by a mob or conspiratorially in confidence but would, nevertheless, fall into the category of space crimes for the *locus* of their commission and would need to be dealt with accordingly.

These considerations of diversity and unmatched perceptions of individuals in pluralistic societies would impel for social justice superimposed on legal justice. This becomes pertinent because positive traits and evidentiary approach of the latter may fail to comprehend the nature of underlying circumstances, mental prefixations, the uncontrollable reflexes, or innate responses of the offender. Ergo, justice in pluralistic societies, apart from being lawful, must be just from all angles and considerations like personal, social, cultural, economic, and political. Such dispensation would reinforce confidence in the process and encourage acceptance of the verdict.

Additionally, there may be a dilemma that the sentencing should be based on whose national criminal code, whether of the offender or of the victim, because both would expect justice of their own belief and understanding. However, a sensitive and sensible opinion may recommend the lesser punishment, in gravity and quantum, or equitable relief for loss or damage to meet the ends of justice. This would satisfy the human sensibilities, pacify the resentment in public mind, address the grief of the aggrieved, and provide a fair restitution to the complainant.

It hardly necessitates a mention that if the prosecution is mired in hassles of jurisdiction or extradition or procedures, then the case may be referred to the International Court of Space Crimes (ICSC). Trial proceedings at ICSC should be *bonafide* and transparent, impartial, and neutral with proper evaluation of defence pleas, judicially and judiciously. Further, the court should brook no extraneous influence or entertain political interference or admit of prejudice or preconception of any kind or for any unsustainable reason. Perceptions may still differ on rule of law and realities of life, yet justice would have been delivered. Certainly, the UN Sustainable Development Agenda 2030 towards justice and crime would have been complied with.

Lately, apex courts have started showing due sensitivity to the criminal in the judicial process and have considered mitigation on points of attendant mental condition, criminal antecedents, and chances of reformation. The Supreme Court of India has emphasised on the courts that they should not puritanically look at a crime in a purist approach but also appreciate the "state of mind and…socio-economic conditions" of the criminal,[44] as also the past history of offences, if any, and probability of good conduct and reformed rehabilitation.[45] This advice appears rather pertinent and relevant in international situations; with an additional understanding about the criminal's knowledge that the impugned act or alleged misbehaviour could tantamount to the charged crime. Perhaps, intention behind the act or *mens rea* could acquire pertinence in the legal process of cases with international ramifications because the criminal may be innocent in belief and the charged conduct innocuous according to one's ethos and mindset.

---

[44] *The Times of India*, (Chandigarh edition), December 11, 2021, p. 14.
[45] Ibid.

However, for better appreciation of local laws of the accused and the aggrieved parties, International Court of Space Crimes (ICSC) could appoint *amicus curiae* from respective countries who could brief the court on the ingredients of the criminal act, national nuances of crime, the germane codified law, the judicial understanding of the crime, and likely components of the punishment and their respective quantum. It may seem relevant here to flag that the rights assured may be equal yet may not be identical, and blind application may lead to patent injustice. For example, the developed need different interpretation of rights while the underdeveloped have different needs and aspirations for fulfilment through these guarantees that solicit social justice and not a sheer positivist verdict. For example, death sentence for murder may be the right sanction but the poor family losing the bread-winner seeks social justice in restitution.

It must, thus, be appreciated that national laws have their own moorings in local ethos and disparities in judicial systems have roots in respective cultures which should be accorded the dignity they command or respect these deserve. Though similar information may be presented by the respective agents of the parties, yet *amicus curiae* could best inform the court more objectively and dispassionately without the influence of client affiliation or sectarian pressures. The objective should not be legalese but social justice. However, the fees for such a court officer could be borne by the honourable court or the litigants themselves or subsidised by the state of nationality or domicile of the respective parties to the adjudication in the court.

Chapter 11
Appraisal and Solutions

11.1 An Appraisal

Some of the modern crimes have existed and persisted since the evolution of humankind. Only, that in prehistoric times, the delinquencies were revenged, avenged, and settled based on emotions and suffering. Down the ages, justice still remained rustic, only method of neutralisation and degree of punishment differed. With the establishment of organised social groups and growth of civilisation, certain norms of justice against crimes were evolved and enforced by the community elders. But given the human nature, graffiti says, some people are never at peace until they are fighting. As nation states emerged with sovereign authority, there was a need for a legal system to maintain and uphold local laws and create a semblance of uniformity in punishment of same or similar crimes. Justice became neutral and equal for all shunning subjectivity, arbitrariness, and discrimination. Law and legal codes had come of age to deter crimes and handle criminals.

In an ambitious stride for development of technology and its applications in the mid-twentieth century, man breached the boundary of Earth's atmospheric envelop to conquer the final frontier of outer space. Soon, astronauts started orbiting in the outer space and visiting the nearby celestial body, the Moon. The astronauts of all countries were generally picked up from the defence forces with ingrained discipline, specialised training, and highest standard of professionalism. Thus, their conduct and behaviour in space missions were impeccable, dedicated to the task, and worthy of their regimented background. That was the class of the fraternity of the astronauts.

Over half a century of "humanned" and crewed operations, the scenario has changed. It turned out that outer space with its characteristic zero gravity, G-factor in launches and manoeuvres, cramped internal spaces within the space vehicle, unergonomic working conditions, and long routines of work at ISS or spaceships have induced high degree of stress and caused unbearable levels of fatigue leading to exhaustion, irritation, annoyance, and mood swings. Thus, the mentally stressful condition has, at times, led to instances of unbecoming acts, passive disobedience, and inadvertent negligence that have reflected patent indiscipline and lack of due diligence, if not really bordering on definable and executable military crime.

Some such cases have been discussed in Chaps. 2 and 3. For the USA, the most significant ones relate to defiance and disobedience by the crew, and for the Russians the major breach of regulations occurred in sexual dalliance by two crewmembers. Another important case of crime concerns the suspected drilling of a hole in Russian quarter allegedly by a mentally unstable US astronaut. This caused leak of pressure at the ISS. Though evidence is weak in this case, yet the case is live from the Russian end. It, however, appears that in most of the cases, the offenders, who otherwise professionally outstanding and cream of the class and having accomplished difficult missions to the glory of the country, were either let off lightly with graceful condonation of misdemeanours or subjected to a modicum of silent punishment.

One such crime committed from the ISS has spilled in the media and splashed in global newspapers. The case relates to Anne McClain, an US astronaut then tenured on a mission at ISS and lodged in the US quarters. This astronaut, while at ISS, accessed the bank account/financial data of her estranged spouse, Summer Worden. The use of privileged network connectivity of NASA and the computer system of ISS could be construed as unauthorised for this personal use. The spouse has alleged that taking out information on financial status from the bank records was patently illegal and tantamount to breach of trust and identity theft. The matter has been reported to Inspector General of Investigations, NASA, and the US Federal Trade Commissioner for inquiry and redress of grievance. Ironically, the case on investigation has turned topsy-turvy and McClain has been exonerated, while her spouse has been indicted for felonies by the authorities. The disposal of the case against Worden has not been made public.

11.1.1 Near Crimes by the States

It needs no vindication that crimes are committed by human beings, whether individually or as bearers of authority in private business corporations or being decision-makers as political leaders governing sovereign states. In the past, state-controlled space agencies have also failed in their duty under the Outer Space Treaty, other space law instruments and international responsibilities *erga omnes*. A glaring example is that of Israel having sent tardigrade organisms to the Moon for experiment on origin and survival of life. The lunar lander carrying this cargo crashed instead of soft-landing on the Moon and has in every possibility polluted and contaminated the surface with these hardy and long-life microorganisms. The pristinely nature of the Moon's environment seems lost though exact consequences and snow-balling effects are yet unknown but are likely to be serious over long period of time.

The US conducted copper-needle experiment, without international consultations, and in a failed attempt, the needles jumbled in lumps and still continue to orbit in outer space. In breach of security check, an astronaut, in a prankish act, smuggled a contraband corn-beef sandwich into his spaceship and caused alarm of possible malfunction with disintegrated floating crumbs under the zero-gravity condition. Or that the astronauts of Gemini spacecraft, in an irresponsible act, threw out into space their dirty linen. In an act of one-upmanship, similar prohibition was breached by the Soviet astronauts. Both acts were in contravention of safety regulations and highly reprehensible. It is immaterial whether condoned with or without remonstration or disciplinary action as these were unbecoming, unauthorised, or irregular acts that, nevertheless, border on crimes in space.

In consequence, astronauts no longer remain a revered sorority of hallowed professionals, highly indoctrinated, long-regimented, and exceptionally disciplined. Regardless of the extraordinary training and the imbibed skills, human frailties are becoming manifest with black marks in their conduct and blemishes in their behaviour. May be, some of the past lapses were committed under the pressure of onerous tasks, exacting routines, the impact of unaccustomed environment or unhealthy influences of the outer space. But despite having been trained for these circumstances, the defence pleas earn no reprieve for them. On the balance, some of the erring astronauts were publicly cheered and heartily congratulated, though internally within the organisation, they were, possibly, meted out with reproof or reprimand under customary military correctives.

11.1.2 The Complexion of Future Crimes

This is just the beginning, and the complexion of future crimes in space may not be fully envisaged as yet because the nature and kind of these will depend upon the character of ensuing space activities, the purpose of humans entering space, and the competing interests within the space economic system. Therefore, activities like space travel and tourism, exploitation of celestial natural resources, specialised industrial production, e.g. alloys, crystals, vaccines, etc. or humans living in planetary habitats as workers or residents; each will pose its own dark side and the resultant crimes. Briefly stated, each type of activity will generate its own typically specific crime genre. Travel and tourism will generate contractual and liability disputes; exploitation of natural resources may create discords in economic interests; business ambitions and entrepreneurial strategies may come in direct conflict; spying on industrial research may cause thefts of intellectual property; and planetary habitations may lead to physical and mental crimes similar to those committed on the Earth.

Space technology is galloping fast with diversity of applications in tow. At the same time, digital technology is getting diversified in numerous apps and broadening in footprint. Beneficial offshoots like digital submission of documents, virtual proceedings in courts, etc., are time and effort saving and still equally effective and validly trusted. Communication and broadcasting systems have revolutionised and have come to provide almost instant and relatively cheap services in daily life. Remote sensing is yielding many advantages in disaster management and is imparting transparency in land records and natural resources. But at the same time, digital technology revolution has given fillip to weaponisation of a different kind that can operate from anywhere: Earth, water, airspace, outer space, or a celestial body. These can be activated in stealth, in anonymity, and from a hiding, and the operator may be a state or non-state actor or even an individual mercenary.

Hence, digital technologies, in their diversity, open floodgates for dual-use devices that can act as weapons for causing system malfunction, satellite destabilisation, or other serious damage, temporary or permanent, if not a total holocaust of humanity. The spectrum of weapons alluded to are cyber-family, directed energy devices, and other similar gadgets that can be operated from anywhere to cause damage to or destruction of space objects or infrastructure on a celestial body. The presently visualised crime potential of these seems well beyond the prohibitions under Article IV of the OST. And their future applications with inimical potential can neither be easily imagined nor assessed, yet should not be underestimated due to ignorance.

Another growing line of technology that can be and has been adapted to space activities is artificial intelligence (AI) and robotics. AI introduces human–machine competition and works on algorithms, comparisons, and self-learning processes. It can imitate human brain's neural network and has a characteristic core competence of integration of technical, mental, and social attributes. Thus, these are dual-use technologies that can act as a double-edged sword, hence considered as weaponry of the new era that can be deployed for defence strategies with far-reaching impact as well as for safety and security benefits. With induced decision-making capability and capacity to imbibe learning and work out new decision algorithms, it may compete with human intelligence. It may even overtake it and go out of control to cause unimaginable harm or create existential threat to humanity. Possibilities seem endless and ominous. And the dead cannot cry for justice. Therefore, let's look beyond doom and gloom to seize the right moment for constructive remedies and workable plans.

Robotics is another put-away, use-away device with similar infused capabilities and control systems. Its potential can be exploited from both edges and for dual purposes. Thus, the risk is from digital transformation and its proliferating mutations. Incidentally, space robots have been tested and deployed in the ISS for dull, uninteresting, and routine duties. Existing laws, ethical, national, and international, are neither sufficiently specific nor substantially adequate to restrict their escape out of human control. In this regard, outer space activities, present and future, will provide an active arena for its deployment and possibly may reap its share of crimes and destruction.

With expanding space transportation of personnel and cargo as well as diversifying space industry, launches are increasing in numbers and becoming capable of putting multiple number of satellites in orbit in one take-off. Further, space activities are becoming diverse in missions, increasingly reaching out to exploit spatial natural resources and establish human residencies on the planets. So are private space players gaining multiple opportunities from state-funded agencies for cooperative ventures and "tycoonic" private corporations are game for the offers. As a result, the character of space activities is shifting towards commercial ventures whether for space tourism or commercial exploitation of celestial mineral resources or tourist habitations or planetary settlements on celestial bodies. The escalating business interests, expanding commercial avenues, and growing diversity of activities due to technological advances can induce situations of cut-throat competition, economic discord, and operational interference leading to disputes and crimes in space that could be complicated and complex.

11.1.3 Challenges of Diversity and Perception

It is logical to expect that space tourists, workers, and settlers would constitute diverse groups with people drawn from different nationalities, ethnicities, cultures, and societies. Each person would thus have different national orientation, ethnic behaviour, cultural norms, and social mores. These dissimilarities would create varying perception of each other in interpreting their verbal nuances, gestural expressions, and behavioural patterns. In fact, the unmatched views and incongruence in understanding of ingrained beliefs and mental fixations may not always be affable or tolerable in mixed company causing provocation, disputes, conflicts, and ultimately crimes. Situations would be endemic with potential for discord. It is not that such dilemmas are not confronted on the Earth, but here national sovereignty provides enforcement with much ease in procedures and equal sway of deterrence in terms of sanctions. In outer space and on celestial bodies, there is no police force for enforcement while international safeguards and remedies are indirect, weak, and labyrinthine.

Discussing of diversity and perception, we may allude to different legal systems operating in different countries. For example, the UK and other countries with British legal tradition follow adversarial system, where both parties present their facts and arguments in the court and the accused is deemed innocent till proved guilty. The French system works on accusation where the onus of defence shifts to the accused who has to demolish the charges fully and completely for acquittal. In most states in the USA, jury system still operates where the judge facilitates the understanding of the jurors and jury returns the verdict on majority vote. The judge, however, still bears responsibility to evaluate the verdict in terms of Statute law before announcing the judgment. Most often the jury succeeds, and it is rarely that the judge modifies or alters the verdict. There are also a large number of Muslim countries that follow Islamic Sharia which has its own distinctive law and logic. This provides "theo-legal" dispensation and brooks no compromises or breaches of Sharia law.

Added to this diversity are differing and even conflicting legal codes in different countries. And these are based on denominational beliefs, social values, and national aspirations. No wonder, differences in thinking tend to creep in for people oriented to different legal ethos and governed by discordant national Statutes. This situation can be further complicated by social mores, experiential reflexes, or empirical fixations. With all this dissimilitude and contrariety, we have created the right recipe for contretemps, conflict, and disorder. Thus, a person governed by a different legal system, brought up in a different social milieu and with different personal experiences, is bound to react and respond differently to the same or similar behaviour in mixed groupings of people. And intolerance to these differences leads to crimes.

11.1.4 Hassles in Adjudication of Space Crimes

It is interesting, that at present, a crime committed in or from space is to be adjudicated on the Earth, based on international law procedures by a competent court and according to applicable law, national or international. The complexity is apparent and needs to be untangled from different aspects of uncompromising jurisdictions, diplomatic over-reach for extradition, procedural hassles in enforcement, contested competence of the court to seize of the matter, and the dilemma to elect the applicable law. The case would get further mired in complications if offenders are more than one and from different countries and the victim from still another country. Such possibilities can be envisaged from multinational groupings in the ISS or an orbiting hotel or a planetary resort or a celestial habitation.

At present, no specific law, Statute or code of rules is in place, internationally or nationally, in most space-faring countries, to handle offensive acts of individuals or business houses committed in outer space domain. Hence, space crimes may involve a matrix of challenges due to the nature of crimes, involvement of multi-nationality offenders, territorial jurisdiction, extradition claims, procedural hassles, and liability nuances. Whatever be the end result of contested claims and cognate legal challenges, the offender must be duly tried under due process of law, by a competent court, with applicable laws, and duly punished to dispense justice to the victim and impart security to the society.

This may not be possible under hassle-ridden rules of jurisdiction or competitive claims for extradition, while the offender may seek and get the choice of forum with advantage to escape trial or punishment or both due to national affiliation or political patronage. In this search, the offender may be helped by legal strategy, ideological commonality, fraternal identity, or denominational commonness. Such considerations may stymie or skew dispensation of justice. Hence, there is need for an international treaty, making it obligatory on states to try the offender wherever apprehended or extradite to the state of nationality or domicile of the culprit or, in ultimate, to that of the victim. Between the countries where mutual extradition treaty does not exist, a new negotiated space crimes treaty could carry the force of a universal extradition treaty[1] and be used for the purpose, in the interest of justice.

Further, international treaties are generally state centric and do not recognise individuals as subjects with independent legal capacity. The same is under space law. Therefore, liability, criminal or civil, incurred by an individual or corporate body does not attach directly and immediately to the criminal entity but rises to the state level. And launching state and/or patron state of that person and/or space object are encumbered with such responsibility and liability, jointly and severally. The respective state accepting such responsibility and consequent liability can, without prejudice, reclaim liability share from the other legally liable state or take appropriate action against the offender under domestic jurisdiction.

On the other hand, having a treaty framework based on sovereign activities does not make sense for the aggrieved individual, and his restricted resort to diplomatic or

---

[1] For example, The Hague Treaty, 1970 for aviation offences has such provision and effect.

sovereign solution yields no quick results and thus gives no solace either. Therefore, appropriate remedies with procedural and jurisdictional simplification need to be devised because justice delayed is justice denied. The illustrative cases, discussed earlier, do give a wake-up call to the international community for timely action and requisite negotiations for resolution of such tricky predicament. It is common knowledge that international negotiations are a protracted affair with political theatricals and diplomatic stand-offs, hence need longer lead time and should get proactive time lead. We now have the opportunity and time to consider the issues holistically, futuristically, and in the right perspective to infuse confidence in international framework and trust in the new proposed institutions. Let us seize this moment of opportunity and succeed. These measures will promote amity among space-farers and provide confidence of due justice to the space tourists, space workers, and space emigrees. It will be a revolutionary step to usher in the second wave of space law; and what is urged here is to identify the challenges, recognise the possibility, and undertake timely preparations.

11.2 Proffered Solutions

11.2.1 *The Scenario*

There can be no controversy on the contention that justice must be dispensed to the aggrieved party and the offender must be punished for his criminal act of whatever kind. It must also be clearly understood and duly conceded by the complainant that criminal justice is not a tit for tat nor vengeance for loss or injury nor is it for restitutio in integrum and also not a compensation for grief or emotional relief. On the other hand, for the culprit it is an opportunity for realisation, repentance, and reformation that may also hold out as deterrence for others. Accordingly, justice imparted for space crimes must display judicial objectivity and transparent fairness; and alongside cogitate on considerations of empathy and sensitivity for multicultural misunderstandings, inadvertent wrongs, and misperceived reactions that led to space crimes while awarding sentence or granting relief.

In the shifting threshold of galloping space technology and its ever-advancing applications, space law stands as a beacon of justice, regulator of activities, and a guide for sustainability. Yet in times to come, not too far distant in the future, crimes in space may become frequent in occurrence, varied in character, serious in gravity, and perilous in consequences. The visualisable ones could be of physical action, mental torture, attacks on dignity of life, economic interference, damage to business interests, mismanagement of rights of the workforce or biased and "inhumanitarian" acts during emergencies, sheltering or evacuation to Earth. These could also extend by consequences to dereliction of duty or incurring of economic loss or denial of a promised privilege or similar remiss. Another foreseeable genre could be digital, cyber, and allied crimes; pollution or contamination of outer space environment to affect its sustainability or graver crimes against humanity. Human ingenuity is too wide, and it may be difficult to list them all, yet these illustrations should suffice to make the point and highlight the dangers. Sagacity lies in finding and implementing the right solutions to our challenges rather than regret the holocaust *post-facto*.

11.2.2 The Need for a New and Specific Treaty

The possible crimes so listed, and those beyond imagination, cannot be appropriately handled under the existing space law instruments. The available legal provisions relating to nationality, territoriality, etc., may fail to provide direct and specific solutions to the riders of jurisdiction, extradition, enforcement, and applicable legal code. Even the remedial avenues offered by the international law, which are equally applicable, *mutatis mutandis*, to the outer space domain, too, falls short of the task, so important, broad and complex. OST, which was crafted, negotiated and has operated for over five decades has stood the test of time and extant technology with its futuristic vision, breadth of scope, and newer interpretations. Given political environment of the then polarised world, necessity for diplomatic compromises, and limited expectations relating to exfoliation of space technology, OST could not have been better in its prescience and forethought and practicality in the sixties of the last century.

Fortuitously or by graceful adherence, space-faring nations and others have all along respected this *grundnorm* regulating activities with an assurance of liberty and fraternity in the space domain. There have been minor irritations like Bogota Declaration of right of subjacent state over geosynchronous slots or the Japanese objection to the ASAT tests[2], but these did not affect the operation or dent the majesty of the treaty. Today, humanity rides the cusp of commercial development that has overtaken the fundamentals of modern space law and OST seems to have gone out of date. This could not have been visualised at the inception and scripting of OST. After all, no one learns algebra in class one. We are wiser today having witnessed the actual growth of space applications, the accumulated experience in space activities and glitches in the operation of OST. Hence, the selected task can now be undertaken with greater wisdom and futuristic vision.

So, the first option among solutions could be to update, renovate improvise, or recraft the OST to become equal to the contemporary regulatory challenges presented by the current expanse of space technology in commercial space transportation, exploitation of celestial natural resources, and the growing inclination towards permanent or temporary residence in planetary settlements. All these developments are recent and would introduce new genre of space crimes. OST did not cater to such exigencies in space activities and their onset so fast in time as also with concomitant repercussions. Ergo, it has lagged behind in vision and content and needs a holistic and revisionary improvement not only to accommodate ensuing exigencies but also to envisage future incumbencies to provide for suitable and adequate legal

---

[2] "Japan voices concern over China's missile tests", Tokyo (Reuters), January 19, 2007.

expedients. But this may turn out to be a herculean task of great dimensions requiring hectic diplomatic parleys with shifting imponderables in its achievement.

Alternatively, an effort can be made to identify relevant treaties operating in other fields of law and make these applicable to this domain; for example, the Hague Treaty,1970 for aviation offences and its flexibility on extradition of the accused even without bilateral treaty between nations on the subject. But few other such germane instruments would be found, and it would make an inefficient patchwork of invited laws which would remain scattered and indexed under the respective titles of their existing tutelage or the subject of parental treaty. Thus, despite the ease in negotiations, this eclectic approach would hardly make for an effective and convenient legal regime to face the new and fast emerging realities of the outer space domain.

Thus, the angst for the weakness of such a contrived legal system is valid and genuine. So, the solution proposed above can be rejected as it may turn out to be cumbersome, ineffectual, and unproductive. And space crime may still remain an adopted child with step-motherly treatment under an "unpaternal" treaty. Again, the major problems to be reconciled in handling space crimes relate to conflicting claims on competitive jurisdiction over the culprit, compromises with understanding of divergent national legal codes, and varying interpretation of the same crime in different countries. Therefore, an apt and appropriate solution would be to negotiate a *specialis* protocol to the OST or an independent treaty that is particular and specific for the intended purpose and capable of resolving extant differences and allied contradictions as also guiding future contingencies that may become manifest in proper handling space crimes. Such a treaty, when drafted and crafted, may consider and include any other cognate posers that may clamour for alleviation through similar or specific regulation.

Secondly, some of the near-crimes listed earlier could be too serious and heinous enough to be ignored or condoned and would need to be punished. Space law and cognate international law may provide a legal opportunity to seek redress for the offence yet for processing a complaint or getting a crime cognised and prosecuted, one may have to enter a labyrinth of conflicting national procedures, wade through contradictory options on jurisdiction over the accused, grapple with diverse legal systems of court procedures, reconcile incongruency in national criminal codes and contend with the divergent understanding of same or similar crimes, and their ingredients and judicial interpretations. These hurdles of common understanding can, at times, become so intractable and insurmountable as to dishearten a determined litigant or defeat even a genuine cause or stall a real grievance and thus foil dispensation of desired justice to the victim.

International law and international courts or tribunal do not acknowledge individual citizen as subjects nor entertain their causes for adjudication and dispensation of justice. Again, judgments of international courts are not binding per se and proper court process may have to be followed for execution of the judgment in the concerned country. This would require a process of legal assistance under international law[3] which takes traction through diplomatic means and modalities that are, in the legendary sense, intrinsically slow in process and non-committal in effect. Thus, the true impact of the court verdict and the granted judicial relief under an international decree may be inordinately delayed or verily frustrated by circumstantial hurdles or diplomatic slow traction. The scenario makes a strong case for a specialised international court with its geographically convenient benches, permanent or sitting as and when necessary, to handle space crimes where an aggrieved individual should have *locus standi* to file one's case for adjudication. This acceptance and permission would disregard the hassles of jurisdiction over the accused, conflicting trial procedures in national courts, divergence of national criminal codes, and the over-riding social ethos for justice.

11.2.3 Overall Governance of Outer Space Domain

Treaties and laws by themselves are usually lame and need policing and enforcement agencies, supporting procedural law and competent courts with defined jurisdiction. Same is the case with the space law comprising a corpus of treaties that have served well as regulatory mechanisms so long as defiance has been ignorable or condonable. But significant crimes in and from outer space or celestial bodies would need effective compliance and significant remedies. Such management would need a suitable and pyramidical organisation for all-round administration of the domain and regulatory remedies with authorised sanctions. One suggestion could be to resuscitate Trusteeship Council of the United Nations and to rename it Outer Space Trusteeship Council (OSTC). It could take on comprehensive responsibility of governance of this ungoverned domain and facilitate growth of all stakeholders in space ventures. Hopefully, this new organ of the UN will succeed in its avowed task and be able to provide impetus to the space economy and work in the interest of humanity.

Despite a limited corpus of space law, treaty, normative, and declaratory, which is still evolving, there is scant regulation and little governance of outer space domain, including the celestial bodies. Though the "space rush" is just beginning, and more prominently by private enterprise with motivation of profit and self-aggrandisement by business tycoons, the space law and space governance are neither geared to nor mature enough to handle impending challenges or see through the moves of the captains of economic engines. To regulate commercial activity and splurging space economy as also to checkmate business acumen on an equal footing, it seems essential to have a competent institutional system for effective governance and supervision of the treaty compliances. Additionally, this institution would supervise operation of lease contracts and agreements relating to commercial uses of outer space and celestial realty (like for space travel and tourism industry) and term leases pertaining to planetary real estate for mining of mineral resources and infrastructure for residencies for habitation.

---

[3] This diplomatic process in Germany is called, *Leistung von rechtshilfe.*

11.2 Proffered Solutions

Despite a regulatory Outer Space Treaty prescribing permissions and prohibitions on space activities, there is no institutional mechanism to oversee compliance of the treaty provisions. Conceding current technology challenges to such a task, the treaty does not even hint at such a need, even in the long run. Fortunately, no major breaches of the space law have occurred over the last half a century; otherwise, such instances would have gone unnoticed and unreported. Hence, the need to evolve an organisational system of governance for the guidance of space activities, management of the outer space domain for regulated activities, and control on prohibited acts and contractual transgressions.

Further, the expanded and diverse uses of the outer space and celestial bodies would need infrastructure like space traffic management, real estate on planetary bodies for spaceports, buildings for hospitality industry, exploitation of mineral resources, manufacturing of special products, and establishment of planetary residencies and their infrastructure. These facilities would require realty for construction and operation, while celestial bodies are common heritage of mankind and cannot be subjected to national sovereignty. Hence, celestial resources of whatever kind that can used for peaceful purposes and to the benefit of humanity shall have to be collectively owned and professionally managed to stem and obviate "the Gold-Rush" by the nations developed in basic technologies of spatial blasting and excavation or creation of spatial infrastructure. Ergo, the need is for a common denominator solution and a level playfield for all, given the global asymmetry in technology.[4]

Nevertheless, the outer space domain which is so precious in commercial utilities and is populated by valuable celestial assets cannot be permitted to lie unused despite dire need for some of the precious mineral available there in abundance. One example is helium dust on the Moon which is useful in generating power,[5] while asteroids are still richer in metallic ores, the sources for which have exhausted on the Earth.[6] The millennial generation is more materialistic, more aware of the quantum of bounty of celestial natural resources and is eager, nay impatient, to commercially exploit this reservoir, whether there is permissive treaty law or no law. Apt examples are the overreaching efforts by the USA as well as the government stimulus by the Duchy of Luxembourg by enacting enabling laws[7] prompting and permitting its citizen and legal entities to exploit such resources, without riders or limitations. This is tantamount to declaration of pseudo-sovereignty leading to colonisation of celestial bodies that may remind humanity of the era of empires and colonies. The US logic for the illegality of their law is indeed, ingenious, and devious.[8]

---

[4] G S Sachdeva, *Outer Space: Security and Legal Challenges*, New Delhi, KW Publishers, 2010, p. 117.

[5] For a detailed study of celestial natural resources, refer G S Sachdeva, *Space Commercialisation: Prospects, Challenges and Way Forward*, New Delhi, Pentagon Publishers, (2019).

[6] G S Sachdeva, *Outer Space: Law, Policy and Governance*, New Delhi, KW Publishers, (2014), pp. 155–204.

[7] For example, American Space Commerce Free Enterprise Act, 2017.

[8] Sachdeva, n. 5 ante, pp. 1–43.

Another parallel proposal mooted by some veteran space law scholars like Ram Jakhu, Joseph Pelton,[9] Guido Lavalle[10], and chaperoned by some think-tanks is based on the premise that outer space and celestial bodies, except the Earth, remain unregulated, unsupervised, and ungoverned. This is because the existing space law emphatically excludes any possibility of "national appropriation by claim of sovereignty, by means of use or occupation, or by other means."[11] Thus, states parties to the treaty cannot exercise sovereignty or jurisdiction in any manner over the whole or any part of the space domain, and it remains beyond private appropriation by nations or nationals. This domain thus loses the tag of *res nullius* and becomes *res extra commercium* or better still, *res communis omnium* and does not lend itself to proprietary or exclusive appropriation.

Space law also proclaims outer space including celestial bodies as "the province of all mankind" and that "the exploration and use of outer space, including celestial bodies, shall be carried out for the benefit and in the interest of all countries..."[12] These concepts reflect the collective, benign, and altruistic values of humanity. Again, the Moon Treaty in Article 11 uses another appellation for this domain to treat it as common heritage of mankind, implying common and collective ownership that would necessitate joint governance ensuring fair, equitable, cooperative, and integrated in interests of all mankind. It thus rightly leads to Trusteeship concept under the aegis of the United Nations.

Another viable modality for such trust-like holding and collective governance can be found in the concept of co-parcenary property of joint, undivided Hindu family, lineally descended from a common ancestor. This doctrine is entrenched in the principles of Hindu inheritance (*Mitakshara* law).[13] This system verily assures joint management, devolution on birth, right by survivorship, and common benefits to and equality of all beneficiaries. It is a form of perpetual and "indissoluble" trust that even acknowledges the legitimate, undivided interest of future generations of beneficiaries. Accordingly, it mandates strict prohibition on division or devolution of co-parcenary into discrete individualisation of assets or dissolution of the functioning trust.

There is another rural custom in India called "*Shamlat.*" This treats common grazing ground of the village as *res publica* in line with *res communis* which could be comparable to "the benefit of all mankind" under the OST. *Shamlat* is a "*panchayati* land which, in an age-old practice with the force of customary law, is open to the entire village as free common grazing ground in timeless lease."[14] This custom also recognises an inalienable right of the future generations as their inherent right

---

[9] Ram S. Jakhu and Joseph N. Pelton, eds., *Global Space Governance: An International Study*, Springer, 2017, ISBN-13: 978-3319543635.

[10] Guido Lavalle, "Bringing Space Law into the 21st Century", ISSSP Reflections, December 15, 2020.

[11] Outer Space Treaty, Article II.

[12] Ibid, Article I.

[13] DF Mulla, *Principles of Hindu Law*, Calcutta, Eastern Law House, (11th edition, 1952).

[14] Sachdeva, n. 4 ante, p. 70.

11.2 Proffered Solutions

apparent to the common and collective property of the village. The *Shamlat* rights comprising free access, permissive use, common benefit, and collective ownership are remarkably similar to the regime of outer space domain. And these public rights of free access and usage to the villagers are obligatory and binding on the state and not merely notional or promissory. Thus, *Shamlat* concept is a broader social reality for common good and cooperative living.

It is proposed that for competent and transparent governance as well as professional management of spatial utilities, the proposed apex space organisation should exist under the aegis of the United Nations. Apart from often made proposals to set up World Space Authority or Organisation,[15] the suggestion to revive the UN Trusteeship Council would appear to be most suitable and appropriate organ. It is suitable because its incumbency would involve duties that appear relatively akin to its previous assigned Charter, which it discharged rather successfully. And the council seems an appropriate option because its resuscitation for the purpose would encounter least diplomatic, political, and ideological hurdles.

Based on the Trusteeship line of thinking and considering the doctrines hallowed in the space law, proposal favours the revival and repurposing of the presently defunct Trusteeship Council of the United Nations[16] and rechristening it as Outer Space Trusteeship Council (OSTC). This could undertake broad spectrum and total governance of the outer space and celestial bodies on the lines and the manner in which it earlier governed the trustee territories for their respective benefit and ultimate interest of humanity. Problems and challenges may be different in the space domain with competing pulls of commercial exploitation for profit and celestial sustenance for posterity; yet the approach and styles of governance, regulation, and management could be similar and experiential. For this reason, the proposal appears feasible and practical to find favour with scholars and diplomats. The tempting logic is that a precedent exists, a new problem has arisen, and a moribund institution that survives as extinct can be repurposed to take on newer challenges and responsibilities which can be matched with its best and fast results.

And it needs no convincing that the existing UN Office of Outer Space Affairs (UN OOSA) is too small in staff, inadequate in purpose and unskilled to perform the envisaged specialised functions of holistic domain governance, regulation of commercial race, and professional management of contractual contingencies in the future scenario. Eventually, UN OOSA could also be put under the Outer Space Trusteeship Council, as a separate working entity with existing tasks or integrated as deemed fit. This would be desirable as OSTC would be an umbrella organisation for total and sustained support to activities in the space domain and as information centre to the states. Hence, the council would have to be vested with a chartered mandate of governance, a roll of authority, suitable organisational structure, professional staffing, and adequate funding with a befitting office edifice.

---

[15] Ibid, pp. 136–40.

[16] Sachdeva, n. 4 ante, p. 35, UN Trusteeship of Celestial Resources. Also refer V. Siddhartha, "The Governance of Outer Space: Repurposing the Trusteeship Council of the United Nations", *ISSSP Reflections,* No. 60, February 08, 2021.

The council could, of course, generate its own sources of revenue from cess, fees and other charges levied on the leases permitted, activities regulated, facilities provided and operations controlled like space traffic management or grant of leases, etc. Additionally, a proposal may be mooted to authorise the council to levy an appropriate charge on the rocket launchings based on the stages shedded and payload carried as also on the number of launched satellites depending upon the size, purpose, life, and inbuilt system for removal from the orbit. This accrual may constitute Space Sustenance Fund (SSF), partly to cater to the expenses for the facilities catered and partly to arrange scavenging and cleansing of the space domain as our bounden duty to the posterity.

11.3 Support Set-up for the Outer Space Trusteeship Council

The Outer Space Trusteeship Council at the apex would want support from specialised subaltern institutions in specific fields for ensuring proper regulation, governance, supervision, inspection of compliances, and to achieve the tasks so allocated by the UN from time to time. One such supporting organisation could be Space Utilisation and Sustenance Regulatory Authority (SUSRA). This authority could supervise commercial and contractual aspects as well as manage space facilities, approve of requisite infrastructure, control celestial reality, and sustain peaceful utilisation of planetary realty through term leases. The second supporting institution may be christened as Authority for Space Monitoring and Compliances (ASMC) to ensure abidance to the international space law.

11.3.1 Space Utilisation and Sustenance Regulatory Authority (SUSRA)

SUSRA could be set up as a multifunctional, multitask institution under the Outer Space Trusteeship Council to take stock of and control of the outer space domain, regulate its commercial uses, and facilitate construction of infrastructure. Its task could include authorisation for release and handing over of virtual possession of usable realty on the celestial bodies on contractual lease basis for specific purposes, determinate term period and possibly rentals for the lease-term. Its second duty could be to ensure sustenance of celestial soil and preservation of sites and craters crucial for its original "pristinity" as also vital for future scientific explorations. For the establishment and effective working of SUSRA, some clues may be taken from analogous organisations like ICAO, International Sea-bed Authority, or the constitution of Global Commons for incorporation in its Charter of tasks and duties. It may have two working wings—Regulations Wing and Executive Wing.

11.3 Support Set-up for the Outer Space Trusteeship Council

Regulations Wing (RW) would formulate technical rules for envisaged space activities and promulgate best practices to be followed by the agencies undertaking such activities. It would thus be responsible for planning, drafting, and promulgation of technical protocols and mandatory instructions suggesting the best mode of compliances to ensure least deviations; and, if at all any, the same are remedied the soonest to obviate incumbent risks. It will also lay down safety standards to minimise operational risks.

RW will enunciate and announce legal framework and operational advisories for the splurging space activities and analyse policy implications for the developing space technologies (like space transportation, hospitality industry, exploitation of celestial natural resources, total prohibition of weaponisation of outer space, militarisation of celestial bodies and infrastructure for space habitations, etc.). This wing may also be tasked to draft a legal regimen for handling of space crimes and other eventualities as may be envisaged or may actually arise pertaining to the outer space domain.

An area of pertinent focus for RW will relate to space debris management. Guidelines for mitigation already exist, but emphasis would shift to remediation of existing accumulations. The operation of this technical mandate would pose legal challenges to compromise and neutralise permanent ownership over space objects and collateral liability issues arising out of accident or damage during on-orbit-servicing and de-orbiting of non-functional or rogue satellites. Again, debris of exploded objects, shreds of blasted nuts, and bolts and small pieces of metal floating in orbits also bear an ownership stamp, as far as identifiable. This needs new thinking by RW to evolve consensus for appropriate changes in the provisions of the OST.

The Executive Wing is a multitask institution to check abidance of and facilitate compliance of the treaty provisions and execution of regulations promulgated by the Regulations Wing. Their sterling role would reflect in space debris management covering both aspects of future reductions and remediation of past accumulations. Guidelines for future mitigation have been declared by the UN and need to be implemented strictly in the larger interest of operational safety, even if "cost-inflatory."

Another area of immediate attention for EW would be space debris reduction by existing technologies and private operators, at least costs and minimal collateral risks. This task could be contracted-out in a cost-effective manner. In this regard, immunities and other legal protection provisions will be arranged by RW. However, EW could encourage by sponsoring and funding new debris removal technologies, as considered economical and feasible. Some efforts in this direction to scavenge space clutter are already well advanced by private sector enterprises in Switzerland and Japan.

It may not be out of place to recommend that there could be a levy on launches based on payload and on satellites based on size and life in orbit as also for the circumstances of non-returnability to Earth due to a system-failed effort or cost-saving expedient. Even aberrations and non-compliances could attract penalties for two reasons: one to discourage recurrence of similar lapses and at the same time to generate funds for innovation and to promote viable space technologies and their applications, as deemed desirable. Maintenance of public order and enforcement of law on the planets as well as procedural handling of space crimes would also come within the scope of its wider functions.

11.3.2 Authority for Space Monitoring and Compliances

The Authority for Space Monitoring and Compliances (ASMC) could be a multi-disciplinary set-up with space technologists and law experts working in synergistic cooperation to supervise space activities and advise correctives on breaches occurring against space law and recommended technical best practices. It will watch for breaches of technical and legal regulations, protocols, and advisories and ensure immediate correction and cogitate on long-term remedies. These faults would also be reported to the SUSRA for consideration of any requisite change in technical practices or the ground rules. ASMC could also be invested with powers for censure and minor punishment of defaulters for alleged violations.

This basic task of ASMC would turn out to be wide in functioning, demanding in responsibility and heavy in authority. It would have to ensure precision in measuring deviations and pinpointing aberrations beyond dispute or challenge. Not many instruments, devices or gadgets are available for such activity; and many specifics and standards may have to be developed for uniformity. Again, monitoring is a serious business demanding sensitivity, transparency, and objectivity in its oft-maligned functions and observations.

In case, any deviations are noticed, and these must be properly recorded and considered by the members for any adverse effect and sustained impact. The results of the in-house review, in summarised form, be brought to the notice of the defaulting state. Should these not be rectified or justified within the prescribed time limit, the authority could exercise the powers of sanction to require removal of the deviation. In case, the violation still persists, the matter could be duly reported to the Trusteeship Council for consideration of remedial options or collective action under the powers of Security Council, as deemed fit and feasible.

11.4 International Court for Space Crimes

A sister organisation of the OSTC, with a specific and complementary purpose, could be International Court for Space Crimes (ICSC). This could be mandated to judicially handle offences committed in and from space and ensure dispensation of justice, objectively and speedily. In addition to space crimes, it could seize jurisdiction to decide and settle on economic crimes and contractual disputes, apart from adjudication on human rights and humanitarian violations. Thus, this court could entertain and adjudicate on cases, which do not squarely fall within the established jurisdiction criteria or get mired in legal hassles or face protracted conflict of interest with consequent delays.

All space crimes may neither fit into the national jurisdiction nor lend themselves to the national judicial procedures like occurrences of international wrongs. To these may be added the generally protracted hassles of cognition of jurisdiction and claims of extradition. Collectively, these will form an intractable legal labyrinth hard to negotiate by the individual victim for timely success. Therefore, to simplify judicial requirements, International Court for Space Crimes (ICSC) may be constituted with a specific Charter for trial of space crimes not squarely falling within the jurisdiction of national courts or cases encountering unnecessary delays due to legal hassles.

Another proffered alternative is to constitute ICSC as a specialised bench of the ICJ[17] rather than as an independent court with support infrastructure and staffing. It will be an economical option yet equally majestic in powers and a pedestal of authority. Further, international courts are state centric and do not entertain complaints from individual nationals unless presented by the state. But ICSC, in its envisaged broad competence and with obligatory jurisdiction over the respondent could also honour a case relating to space crime if invoked by the victim party, irrespective whether it is a state, an agency, a corporate body, or an individual.

11.4.1 Support Structure for ICSC

ICSC could be supported by the Office of the Registrar General (ORG) who could help the court with administrative tasks and para-legal duties as is usual with similar offices of national apex courts. ORG would entertain and record complaints, call for investigation records, check completeness of the case as also scrutinise, and prepare briefs for the court. ORG shall maintain all files of cases registered, issue listings for hearing, notify final orders of the court, and release judgment records to public domain. Needless to mention that ORG shall take full advantage of the digital technology, e-meetings applications, and online facilities for the convenience of all concerned.

The second support set-up for the ICSC could be a Dispute Redressal Forum (DRF) to officiate as first-step solution for *in limine* dispute redressal. Wherever relevant and within competence, ICSC may, as a first step, refer a case to its subaltern set-up, Dispute Redressal Forum, for consideration, explication, negotiation, and settlement. This could apply to all types of complaints relating to space operations, interfered activities, breached contracts, human crimes, and violations of the treaties by states. It could, if necessary and suitable, work on the lines of the jury system with invited members who are specialists in the core content of the dispute. The DRF, as a jury, could also take into consideration non-legal aspects and social nuances of the dispute

---

[17] The Charter of the United Nations is already part of international space law under Article III of the Outer Space Treaty; and Statute of the International Court of Justice is integrated in the Charter. So, creating applicability in this regard would be a matter of concurrence by the Court and the rest would be a procedural formality.

to dispense social justice and not merely send a positivist verdict. For the designated jury, there need be no distinction between commercial disputes and criminal cases.

11.4.2 Character and Competence of ICSC

In view of the above solicitude, ICSC is proposed to be a court of adjudicature of first instance entertaining states as well as individuals as complainants. The judgments of the court will be final and enforceable; and it will not act as an appellate court. Thus, it will be a court of a different type and competence than the ICJ. First, it may directly accept aggrieved individual as complainants and litigants, despite individuals not being subjects of international law. Secondly, apart from the affected individuals, the court may also entertain pleas from the states espousing cause for its nationals. In case of duplication, these could be clubbed, if factually same or similar in their prayer.

Thirdly, its jurisdiction could be compulsory, if a crime is cognisable and presented by law enforcement authority or a formal plaint is lodged by the aggrieved party. Thus, the court shall have competence to seize jurisdiction over such complaints and crimes committed or caused in space against resident humans, space workers, or space objects. Fourthly, this court could adopt the established doctrine of *res ipsa loquitur* for evidentiary responsibility and burden of proof. This concept has already found acceptance in Air Law treaties and demonstrated its validity and usefulness in litigation.

And lastly, the court may sincerely ensure that there is no miscarriage of justice due to conflicts in national legal codes or divergence of social norms, cultural beliefs, and community customs of the parties. The court could invite one Judge, as co-opted and ad hoc, from the respective country of each party to the crime or litigant. Alternatively, to appreciate the case and its causation better, it could appoint an *amicus curia* for each party to inform the court of local legal nuances and other non-legal factors influencing the same.

The competence and jurisdiction of ICSC would cover space crimes those are committed from space to space, in the air or on Earth causing damage or destroying space object/s physically in any manner or bringing about adverse impact on their operations or functionality even without inflicting any apparent physical damage to these objects. This category could cover artificial intelligence, cyber, laser, directed energy, or robot attacks. Another genre of space crimes could relate to offences of economic nature, financial losses, concerning interference in business operations, piracy of intellectual property secrets, or demolishing brand value of research and the like. These can be, by and large, stalled with injunctions or restituted with monetary compensation. Disputes pertaining to contracts and leases of realty and resource exploitation, which are not sorted out and settled by Disputes Redressal Forum can be placed before ICSC for proper adjudication. In such eventualities, it can act as Court of Appeal. Further, space crimes committed by humans against human beings would, normally, find jurisdiction under international or national laws and resort to

11.4 International Court for Space Crimes

such an option. However, should such a person approach ICSC for denial of justice beyond its control, ICSC may seize of the case and ensure adjudication.

Another category of cases could relate to human rights and humanitarian rights. With expanding space activities, space workers may be employed for excavation of natural resources or industrial production of space-specific products and to maintain tourism facilities. Normally, it may be expected that they return to the Earth on expiry of tenure or contract. But for repatriation in health emergencies, accidents, and disasters, respective contracts would have appropriate provision regarding promised and planned corporate responsibility or as part of labour welfare policies or under corporate social responsibility (CSR). But any physical restraint or unjust discrimination or undue bias during evacuation in defiance of human rights as per international convention[18] may be treated as violation of international law and accordingly punishable by ICSC, if so complained. Similarly, tourists and residents of planetary habitats would have their own contractual arrangements for emergency evacuation to safety, but for any breach of contract or exercise of discrimination, the survivors or the legal heirs of the deceased would have the right to resort to ICSC for award of compensation for mental agony and torture, bodily injury, or for loss of the deceased person.

It is conceded that international adjudication is an expensive proposition and a costly option,[19] but space travellers and space industry captains would be no paupers either. The main advantage would be that it will cut away the hassles of jurisdiction, national judicial protection, and transnational criminal procedures. The motto should be to see that the guilty are not spared, while the innocent victims are not harassed. It would thus bring the victim of crime or the aggrieved party face to face with a court that is competent from all aspects to seize the presented case rather than face conflicting claims on jurisdiction or extradition over the offender and thus lose time and evidence which may weaken the case.

Further, in modern times of digital technology, Internet of Things, e-mail communications, and virtual pleadings and hearings in the court may, in fact, turn out to be a more convenient and relatively cheap mode of adjudication or for settlement of disputed claims. Based on technological reach and Internet facilities, the court should be easily accessible rather than victims groping for a hold to get justice. Thus, the highlighted benefits from an adjudication by ICSC would far outweigh the expenses on international judicial option and also provide uniformity in judgments and dispense social justice. So, the trade-off would be cost effective and essentially helpful in affording economical and speedy disposal of the cases with finality.

It may also be suggested that the costs of initiation of proceedings in ICSC may be partly funded by the state of nationality or domicile of the victim on certain criteria for funding and its quantum. This reference for financial aid to the state authority will also lend the case to an initial legal scrutiny by the state solicitor and confirm its *prima*

---

[18] International Convention on Civil and Political Rights (ICCPR).

[19] Article 64 of Statute of the International Court of Justice states, "Unless otherwise decided by the Court, each party shall bear its own costs." Here parties are the states in litigation. Similar provision for ICSC can be suitably amended for a part of costs to be borne by private parties or individuals to the dispute and balance by the concerned state.

facie credence. In addition, the state diplomatic machinery may help in compliance of pretrial procedures till a charge is preferred in the court. This, however, would need sharp acumen in diplomacy to handle tricky legal issues with interlocutors. And on finalisation of the case, the initial funding by the government can be partly reimbursed from the awarded amount on execution of the decree or from penalties imposed on and realised from the guilty as part of the judgment.

Apart from crimes and serious conflicts fit for adjudication by ICSC, there may be a range of economic disputes on sharing of proceeds or compensation for liability, breach of intellectual property, etc., in which cases the parties may, for certain reasons, prefer international arbitration over the judicial option. In fact, alternative dispute redressal procedure has been resorted to in some cases with useful results to the satisfaction of parties involved. This procedure seems viable and eminently suited where arbitration clauses integral to contracts, e.g., launch contract, insurance contract, investment contract, contract for supply of parts or services and the like, could be rightfully invoked. The results could, thus, be amicably obtained, which would be mutually satisfying and with speeder processes.

A survey conducted recently and analysis of empirical data on the subject reveal a trend of industry preferences for the future development of arbitration as a form of dispute resolution in the space sector.[20] The survey also shows a preference of the contracting parties for known seats of arbitration, reputed institutions of arbitration, selection process from empanelled arbitrators, and a choice of procedural and substantive rules. Furthermore, the results over a period will allow us to evaluate the success of existing arbitration infrastructure for space-related disputes, including the PCA Optional Rules for Arbitration of Disputes Relating to Outer Space Activities and the Panels of Arbitrators and Experts for Space-related Disputes.[21] Therefore, empirical data and revealed trend may be indicative and useful to scholars, policymakers, and practitioners to anchor policy issues and cull out future recommendations.

Realistically speaking, the proposed organisation, institutions, and mechanisms may not be able to change human propensity to crimes and end the occurrence of space crime but at least would usher better prospects of peace, order, and security in the space domain. These may, thus, collectively achieve two basic objects of governance: first, by inducing a certainty that offenders of space crimes will not be able to escape due process of law for their actions and the second objective of infusing deterrence that the crime would be properly adjudicated and would entail penalty and/or punishment.

---

[20] Eytan Tepper, Viva Dadwal, "Arbitration in Space-Related Disputes: A Survey of Industry Practices and Future Needs", a presentation at *IISL Colloquium on the Law of Outer Space* (E7), 70th International Astronautical Congress, 2019, (ID 50661).

[21] Eytan, ibid.

Chapter 12
Some Conclusions

In conclusion, let us accept at the very outset that crimes are committed by human beings while animals, birds, and sea-creatures commit no crimes according to their natural laws. Therefore, crimes occur due to human decisions made as individuals or collectively or conspiratorially. And most of the crimes so committed reveal either instinctive reflex or motivation by mens rea. Therefore, most of the crimes, whether physical, psychological, mental, sexual, economic, or against the state, have been codified in national criminal laws for abidance and deterrence. In modern times, however, crimes are committed with technology tools, gadgets, devices, or weapons. Nevertheless, the ultimate criminal remains a human being, the wielder, whether for a planned or provoked act, direct or a causation. And crimes, in whatever form or character, shall persist wherever human beings exist.

The old dictum needs no convincing that there cannot be a crime without a criminal, who may be in any domain: outer space, on a celestial body, in atmosphere or on the Earth. It is also a different matter whether the criminal remains anonymous and hidden or may not be traced and apprehended or that the evidence is scant, broken, and unreliable. Thus, the guilt may not be substantially proved or at least beyond reasonable doubt. Nevertheless, a criminal exists behind every crime and should, as far as possible, be brought to book for the impugned act and to suffer its consequential repercussions and sanctions.

Crimes in space have been committed in the past and by astronauts also who are expected to be disciplined, experienced, trained, and regimented. Some such cases of near-crimes have been narrated in Chaps. 2 and 3 though in most cases the misdemeanours of offenders have been condoned, and in isolated cases, their achievement has been glamourised while only a few punished internally and meekly. A couple of other incidents of space crimes were weak on judicial evidence or legal reasoning and were let off rather lightly. Nevertheless, it is pertinent and important enough that space crimes should be brought to book in the interest of discipline, safety, security, justice, jurisprudence, human rights, and humanitarian causes. This flags enforcement of law in outer space domain as an important issue.

Returning to the space crimes, it must be acknowledged that given the human nature and the attendant circumstances, whatever be the level of education, indoctrinated discipline, efforts at reformation or gravity of deterrence, the occurrence of crimes cannot be completely eliminated; it may at best be minimised. Therefore, once the crime is committed, both the parties; the culprit and the victim, are in search of justice that may seem elusive as either of them may be accustomed to a different legal system or familiar with a different legal code. Each has misgivings and apprehensions; the culprit of victimisation for whatever reason and the victim about the sufficiency of sentence or restitution of loss. Their search may pursue different routes; they may also harbour doubts due to different perceptions yet justice is traditionally neutral and objective and just in essence and purpose.

Space crimes get posited with certain ticklish issues. First relates to the election of the legal system of which country, that of the victim or of the offender. Different legal systems like British, continental, jury, or Islamic Sharia prevail around the world and may not mean the same to both parties. Secondly, there are differences in legal codes, cultural beliefs, social norms, and acceptable behaviour resulting in that the gravity of a crime may be understood differently and views on justice dispensed may also be divergent in perception. Thirdly, in international crimes, jurisdiction of the appropriate court may be a matter of competing tussles, and claims for extradition of the offender may be parallel and even conflicting. Therefore, these hassles seek remedies.

12.1 The Need for a Specialised Treaty for Space Crimes

The existing corpus of space law comprising Outer Space Treaty and supporting conventions, agreements, soft law guidelines, declarations, and principles is deficient to confront these tricky challenges squarely and effectively. Accordingly, the current legal regime of outer space requires either amendment to the OST to incorporate necessary additional provisions or a special protocol devoted to tackling of space crimes or that a changeover to a new specialised treaty would seem necessary.

The option of tinkering with the OST can be considered because the phenomena of change and growth are neither new nor unique but may be ruled out for various reasons so enumerated. First, OST proclaims some fundamental principles and universal tenets of sharing, caring, and cooperation among space-faring nations. Secondly, concepts of commonness, province of all mankind, and altruism in partaking of benefits from space activities, of whatever kind, with other nations exude an urge for sharing, a tendency towards cooperation and nobility of gesture. Thus, every space activity must anticipate and promise common benefit, whether in exploration or use. But in the eyes of the millennial generation, the future of this domain lies beyond in commercial uses, exploitation, and appropriation. This view would need to be appreciated in the current context of economic values and reconciled with the existing law.

Thirdly, OST as basic constitutional law of outer space has stood the test of space activities and abidance in state practice for over half a century. Thus, OST carries an honourable legacy of trust and compliance of space-faring countries. Hence, it will not be wise to disturb its constitutional character nor neutralise the impact of embedded ideological tenets. Fourthly, with consistent state practice and growing *opinio juris*, OST has crystallised into customary law of space with greater obligatory force for space-farers. Therefore, a considered view would be that stabilised and enduring law of OST may not be mutated to accommodate contemporary contingencies; and it must be permitted to operate and govern as *grundnorm* and be accorded the dignity and reverence it deserves. Ergo, this proposal lacks justification for acceptance.

The next option is to negotiate a protocol to OST. It certainly appears tempting in garnering consensus and rapidity in negotiations but this, too, has certain drawbacks. First, the postulation of space crimes is new and emerging so there is no provision in the treaty to afford nexus and support to this protocol. Secondly, a short protocol cannot do justice to the legal imperatives of handling this branch of law and jurisprudence in a new environment and for crimes assisted by technologies like directed energy, artificial intelligence, cybernetics, kinetics, and others. Thirdly, jurisdictional conflicts in the process of law, claims on extradition of criminal, variants of legal systems, differing criminal codes globally, divergent perception on crimes, as discussed earlier, may not be tackled properly in a sketchy protocol. Thus, the loopholes in the skeletal document may afford ample opportunity to the accused to foil or foul justice. Hence, the option of a protocol to OST, so mulled, does not fit well into a viable and effective solution.

The last option is to have a new, detailed, and independent treaty to tackle this growing proclivity among astronauts as also future occurrences among space tourists and celestial residents. Commercial space travellers would be still less disciplined by temperament and training and thus more prone to objections, conflicts, and crimes. Commercial exploitation of celestial bodies would introduce a different genre of economic crimes and neglect of space workers in outer space by the employer-corporates may tantamount to breach of contracts and violation of human rights. Crimes by cyber-attacks, artificial intelligence, and other allied technologies and applications may occur from any domain into outer space domain wearing a cloak of stealth and anonymity. And some of these crimes may be capable of creating catastrophic impact not only in space or a celestial body but overall, for the entire terrestrial community also. These may, thus, constitute a veritable threat to the very survival of humanity.

At the same time, it may be conceded that it is difficult to presage the total range of future space crimes, yet a rough visualisation described earlier should suffice for our discourse. Therefore, irrespective of the nature, character, complexion, or impact of the crime, it may be asserted that the primary purpose of the proposed specialised treaty on space crimes is to lay down a legal regime for effective handling of crimes in space domain from anywhere. Further, as an ancillary benefit in the wider interest of the diverse nature of expanding activities in the outer space, the proposed treaty may be enlarged to accommodate and cater to other hanging issues of space tourism, commercial exploitation of natural resources, manufacturing of special products, and human residencies in outer space and celestial bodies. So, the final choice falls on a new specialized treaty.

12.2 The Need for Governance of the Space Domain

Apart from a new treaty law for global regulation and compliance, there appears a dire need for proper governance of the outer space domain for check on compliances, regulate commercial utilisation, and to maintain its sustainability for posterity. Hence, a proposal has been made to revive the erstwhile Trusteeship Council and rechristen it as Outer Space Trusteeship Council (OSTC) to materialise the avowed principles of space jurisprudence enshrined in "province of all mankind," sharing of benefits, maintain common heritage of mankind as also in the denial from claiming national sovereignty over celestial bodies in any form or manner. Thus, in deference to the espoused ideals of the treaty, OSTC could take up the task and responsibility, in principle, for the total governance of outer space and the celestial bodies on the lines of trustee-territories. Similarity in the task seems apparent and striking.

The OSTC could be structured to have two supporting establishments to help in regulation, governance, sustenance, control, and inspections. First is Space Utilisation, Sustenance, and Regulatory Authority (SUSRA) and is missioned to regulate use of celestial real estate through licensing of leases for commercial space activities and for infrastructure for habitations. Its other important duty will be to ensure sustainability of space environment through management of space debris, in both mitigation and remediation tasks. This task is imperative to facilitate safe operations for exploratory and commercial uses as also by the future generations.

SUSRA shall have a sister organisation by the name, Authority for Space Inspection and Compliances (ASIC). The latter authority could be a multi-disciplinary set-up with space technologists and law experts working in cooperation to inspect space activities for compliances and to advise correctives on breaches against space law and recommended technical best practices. Not many instrumentalities, measuring tools or facilitative gadgets are available for this purpose and would need to be developed because inspection of compliances is a serious business of importance. It would demand sensitivity, transparency, and objectivity in its delicate duty in order to induce greater trust and confidence in its institutional functioning.

12.3 The Need for Sustainability of the Space Domain

The space domain comprising outer space environment and celestial bodies is highly vulnerable. With escalated launches for tourism and other commercial activities, the space highways and common launch trajectories may get crowded and denser in traffic. Even today, the low-earth orbit is highly cluttered with space debris reducing the windows of opportunity for launches. Same way, geo-synchronous orbit is habited by a high density of satellite population, both functional and non-functional. This problem may eventually plague other orbits and nor are the risks from other floating debris going to abate. Causing non-sustainability of space environment, even if by inadvertence yet fully knowing its consequences, will be a crime against posterity. Therefore, to turn the situation around, space debris must be perceived as a common goal by all the major stakeholders who should actively participate and financially contribute in its management: mitigation measures for the future and remediation of past accumulations.

Thus, the situation seems hazardous and may become graver with time and increased commercially exploitative uses of outer space. This predicament calls for stern measures in mitigation of space debris as well as management for remediation of existing space debris. A Space Sustenance Fund (SSF) has been mooted, partly for this purpose. Additional funds may be mustered on the principles of "polluter pays" and "proportionate responsibility" from the polluting countries or space agencies who left the debris in space in the past. And the task of scavenging of outer space and the celestial bodies can be outsourced to competent enterprise. Such companies for outer space cleaning are gaining expertise and coming up in Japan and Switzerland. They only need payment for the job and legal immunities against any damage caused to a third party during such operations.

12.4 The Need for Judicial Set-up for Space Crimes

Alongside OSTC, International Court of Space Crimes (ICSC) may be positioned as an independent court of adjudicature or as a specialised bench of the ICJ to entertain and adjudicate on all kinds of space crimes as also business and economic disputes presented before the court and dispense due justice to the parties in quest for the same. International courts are state-centric and do not recognise individuals or business corporations as litigant parties. But ICSC may be chartered to acknowledge individuals or corporations as parties under certain circumstances. It is, therefore, essential to be ensured that justice is dispensed objectively, impartially and speedily to the approaching parties.

Further, justice should not only be done as formalism of positive law or a mere judicial function but accepted as a social necessity and, as far as possible, perceived by all concerned to have been fairly dispensed. The court proceedings should be transparent and sentence proportionate to the gravity of the crime and in full consideration of the defence pleas of the accused. The court may also conform to the legal maxim that justice delayed is justice denied. In consequence, efficacy of the proposed *specialis* treaty and the lofty image of the institution of ICSC should infuse confidence and motivate the victims as well as the aggrieved parties to invoke the proposed treaty and approach ICSC with an earnest hope that justice and equity (*aequitas*) shall prevail.

Please permit a reiteration that justice in international milieu is not a mechanical exercise in binaries but a social process with corrective motivation, sensitised reformation and emotional overtones. A fundamental principle of justice is that guilty should be rightly and appropriately punished but also to make sure that innocents are not harassed, demonised or victimised; even though an alleged accused or assumed culprit is let off as "not guilty" under benefit of reasonable doubt. Thus, law and procedures should pin the accused on evidence of actions, facts of the event and *mens rea* or motivation; and law should not become a tool for condemnation of the innocent or harassment of the aggrieved. Legal tricks and twists are too well-known to be hidden by the practitioners and the judges better remain alert and strive to unravel them in search of justice.

At the same time, it needs to be appreciated that in international scenario of collective interaction and joint living, justice is not tit for tat or proclaimed as per codified law but modulated by the national habits, cultural attitude, and social background of the accused. Therefore, there should neither be politicisation of judicial proceedings nor abuse of a licit right by the complainant. Thus, a *bonafide* image of exclusion of politics or racial bias from proceedings and observance of professional objectivity and highest integrity should be cultivated through sustained trust in the success of initiated cases and confidence-building judgments of ICSC.

In tandem, it also becomes incumbent on states, space faring or otherwise, that measures for avoidance and steps in handling of space crimes should be perceived as a common goal and collective responsibility globally. This imperative, in turn, mandates international cooperation and reciprocal facilitation to curb and control as well as trial of space offences. This attitude is also ordained in the Outer Space Treaty under Articles X and XI. Political fissures or nationality affiliations or other prejudices should not make us complacent of or oblivious to the high level of impending risks of trust or the gravity of possible catastrophe pregnant in actions of such crimes or even advertent misdemeanours. Hence, the need for a genuine change in the mindset to create synergy in management, to evolve a consensual strategy for control of space operations as also observe absolute seriousness in the matter of space activities.

It deserves to be appreciated that the genre of space crimes though apparently similar to those on Earth yet are different in character, distinct in impact and, at times, in contradistinction to the gravity of consequences from those committed on Earth. Some such space crimes may not even require the physical presence or proximity of the criminal in space and the criminal act may be committed from anywhere in the universe, depending upon the range of coverage of the device. So, the anonymity or spatial spacing of the criminal would be another imponderable in investigation of crime and apprehending the criminal, who could be anonymous or invisible, particularly in artificial intelligence and cyber-attacks. The dilemma in prosecution may remain intractable.

The norms of evidence may also have to be revised to accommodate circumstantial probabilities and technological findings which may not be incontrovertible proof. Perhaps, it would be equally necessary to invoke the doctrine of *res ipsa loquitur* (meaning fact speaks for itself) to determine the *onus probandi* in crimes which occur so fast to even confuse and defy eye witness. Conjecturally, some of these acts of commission or omission by humans could be committed under stress of flight or angst of safety or under the unaccustomed and debilitating influences of zero-gravity, discomfort of cramped spaces, aromatic distress of enclosed areas, lack of privacy, differences in social values, unidentical cultural mindset, and so on. It may, of course, be difficult to presage or envision the total range of likely space crimes and their causation yet a visualisation of their future complexion and diversity of motivations has been attempted and described in the book.

Therefore, most of the space crimes should be seen from sociological angle with humanitarian approach rather than mechanically implementing juridically rigorous codes in a formal binary mode based on holed evidence. This valuable consideration, sure, calls for sensitivity, empathy, honesty, integrity, and flexibility in handling adjudication of space crimes. Ergo, the expectation is for compatibility between universal need for justice, neutrality in procedures, transparency in proceedings, fulfilment of legitimate rights of all the parties, and ultimate dispensation of justice that is legally just and socially welcomed.

At the same time, there is need to be cautious about recidivism which is a tendency or proclivity of the offender to relapse and repeat crimes. Thus, sentencing for a crime becomes a compulsion of judicial process for social protection and common security. It concurrently evokes an emotional relationship of the offender with justice soliciting sympathy and mitigation due to differences in understanding of others' sensitivities while interests of security and deterrence for safe social existence cannot be forsaken. All this discourse calls for a future vision as also aetiology for legal strategy and judicial planning to curb, control, and tackle crimes occurring in outer space.

12.5 The Need for National Legislation

The governance architecture for space activities must elicit the support and cooperation of the space faring as also other space-using states in the governing complexities. In fact, states, their space agencies, private enterprise entities, and non-governmental organisations[1] are all direct stakeholders in the regulation and governance of space domain and should not shirk their duties as responsible users of the domain. States, in particular, are required under the treaty to undertake "authorisation and continuing supervision" of its national space activities. Effective performance of this mandated responsibility can act as the first filter for crimes in outer space.

Accordingly, an essential part of this mandate under the OST is to contribute to the safety and security of space operations, assets and space personnel by ensuring proper intelligence clearances before authorisation and equal vigilance during continuing supervision. This effort will, in a large measure, obviate crimes in outer space under the future uncertainties. Thus, this calls for subglobal governance of space stakeholders at national level. Towards this end, national space legislation will help

---

[1] Like ASGARDIANS and For All Moonkind, etc.

thwart criminal intentions by strict laws forewarning of the consequences and deterrent punishments provided therein. This strictness seems pertinent because even a minor mischief or misdemeanour in space can cause or initiate an existential threat.

Therefore, this wisdom must also visit the heads of the entrepreneurs of private space activities in order to create a realisation that cost-cutting measures or concessions on operational safety of space activities would be crime in law, a breach of business ethics and a guilt of conscience. Terminology may differ, but the conceptual core and the empirical significance of this assertion remain valid. Thus, private sector owes this sincerity as corporate social responsibility (CSR) to humankind. Because ominous threats from such economic and value-infringed compromises, intentional or inadvertent, may materialise sometime leaving us little chance of escape or survival. And the dead do not cry for justice. National space legislation can help avert such a predicament.

12.6 Timeliness of the Topic

Some scholars may consider this discourse premature but this objection can be partly refuted because the first media-reported crime in space has been committed by an astronaut Anne McClain in 2019, although investigations have cleared her of the allegations. It is also pertinent to allude to the past near-crimes discussed in earlier chapters. And interestingly, these are not confined to any single nation but extend to more space-faring countries. It is only that much information on this topic has been kept classified by space agencies and is not presently available in public domain. Moreover, most of the impermissible conduct and near-crimes of astronauts have been graciously condoned in view of the glorious achievements for the nation in their instant mission or overall career, and they were possibly punished or reproofed based on non-conventional investigations.

In view of the recurrences of and repeated misdemeanours even by the disciplined military astronauts, there is no reason to be complacent about the oncoming eventualities with commercial tourists, workers and residents. In fact, this possibility may escalate with fare-paying civilian travellers who may demand much value for their money while discipline not being their forte. The not-too-spacious passenger cabin in the space module may provide little elbow room for a delightful, or even comfortable experience. Hence, nudges may turn into disputes and grow into conflicts. We may not, therefore, forget the old adage that a stitch in time saves nine. Our preparedness for smooth redressal procedures and a judicial system for space crimes must begin soon. Experience tells that treaty negotiations tend to stretch over long periods for various reasons like political theatrics, diplomatic deadlocks, unwanted compromises, or deliberations on the side-lines. Therefore, let us learn from experience and be wise by hindsight.

It may not be out of place to also acknowledge that this discourse truly adopts a proactive approach to the ensuing challenges and identification of gaps and grey areas in space law. Military wisdom reminds that to be forewarned is to be forearmed for the eventualities, and the latter is the winner. It is also worth believing in the sagacity of an ancient Biblical reference that Noah did not build the Ark to escape deluge when it was raining. So, to be prepared to effectively curb or handle space crimes and at the same time enable the involved to tackle and negotiate the labyrinths of jurisdictional proceedings, incongruent legal systems, different prosecution procedures, divergent perception of crimes, and unequal punishments in national criminal codes seems more sensible and highly advisable.

Printed in the United States
by Baker & Taylor Publisher Services